Your Life
as Story

ALSO BY TRISTINE RAINER

The New Diary

The Autobiography of Alice B. Toklas, Ge

I Know Why the Caged Bird Si

Angelou * Growing Up, Russell Baker

Flying, Erica Jong * Down and Out in

London, George Orwell * Leaving

Buchwald * Nobody Knows My Na

Baldwin * A River Runs Through

Maclean * An Unfinished Woman, Lillia

The Lover, Marguerite Duras * Dance

Agnes de Mille * Shot in the Heart, Mikal

The Autobiography of Malcolm X, Alex

Diaries, Anais Nin * Refuge, an Unnatu

Family and Place, Terry Tempest Willi

Life, Elia Kazan * Cowboys Are My

Pam Houston * Remembrance of Things

Proust * Under My Skin, Doris Lessing

Survivor's Tale, Art Spiegelman *

Warrior, Maxine Hong Kingston * The

hy, Benjamin Franklin * Portrait of the

Young Man, James Joyce * Autobiograph

Paramhansa Yogananda * The House

Street, Sandra Cisneros * Sex Death En

A True Story, Mark Matousek * Autob

Tristine Rainer

Your Life as Story

*Discovering
the "New Autobiography"
and Writing Memoir as Literature*

JEREMY P. TARCHER/PUTNAM
a member of Penguin Putnam Inc.
New York

Most Tarcher/Putnam books are available at special quantity discounts for bulk purchases for sales promotions, premiums, fund-raising, and educational needs. Special books or book excerpts also can be created to fit specific needs. For details, write Putnam Special Markets, 375 Hudson Street, New York, NY 10014

Jeremy P. Tarcher/Putnam
a member of
Penguin Putnam Inc.
375 Hudson Street
New York, NY 10014
www.penguinputnam.com

Library of Congress Cataloging-in-Publication Data
Rainer, Tristine.
Your life as story : discovering the "new autobiography" and
writing memoir as literature / by Tristine Rainer.
p. cm.
Includes bibliographical references and index.
ISBN 0-87477-922-7
1. Autobiography—Authorship. 2. Report writing. I. Title
CT25.R34 1998
808'.06692—dc21 98-10091 CIP

Book design by Deborah Kerner
Cover design by Isabella Fasciano
Cover illustration: *Untitled* by Lenore Tawney © 1983

Printed in the United States of America

20

For Barbara Dixon

Long friendship is sustained by banking our personal stories,

episode by episode, in each other's memory.

What baubles we girls have put away!

Acknowledgments

I am deeply grateful to my own writing mentor, Leah Appet, who would be appalled by this clichéd phrase; to my dear friend, James Cass Rogers, who offers me the understanding and love that only another writer can give; to Richard Beban for reading the manuscript before it was one; to Deanne Barkley, who kept saying, you have to write a book on how to write autobiography. (This is for you, Deanne, so you'll finally write yours.)

I wish to thank Jeremy Tarcher, who gave what I could not provide for myself: faith and support for my writing, not once, but twice; Robin Canter Cook for her gentle editorial suggestions; Irene Prokop and Joel Fotinos for delivering the book to the light; and Jennifer Greene for helping with all the odds and ends while sharing a laugh.

I am most indebted to my beloved daughter, Jamie, for the time I took away from her and can never return; to my ex-husband, Jeff, for not discouraging me from this project; and to my father, Warren Rainer, his wife, Bette; and Jack Fletcher; to my brother, sister, and, of course, to my magnificent godmother, Lenore Tawney, for their encouragement.

I also wish to thank Dr. Linda Venus and all the wonderful people who work in the administration of the UCLA Extension Writer's Program, Hannelore Hahn and the International Women's Writing Guild, and Judy Reeves at the Writing Center in San Diego for allowing me to generate on my feet the exercises presented in this book. Thanks, as well, to Renate Druks, Ellen Snortland, and John Gillis for speaking to my classes about their own first person writing, and for so much more. My continuing gratitude goes to the members of the Center for Autobiographic Studies for their support and faith, particularly James Ingebretsen, Lois Henley, and Dr. Dianne Freund.

The saw is true: by your students you'll be taught, so I want to thank all my students and clients, especially Hanh Hoang, Lianne Clenard, Marlena Fontenay, Susan Golant, Adrianna Nery, Brason Lee, Linda Garbett, Luisa Fels, and Philomene Long.

Most of all, I wish to acknowledge my mother, Marie, who gave me life, who gave me my name, who gave me unconditional love. If my mother is ever canonized, it will only be by me, but she deserves it, for she was a saint.

Contents

1   The Story Only You Can Tell   *1*

2   The Evolution of a New Autobiography   *20*

3   What Is a Story?   *37*

4   A Story Depends Upon How You Slice It   *47*

5   The Nine Essential Elements of
Story Structure   *65*

6   Genres of the Self   *83*

7   Tricks Memory Plays on You and
Tricks You Can Play on It   *100*

8   Finding Your Voice   *123*

9   Portraying Yourself: You Are Your Hero   *140*

10   Portraying Others: Casting
Your Story from Life   *152*

11   Truth in Autobiographic Writing   *173*

12 How to Write What You Dare Not Say *184*

13 Dealing with Your Dark Side *192*

14 Writing the Body *202*

15 Theme: String for Your Pearls *212*

16 Scenepearls *231*

17 Anatomy of a Scene: Description, Inner
Responses, Dialog, and Structure *244*

18 Jumping and Leaping through Time *267*

19 Humor *289*

20 Dressing Up before Going Out *300*

21 Emotional, Legal, and Ethical Concerns *306*

22 Finishing the Unfinished Story *323*

Appendices

1 Forming or Finding a Memoir Group *327*

2 Selling Your Story for Fame and Fortune
and Other Good Alternatives *329*

Bibliography of Autobiographic Works and
Critical Works on Memoir Cited in the Text *337*

Index *345*

Your Life
as Story

1

The Story Only You Can Tell

Imagine you could trace your course through time and space as an astronomer tracks a planet's orbit or a comet's path. Imagine you could get back far enough to see the shape of your life. Would it be pitched like a camel's back, straight as a projectile, coiled like a pig's corkscrew tail, or would it make a nimbus, a cochlea, a zigzag?

If you could see your life's shape, you would find its features to be, like those on your face, universally human yet completely unique. Although the pattern of your experience might resemble certain categories—a mandala? a parabola?—it would have contours that have never before existed and will never exist again.

Now imagine that within your life's unique path you could recognize a story or stories—the way a stargazer recognizes constellations. A story is a *meaningful* pattern of events. Through finding a story's shape within your life's shape, you could know what your life means. It would be an individual meaning, unique to you. As Anaïs Nin said in *Diary II:*

> What makes people despair is that they try to find a universal meaning
> to the whole of life, and then end up by saying it is absurd, illogical,
> empty of meaning. There is not one big cosmic meaning for all, there
> is only the meaning we each give to our life, an individual meaning,
> an individual plot, like an individual novel, a book for each person.

This is what the New Autobiography is: the discovery of the unique story or stories your life makes. It is the application of story structure to your life experiences to give them meaning. It's reading your life as if it were a dream, asking, "What hidden significance do these characters and these events have for me?" It's shaping those elements into what is as compelling to read as a contemporary novel. The New Autobiography asks that you perceive your life as a writer would, not simplistically, but with the mystery and complexity of literature.

The purpose of this book is to give you the tools to see story in your life, and then, if you choose, to give it shape in writing so it can be shared. In this work I am indebted to Joseph Campbell and Clarissa Pinkola Estés, who have taught us the importance of story to our lives. My work builds on theirs, although I do not, as they do, rely on the myths of other eras and cultures as models. Rather, I show you how to overlay your life experience upon the timeless principles of story structure that underlie all myths. Campbell himself recognized that the old myths don't work anymore for the conditions of our modern lives. Our job is to find in our contemporary lives myths for our times, and that is what New Autobiography seeks to do.

No longer the exclusive privilege of the famous or infamous, the luxury of established writers, or simply a hobby for grandparents, New Autobiography is available to everyone. It is a new concept of autobiography that changes long-held assumptions about who may write it, why, and how. Just as diary writing is now radically different from how it was practiced before the late twentieth century, so autobiographic writing has evolved into new contemporary forms.

Perhaps you notice that I differentiate diary and autobiographic writing. The difference is not that a journal is kept for oneself and autobiography seeks an outside audience. In fact, diaries can be written with an audience in mind, and autobiography for one's self alone. Nor is the difference that autobiography covers the whole life, because as I am using the term, autobiography includes short narratives of pieces of a life. No, the difference between diary and autobiography is that elusive partner in the process, time. The diarist writes from an *ever-moving present*. Autobiographic writing is written from a later point in time, *in retrospect*. The autobiographic writer, to a far greater extent than the diarist, re-members the past to find within it thematic continuity and coherent meaning.

You might think, then, that autobiographic narrative is most appropriate to old or middle age. Yet as many students in their twenties and thirties have attended the autobiographic writing classes I've taught for UCLA Extension's Writer's Program as forty- to eighty-year-olds. My younger students and clients know that writing and reading memoir written with fictional devices is the latest literary trend. In fact, there's been a shift within all generations so that we now want to read about real-life experiences rather than about someone's fantasies. The autobiographic works I cite in this book are from pre-prime as well as post-prime writers, both published and unpublished.

I myself, though, didn't feel the autobiographic urge until I turned forty. I even know the day it began, with a scene that was an *initiating incident* (that, you'll learn, is the first of nine essential story elements). I was working as an executive producer of television movies, which may surprise those readers who know me as the university instructor who wrote *The New Diary*. I say surprise because a few years ago I read a survey in which Americans were asked to rate the honesty of those in sixty-three different professions. A majority rated college professors most honest (second only to clergymen) and named television producers most dishonest (next to used car salesmen and politicians). So—trust me—people can have a hard time forming a coherent image of me.

When the initiating incident took place, I was having a hard time forming a coherent image of myself. I saw myself as through one of those camera viewfinders that you focus by trying to reconcile a double image, one figure floating beside its twin. Mine wouldn't go together. On the occasion I'm referring to, though, someone else had no trouble seeing me straight.

It was a sweltering July morning and I was camped outside the Santa Rosa county courthouse. It was the last day of the trial of a jealous fifteen-year-old who had stabbed to death her more popular classmate. I was waiting for the victim's mother so I could talk to her about the movie rights to the dead girl's story.

This was not the kind of movie I'd produced before. I'd developed movies based on true life stories, certainly, but they'd been comedies and social dramas. In the late 1980s, the networks abruptly stopped buying those. They only wanted "hard edged" true crime stories, r-r-r-ripped from the headlines, and if I was going to stay in the game and keep my six-figure salary, I had to get some. The grieving mother had not answered my mailgram or phone calls, but I'd spoken with her attorney and he'd encouraged me to try to talk to her in person. I already knew if I could get her to give me the rights, I would have a deal at ABC.

There! Coming out the door! A slender, chiseled woman in a navy dress with a white collar, her tall, athletic husband holding her arm.

I rush up. I ask for fifteen minutes to tell her that her story is important to share and why. Her head tilts up to her husband's face.

"It's up to you," he demurs.

She nods to me, compliant, helpless against the force of events that are carrying her reluctantly into her fifteen minutes of fame. She agrees to meet me at her lawyer's office at four thirty.

The room is like a stage set, large and empty, a carpet, a couch, a chair, tall sealed windows evenly filled by a dimensionless sky. The mother and father of the murdered girl sit side by side on the couch, clasping hands.

"Your daughter's story is not just about her tragic murder. It's about a crisis in values and the failure in our schools." I lean forward toward the mother, my gaze steady, my voice even, explaining that the personal tragedy of her daughter's murder contains themes that we all need to look at, that something valuable can come out of their terrible tragedy . . . if only they will let me purchase the rights . . . no, no, we don't need to discuss money now, though I think this story would bring $100,000. "I understand that you don't want to profit from your daughter's death. You could arrange to have the money contributed to your chosen charity."

I am well-rehearsed. I make my peroration.

". . . It will be a way for your daughter's life to have meaning to so many others."

The mother takes a Kleenex from her purse. Stanches the tears that leak down her face. Composes herself. Reclasps her husband's hand.

"No."

What!? But . . . ?

"No."

I look into her tired blue eyes. I see steel. I see that nothing I say will change her mind. I see that not only will I not get her rights—no one will get her rights. I see myself through her eyes. I am transported into her grief. I see myself as she sees me, this intruder, this alien creature in a business suit, this, this ambulance chaser. Who are you—you without tragedy, how dare you come here now while the earth on my daughter's grave has yet to settle, while I am still in the center of my mourning, you who do not know what it is to lose a child, you who can get up in the morning as if the world still continued, *you* who want to make a *movie!*

I leave my card. I back out the door. I rush to the elevator.

I cannot do this, I tell myself. I can't do this.

I loved working with people's true life stories, but only if *they* wanted to tell them, only if they came to me. With television movie companies in escalating bidding wars and tabloid reality shows joining in hot pursuit, no one was going to drop salable true story rights on my doorstep like a foundling baby. "So you haven't the stomach for the TV movie chase?" I goaded myself. "So *now* what are you going to do?" I had changed professional directions so many times, there were skid marks all over the road. Could I really take another sharp turn? I started to have nightmares of careering along a mountain pass, of speeding blindfolded through a freeway interchange.

This is where my autobiographic process began; and with the disturbing reflection that though I had been making story from other people's lives for over a decade, I could not see any story in my own. My life was too fragmented, and not only professionally. I'd married late, and after too many temporary relationships that would never add up to a satisfying narrative. When I looked at myself, I saw a woman flying apart like Marcel Duchamp's *Nude Descending a Staircase,* a woman who desperately needed to glue herself together. I no longer wanted my episodic life; I wanted it to have a coherent flow. I wanted to recognize my *daemon,* that unique but continuous spirit which, according to psychoanalyst James Hillman, gazes from the eyes of the little boy and the old man unchanged. Besides, like a thrifty cook who doesn't want to throw out the turkey carcass, I wanted to find some use for the years I'd spent in television movies learning dramatic structure. So I got the idea of trying to apply to my own life what I knew about story.

The first thing I knew is that the central character should have a clear desire line—it can bend, it can turn unexpectedly, but it should not break; it should be intense and continuous. But I was in this fix because I lacked a consistent line of desires. Rather than a heroic or even unheroic journey to a longed-for goal, my life, like those identified in Mary Catherine Bateson's *Composing a Life,* had merely been a "kind of desperate improvisation" in response to what had been thrown my way. Diary writing had served my constant and ongoing self-invention because it didn't require the continuity of story, but now it was that continuity I longed for.

I'd done so many different jobs, each of which suited me at the time; none of which could be said to follow a career progression. I'd been a waitress, a receptionist, a job counselor, an amateur actress, a university English literature lecturer and film and women's studies' instructor, an author and advisor on journal writing, a private writing teacher and editor, a writer of fiction, nonfiction, screenplays and teleplays, a network television movie producer, a film company executive. . . .

I made this list as if to prove how futile it would be to find within it a thread of continuity, but when I read it, I was amazed to detect throughout my fascination with people's stories: listening to people's stories, observing how people's lives made story, and discovering, teaching, and practicing how to make story out of people's lives.

I knew that an abstract interest in life stories was hardly a story and not promising material for one. Nonetheless, I could not suppress a soaring delight in finding a line of continuity in my life, any continuity. It was followed by mild horror. Standing outside and seeing myself at a distance this way, I became aware of how peculiar my passion for life stories and my compulsion to get other people to tell theirs might seem. I found my own obsession as eccentric as the entomologist's fascination with beetles or a collector's enthusiasm for plastic PEZ candy dispensers. I heard Herr Freud pronounce with a Viennese accent the kinky, accusatory sentence, "You're a voyeur encouraging exhibitionists," until I sassed him back, "Like you." I had come face to face with my own peculiarity, my own uniqueness, yes, my own eccentricity. Now I could only walk outside my own shoes or choose to put them on.

I tried to put them on. I admitted to myself my obsessive interest in life stories, though I was still no closer to seeing story or purpose in my own life. I'd found a line of continuity, but not the kind that lends itself to traditional autobiography. When I began, I held the common assumption that autobiography was reserved for the famous and infamous or those who were writing a family history for their descendants. I'm not famous, nor wish to be; and my only child is adopted, so she wouldn't be much interested in my bloodlines, of which I have scant knowledge anyway. No, my need was to make sense for myself out of the scattered pieces of my life—to see the pattern in the quilt, to use Mary Catherine Bateson's metaphor—but there was no established methodology.

Bateson had suggested that the linear story structure of the heroic quest could not apply to contemporary stop-and-start lives. It might pertain to tycoons like Lee Iacocca who write autobiographies of their struggle to a pinnacle of success. But I certainly was not, as they say in Hollywood, failing upward. I was failing down. This turned out to have a benefit. It gave me the time and desire for introspection, to explore in my journals a method that might work for me and others to understand life as story.

So I made myself my lab and then, having returned to the classroom, tested on my adult students the exercises and constructs that had worked for me. I was traveling at high speed in the dark, but as happens when you are on your path, other people believe you know what you are doing. They did deliver true life stories to my doorstep like foundlings (though for writing guidance, and only a few were true crime). I wasn't making six figures, but somehow I was working as an autobiographic writer's coach and surviving, barely.

Meanwhile, I was reading every noncelebrity autobiographic narrative being published—there were a remarkable number—and I noticed that in subject matter and technique, they were quite different from memoirs of the past. Autobiographic writing that I'd been exploring on a personal level was emerging as a vibrant new form of literature. I began to realize that a whole new consciousness about autobiographic writing was going on, and that my interest in it was part of a much bigger picture, what I came to call the New Autobiography.

Hungry now for anything I could find on the subject of autobiography and memoir, I visited the UCLA Research Library as I had so frequently when a grad student. My heart sank. When I had been researching diary writing twenty years before, there were only two books on autobiography. Now there were almost a hundred. In my absence, while I was lunching at Le Dome and waiting for my network calls to be returned, autobiography had become a hot interdisciplinary topic in the university. If only I'd stayed within the academy's ivy-covered walls, I'd be in my element now, tenured, at the apex of my career, instead of nabbing the occasional script or screen treatment to maintain my Writer's Guild Health and Pension, teaching extension classes for a pittance, and calling myself an autobiographic writer's coach ... say what? My life made no sense. No wonder I couldn't get what the screenplay structure people were calling "the hero's journey" to fit my life. No wonder I couldn't get the kinks out of my *formula for finding story in your life* I'd been testing on my baffled students. Life is not a drama, I despaired; it is haphazard, unstructured, especially mine.

I read the feminist critics of autobiography. They observed that women wrote more fragmented, less structured memoirs than men did. After all, unlike men, women were not encouraged to pursue their life desires directly (unless the goal was a man). So women's desire lines were often interrupted, shattered, or bifurcated. Probably that was why I couldn't find a coherent story in my life.

Some feminist scholars altogether dismissed the goal/quest thing leading to a crisis and climax at the end, as a male construct. The dramatic structure of the hero's journey might work for men because they were so linearminded, these theorists said, but not for women. But what did that mean in a practical sense? That women couldn't have stories? That they could not write dramatically about their lives? That wasn't what I was seeing in the personal, creative nonfiction that women were publishing. But then, all those academic studies I was reading were based on research of the past. Most began in the Middle Ages with Dame Julian of Norwich or Margery Kempe, and if they got to the twentieth century at all, they stopped halfway through. I already knew that the way both women and men wrote autobiography had taken an evolutionary leap in the second half of the twentieth century, and that recreating one's life as story was part of that change. And anyway, as I understood story, it was about having desires and crises and climaxes, and why should that be male? Screw the hero's journey! The structure of a story is *orgasmic,* and that, thank goddess, is not the sole province of either sex.

With that breakthrough, the two irreconcilable images of me—the English lit. instructor and the TV movie honcha—converged, and my wayward life began to make sense—and a spiral. I realized I'd *had* to leave academia in order to learn hands-on about writing contemporary true life stories. Only when I'd mastered in the field what no one I'd known in the university understood—story structure—could I couple it with what I knew about first person writing. The product of that coupling is this book on seeing and writing your life as story.

You say, well, that appears to have been therapeutic for you and an odd sort of career self-counseling, but why writing? Why not just seeing?

Good question, I say, because actually you can use this book and exercises in it simply to see and understand your life as story, which in itself is fascinating and valuable. But it's also about writing, because we depend on language in order to evolve as human beings and because writers for centuries have been developing language in extraordinary ways to express what otherwise could not be expressed or even perceived. So this is also a book on the craft of writing autobiographic narrative, and not a watered-down book on craft, but the most complete and advanced book on the subject you are likely to find. It asks that you experience your life with the levels and complexities of literature.

School taught you how to write to get through school and for commerce. Autobiographic narrative teaches you how to express what you've experienced, what you feel, what you remember, what you understand, who you are, what you believe and why, in a way that someone else would relish reading—reasons to learn this type of writing as valid as school or commerce.

But will it sell to a publisher? Will my grandson like it? Will I get sued? you ask. And I answer: Maybe—yes—and no, in that order.

Why are you putting words in my mouth? you finally say.

It's my job to give you your voice, my role as your personal writing coach.

Of course, in a book it is difficult to reproduce the individualized, intuitive process of one-on-one coaching. So I have written this study to work like glasses with progressive lenses that will allow you to focus on what you need to see at the moment no matter what your prescription. It is meant to be helpful to experienced and professional writers as well as to beginners, to those with only one story to tell as well as those with many. Some may begin with a spiritual yearning to understand the purpose of their life, others with the desire to publish and sell movie rights. Some will start with a desire to write only for oneself, and as the writing develops, discover a wish for readers. Some will want to create a memoir for descendants; some will turn their stories into fiction. In reading this book, you may come across places that do not immediately pertain to you, but if you keep going, you'll find what you seek.

Rather than read passively, I encourage you to use the table of contents and index to navigate through the book to satisfy your immediate concerns. If you are a curious beginner, you may wish to skim the entire book before you try any of the exercises, but do know this: The exercises have an intended arrangement, so if you wish the benefits of the autobiographic act without actually writing a complete work, or if you seek step-by-step guidance in writing your first autobiographic work, I recommend doing the exercises in the order presented.

Starting with Chapter 3, I will encourage you to start writing, or rather prewriting, in a creative journal. Don't confuse this journal with your intended autobiographic work; think of it rather as the turned soil in which to grow your eventual work. As a personal diary serves your life, a creative journal serves the generation of a work. Your creative journal may be a bound blank book, a spiral notebook, or a loose-leaf binder. Like a personal diary, it is a place for spontaneity, play, creative risks, and total freedom from judgments. In addition to holding the exercises I will suggest, a creative journal is a safe, private place where you can capture memories out of order as they come, experiment with different ideas for structure, or sketch alternative ways to approach a scene. It's a place to make mistakes, write clichés, wallow in self-pity, split infinitives, rant, be unfair, and have flashes of brilliance that turn out to be inflated abstractions. It is meant for no one's eyes but your own and can be destroyed when your autobiographic work is finished.

Eager as I am for you to start writing and learning from your writing, this chapter and the following one are devoted to laying groundwork. Because the New Autobiography is a new concept, it requires definition and some understanding of its evolution. So get ready for some definitions, and bear with me. Yes, definitions are as dull as overprocessed hair, but at the roots, still alive.

AUTOBIOGRAPHY: *the description (graphia) of an individual human life (bios) by the individual (auto).*

THE NEW AUTOBIOGRAPHY: *a late twentieth-century liberation of the established genre of writing.*

The New Autobiography is a vibrantly democratic and deeply personal type of narrative writing that, while little understood, is becoming popular in our culture. It is new because it is being written by new voices, not only those who represent the official and dominant view from the top. It is new because it is written as self-discovery rather than self-promotion. It is new because it beholds the individual's life, not through Puritan mandates of moral edification, nor nineteenth-century credos of materialistic success, nor twentieth-century formulas of reductionist psychology, but through the cohesion of literature and myth. Stylistically it is new because it employs storytelling devices, such as scenes and dialog, that are borrowed from fiction.

In publishing, New Autobiography (sometimes called personal nonfiction narrative or literary memoir) is the hottest event around. The May 12, 1996, issue of *The New York Times Magazine,* that harbinger of what's in, devoted itself to short memoirs by literary lights such as Mary Gordon, Susan Cheever, Joyce Carol Oates, and Leonard Michaels. In the lead article, "The Age of the Literary Memoir Is Now," James Atlas declared, "Fiction isn't delivering the news. Memoir is. At its best, in the hands of a writer able to command the tools of the novelist—character, scene, plot—the memoir can achieve unmatchable depth and resonance."

The New York Times Magazine, though, touched only the tip of the iceberg. Publication of memoir by noncelebrities as well as big shots is the real news, and the value of the new memoir writing doesn't even depend on publication. For New Autobiography transforms how we view and value even the most private and seemingly insignificant lives. It is a complete redefinition of who may write about their lives, who they write for, the reasons they write, how they write, what they write about, and what they do with the writing.

WHO DOES IT

"Plebeian autobiography" is the term Jill Johnstone used to describe "a new autobiography" in *The New York Times Book Review,* April 25, 1993. "A revolution is taking place, a form is under development," and with it, she wrote, a revised notion of "who has rights, whose voice can be heard, whose individuality is worthy."

In fact there has been a trend toward increasing democratization of the genre through the centuries, particularly in the United States and especially since the last half of the nineteenth century. As the form of writing favored by African-Americans and other ethnic minorities, autobiography carries forward a rich tradition of self-affirmation through finding one's voice. It has served as a form of revolution when seized by those whose lives and selves would otherwise be invisible: women, minorities, immigrants, homosexuals, disenfranchised youth, gang members, the blue-collar father, the romantic eccentric, the elderly, the women and men whose lives have taken the unpaved road, those who have felt silenced—all those who feel the need to bear witness to their truth. It is a way of saying, "I matter; this life I have lived has meaning! And because I tell it from my perspective, because I frame it, it has the meaning I give it."

The purpose of this book is to push this tendency toward democratization one step further so that, as Carolyn Kay Steedman writes in her autobiographical novel, *Landscape for a Good Woman,* "the people in exile, the inhabitants of the long streets, may start to use the autobiographical 'I,' and tell the stories of their life."

Those who revere language may clutch, may fear this means a lowering of standards. Yet the emergence of a New Autobiography converges with a broadening, not a devolution of what we consider literature. No longer does literature have to be written by recognized writers with a body of work. It can be an unpublished book or one autobiographic story by a man who never wrote anything else. Its value may be measured not in how many people it reaches or good reviews it receives, but in the experience creating it gives the writer.

As a grad student in English literature, I was taught to revere a literary canon that consisted mainly of dead white males; I still revere them. I never expected, though, to find writing all around me that would awe me as the classics did, written by women and men I know, by people of every hue, by students who come to my classes, young women who hold down jobs as exotic dancers, business executives, kindergarten teachers, secretaries, and shopkeepers. What these unknown writers can do with language makes me envious. The way they bare their hearts makes me love them as I fell in love with Shakespeare and the authors of my favorite novels. The way they can take a writing principle and use it like a pool shark uses a cue makes me weak with admiration. This kind of writing is going on in writing centers and church basements and bookstore back rooms all over the country. And part of this, a big part of this, is New Autobiography.

⟨ WHO WE WRITE FOR

Like older kinds of memoir, New Autobiography may be published or given to grandchildren, but it need not be. It can be written for friends; self-published or live disembodied on the Internet; it can be written for oneself as a gift of wonder.

⟨ WHY WE WRITE IT

The possible reasons are so many, I'm going to list just some:

You want to see how your life makes a story by setting it down.

You want the catharsis and self-forgiveness of an honest and complete confession.

You are in midlife and want to gain from the life behind you the wisdom to mold the life still before you.

You are nearing the end of your life and wish to understand and share what it has meant.

You desire to change the myth that has been driving your life, so you want to catch and preserve it like a fly in amber.

You are a student, a journalist, screenwriter, or novelist who wants to find your personal voice.

You want to touch the sacred, to find the eternal form of myth in your own contemporary life.

You are motivated by familial love to leave for your descendants knowledge of who you were and the life you lived.

You are motivated by desire to relieve the loneliness, fear, or ignorance of others who may find themselves in a situation you've been through.

You have a whopper of a story to tell and you want to make a bundle by selling it.

You wish to write about your family as a way of ending destructive cycles and creating cohesion based on truth.

You are a notable person who has been invited by a publisher to write your life story and don't wish to rely on a ghostwriter.

You are a not-at-all famous person to whom life has given experiences too valuable to fade into oblivion.

You want to know what is true, true for you.

You never enjoyed writing in school, but you want to experience the pleasure and sensuality of writing like the contemporary authors you enjoy reading.

You want to relive and relish the best years of your life.

You know that the only thing that death cannot destroy is memory, and you wish to preserve from forgetfulness those you have loved.

You can endure your life only by transforming it into a work of art.

Your way to cope with your troubles is to make yourself and others laugh at them.

You wish to celebrate the mystery and complexity of your life.

You want the intimacy and adventure of being in a memoir club.

As a bird must sing, it's your human nature to tell your story.

How We Write It

Like the New Journalism developed by Tom Wolfe and other magazine writers in the late 1960s, New Autobiography appropriates storytelling devices from the realistic novel. It is often written in dramatic scenes with dialog and interior monologs. It uses novelistic devices to reach inner truths, not just the truth of facts.

New Autobiography revitalizes traditional forms such as memoir, confession, full autobiography, vocational memoir, spiritual autobiography, personal essay, and meditation, and is creating new forms of first person narrative. It includes the most commercial types of creative nonfiction as well as the newest wave of artistic experimentation. This book concentrates on the written word, but artists are exploring the principles of New Autobiography in photography, poetry, as solo performance pieces, and through mixed media.

What We Write About

Just as it can be written utilizing traditional forms, New Autobiography can cover any of the traditional themes of autobiographic writing, such as adventure, spiritual quest, racial injustice, or overcoming adversity, but it is distinguished by greater intimacy and emotional authenticity than autobiographic writing in previous eras. Recently published works penetrate new territory, some of it dark and dangerous: autism (Donna Williams, *Nobody Nowhere*), depression (William Styron, *Darkness Visible* and Elizabeth Wurtzel, *Prozac Nation*), the loss of a beloved to AIDS (Mark Doty, *Heaven's Coast*), family violence (Mikal Gilmore, *Shot in the Heart*), intergenerational substance abuse (Carolyn See, *Dreaming: Hard Luck and Good Times in America*), and adolescent gang life (Nathan McCall, *Makes Me Wanna Holler*). New Autobiography at the same time explores the spiritual depths of common experiences (Terry Tempest Williams, *Refuge*, and Nancy Mairs, *Ordinary Times*.)

New Autobiography is more naturalistic than the old; it is grounded in the daily realities of people and events. It also differs in the degree to which it shapes life into story, into personal myth. Carl Jung asked, "What is your myth—the myth in which you live?" New Autobiography answers that question.

⌒The Passages of Writing Life Stories

Autobiographic writings may go through many stages and need not progress beyond the initial step or steps.

⌒DISCOVERING STORY IN YOUR LIFE
AS A HEALING PROCESS

Whether or not you complete or even attempt a written work, you can use the exercises in this book to contemplate your life's path and learn its encoded wisdom. In a sense, this first passage of the autobiographic process is a kind of therapy. For although therapy is seen as a healing science and autobiography as a literary form, there have always been intimate links between psychotherapy and the restorative powers of personal narrative. In traditional Freudian analysis, for instance, the subject through recollection and the analyst through interpretation fashioned a therapeutic narrative. Freud held that his "cure" was accomplished when the patient finally understood himself as the central actor in a drama of inner and outer events which have meaning.

Actually, sixteen centuries before Freud, Saint Augustine used the autobiographic process of reviewing his past in order to heal himself. Written ten years after Augustine's conversion in a garden in Milan, the *Confessions* begins with him lamenting that his soul again "lies in ruins"; in writing his narrative, he hopes that God will help him to "build it up again." Augustine wrote his narrative of wantonness and subsequent conversion in order to heal himself, and others, in the present.

Today psychologists have rediscovered personal narrative and its healing potential. James Hillman's "acorn theory," explained in *The Soul's Code*, asks that we look for the line of continuity in our lives in order to know ourselves, our unique character, our *daemon*. To find it he suggests that we read life backwards, which is what one does in the autobiographic process. When

I looked backwards to find some continuum in the scattered pieces of my life, I found it in my fascination with seeing life as stories. This was the yearning that had pulled me to read and daydream about fairy tales and myths, write, study literature, read diaries, make movies, teach writing. This *desire line*, as I call it, had for me the shimmering romantic energy of Hillman's *daemon*. There was within it a sense of providence in which my life spirit was the driving force.

Since you must use a desire line to shape an autobiographic story, in the process you recall your yearnings and dreams and their place in your destiny. You are led away from perceiving your history as a series of accidents or calamities that wrongly formed you. "We are less damaged by the traumas of childhood," Hillman writes, "than by the traumatic way we remember childhood," and "We dull our lives by the way we conceive them. We have stopped imagining them with any sort of romance, any fictional flair." Through the autobiographic process you restore the "romance" and "fictional flair" of story to your own life, and you replace old stories of powerlessness with stories of consciousness and revelation in which you are the protagonist.

In this sense, the autobiographic process has features of another current school of psychotherapy that sees neuroses as unconscious scripts that people have been told or told themselves and lived out either by compliance or rebellion. Once you recognize your preconditioned scripts, the theory goes, you can accept or reject them and create conscious stories of your own making to guide your life.

By applying story structure to your life, as you will learn to do in this book, you necessarily replace unconscious, unexamined scripts with consciously chosen stories. The old scripts are self-defeating personal myths repeated to oneself until they seem to fit perfectly—as a straitjacket. In working with students, I recognize these scripts as *story fragments* that have a self-pitying, blaming, or repetitious tone and which run in a circle like a dog biting its tail. True, complete stories have many tones, dark and light, and are orgasmic in structure. True stories lead to a climax which is a point of transformation. Story structure pushes you past the circular logic of impairment because it requires you to move forward to a climactic realization in order to give the story a meaningful conclusion. Though not necessarily religious in the sectarian sense, it is also a spiritual process because story structure, the essence of myth and literature, engages you in the mysterious ritual of psychic death and rebirth.

Yet while the autobiographic process offers profound healing benefits, it is important to distinguish it from therapy. It's not a substitute for people who need medical intervention, and, in one respect, it could not be more different from the discipline of psychology: in its approach to language. Psychology deals in theories, generalizations, cases, and categorizations. In autobiographic writing, you need to eschew all diagnostic labels, reductionist theories, and psychological language, and instead seek what in yourself is most individual, most unique.

So the first passage of autobiographic writing, outlining your stories using the exercises in this book, is full of rewards, but if you go on to complete for yourself a draft of even a one or two-page work, you'll discover increased gains which are side effects, so to speak, of attentiveness to craft and language. If you complete even one short autobiographic story or essay, you will know the delight of creative alchemy, of making a gem out of life's dross.

WRITING LIFE'S STORIES FOR YOURSELF

Most of the pleasures of autobiographic writing do not depend upon having a reader other than oneself. No one has expressed the delight of the experience better than Virginia Woolf in her own unpublished autobiographic writings. This passage is taken from a piece titled "A Sketch of the Past."

> Perhaps this is the strongest pleasure known to me. It is the rapture I get when in writing I seem to be discovering what belongs to what; making a scene come right; making a character come together. From this I reach what I might call a philosophy; at any rate it is a constant idea of mine; that behind the cotton wool [of daily life] is hidden a pattern; that we—I mean all human beings—are connected with this; that the whole world is a work of art; that we are parts of the work of art. *Hamlet* or a Beethoven quartet is the truth about this vast mass that we call the world. But there is no Shakespeare, there is no Beethoven; certainly and emphatically there is no God; we are the words; we are the music; we are the thing itself.

Woolf is describing the pleasure of seeing the patterns in one's experience. Another writer might see that pattern as the hand of God, as the revelation of God's existence, but for Woolf the discovery was purely aesthetic. Pattern, shape, form in life for her was the great spiritual mystery.

The ability to find this aesthetic or spiritual shape in one's life through writing is a unique gift of the genre to its practitioners, even if they never share it with anyone.

⌒SHARING YOUR WRITING WITH SELECTED OTHERS

As some of us feel our stories are not complete until written, many will feel they are not complete until told to selected others. You may not really be able to understand what it is you have written until you have a compassionate reader who will reflect back to you what it is you have said. You may wish to read this book and do the exercises in it with others in a self-formed memoir club. The best place to find helpful listeners for your work in progress is with others doing autobiographic writing. The intimacy of sharing life stories in many cases creates alternative families, and you may discover that the humane spirit of community in a memoir group is more valuable to you than even the writing itself. I offer suggestions for forming or finding a memoir club in Appendix 1.

⌒EDITING AND REWRITING FOR PUBLICATION

Two of the benefits of publication are obvious: an added boost in self-esteem and, in some cases, financial reward. There are other benefits not so obvious. When you publish experiential writing, it enters the hearts and minds of people you would never otherwise meet. For some people, publishing autobiographic writings helps them discover their "tribe," or rather, helps their tribe discover them. Those with whom you have the most in common and those who most need to hear your story may not be your family members, may not live in your neighborhood or even your state. To reach them, you need to publish, and, fortunately, there are now many opportunities. Shorter pieces can be placed in newsletters, magazines, and journals (some are dedicated to experiential writing). You can self-publish inexpensively with desktop publishing or on the Internet or offer your work there through an electronic publisher.

The desire for publication is natural, and for many people will be an ultimate goal; but it is important to realize at the outset that just as a draft written for yourself is not the same as one meant for your family, a draft written for family or friends will not be the same as one written for publication.

If you never publish a word, however, or even share a phrase from your writings with another person, there is a major, unforeseen benefit in practicing New Autobiography. With new forms of writing come new paradigms for seeing life. Through New Autobiography you may begin to see yourself as the hero of your own story, even as it is happening. For me this is an enormously positive.

When I view myself as the heroine of my own story, I no longer complain about the conflicts in my life and in myself. I am no longer a victim of circumstances. No longer am I caught within the psychological paradigm of neurosis. Instead, I am full of anticipation for my journey into the unknown. I am a protagonist in a world of unending dilemmas which contain hidden meaning that it is up to me to discover. I am the artist of my life who takes the raw materials given, no matter how bizarre, painful, or disappointing, and gives them shape and meaning. I am within each scene and each chapter of my life, defining my character through the choices I make. I am on my own side, rooting for myself, aching for myself, celebrating my sensual experiences, marveling in the exquisite subtlety of feelings in my life that novelists have made me aware of in their books. I am as engaged with the ongoing story in my life as is a reader who eagerly turns the page.

When my mother is dying of cancer, as she is as I write this, I recognize my desire to flee the pain of watching her lose her memory, each day becoming less vital, and I do not flee. I embrace this sorrow because it, too, is life's story. I have always been terrified of death; my own and hers. My fear has made me cowardly. My friend Dianne believes that when we die, there is a sudden burst of energy released and that we have a perception we could not have imagined before that transformation. I doubt most beliefs about death—that we are reincarnated, or go to an eternal afterlife, or have a disembodied consciousness. But I believe Dianne's description of an ending because it is what happens at the end of every story: There is a climax, a burst of energy, a transformation, and a new, shattering realization. Something dies so that something can be born. And since I believe every life is a story, I believe Dianne about the end. My understanding of life as story has even shifted my conception of death.

Of course I cannot promise you my rewards; only that in expressing your life as story, you will gain your own. And it's nice to know that with all its benefits, autobiographic narrative is the easiest type of writing at which to succeed. You don't have to do research; you know your protagonist and your main characters intimately; and the rewards are so immediate that once you get going, it carries you along.

It is, though, the form of writing that demands the most courage and personal compassion. Moreover, unlike diary writing, autobiographic writing is not a purely spontaneous activity; to do it well requires the ability to endure dissatisfaction and frustration as you write, to learn from your writing about your writing and yourself.

You may already be getting cold feet; you may already be thinking, Who am I to write about my life, I'm not important enough, or I'm not capable enough, or my story isn't unique enough—or any number of other self-doubts that will specifically be addressed in this book. For right now, as your writing coach, I want to give you a touchstone, in the form of a quote from Martha Graham to her student Agnes de Mille, which is recorded in de Mille's memoir, *Dance to the Piper*.

TOUCHSTONE 1

There is a vitality, a life force, a quickening that is translated through you into action, and because there is only one of you in all time, the expression is unique. And if you block it, it will never exist through any other medium . . . and be lost. The world will not have it.

It is not your business to determine how good it is nor how valuable it is; nor how it compares with other expressions. It is your business to keep it yours clearly and directly, to keep the channel open.

You do not even have to believe in yourself or your work. You have to keep open and aware directly to the urges that motivate YOU. Keep the channel open. . . . No artist is pleased. . . . There is no satisfaction whatever at any time. There is only a queer, divine dissatisfaction; a blessed unrest that keeps us marching and makes us more alive.

The reason people are beset with self-doubts when engaged in autobiographic writing is not only personal, however. Often they are the result of internalized misconceptions about autobiography, misconceptions that come from outdated notions. So before you begin writing, I want to give you a brief history of the genre you are about to embrace.

2

The Evolution of a New Autobiography

Like language itself, forms of expression adapt themselves to the values and needs of each historic era. Autobiography has always crested the wave of society's progress, wiser about itself in most ways than the diehards who try to safeguard it from change. Our English language tradition of autobiographic writing comes most directly from the Puritans, who wrote autobiography to edify others and to record their history as God's elect. At present, autobiography is serving quite different needs: for intimacy, the telling of private truths, the discovery of inner meaning, self-definition as opposed to external definition, and the sharing of new wisdom gleaned from contemporary life stories. Not surprisingly, autobiography today looks and reads unlike previous modes.

It's as if between old autobiography and the new, there has been an evolutionary leap, making them as different as Cro-Magnons were from Neanderthals. The New Autobiography is almost a new genre, distinct from older forms of autobiography, which continue to exist with it side by side. This makes things confusing because old autobiography shares the same bookstore shelf with New Autobiography. In order to distinguish between them, you need to recognize the conventions of old autobiography, and that requires some history.

I have debated in my mind three dozen times whether or not to include this chapter on literary history. It reads more like nouvelle scholarship than the intimate, practical coaching of the rest of this book. This is particularly problematic because it's at the beginning. Incongruously, this historical chapter is like those dutiful ones on "my forebears" that often introduce an old-fashioned, traditional autobiography. I find those chapters on deceased ancestors hard to get through, and, I confess, usually skip or skim them. They lack the intimacy that emerges as soon as the author begins to write from firsthand experience.

I decided to keep this chapter because I think you need to know something about the history of a craft you wish to practice. Without realizing it, you might have quite outdated assumptions about autobiographic writing, assumptions that were apt two hundred years ago, but that have little relevance now. My reasoning is this: if you understand New Autobiography's evolution, you will be able to embrace its freedoms without guilt.

The extant history of autobiography begins around 3000 BC with the Egyptians, who were obsessed with preserving themselves past death. The furnishings for a rich man's tomb included statues and pictures of himself, and a first person account of his life carved on tablets and walls. These formulaic records of pharaohs and their cohorts all followed the same pattern of monotonous boasting: "I was the favorite of the king. I had the most fruitful orchards. My house was the largest next to the king's. My praise ascended to the skies. . . ." You could say that such unabashedly self-promotional autobiographies continue in our own day as the publications of a Donald Trump or Maggie Thatcher.

Egyptian autobiographies changed a tad several thousand years later. In the era of the New Kingdom mummies were entombed with their autobiographies clutched to their breasts. The privileged royals who could afford well-made tombs believed they would need their memoirs close at hand as testimonials to present to the god Osiris, who along with his sister Isis, would judge the deceased's worthiness to enter the afterlife. The self-justifying autobiographies of the New Kingdom were really elaborate denials of wrongdoing, and, like the earlier bragging inscriptions, were formulaic: "I have done no sin against men. I have done nothing that the gods abhor. I have let no one starve. I have done no murder," etc. The fundamental attitude toward self-presentation was: never admit to any flaw in one's own character. This type of memoir also survives in our own time as the "as told to" books of an O. J. Simpson or Lyle Menendez.

Based on Egyptian tomb inscriptions, we find another trend established: a difference in how women and men write about themselves. Feminist scholar Estelle Jelinek argues that although there are exceptions, throughout written history women have favored personal and subjective subjects and a more piecemeal, fragmented, less linear style than men. These differences, she believes, are apparent in the first extant autobiography by a woman, Ahuri, the daughter of an Egyptian pharaoh.

Ahuri's autobiography is far more personal than the male autobiographies of the time. Ahuri writes of her courtship by her brother, how she "got around" her father to obtain his permission to let her marry her brother, and her subsequent marital difficulties and burial arrangements. Although it is the first full autobiography from birth to death, the narrative is frequently interrupted by flashbacks, making it more disjointed than the more chronologically linear autobiographies of men at the time.

What I find particularly interesting about Ahuri's autobiography is that it is the first to have introduced fiction into the form. Ahuri tells her life story in the first person as if she were already dead and recalling her life, certainly a fiction. She writes as if she herself is addressing the reader, and this is also fictitious. In her text Ahuri admits that, like most Egyptian women, she has not been taught how to write, so we must assume she dictated her autobiography or used a ghostwriter.

After Ahuri, the use of the first person narrative clearly splits into fictional and fantastic fables on the one hand and nonfiction, historic accounts on the other. Fact and fiction do not openly complement each other in autobiographic writing again until the twentieth century.

The Christian Confession

In the most cursory way, I'm going to fast-forward through the Western tradition of autobiographic writing, which for all intents and purposes skips from the Egyptians right past the Greeks, who were more interested in a collective ideal than the unique self. Historically, autobiographic writing seems to be tied to an interest in the individual and individuality, which may also be why autobiography is far more prevalent in the West than in Asian cultures.

Although his is not the first autobiography, the father of the form in the Western tradition is said to be Saint Augustine, the fornicating, thieving, carousing, then converted sinner/saint. His *Confessions,* written about 399 AD, establishes the dominant type of autobiographic writing for fourteen centuries. Unlike the Egyptian denials, the Christian form of the confession is an admission of sin in order to be saved. The author offers the details of his misdeeds—whether wantonness, drunkenness, or crime—for the reader's enjoyment, and then recounts how and why he mended his ways.

The conventions of the confession remain popular in our own time, especially among recent graduates of the Betty Ford Clinic.

The stated intent of such confessions is to warn or inspire the reader through the example of the author's life. Saint Augustine tells us that his life was altered by reading Paul's Epistles, and he intends that the reader will likewise be changed by reading his personal account of conversion to holiness. Until the Renaissance, all autobiographies followed Augustine's example of presenting one's life as a dramatic spiritual duel eventually resolved by God. However, women seem not to have practiced the form, probably because in the Middle Ages a woman who confessed to sins like Augustine's would have been stoned to death.

The First Secular Autobiographies

It was the Renaissance goldsmith turned sculptor, Benvenuto Cellini (1500–1571), who first shaped a nonreligious autobiography as a work of art for its own sake and as a reflection of self, rather than as an instrument to convert the reader. Dictated to an amanuensis in the rough vernacular then spoken in Florence, Cellini's memoir feels remarkably modern because it is crafted like a Florentine novella, each incident and chapter seeming to grow out of what has come before. Cellini portrays himself as a swashbuckling soldier/artist, a celebrity in his own time. His description of his escape from prison is full of boasting and exaggerations, but is undeniably the work of a man skilled in entertaining his audience. Cellini's masterpiece did not establish a tradition of autobiographic writing in his time, but bears resemblance to the self-celebratory memoirs of some music and film stars in ours. Reprinted and translated into English and French in the eighteenth century, it may have influenced the development of the novel in England.

However, the development of the realistic novel was more directly influenced by British women's secular autobiographies. Prior to the late seventeenth century, only religious women and noblewomen wrote memoirs. These were either about spiritual ecstasy or the advantages of domestic propriety. With the advent of cheap, popular publishing, though, impoverished women, desperate for money, wrote and sold confessions about their sexual indiscretions. These "independent" women (usually divorcées or actresses) begged understanding in their memoirs, explaining that economic circumstances had forced them into lives of sin. Their racy confessions sold like hotcakes—not unlike the confessional memoirs written by actresses today. They led directly to the novel. (Samuel Richardson's *Pamela,* and Daniel Defoe's *Moll Flanders* although written by men, closely imitate the female first person confessions of the time.)

Jean-Jacques Rousseau's *Confessions* further broke new ground in frankness. Begun in 1766 by the man without whom, Napoleon supposedly said, there would have been no French Revolution, the *Confessions* at first seems to contradict its author's famous philosophy: that human nature is inherently good; it is the inequities and abuses of society that corrupt humankind. But perhaps only a man convinced of his inherent goodness could admit to the appalling private offenses that Rousseau does. He admits to stealing when he was a lackey and allowing a servant girl to bear the blame. He tells us he did not try to help his benefactor who fell down on the street in a fit. He reveals that he consigned five of his natural children to a foundling hospital, having taken precautions that he should never hear of them again.

Rousseau's intent in writing strikes us as peculiarly modern: to make a clean breast of it, to keep nothing back, even the most private incidents of his life—not to convert the reader, but to enable the outside world "to behold a man as he really was in his inmost self." Such candor will not be found again until the twentieth century, when it reappears as the "tell all" book, such as producer Julia Phillips's *You'll Never Eat Lunch in This Town Again.*

Autobiography in America

Even before the proprieties of the Victorian era stifled other forms of Romantic self-exploration, the secular intimate confessions disappeared. Instead what prevailed during the late eighteenth and nineteenth centuries were conventional types of autobiography that were already prevalent: the memoirs of soldiers and statesmen, the modest autobiographies of wives of prominent men, and religious confessions, now written especially by Puritan ministers and Quakers for the edification of their congregations.

When the Puritans sought refuge from persecution in the American colonies, they brought their tradition of religious autobiography with them. They wrote autobiographies for the same reason they kept diaries: to preserve the congregation's history as God's elect. Given this historic function, factual accuracy was understandably of great importance.

But the Puritans and Quakers did not simply value truthful life records— they out and out distrusted fiction writing and novels as frivolous and morally suspect. The only stories you were supposed to read in Puritan America were true stories that set an example for an exemplary life. This resulted in plenty of edifying and factual autobiographies, but also in some fake, outlandish ones. Just as repression of sex may impel perverse expressions of it, so puritanical repression of the imagination led to some perversely phony memoirs.

In fact, "pseudo memoirs" became quite popular in colonial America. In a climate officially hostile to fiction, romances and adventures that disguised themselves as autobiographies could find a place on sparsely filled bookshelves because they professed to record, not what the writer imagined, but what had actually happened. They offered a stirring adrenaline ride by incorporating fictional embellishments within the authentic accounts—but not openly. Like the first person stories found in soldier of fortune magazine today, both publishers and readers pretended they were completely factual.

The earliest of the falsified autobiographies were Indian captivity narratives. The form had begun authentically as a variation of the spiritual confession. Often written by women, they asked for absolution for the sins forced upon them by their "savage" captors. Because such forced sex with pagans was considered utterly shameful, most captivity narratives were published after the author's death. They became so popular that they were frequently reprinted and, in the eighteenth century, they were inflated and sensationalized by editors eager to capitalize on any evidence of Indian brutality, in order to justify exterminating the Indians and confiscating their lands. By the nineteenth century, those who wrote Indian captivity narratives were defensive about the authenticity of their accounts, sometimes attaching affidavits from military personnel as evidence that *this* account was really true.

Also by the mid-nineteenth century, a new wave of feminism had begun in the United States, and with it new forms of the "thrilling" confessional autobiography initiated by those long-forgotten British actresses nearly two centuries before. Women in America were daring to write about their unhappy marriages, often in order to vindicate themselves for having committed the social taboo of leaving a husband. Like the captivity narratives, these thrilling domestic confessions were sometimes authentic, but once successful, were often copied by other writers who began to include exaggerations and fabrications. Thus developed the "pseudo confession," which continues into our day as the fabricated stories in *True Confessions*–type magazines.

The "thrilling" autobiography became popular in other forms as well. Men continued to write adventure stories of exploration and war, and women began to write about disguising themselves as men to have adventures in wars and at sea. Women also wrote about their incarceration in prisons, mental institutions, and (as part of an antipapist movement) in convents.

Curiously, these autobiographies, which often mixed fiction with fact, gave a more open, diverse, and frank account of women's real feelings than had the earlier, more strictly factual edifying autobiographies. As with the Indian captivity narratives, the editors of sensationalized thrilling autobiographies believed that their means of exaggeration and fabrication were justified by their social ends. In some cases it is hard to disagree.

For example, in the mid-nineteenth century, a new type of thrilling autobiography, the ex-slave narrative, began to rival disguise and domestic autobiographies in popularity. A number of these flight-from-slavery narratives were actually written by white northern abolitionist editors who, in their zeal to get their message across, shaped their "as told to" narratives with digressions on the evils of slavery, long dialogs, and highly dramatized descriptions of the slave's escape. These thrilling ex-slave narratives, like the autobiographies by unconventional women, used fictional devices to heighten the action and hold their audience's attention, thereby delivering their important social message.

After the Civil War, the thrilling ex-slave autobiographies were replaced with more sedate life studies by literate African-American men and women. They had to write for a white audience because most of the recently freed slaves could not yet read. Never openly critical or angry, the authors tried to prove by example that blacks could succeed in the white world. By today's standards these inspirationals strike us as overly amiable.

But it wasn't just successful African-Americans who felt they had to be insistently positive, upbeat, and uncritical in writing inspirational autobiographies. Even the most radical suffragists, like Elizabeth Cady Stanton, wrote autobiographies that by today's standards seem to do somersaults not to offend. These early reformers believed, rightly, that they would be judged as representatives of their entire group or cause. So anything that could shed a negative light on that important cause was omitted: the rifts within the suffrage organizations, discord in their personal lives, their despair of ever achieving women's emancipation. Elizabeth Cady Stanton, for example, though radical and assertive in her other writings, in her autobiography presents herself as a nonthreatening comfortable wife and doting mother who happened to have founded and led the fight for woman suffrage. She omits any mention of her separation from her husband or that they lived in separate houses. She presents as unqualified successes all her efforts at organizing and petitioning for women's emancipation, never admitting defeat though in reality she never saw the success of her life's work, having died eighteen years before women were finally granted the vote in 1920.

Nowadays, early African-American and suffragist inspirationals seem insincere by their omissions. But they seeded today's rich African-American protest literature on the one hand and an emerging, uninhibited body of women's autobiographic writing on the other.

DEVELOPMENTS IN THE TWENTIETH CENTURY

Before the tradition of African-American autobiography could flower into contemporary masterpieces by James Baldwin, Maya Angelou, or Alex Haley, and feminist autobiographic writing could take off with Erica Jong's *Fear of Flying* or become the complex voice of Alice Munro, the freedoms of fiction would have to be introduced into autobiography—not as the exaggerations and fabrications of the thrilling autobiographies, or as the conscious omissions in inspirationals, but as an appreciation of naturalism and intimacy. Writers of the realistic novel had been developing techniques for conveying the significance of ordinary happenings in an everyday world. In the late nineteenth century, these new techniques were making the novel feel more real than autobiography.

Even as Dickens and Dreiser were taking the novel to new heights by exploring the drama in everyday life and characters, autobiography was floundering. Despite its emerging African-American and feminist traditions, autobiography in its dominant forms hit an all-time low. Although there were exceptions, one finds in the late nineteenth century and in the early twentieth century, a great many well-educated men publishing puffed-up accounts of their accomplishments. Since the values in that gilded age were increasingly materialistic, autobiography lost its focus on life as a spiritual duel. Instead, it fulfilled the need of the times to understand how success, status, and wealth are achieved. The authors felt they had to hide their vulnerabilities and failures, and thus many of their autobiographies were guilty of rationalizations and self-justification.

By the middle of the twentieth century, the novel and autobiography had switched positions. The novel had risen from its lowly place as a suspect and frivolous genre to its status as crown jewel of American letters. In an introductory essay to a collection, *The New Journalism*, Tom Wolfe recalls the pinnacle of adoration to which the novel had ascended.

It's hard to explain what an American dream the idea of writing a novel was in the 1940s, the 1950s, and right into the early 1960s. The Novel was no mere literary form. It was a psychological phenomenon. It was a cortical fever. It belonged in the glossary to *A General Introduction to Psychoanalysis*, somewhere between Narcissism and Obsessional Neurosis. . . . Not so long ago, I am willing to wager, half the people who went to work for publishing houses did so with the belief that their real destiny was to be novelists. Among people on what they call the creative side of advertising . . . the percentage must have reached 90 percent. . . . Such was the grip of the damnable Novel. Likewise among people in television, public relations, the movies, on the English faculties of colleges and high schools, among framing shop clerks, convicts, unmarried sons living with Mom . . . a whole swarm of fantasizers out there steaming and proliferating in the ego mulches of America.

Now the novel defined one as a real writer; autobiography was for everyone else, for amateurs. And the amateurs embraced it wholeheartedly. In the twentieth century, autobiographies have been published by atheists, con men, boxing referees, store detectives, widowers, veterans of the Vietnam war, sports figures, immigrants, people with mental or emotional illnesses, people who are blind or deaf, teachers, prostitutes, singers, dancers, survivors of concentration camps in Europe and internment camps in America, priests, servants, social workers, activists, nurses, convicts, factory workers, and nearly every other profession or social identification.

Gaining vigor from its sweeping diversity, autobiographic writing, considered a "subgenre" by academics in the 1920s, '30s, '40s, and '50s, picked up any literary writer who would have it: lesbians like Gertrude Stein, impoverished scoundrels like Henry Miller, blacks in Harlem like Zora Neale Hurston, lowly enlisted men like James Jones, and bohemians like Jack Kerouac. They wrote with the freedom of those who are marginal to the establishment; they wrote with the zeal of those who are creating and affirming themselves by writing.

Because these literary outsiders were, like everyone else, enamored of the novel, they began to create of autobiography an amphibious creature, neither fish nor fowl, neither autobiography nor novel, but a New Autobiography. At first this meant the incorporation of frankly fictional techniques into the traditional form of autobiography. Gertrude Stein, for example, experimented with a fictional point of view in *The Autobiography of Alice B. Toklas*. The book was really about Gertrude Stein's life and written by Gertrude Stein, but the first person narrator is her companion, Alice B. Toklas. The use of this fictional device solved several problems for Stein. It allowed her to praise her friends without appearing sentimental, to criticize those she disliked without attacking them directly, and to present herself as a genius without appearing egotistical. It seemed to be Alice who was saying Gertrude was a genius.

> I may say that only three times in my life have I met a genius and each time a bell within me rang and I was not mistaken, and I may say in each case it was before there was any general recognition of the quality of genius within them. The three geniuses of whom I wish to speak are Gertrude Stein, Pablo Picasso and Alfred Whitehead.

Putting her autobiography into the mouth of Alice also allowed Stein to present in a discreet way the centrality of their lesbian relationship without ever explicitly stating it. Her use of fictional techniques allowed Stein to be more open in her memoir about her personal life than she felt she otherwise could be.

Other American expatriates such as Henry Miller and Christopher Isherwood, influenced by Marcel Proust, wrote autobiographical fiction. Their novels and short stories demolished the boundaries, which had been so important to the Puritans, between fact and fiction, memory and imagination. In subject they were intimate and revealing, in style they were novelistic. Innovators like Miller and Isherwood paved the way for autobiographical novelists like John Nichols and Pat Conroy, who would fully accept the bastard form and give it a seamless literary polish.

As our best contemporary writers took to autobiography, academics and literary critics, who had turned up their noses at the form, got a whiff and started to wag their tails like devoted dogs. Paul John Eakin in *Fictions in Autobiography: Studies in the Art of Self Invention* (1985) observes that twentieth-century autobiographers "no longer believe that autobiography can offer a faithful and unmediated reconstruction of a historically verifiable past." Instead, modern autobiographies express "the play of the autobiographical act itself."

Nowhere is this more true than in the recent works of Philip Roth. He has become so preoccupied with the postmodern terrain between the novel and autobiography, between fact and fiction, between what he terms "the written and the unwritten world" that he has made it a literary game. Defensive over having the term "autobiographical novel" applied to his earlier work such as *Portnoy's Complaint,* he wrote *Operation Shylock: A Confession* about "another" Philip Roth who was a spy in Israel. Roth's publisher and readers call it a novel, but Roth, perversely, insists that *Operation Shylock* is completely factual autobiography. Roth's books have become "metafictions," intellectual and self-conscious explorations of the relationship between fiction and autobiography.

It was one thing to write about one's life and call it fiction; it was another to incorporate the imagination into writing about one's life and call it autobiography, and it took more courage. Mary McCarthy, in *Memories of a Catholic Girlhood,* wrote each chapter of her memoir with novelistic devices of suspense, character development, and thematic unity, then Monday morning quarterbacking herself, added an analysis of just how she had mythologized her memories. For example, after a chapter set in her convent school where she'd pretended to have lost her faith in order to get attention, McCarthy reveals how much of the chapter was fictionalized.

This story is so true to our convent life that I find it almost impossible to sort out the guessed at and the half-remembered from the undeniably real. . . . I am not absolutely certain of the chronology, the whole drama of my loss of faith took place during a very short space of time, and I believe it was during a retreat. The conversations, as I have warned the reader, are mostly fictional, but their tone and tenor are right. That was the way the priests talked, and those, in general, were the arguments they brought to bear on me. . . .

The proofs of God's existence are drawn from the Catholic Encyclopedia. My own questions are a mixture of memory and conjecture. One bit of dialogue was borrowed from an Episcopal clergyman: "There's a little gap that we have to fill with faith." My son, Reuel, came home one day and quoted this from his Sacred Study teacher. I laughed (it was so like the way my priests had talked) and put it in.

McCarthy felt she had to confess to her readers when she was taking imaginative leaps, but Maxine Hong Kingston incorporated wild fantasies into her memoir *The Woman Warrior* and made no explanations. To fill in what would otherwise be missing in her multigenerational story, Kingston imagined what she did not and could not know about her ancestors, yet felt she must know in order to understand herself as a Chinese-American. She writes:

Chinese-Americans, when you try to understand what things in you are Chinese, how do you separate what is peculiar to childhood, to poverty, insanities, one family, your mother who marked your growing with stories, from what is Chinese? What is Chinese tradition and what is the movies?

She knows only what her mother has told her about the family history, and it is not enough to truly be helpful. She cannot ask her mother for more details.

If I want to learn what clothes my aunt wore, whether flashy or ordinary, I would have to begin, "Remember Father's drowned-in-the-well sister?" I cannot ask that.

So using her imagination, Kingston tries on different stories about her aunt to see which provides the "truest" history to fit the bits of information she has been told. Moreover, she uses outright fantasy to create woman warrior ancestors for herself. She imagines the autobiographic past she needs and can get no other way. Some critics in the Asian-American community reproached Kingston for distorting Chinese mythology, but it was never her intention to write a verifiable account. She was creating a new mythology for Chinese-American women.

Kingston and other innovative twentieth-century novelists, poets, and playwrights brought a spirit of creativity and experimentation to New Autobiography, while another group, the New Journalists, influenced its popular voice. In the 1960s, some young New York journalists discovered that they could write journalism that read like a novel. They used extended dialog and scene construction, character development, and subjective as well as objective ways of knowing. Suddenly, they were reporting real events with the drama and detail readers had enjoyed only in fiction. It made nonfiction so much fun to read that almost overnight readers switched their allegiance back from the novel. Gay Talese's *The Kingdom and the Power* about *The New York Times,* Joe McGinniss's book on Nixon's 1968 campaign, *The Selling of the President,* Adam Smith's book on Wall Street, *The Money Game,* Gail Sheehy's book on the Black Panthers, *Panthermania,* and Tom Wolfe's book on black–white confrontations, *Radical Chic & Mau-Mauing the Flak Catchers,* all became best-sellers.

When journalists writing like novelists stole the spotlight, novelists jumped over and started to write journalism. However, when novelist Truman Capote wrote *In Cold Blood,* he didn't call it journalism; he said he had invented "the nonfiction novel." Then in 1968, nonfiction lured another novelist, Norman Mailer. In *The Armies of the Night,* he wrote about an antiwar demonstration he had become involved in. It was New Journalism because it was written soon enough after the event to have journalistic impact, but it was also New Autobiography because it was in the first person and primarily about Mailer himself. It was memoir, it was journalism, and it was written like fiction. Later, Gay Talese was to copy this hybrid in *Thy Neighbor's Wife,* adding yet another aspect, conceptual autobiography. Like George Orwell who made himself destitute to write *Down and Out in Paris and London,* and Cameron Crowe who pretended to be a high school student to write *Fast Times at Ridgemont High,* Gay Talese went out and lived an experience, in his case, playing the part of a sexual swinger, in order to write about it.

So New Journalism taught New Autobiography some hijinks and stylistic tricks for making memoir fun to read. Serious New Autobiographers such as Maya Angelou, *I Know Why the Caged Bird Sings,* Mikal Gilmore, *Shot in the Heart,* Susanna Kaysen, *Girl, Interrupted,* and Carolyn See, *Dreaming: Hard Luck and Good Times in America,* have gone even further. These New Autobiographers haven't just taken the trappings of the novel. They have seized its heart, its narrative structure—story. It is as if they knew that at the end of the twentieth century, we needed the meaning and romance only story can bring to redeem otherwise futile, flattened, or brutalized lives.

Or perhaps these New Autobiographers are just taking story back. For before the networks, cable companies, film studios, and publishing conglomerates determined what stories would be told, before the printing press put story in the hands of only those who owned the means of production, and even before those privileged Egyptians hired rock carvers to preserve their autobiographies in stone, story belonged to the people. All the people. Or at least I imagine it did. Like Maxine Hong Kingston inventing female warrior ancestors because she needed them, I can only imagine how stories were told before they were written down.

So I visualize Rousseau's natural paradise, and a tribal people who, after a day of hunting and gathering, shared a meal in a shelter made of logs and animal skins, then around a blazing fire joined in a circle for warmth and amusement, much as we now relax in front of the light of the tube. The entertainment then at the dawn of history was stories, too, created by the members of the tribe for the members of the tribe.

On some occasions men and women formed separate circles and told stories meant for one gender only, but most of the time, the stories were for everyone. Perhaps they passed a talking stick around their circle, as storytellers yearning for that mythic time do at conferences and retreats today. Perhaps a ritual chant was repeated by each speaker that, like the flyleaf at the beginning of a book, was meant to empty the listener's mind in preparation for the actual tale. Perhaps each speaker sang:

> This story was entrusted to me by the god who gives us life and guides our path. I tell this story so that we may see the sacred connections in what happens to us and in what we feel and understand. It is a story made from my life, my heart, my imagination, and my eternal mind. I give it to our tribe and to our tribe's children as long as they wish to remember it.

then began the particular story . . .

> I was hunting by the shore of the Great Lake when I saw a snake, the kind that killed cousin Oko. We locked eyes and that snake said to me, "You need to find the child your sister bore with the people across the mountains. That child must know you."
> I asked myself, how does that snake know about my sister and her child? I guessed a god must have told him. So I set out across the mountains. . . .

The story would continue with heart and mind, imagination and soul all engaged, with a combination of fact ("I was hunting by the Great Lake when I saw a snake") and the openness of wonder that allows one to hear what an animal is telling them. The member of the tribe, who did not own houses or servants, did not have a name known from coast to coast, and did not even desire this, had only one thing to give—her life, her wisdom, her experience. She did not give it exclusively to her biological children. The member gave it to the tribe, to whomever in the tribe it could benefit.

We are no longer a tribal people, but we are entering the age of the global village. We now have a technological campfire, the Internet, that allows us to find other members of our tribe—people who share our general mythology about life. We could use our technology to enrich our collective wisdom through autobiographic storytelling—but we have lost the skill.

If you had been a child in my imaginary tribe, you would have learned at your mother's knee the requisite steps to telling a good story. You would have known to begin with an initiating incident and to end with a climax, though you would not have used those terms. You would have known many types of stories: trickster myths, inspirationals, tales of ancient wisdom—and what stylistic and contextual expectations your audience would have for each.

Likewise, if, like my friend Renate Druks, you had grown up in Vienna, a neighbor of Sigmund Freud, you would have acquired as a child skills as a storyteller. It was considered as necessary in Renate's polite society to be able to tell a good story as to know the proper terms of address and how to play a musical instrument. Dinner conversation was considered an art, and when Renate's father said, "How was your day?" she was expected to turn her response into an entertaining story with a point, not just recite a list or issue a grunt.

At this point, some readers will be feeling disturbed at my mixing literary history with a personal fantasy of prehistory and my friend's childhood dinner table. Similarly, some people are offended by the fusion of memory and imagination, fact and fiction in New Autobiography. The Puritan concept lingers, echoing in our heads, warning us to demarcate fact from fiction, alarming us to the danger of blending experience and imagination, predicting that the dissolution of genre distinctions is symptomatic of a breakdown of society itself, panicking that mixing true stories with fictional techniques is like intermixing the races . . . it's . . . it's . . . *impure.*

Just as there are fundamentalists who still do not accept the theory of evolution and consider it dangerous, there are many people who still insist that autobiographic writing has to be verifiable fact, has to be chronological, historical, just the way it really happened, and that only certain people may do it. A hundred years after Copernicus's theories had been accepted by astronomers, many people, including learned and influential people, clung to the belief that the sun circled the earth. People get used to a nice, simple idea, and after centuries of seeing it that way, it's hard to change. So even though autobiographic writing as practiced now fulfills important functions that have nothing to do with edification, many editors and agents still insist that autobiographic works should only be attempted by preeminent or famous people. They seem to forget that many writers have become well-known thanks to their autobiographic works published when they were no-names, writers like Christopher Isherwood, Maya Angelou, Erica Jong, Carlos Castaneda, Robert Pirsig, and Bret Easton Ellis.

Even though the best-seller lists are now full of personal works that cannot be classified definitively as either nonfiction or fiction, publishing houses and *The New York Times Book Review* still all divide books that way because they always have. Similarly, the television networks divide their programming into "news" and "entertainment," while much of it is a combination of both. In practice, both the publishing industry and the networks provide what people want. And more and more, what people want is true stories told as entertainment.

In actuality, contemporary readers accept a large portion of fiction within nonfiction and a large portion of nonfiction within fiction, *as long as they understand what the writer is doing.* Readers swallow up the autobiographical novels of Pat Conroy knowing they are based on his childhood and personal experiences and that he has fictionalized episodes and characters to heighten the melodrama. They enjoy "conceptual" autobiographies admiring the chutzpah of the authors who go out and live an adventure in order to write a book about it. They even accept without blinking the authenticity of autobiographies written not by the subject but by a collaborator or a ghost writer. *The Autobiography of Malcolm X* written by Alex Haley is recognized as a literary classic.

The lie is not in the new popular forms: factions, docudramas, nonfiction novels, personal journalism, dramatic nonfiction, the literature of fact, creative nonfiction, autobiographical novels, nonfiction narrative, and literary memoir. Mixing of fiction and nonfiction has been enjoyed by other cultures for centuries. The art of the earliest Japanese diaries lay in blending the author's experience with imagination so the reader could not tell where fact ended and fiction began. *The lie in our culture is in not recognizing that we are now sophisticated enough to enjoy this kind of writing and entertainment, and that this is what we are doing.*

Indeed, even my cursory review here of autobiography through the centuries suggests it has never been as pure a form as people like to imagine. Truth in autobiography has always been a complex question. If you believe everything that those Egyptian braggarts wrote in their autobiographies, you might as well believe that Ahuri really wrote her autobiography after she was mummified. We know that even the most respected Puritan ministers frequently left out embarrassing facts from their popular autobiographies, that fiction within autobiography was used for sensationalistic purposes in Indian captivity narratives, and that women, African-Americans, and others have used omissions and invention to tell first person stories they otherwise could not tell.

Which is not to say that most autobiographies are untruthful nor that the New Autobiography is less truthful than earlier forms. It is to say that there is no such thing as journalistic objectivity in autobiography. It is to say that

while readers should insist on verifiable facts from journalism, including New
Journalism, in autobiography they may appreciate deeper psychological and
poetic truths. Although New Autobiography has been influenced by New
Journalism, it is not a form of journalism, and though, like any genre of writing, it does have ethical responsibilities—such as the responsibility not to tell
emotional lies—the responsibilities of the memoirist are not those of the reporter. Like it or not, journalists have taken on the role of popular historian,
a role that autobiography is abandoning. Journalism, even the New Journalism, is obligated to the small truth of fact, whereas New Autobiography,
having moved into the literary arena of poetry and fiction, is now concerned
with the larger truths of myth and story, which permit, and sometimes require, imaginative reshaping.

Like new, powerful technologies, new forms of expression can be disturbing; they can be used for good or ill. But it isn't necessarily a bad thing
that our contemporary culture has developed a New Autobiography to
bring the spirituality of myth and story into our stress-filled lives. It may be
a way to recall that although each of us gets a different life story—a different piece of the puzzle—our tribe needs the wisdom of us all for truth to
emerge.

3

What Is a Story?

hat is a story anyway? We all know intuitively. As children we gobble them up and never feel too full for more. Myths are stories, fairy tales and folktales are stories; so are novels, movies, and sitcoms. But you can't touch, taste, smell, hear, or see a story—only the images and words it assumes. To say what a story is, is like trying to get your hands around a ghost shape.

Though they are intangible, stories are powerful and their power seems to come from another realm. They appear to be a way in which the sacred enters our lives. Myths, stories to explain how and why we are here, begot religion. The morality tales of Moses, Jesus, Mohammed, and Buddha— stories that tell us what to value and how to live—have determined the course of world history for more than nineteen centuries. Stories remembered within a community or family transport the beliefs and values of past generations into the future. The individual stories of our own lives tell us who we are and infuse our personal existence with excitement, meaning, and mystery.

Myths, parables, family stories, and the innumerable media stories of our popular culture are offered to us already embodied in the words or images of others. However, the stories of our own lives require active searching— learning to look through our memories in a new way. To find story in your life, you must engage imagination with memory; you must invent a line of continuity—not from nothing, but from the raw materials of your life. It's like reading a pattern in DNA or figuring out the possible anagrams in a word. To find story in your life, you have to know what you are looking for.

Fortunately, though you can't see a story, if you learn what its features are, when you look you will recognize one—and then many.

So what are the features of a story? A story isn't just a plot, a series of interconnected events. A story is a meaningful narrative with a beginning, a middle, and a conclusion. You started out at point A, the beginning, and because of what you did and what happened to you in the middle, point B, you ended up at point C, the conclusion. At point C you were a different person than you were at A, not just because you were older, but because you saw things differently.

In its simplest form a story is: what you wanted, how you struggled, and what you realized out of that struggle. A story is a series of interrelated events that you made happen and that happened to you, and the consequence. The consequence is a change in you. In an autobiographic story, change may occur in other characters, but it must also occur in you, because you are the protagonist. The change may come from an event (you married, you got old), but it is also a moral change. You had a realization, a shift in values or perception.

In other words, within the story you made a "character arc," you had a change in character. Gradually, because of what happened to you in life and the minirealizations you had along the way, you went from "there" to "here" as a person. What you believed, what you valued, and how you acted toward others changed, even if only slightly. You track this character arc in an autobiographic story by including your feelings, reactions to the events you experienced, and your realizations. You give the events of your life significance because of what they meant to you and how you changed from your engagement with them. An autobiographic story is not just an account of events; it is the charting of your emotional, moral, and psychological course, which gives meaning to those events.

It is worth taking some time to think about the inner course you wish to trace before you start putting down everything you can remember about your past. It is worth considering what story you want your life to tell. Why? Why not just write down everything you can remember, like so many people do? Because it won't be alive, it won't tap into the power of myth, it won't participate in the kind of truth that we read narratives for.

Columnist Russell Baker illustrated why a memoir needs to tell a story in a talk he gave at the New York Public Library, which is included in an anthology William Zinsser edited, *Inventing the Truth*. Baker told his audience that although his memoir *Growing Up* eventually won him a 1982 Pulitzer Prize, his first attempt at writing it was a disaster. Being a good storyteller, Baker made his point by couching it as a story. (A story, remember, can be as long as *War and Peace* or as short as this Russell Baker anecdote, provided it contains the basic story ingredients: beginning, middle, and conclusion, i.e., desire, struggle, and realization.)

Baker said that though he'd been thinking for a long time about writing a memoir about the Depression years, his mother's sudden loss of memory impelled him finally to start it, in order to preserve with words what she was losing. He approached the writing as the newspaperman he was: he took out his tape recorder and interviewed his older relatives, transcribed the interviews and his notes, and accurately reported in a 450-page manuscript what it was like to grow up in America during the Depression. Excited at having finished it, he sent it off to his agent and editor and waited for their praises. Two weeks went by, a month, several more months without any response at all. Finally, sensing that something was wrong, he took the manuscript out of a drawer and sat down in his office to read it. On page twenty, he nodded off.

He realized that in trying to be objective he had essentially left himself and his mother out of the book. "What I had written, though it was accurate to the extent that the reporting was there, was dishonest because of what I had left out."What he had left out was the emotional meaning of the events and how they were part of the pattern of his relationship with his mother. Thus he came to the point of his talk: *"although nobody's life makes any sense, if you're going to make a book out of it you might as well make it into a story."* He told his wife, "I am now going upstairs to invent the story of my life."

It's comforting that a writer as adept as Russell Baker fell into the same trap as many first-time autobiographic writers. Attempting to be objective and thorough, he had first written an intensely responsible *account,* which was as interesting to read as the *Congressional Record.* There were events, but there was no story: no *meaningful* sequence of beginning, middle, and end, and no personal character arc—which *are* present in the anecdote he told about making that mistake.

Now, you may object that Baker had to write those 450 boring pages before he could realize he didn't have a story, and that may well be true. It is certainly true that many writers just have to get down on paper what is in their heads and hearts before they can stand back and see the story buried in all those words. Still, I like to get my students to start feeling the shape of their stories before they write 450 boring pages (if only to save myself from having to read them). So in our first class, I ask them to write a fairy tale about their life. A fairy tale? Yes, because you can't tell a fairy tale without including the basic parts of a story: In the beginning something happened so that a character had a problem and a need, thence a struggle ensued, but in the end there was a crisis that was resolved when a transformation took place.

A lot of people think I mean that they should choose a fairy tale or a myth that already exists and try to fit their life into its template, but this isn't what I mean at all. I'll admit that seeing yourself as Persephone or Sisyphus can be a fascinating exercise, and it is one that a number of New Age psychologists encourage people to try, but I'm convinced it's flawed. Let me tell you why with an anecdote of my own.

One evening my friends and I were waiting forever it seemed for our reserved table at a restaurant. To while away the time Jim suggested a sort of parlor game. "It's said that your favorite fairy tale or children's story turns out to be the key to who you are."

"So what was yours?" I asked.

"*Ferdinand the Bull*," Jim said. It was perfect. He is a burly bull who just wants to smell the flowers all day. He sweats through the San Fernando Valley summers turning his fenced backyard into a garden that would inspire Monet.

Ellen said that her favorite kid's story was *The Pokey Little Puppy*, and her husband, Greg, said his was *The Velveteen Rabbit*. I had to admit these, too, seemed apt for my very nonthreatening friends.

"I'm ashamed to admit mine was 'Cinderella.'" I blushed through my age-defying foundation.

"It's perfect!" said Ferdinand the Bull.

"I don't see how!" I protested.

"You are always waiting for the prince to come save you." This from my closest male friend who has known me for twenty years, who knows how I have struggled to be independent, and that the only prince to have visited my humble abode complained about my housekeeping and kept his kingdom to himself. I was willing to admit that the idea of becoming suddenly rich is quite appealing to me (and, I'd venture, to at least ten million other Americans who promptly return their Publisher's Clearinghouse sweepstakes entries). But most certainly Cinderella is not a template for my life story.

Coincidentally, that week I was finally unpacking my books from a move I had made eight months before, and I came across a hardback I'd bought but never read titled *The Cinderella Complex*. The author, Colette Dowling, began with her autobiographic story—how she had been successfully self-supporting until she moved into her country dream house with her boyfriend, and how despite her feminist convictions, she'd found herself luxuriating in the relief of not having to struggle to make a living. Her paralysis when it came to finding work obliged her boyfriend to take on the lion's share of financial responsibilities, though that had not been their arrangement. She said it embarrassed her to admit her unconscious manipulativeness, and went on to show how in many other women's lives the deep-seated desire to be taken care of, which she called the Cinderella Complex, had disempowered them. As I read Dowling's story, I recognized times in my own relationships with men when I had dwindled into financial dependence because it was easier than having to struggle assertively in the marketplace. Like Dowling, I felt embarrassed at the recognition.

So I had to ask myself—was Jim right, after all? Was the Cinderella myth my life's theme? Certainly there was a key to some of my relationships with men in the complex Dowling had identified. As a girl, I had suckled that fairy tale like mother's milk. Unfortunately, it contained no nourishment. The Cinderella myth had deceived me by making false promises about what the realities of my life would be. It taught me that if I sat in a corner and waited, others would come save me: a godmother, a prince. In the Disney animated version, which had the greatest impact on me, Cinderella didn't even make her own dress; the birds and the squirrels sewed it.

I realized why I'd reacted so defensively to Jim's assertion that I was Cinderella still waiting for the prince. It wasn't just that there was something there for me to face about myself that was uncomfortable; it was also that I knew that if I identified with this myth, I would be snared in its outdated assumptions. Though powerful, "Cinderella" is not a contemporary woman's story. Its wisdom does not come out of the experience of modern women's lives.

I have to thank Jim. His jab that I was an aging Cinderella made me recognize why I am passionate about the concepts presented in this book. The intensity of my reaction reminded me why I feel a mission to teach the underlying structure of story and not the application of preexisting myth as the key to finding meaning within each person's contemporary life.

Even Joseph Campbell, whose body of work demonstrates how the myths of other eras and cultures offer us the experience of life's great mysteries, recognized that the old myths don't work anymore for the conditions of our lives. He told Bill Moyers in *The Power of Myth,* "This I believe is the great Western truth: that each of us is a completely unique creature and that, if we are ever to give any gift to the world, it will have to come out of our own experience and the fulfillment of our own potentialities, not someone else's." Terry Tempest Williams put the same realization more colloquially in

Pieces of White Shell, an autobiographic work she wrote about her attempt to assimilate Navajo stories into her own life: "I am not suggesting we emulate Native Peoples—in this case, the Navajo. We can't. We are not Navajo. Besides, their traditional stories don't work for us. It's like drinking another man's medicine. . . . We must create and find our own stories, our own myths, with symbols that will bind us to the world as we see it today."

We must create our own mythic stories out of our familiar, contemporary lives, so we can know how to live, how to *be* life, here and now, within the conditions of our times. Though he pointed the way, Campbell could not tell us how to find the myths of our own lives, because the work of finding and creating these new myths is our work as autobiographic writers. In order to give the gift of our story, of our personal embodiment of the mythic, we need to understand how our own lives make myth. Modern women, especially, need to tell the true myths embedded in our contemporary lives so our daughters and theirs will start out with desire lines more rewarding than Cinderella hoping for a prince to save her.

So in every autobiographic writing class and consultation, I begin with the following exercise. It consists of two parts, a fairy tale and an unsent letter. I can pretty much guarantee that if you do both parts, you will find a meaningful story in your life that concludes with a truthful realization.

EXERCISE 1: *Once Upon a Time*

People have an instinct for what a story is—beginning, middle, and conclusion—and when writing a fairy tale, they intuitively use the essential ingredients in the right order. Remember, though, you are not trying to find a shape in your life by imposing on it a preexisting story. This will be a fairy tale never told before, one inspired by your unique life concerns.

PART ONE: THE FAIRY TALE

In writing this fairy tale, use "altered point of view," that is, refer to yourself as "he" or "she" instead of "I." This allows you temporarily to step back and see story in your life from a distance.

Begin with one of the following:

- *Once upon a time there was a little girl who . . .*
- *Once upon a time there was a little boy who . . .*
- *Once upon a time there was a woman who . . .*
- *Once upon a time there was a man who . . .*

Your fairy tale need not be longer than a page, at most two. It can be as brief as three lines, if they contain the three parts of a fairy tale:

1. *In the beginning something happened so that a person had a problem and a need.*
2. *As the person pursued his or her desire a struggle ensued.*
3. *And in the end the person changed with a realization.*

You don't have to think about these parts, however. If you just begin with Once Upon a Time . . . a story will follow. Try it.

PART TWO: LETTER TO A GRANDCHILD

Imagine that you are writing a letter to a grandchild, real or imaginary, or to any child you know and care about. In this letter, you are going to share what it is you have learned from living your life. It should be a short letter that contains the most important insight, vision of reality, or wisdom you have learned and wish to pass on. Begin . . .

Dear _____

When you have finished your letter, reread it. Then reread the fairy tale you wrote. Ask yourself:

- *Does the story in the fairy tale convey the insight contained in my letter?*
- *If not, what story from my life could convey this insight?*
- *If not, what insight does the story convey?*

In all likelihood your fairy tale and your letter convey the same insight. The story you have just identified may not be the autobiographic story you choose to write, but be assured it is a core story for you. Whatever story you ultimately choose to write, see if you can express it simply, as a fairy tale with a beginning, a middle, and a conclusion.

Deborah Taylor, a student in a class I gave in San Diego, kept her fairy tale to three sentences, yet it contains the essential parts of a fairy tale.

THE BEGINNING:	
a person	*Once upon a time there was a little girl*
and her problem	*whose mother was dragged away kicking and screaming by men in white coats.*

THE MIDDLE:

a struggle

The little girl then began to hate her mother and to wish that she would die in the hospital and never come home.

THE CONCLUSION:

a transformation
and realization

In the end, though, she felt compassion and loved her mother as she had always really wanted to.

Now read Deborah's letter to a child and see how it conveys the same lesson as her fairy tale:

Dear Mimi,

Dear little granddaughter, I want you to know that there is something you must do. You must trust me on this, because I have learned it from my long life.

Do not pretend that everything is O.K. Please talk to your Mama about her sickness. Tell her that you love her and that you do not blame her for what has happened.

In this same class there was a Latina woman who said she could not complete the exercise because she couldn't find a conclusion for her fairy tale. In fact, she said, that is why she had come to the class. She was not interested in writing her life story; she was simply hoping I could help her know what her story was. She then told us about a real incident in her childhood that certainly sounded like the beginning of a fairy tale. It seems she was very ill as a little girl and almost died in the hospital. When she miraculously recovered, her mother and other members of her family said to her, "God saved you for a reason. You are meant to do something very special in your life." They did not tell her what that special deed was, and her desire through the rest of her life had been to discover what it was that she was to do. Now in her fifties, she was convinced that it had been just a metaphysical hoax; there was nothing special she had ever done or intended to do. "I never did anything but become a wife and a mother," she said, "so, you see, I couldn't complete the fairy tale."

"Were you able to write the letter?" I asked.

Why, yes, that had been no problem, she said. She had written it to her adult daughter telling her how she loved her more than anything else in the world, that being a parent was the one thing she felt she had done right in her life, and that she was deeply gratified that all her children had grown up to become decent, self-sufficient, and moral people. Several class members smiled at each other and at me. "Your letter contains the answer," a young man offered, but the woman did not understand.

"Let me tell you a story," I said. "It is the mirror image of your story, and it is happening to me right now. It is as if you and I were meant to meet in this class to hear each other's stories.

"My mother, who is almost eighty, is dying. I think the reason I've always been horrified by the thought of her death is because I feel she never lived her life. She had been a captain in the WACS but she quit to marry my father on the condition that they have children. Though she was a gifted and beautiful woman, my siblings and I were her entire life from then on. She sacrificed her life to us, while her own life turned out to be terribly limited and difficult.

"A few weeks ago I was talking to a wise man who is eighty-nine and has successfully lived his life to the fullest and written about it. I choked on tears as I told him, 'What's so hard with my mother is that it's like a child dying. What hurts most is that she never fulfilled her potential.'

"He was quiet for so long I was worried about him, but when he spoke I realized he'd been thinking about his beloved late wife. He said, 'Your mother reared three children who are capable of loving and contributing to the world. Maybe the problem is a society which doesn't recognize the value of what your mother did.' I felt relieved by his words."

I told the Latina woman, who had brown almond eyes like my mother's, that I thought she had already done something very special: she had been a good mother; she had raised children who weren't criminals, who were adults she admired. I told her that if she could write a memoir about how she had done it right, been a successful mother, *that* would be a worthwhile book.

She smiled sweetly and I could tell it was for my benefit, so I would feel good. In fact, she still did not see how her life made a story at all, let alone a worthwhile one. As a last resort, I pulled out my story mantra, my favorite mnemonic for the nature of each part of a story, beginning, middle, and conclusion. If you are still having difficulty finding a fairy tale in your life, this may be the key that makes the pieces fall into place. You can hum it to yourself like a grown-up nursery rhyme. It's the Rolling Stones lyric:

> *You can't always get what you want,*
> *but if you try some time,*
> *you just might find, you get what you need.*

In the beginning of a story, you have a problem and a desire: "You can't always get what you want." In the middle you have a struggle: "if you try some time." In the conclusion you have a transformative realization: "you just might find, you get what you need." Very often in autobiographic stories the realization is that what you really needed is what you actually got from life, rather than what you thought you should get.

Now that you know what a story is—a beginning, a middle, and a conclusion; a desire, a struggle, and a realization—you can begin to look for stories within your life. A story can be decades long or take place within a single day. A story may be found in your relationships with your parents, your siblings, your children, your friends, your pets, your house, your boss, the people you've dated, the gardener who mows your lawn, or the cobbler who soles your shoes. Stories are everywhere, and although you cannot touch them, you may see them like fireflies in your backyard; they fill the night with magic.

4

A Story Depends Upon How You Slice It

Your life can make many different fairy tales, since there are numerous beginnings and conclusions within it. There are many consecutive stories within the course of your life, and within any particular period there can be alternative stories depending on the different meanings you choose to give the same events. Further, there are limitless ways to pull out sections of your life in order to assemble them into different stories.

To identify the stories within your life, you need to alter the way you look at it. Throw out your attachment to uninterrupted chronology—this happened and then this happened and then this happened. The ability to find story in your life depends upon cutting it into pieces, and the nature of the stories you find depends on how you slice them.

Let me give you an obvious example. I wrote a TV movie about Judy Shapiro, who in 1979 went to China to teach and had a secret affair with one of her students, Heng, a political dissident. Judy's character arc in that story included these emotional steps: She went to China wanting an adventure; she desired the pleasure and excitement of an affair with Heng; she was angry that due to Heng's carelessness, their affair was discovered; she wanted to avoid marrying Heng because she felt coerced by him and the college authorities; she realized that she really loved Heng and was afraid it was too late; she chose to marry Heng to keep him from going to prison camp. At the end of the story, Judy and Heng celebrated a Chinese wedding, and he returned to the United States with her.

The story I wanted to tell took place in only two years of Judy's life. It began with her arrival in China and ended with her departure because that was how I sliced it. One day, while I was writing the script, Judy phoned.

"I don't know how to tell you this because it is going to ruin the story. Heng and I are getting a divorce."

"Oh," I said. One never knows the right thing to say to this announcement, but I've learned that "I'm sorry" isn't it.

"We were afraid to tell you."

"Why?"

"Will you have to tell the network? Won't they cancel the film because it's no longer the love story they wanted?"

"It's still a love story," I assured her.

"But it doesn't have a happy ending now."

"Yes, it does. The story still ends when you and Heng got married, when you were most in love. What happens later is another story."

"But reviewers will say it's a lie if they find out we're divorced by the time it airs."

"It's not a lie. It really was a happy ending, if you end the story where I am going to end it. Nothing has changed in the period of time of the story we are telling."

Ultimately the film that aired was a forbidden love story with a happy ending, because that was how I sliced it. Judy, if she should choose to write her story autobiographically, might slice it another way. She might begin at the same place, going to China, but end eight years later with the divorce. Or she could begin earlier when she was a defiantly independent grad student at Berkeley and end twelve years later when she was independent again, her relationship with Heng having become a respectful friendship.

These are entirely different stories based on the same person's life, not just because one has more events, but because the point each story makes is different. In my screenplay, the point was that sacrifice doesn't feel like sacrifice when you truly love someone—it just feels like love. In the second story, the point might be that the cultural differences that initially created a strong attraction inevitably caused the marriage to end. In the third story, the point might be that the nature of love between a couple evolves and changes even when a marriage is over.

In life, a realization at one time may lead to—or contradict—a realization at a later time. Sometimes, blinded by certain beliefs or emotions, your convictions are deficient; and sometimes a perception comes that, at least for a moment, allows you to glimpse your full humanity. How you track, order, and select such moments, where you choose to begin and where you choose to end, determines the story you tell. So in this sense, though you may remain completely honest and never alter an event, reaction, or feeling, you are "making up," crafting, your life into story. You are deciding what story or stories you want your life to make.

A story may come to you simply by thinking about where it might begin and where it might end. In your creative journal, you can jot down ideas for beginnings and endings. You can play with different choices until you find the one that gives you the story point you want to make.

There are three basic options for cutting up your life to find story in it, which I have labeled the *Submarine Sandwich,* the *Single Slice,* and the *Embroidery Thread.* The Submarine Sandwich option is often used for full autobiographies written for descendants; the Single Slice and the Embroidery Thread are more apt for literary memoirs. Which you choose will depend on your purpose in writing your work, and the intended length and nature of your story.

It is also possible to employ more than one slicing method within the same work. Though it is an unsavory image, a Submarine Sandwich or a Single Slice could have an Embroidery Thread running through it. This sounds complicated, but I've found that as soon as students hear what the slicing options are, they recognize which is right for their work. Read through, and if you find one or more techniques that interest you, try an accompanying exercise.

The Submarine Sandwich

The Submarine Sandwich is the shape of most traditional full autobiographies. It asks you to imagine your life as a continuous line (a long loaf) stretching from birth to the present:

birth————————————————————————*present*

You cut this loaf into slices of more or less proportional size—into chapters, each covering a number of years placed side by side in chronological order. You might visualize it as:

childhood,   *adolescence,*   *young adulthood,*   *your 20s,*   *your 30s,*   *your 40s . . .*
ch 1   *ch 2*   *ch 3*   *ch 4*   *ch 5*   *ch 6*   *ch 7*   *ch 8*   *ch 9*   *ch 10*   *ch 11*
———   ———   ———   ———   ———   ———   ———   ———   ———   ———   ———

birth————————————————————————*present*

This is the structure taught in most books and classes on writing autobiography. It's good if you are writing a family history for your descendants or if you are at a point in your life where you want to look back and sum it up for yourself. Even if it is not the option you choose for your autobiographic work, you may find it revealing to look at the path of your life as a whole by trying one of the following exercises.

EXERCISE 2: *Dividing Your Life by Years*
Since seven years seems to be a natural cycle, divide your present age by the number seven: 1–7, 7–14, 14–21, 21–28, 28–35, 35–42, 42–49, 49–56, 56–63, 63–70, etc. You may end up with some extra years at the end; if you are fifty-eight, you would have eight chapters and two years left over. Just include the two years in your eighth chapter, or create a ninth chapter to cover these last two years. Give each chapter a title that characterizes the overall theme of that period.

If, subsequently, you were to list the major pivotal events within each seven-year-period chapter, you would have an outline for a full autobiography that would have a major benefit: It would move you out of childhood within a reasonable amount of time. People who sit down to write a full autobiography often fall into the trap of never getting out of childhood, even though the most interesting part of their life has been as an adult.

If you are much younger than forty-nine, you should use a smaller number than seven so you'll have enough chapters. Better yet, use the Pivotal Events method for dividing your life (see Exercise 4).

EXERCISE 3: *Dividing Your Life by Decades*
Since social historians divide the twentieth century by characteristic decades, this can provide a fascinating grid through which to view your life as a whole. Try to make the decades of your life correspond to particular historic decades to see the interrelationship between the themes that occupied you and the social forces that affected your values. You can then study how you were a part of your times or apart from your times. For example:

- *3–13 the 1950s*
- *13–23 the 1960s*
- *23–33 the 1970s*
- *33–43 the 1980s*
- *43–53 the 1990s*

Whatever slicing method you ultimately choose, your work will be enlarged if at some point you chart your personal history alongside its historical context. In one column, you can create for yourself a chronology of important political and cultural events by consulting a contemporary history such as a Time/Life or Newsweek retrospective series on the decades. In a parallel column, you can list the major stepping-stones of your personal history. Doing this will give you an overview of your life in relation to your times.

Dividing your life by years or by decades can get you started and stimulate your imagination, but both are arbitrary methods of Submarine Sandwich slicing and you needn't let them restrict you. If you recognize an alternative division that works for your life—for example, if you moved to New Mexico when you were thirty-two and that makes a natural chapter break—follow your instincts.

EXERCISE 4: *Dividing Your Life by Pivotal Events*

Arbitrary methods of dividing your life can jump-start the creative process, but I prefer a more organic, intuitive technique: the diary device of spontaneously listing the major stepping-stones of your life. (You will find that many journal devices will prove useful in developing an autobiographic work.)

Stepping-stones are a list of the marker events that surface when you overview your life. You simply put down a phrase or sentence for each significant pivotal event in your life as it comes to you. Begin with "I was born" to get you started, and then think of the next important turning point in your life, and the next, and the next, up to the present.

Your list can be any length, but if you wish a guideline, try to keep it between ten and twenty items. After you have finished writing your life stepping-stones, reread your list to get a sense of the continuity and movement of your life. Are there any themes that appear?

For some people this list of stepping-stones will be sufficient to suggest how to divide their life into chapters. Each item, each pivotal event on the list, could be the gist for a chapter in a full autobiography. You may wish to go back and transform each item on your list into a chapter title.

However, I encourage you to try a companion exercise that will give you a stronger sense of story running through your life. The second exercise is as easy as the first one. It is simply another list, this time of your desires as you moved through life. Each item on this list will begin with "I wanted . . ." Think back to your infancy. What did you want? Your mother's love and attention? To be able to explore an unfolding world without limitations? Then list the next major desire that impelled you (e.g., "I wanted to become a missionary") and the next, and so on. This list may be shorter than the previous one of stepping-stones.

The third part in this exercise is to combine both lists by sensing which desires preceded which pivotal events. Some desires may be followed by only one stepping-stone event—for example, "I wanted to get married" by "I got married." Other desires may be followed by numerous events—for example, "I wanted to become an actor" might be followed by "I moved to New York," "I enrolled in the Actor's Studio," and "I got fired from the play in which I had the lead because I was drinking and missed performances."

Now read your blended desires list and your list of stepping-stone events as one merged list that tells a story. What do you notice about the relationship between your desires and your actions?

Some people will find from reading their merged lists that they consistently ignored their desires while serving those of others; some will see that their own desires always drove their actions. Still others will discover that sometimes they served their own desires, and sometimes their sense of responsibility to other people took priority.

Also, when you have blended your desires list and your stepping-stones list as one list, you may see how in your life there have been turns in your desire line—that is, places where one desire died out and another emerged. Your life's energy, desire, didn't end; it took a different direction; you began a new life season. The turns in your desire line give shape to the overall story of your life. As you sense this shape, let yourself play with your combined list. *Are there missing desires or events that will create greater continuity? Add them. Are there clusters that seem to go together, marking distinct seasons in your life, periods that were devoted to the same desire? Delineate them.*

As winter leads to spring, each life season leads into the next. Each has its own beginning, middle, and conclusion, and is part of a larger cycle. The purpose of identifying your personal seasons is to appreciate how each may contain its own story. At the beginning of a new life season, you have a new desire, then you struggle to achieve it, and in the end you change with an accompanying realization.

Some of your seasons may bear similarity to the predictable life passages outlined by Gail Sheehy in *Passages* and *New Passages,* although their timing and sequence will be unique to you. The goal of Sheehy's work was to determine what passages people have in common, whereas the goal of your autobiographic work is to discover and embody what individualizes you. So if you vary from the imaginary norm—say, in your twenties you did not mate—there is no need for self-judgments.

As you come to view your life as evolving stories, you may begin to appreciate that, from the perspective of story, all desires are equal. It doesn't matter if the desire was to get rich, marry, build a dam in Ethiopia, get a job, or find spiritual centeredness. All are equally valid in that they are equally the expression of the life force. Your desires may assume many faces in your lifetime, but in the Platonic world of pure form, desire is simply the beginning of a cycle, that which propels you forward to a destined realization.

Regardless of how you have sliced your Submarine Sandwich, by years, decades, stepping-stones, or personal seasons, you will have the benefit of having approximated in advance your chapter divisions. You can use these divisions as containers in which to collect memories. Look again at your list of life slices, and if you have not already done so, give each a provisional chapter title. Then get a three-ring binder with dividers and label each divider with a chapter title. As memories come willy-nilly and out of order, as they will, you can record and place them in the labeled section of your binder where you think they belong. These memories will be there waiting within each slice of your Submarine Sandwich for when you are ready to digest them.

The Single Slice

While most celebrity and familial autobiographies are Submarine Sandwiches, the majority of literary and adventure memoirs are Single Slices. You can imagine it as cutting a single period of time out of your life as you would choose a slice out of a long strudel. You get to pick the very best piece, whether it's right in the middle or near either end.

With the Single Slice, you choose one period of your life only and leave the rest. Childhood memoirs are slices of childhood only. Susanna Kaysen's memoir, *Girl, Interrupted,* only covers her two years in a mental hospital. Molly Haskell's *Love and Other Infectious Diseases* is a wry memoir about the six-month period when her husband, film critic Andrew Sarris, was hospitalized for a near-fatal brain fever.

You may wish to choose a portion of your life that you know will make a good story—your tour of duty as a nurse in Vietnam, your two decades as a special ed teacher, your adolescence, your first two years of retirement, the months you spent researching in Antarctica. The section you choose could be twenty years, seven years, two months, a day, one afternoon. If you are writing an autobiographic short story or novella, you will certainly need to narrow the time period covered.

single slice

birth————————————————— / ——— / ————————————————— present

The compression of the Single Slice has a literary advantage in that it comes closer to the Aristotelian dramatic unities of time and place. Rather than trying to find story in your life as a whole, you explore in greater depth the mystery of story within one part. The story formula in the next chapter will help you give a dramatic structure to the slice you choose. This preliminary exercise can help you determine if the slice you have selected contains a story you wish to tell.

EXERCISE 5: *Finding the Story That Surrounds a Pivotal Event*

Choose a pivotal event in your life that you wish to serve as the conclusion of your Single Slice. It should be a turning point after which you felt differently or lived differently in the world. It might be the day you gave up trying to be accepted as the only girl on the high school football team, the night your daughter moved out of the house, or the moment you realized you no longer felt anything for the lover who had obsessed you. If you wrote a list of life stepping-stones (the first part of Exercise 4), you could choose one pivotal event from that list to mark the end of a slice.

In your creative notebook, write freely about what comes to mind in response to each of these questions:

- *What did you desire in your life before this ending pivotal event?*
- *When and how did this desire begin or intensify significantly? Could this be the beginning of your story?*
- *Did you have a struggle in trying to fulfill this desire?*
- *Did you learn anything from the struggle?*
- *How did you change after the final pivotal event?*
- *What did you do that indicated this change?*
- *What did you realize when this stage in your life came to an end?*
- *What do you perceive now as you remember it?*

When you read over your answers, you may begin to sense a story: a desire, a struggle, and a conclusion.

❧The Embroidery Thread

Unfortunately, I have to change metaphors from food to needlework. It's crummy, but try to brush away thoughts of sandwiches and strudel, and imagine a piece of fabric on which a design has been created with colored embroidery thread. The embroidery thread runs through the cloth but comes to the surface only where the pattern is. With the Embroidery Thread technique, you select as your story only the particular hours, days, months, or years that belong to the theme and dramatic line of your story. You skip over months, years, and even decades that bear no relevance to that particular story.

Thematic memoirs, whether about work, a relationship, or an idea, use the Embroidery Thread technique, leaping through the narrator's life featuring only what is relevant to the chosen theme. Elizabeth Marshall Thomas's *The Hidden Life of Dogs* is a thematic memoir about what the author calculated to have been a hundred thousand hours of dog-watching. It is a large Single Slice with an Embroidery Thread—her interest in canines—running through it. Certainly other things went on in her life at this time, but she only writes about her observations of dog behavior. Her husband gets scant mention, and then only in relation to the pups.

It seems that a majority of my students with literary aspirations choose to write Single Slice memoirs with the Embroidery Thread technique. One student wrote about a twenty-year slice of her life as an adoption worker, only highlighting those parts of her life during that period that had to do with her being a childless woman working with parentless children. When you read a work that runs an Embroidery Thread through a Single Slice, it can feel much like a modern novel. For as in a novel, in this form of New Autobiography, you have the freedom to move through time as you wish. Like the novelist, you can play with time, stretch it and condense it, jump over years that are irrelevant to your story, then slow down to delve for a dozen pages into a scene that in life took only five minutes.

The Embroidery Thread technique is also a contemporary way to deal with the expanse of intergenerational sagas. This is what novelist and critic Carolyn See did in her memoir, *Dreaming,* which explores the theme of intergenerational substance abuse. "I want this book to fall like a plumb line down through four generations, tracing that history of drugs and drink, depression and divorce," See writes. "I just want to take a look at it, see how it works."

Like See, you could use the Embroidery Thread technique to look at a particular issue or conflict in your life. Imagine your life as a long bolt of cloth upon which a particular conflict surfaces intermittently. It could be for two months when you were nine, for three years until you were nineteen, for a week when you were twenty-five, for six years when you were in your thirties, for a day when you were sixty.

2 mo (9)   *3 years (19)*   *1 wk (25)*   *6 years (30s)*   *1 day (60)*

_____   _____   _____   _____   _____ __

You can also use the Embroidery Thread technique to write about a particular relationship. For instance, you could trace your relationship with a certain lover that began during a summer when you were nineteen, resumed as an adulterous affair when you were in your thirties, ended after twenty years, and began again in your fifties as a second marriage.

summer 1959   *winter and spring 1974*   *fall 1991–present*

____   _____   _____

Let me give you a sense of how this works with a choice of two different exercises. In the first, you will be tracking a particular theme throughout your life. In the second, you will track a particular relationship.

EXERCISE 6: *Stepping-Stones for a Thematic Memoir*
First make a list of conflicts that you feel have pulled you in different directions in your life. State the conflicts as a pair of opposed values or feelings, if you can. For example, one student wrote:

- *money/spirituality*
- *appearances/truthfulness*
- *my family/me*
- *making a good impression/pleasing myself*

See if any of the oppositions cluster together and could be expressed by one general conflict of values. In this case, the writer was able to gather them all under a conflict she expressed as being a Collins (her family name) versus being herself. The values of money, appearances, and making a good impression were all values that were important to members of her affluent family. She felt separate and isolated when she did not share their values.

If you cannot subsume two or more of the value oppositions on your list into one larger thematic conflict, then choose one pair of opposing values to work with.

Now make a stepping-stones list of times the conflict has surfaced in your life. Begin by trying to remember the first time you became aware of the conflict. The writer of the list above recalled an incident when she was seven on a private beach in the south of France. She was sitting inside a cabaña, covered from head to toe to protect her sensitive skin from the sun. On the beach were her parents' friends, the famous, rich, and beautiful people of Europe. This was the first time she was aware of feeling cut off, different from them.

The first occurrence of your thematic conflict becomes the first item on your list. Move forward through your memory, noting each occasion when the conflict became an issue for you. In other words, write a chronology of this conflict as it has developed in your life. When you have finished your list, read it and write a paragraph noting whatever insights come to you. If you believe your list suggests a story you would like to pursue, go to the next chapter to see if you can give it more shape by applying the nine essential elements of story.

EXERCISE 7: *Relationship Stepping-Stones*

Just as a particular conflict in your life evolves over time, so a relationship has a line of development. In order to see that development, you need to set it off from the rest of your life with the Embroidery Thread technique. To feel how this works, choose a relationship you would like to explore, perhaps with a sibling, friend, mate, or parent. Write the stepping-stones of this relationship, that is, the main emotional incidents and pivotal events in the relationship.

Begin with where your connection began, when you first met, or your first memory in relationship with that relative.

1. I was born. My mother's joy. Her reason for leaving the military.
2. I was a colicky baby, the first wedge in my parents' passionate relationship.
3. My mother had to do a balancing act, giving me the attention she knew I needed without angering my father, who was jealous of that attention.
4. I adored her. I thought she was the most beautiful and the best mother in the world.
5. It was her side I took in her arguments with my father.
6. When he left, I thought I was glad. Now they would not fight.
7. I was ashamed of her grief. I distanced myself. I would never be like her, I told myself. I would never marry.
8. I was ashamed of her shame as a divorcée. Why did she have to date men? Why did I have to be nice to them?

9. When I discovered Peyton Place *hidden in her closet, I knew she was a hypocrite. She had been so protective of me. She would not say the word "sex."*

10. *When I got my period and I thought it meant I had cancer, she cried and said, "I should have told you." Why didn't you? I thought.*

11. *As I became interested in boys, she distrusted me, accused me of wanting to have sex with them. I hated her for restricting my freedom.*

12. *Jack, her boyfriend, told me she was going to marry him. I said he was lying. He said she had to. She was pregnant. I felt sorry for her and I despised her for being foolish. She had been so afraid I would get pregnant, and she was the one who was careless.*

13. *I distanced myself as her life closed in on her. I left as my father had. She called me by his name when we argued.*

14. *I knew that she did not have enough money, that she was cleaning people's houses to keep the family going. I was a college scholarship girl. I told myself she was stupid, I'll never be like her.*

15. *When I did get pregnant at twenty, I got an abortion. I never told her. By then I had begun to protect her and myself from her hysterical concern.*

16. *She continued to give me unconditional love. When I came home to do my laundry, she fixed my favorite foods. Sometimes she would visit my apartment and clean it and stock the refrigerator.*

17. *When I became a feminist, I began to understand my mother's rage.*

18. *When my house at the beach was flooded, she and Jack sloshed through the mud with me to help me move out.*

19. *The love I had for her as a child returned. I saw that she was, indeed, the most beautiful and wonderful mother in the world.*

20. *I was sorry that she had not pursued her dream. I wanted to become rich and successful to give her all she longed for but never had.*

21. *She began to have health problems. She would collapse walking through the parking lot to work. I wanted to scream that her life had been too full of sacrifice. That it seemed to me it had been all work.*

22. *I resented that my sister let her pay her student loan.*

23. *I resented that she always saw me as the strong and capable one and my sister as poor Deirdre.*

24. *She had a stroke cooking in a hot kitchen on my birthday. I howled with anger and pain.*

25. *She survived that stroke and others. I felt her doctors did not treat her with enough concern and respect.*

26. *She developed breast cancer. I tried to help her find a good surgeon. I took her to all her appointments.*
27. *Once the crisis was over, I was so busy I did not see her often.*
28. *I moved into my own house. I was happy that she could come see my house and that she liked it.*
29. *My mother's cancer came back in her brain and her lung. I had to care for her, changing her diapers when she came back from the hospital.*
30. *My mother found a cache of old photos and my baby book. I saw with what care she kept that baby book. I saw that I meant as much to her as she has meant to me. I saw that she had once been young and beautiful and happy, and I had been a part of her happiness.*

When you have finished writing your list, read it through; if you have any insights, add them in a reflective paragraph. Is there a part of this list that clusters together to make a story? Would you want to cover the entire period that the list covers? Would you want to concentrate on one period within the list and allow what precedes it to filter into your story as memories? Are there pivotal points within the list? Could any of the pivotal points be the end of a story?

Be aware that a relationship may continue to develop when you no longer have physical proximity with the person. Even after someone has died, your relationship evolves. I wrote the stepping-stone list above of my relationship with my mother when I was working on a first draft of this book. Were I to write such a list now, there would be several steppingstones to our relationship since her death.

⌁Alternative Models for Assembling the Pieces of a Life

We have explored the three basic ways to cut your life into pieces: as a Submarine Sandwich with many slices; as a Single Slice; or as the selection of pieces of your life that relate to a particular theme or relationship, the Embroidery Thread technique. Now that you have all these pieces, just think, there may be more than one way to assemble them into a work.

⌁QUESTS

We ordinarily think of a story as a linear quest where a character with a desire searches like a knight for his Holy Grail and has adventures on his way to his ultimate discovery of the Grail and its wisdom. Many life stories, especially religious quests, adventure stories, and success stories in a chosen vocation or profession, lend themselves to the quest structure. In a quest there is one main and continuous character arc.

POINT A   POINT C
the hero's goal set   *the hero's goal achieved (or not)*
                                                                  and wisdom attained

QUILTS

However, as Mary Catherine Bateson pointed out, many modern lives do not look like a quest; they are too full of unrelated stops and starts. Women's lives, especially, are fragmented by constant interruptions. You are pursuing a career, then stop for a while to raise your children while they are young, then you may work with your husband in his office, stop to care for an invalid relative, divorce and remarry, go back to school in an entirely new field. Men's lives now, too, are more fragmented than they used to be. You may be following a quest in your chosen career only to find that it has been eliminated by new technologies; you retrain and find a new job only to be laid off; you may live with periods of unemployment and incrementally lowered salary expectations, which makes the hero's linear quest an inapt model for your life.

Bateson's image of the quilt patched together from fragments worth saving provides an alternative image for a life's structure. It bears similarity to a particularly modern literary strategy of assembling many short pieces (often short stories) into an extended work. When you follow the quilt model of assembling a work, you spontaneously write and collect pieces that seem to you thematically related. As you proceed, a pattern or story begins to link the pieces. Certain areas will easily cluster, but you won't have the whole picture until it is all in place.

Contemporary autobiographic story collections such as Christopher Isherwood's *Berlin Stories,* Pam Houston's *Cowboys Are My Weakness,* and Susanna Kaysen's *Girl, Interrupted* follow a quiltlike structure in that each story stands on its own, and looked at together, the assembled stories tell a larger story. In quiltlike structures, the attempt to create smooth transitions is dispensed with in favor of tighter unity within each story or chapter. Transitions are often like cinematic cuts, which leave it to the viewer to read-in links between disparate pieces set side by side.

In a quiltlike book there is often a series of discrete minor character arcs instead of one major one. An unresolved problem expresses itself first in one story and then in another. The final realization in the last story is possible because of all the realizations in the stories that have led up to it. It may be visualized as:

Point A	*Point C*	/	*Point A*	*Point C*	/
problem and desire	*realization*	/	*problem and desire*	*realization*	/

Point A	*Point C*	/	*Point A*	*Point C*
problem and desire	*realization*	/	*problem and desire*	*final realization*

It could be said that the edited diaries of Anaïs Nin are another type of autobiographic quilt. They were set down spontaneously as natural diaries, but when Nin chose to publish them, she went back and edited and rewrote from the perspective of a later point in time. She decided what her themes would be in each volume and edited for those themes, eliminating whatever did not seem relevant. In the first edited *Diary* (1931–1934), her central theme is the young woman becoming an artist; in *Diary II* (1934–1939), it is the discovery of inner time as opposed to outer time. Later volumes lack comparable unity, but the importance of Nin's work is not so much in her skill as writer/editor and not in her faithfulness to literal truth. Although overlooked, Nin's importance is in creating a new hybrid literary form, something between diary and autobiography.

The quiltlike structure of journal writing has influenced autobiographic narrative writing in other ways. In San Diego, there is an artistic school of writers, painters, and sculptors linked by their interest in journal writing. The diary process has been the common source for their diverse paths of artistic expression. Out of her interest in journal writing, Joan Crone discovered book art, the making and binding of limited edition books. Joan handmade twenty-five copies of *Letters of My Life,* a twelve-page intergenerational memoir that uses a quilt structure. Each page of the book is an envelope containing a photocopy of a handwritten letter sent to her by her grandparents, her parents, an uncle, a stepmother, or a friend.

In *Letters of My Life*, one never sees a word written by Joan herself, yet we feel her feelings as the recipient of the twelve letters. We read into the space between each letter that as a girl she was a talented photographer who never received encouragement or financial support from her parents. Having had to quit art school, she married and raised two sons, but the marriage ended when she realized she had become an alcoholic. Letters from her fa-

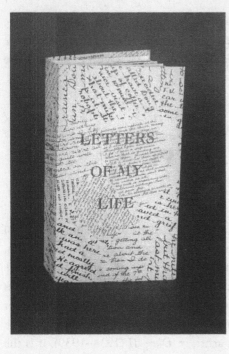

ther and stepmother admonish Joan for joining AA, insisting she should have kept quiet about her drinking problem instead of embarrassing them and herself. However, the last letter, from a childhood friend, recognizes how Joan has turned her life around and recreated it successfully on her own terms. It is the only letter of encouragement she received.

Joan created New Autobiography without writing a word, simply by assembling "found art." Using the quilt structure, she selected and arranged twelve letters from different people telling a coherent story: desire, struggle, and transformative realization. It suggests that even with quilts, it is helpful to understand the basic structure of story in order to arrange the pieces dramatically.

TRANSPARENCIES

While the quest structure and the strategy of assembling a story as one stitches together a quilt is common, very few autobiographic writers will ever use the transparency technique. Although it can begin intuitively, a transparency (unlike a quilt) cannot be completed without a plan. A transparency is a complicated structure that superimposes two or three single slices of time to tell multiple, complementary stories. Isabel Allende uses it in *Paula* to tell four stories concurrently: (1) her story of watching over her comatose adult daughter in the hospital, (2) her grandmother's and grandfather's stories, (3) her mother's story, and (4) her own story.

The transparency technique is more difficult than setting complementary stories side by side as in a quilt, and more ornate than imposing the perspective of the present upon the past, which every autobiographic writer does. The transparency technique is a very artful and somewhat mechanical approach that overlays different periods of time as a graphic artist overlays two or three color transparencies to make one picture.

The transparency technique should never be attempted simply for the sake of being literary or artistic. It should only be used when it is the only way your story can be told. Pat Conroy uses it effectively to tell a psychological mystery in his autobiographical novel, *The Prince of Tides*. He overlays three different time frames: the distant past, his recent past, and the present. He begins with the distant past of his childhood, then moves in the first chapter to the present as an adult going to New York to see his sister. The second chapter jumps to the recent past of ten years before. In the following chapters, three through twenty-four, the narrator moves back and forth between the adult present-time story of his love affair in New York and the distant-past story of his childhood. Chapters twenty-five through twenty-seven are set in the recent past, of about ten years earlier, and the epilogue is in the present. In all, there are four segments set in the recent past, twelve set in childhood, and thirteen in the narrator's adult present.

The complex integration of overlapping stories in different time frames runs the risk of becoming terribly confusing. If you find that it is the only way your story can be told effectively, you will at some point need to map out the sections as indicated here for *The Prince of Tides*. You will need to make sure that you have protected the chronology within each section and that you've made your transitions between sections clear.

The exercises in this chapter offer ways to cut your life into pieces and ways to reassemble the pieces. They suggest ways to see the arcs your life makes. Your results are proto-stories, the gathering together of associations that can lead to stories. In the next chapter, you will learn the nine basic components of a complete story, and a formula for creating a dramatic story outline.

5

The Nine Essential Elements of Story Structure

To give the gift of your story, you need to understand dramatic structure and how to apply it to your life. Why dramatic structure? Because dramatic structure is the essence of myth, and through it you bring the mythic into ordinary, temporal life.

Some of the secrets of dramatic construction have been known at least since Aristotle (384–322 BC) wrote his *Poetics*. However, like the Scholastic discipline of memory, the rules of dramatic construction went underground during the Middle Ages. By the Renaissance the laws of drama were considered by the educated elite to be privileged knowledge, as protected and cryptic as the Cabala and Rosicrucian lore. Sir Francis Bacon warned that the masses were not ready for these secret mysteries. Hence, the relationship of dramatic structure to our everyday lives has remained hidden.

If someone had only taught me what I am going to teach you in this chapter, it could have saved me twenty years of searching for how to construct a story. I studied literature to get a Ph.D., but I never learned the essential components of a story at university. When I became a screenwriter, I had to piece it together bit by bit from other writers and teachers. Even then, what I was able to glean about dramatic construction seemed only to apply to fiction, not to real life.

What I am going to give you in this chapter is a formula for constructing story out of the pieces of your life, a formula for taking your unique experiences and fitting them to the eternal shape of myth. What do I mean by the eternal shape of myth? There are certain elements that all myths and powerful stories have in common, in an invariable order.

Joseph Campbell found the same elements in myths of diverse cultures scattered over the face of the earth. For instance, he found repeatedly that at the climax of a myth there is a transformation which involves a death and a rebirth, the phoenix of renewal emerging from the flames of destruction—the consummation of opposites into the creation of new life. All myths, he said, share this thesis: There is an invisible plane supporting the visible one, and the world of the spirit parallels that of the body.

What does that mean, the world of the spirit parallels that of the body? I think it is a rather delicate way of saying that myth—like all rites of sacrifice and all drama—has an orgasmic structure. The act of ceremonial sacrifice from which drama evolved is structurally like the sexual act.

That is the safeguarded secret. The terms the dramatist uses to describe parts of a story—crisis, climax, and resolution—should give it away, but generally only confuse and intimidate. Through the friction of thematic conflict, the constriction of crisis, and the high point of dramatic climax, we copulate as bodiless angels do. The universal mythic experience of dramatic intensification, crisis, and climax is sex for the mind. No wonder people who can't afford food manage to buy television sets; no wonder we never tire of being entertained at movie temples. Though the particular people, words, or deeds on the screen differ drastically, from monsters in horror films to ingénues in comedies, the dramatic sequence through which the spiritual orgasm is accomplished remains constant as a law of physics. This constancy of dramatic structure and its universality ensures that you can apply it to your life.

So what are the laws of dramatic structure? You've already learned the basic tripartite structure in writing a fairy tale: a story is a beginning, middle, and conclusion; more specifically, a character who has a desire, a struggle, and a realization. Here, now in more detail, are the ingredients of a story. For autobiographic writing, I have found it most helpful to identify them as nine basic components.

THE NINE ESSENTIAL STORY ELEMENTS

BEGINNING	*Initiating Incident*
	Problem
	Desire Line
MIDDLE	*Struggle with Adversary*
	Interim Pivotal Events
	Precipitating Event

CONCLUSION   *Crisis*
                      Climax
                      Realization

I will define each of these elements and illustrate how they work similarly in a fairy tale/myth and in a memoir. Given my discomfort with "Cinderella," you may be surprised that it is the fairy tale I've decided to use as a vehicle. I chose it because it's classic in structure and universally known, and, all right, because I'm so intimate with it. I've also chosen one of my favorite memoirs by a white, Anglo-Saxon man, Russell Baker's *Growing Up*. It has an evenness of tone and easy humor that I think is only possible in memoirs by accomplished Anglo-Saxon men. Nevertheless, the structural principles at work in it are to be found in autobiographical narratives by women and men from every background. The basic structure of story is, remember, orgasmic, which is not the exclusive province of any particular race or gender.

What follows is a detailed breakdown of the basic elements in a complete story. Don't worry if you have a hard time grasping these abstract concepts. Read through them and absorb what you can. When you are writing, you can return as needed to these definitions and illustrations for guidance. At the end of this chapter is a thirteen-step formula that will guide you to find these basic story components within your own life.

⌒The Beginning: What You Wanted

What's required in a beginning? *A character, a protagonist*. This is the easy part in autobiographic writing. The protagonist is *you*. What else is required? A time and place in which *something happened to you* and (whether you realized it or not) caused you to have *a problem and a need*.

⌒INITIATING INCIDENT

The something that happened to you that incited your problem is the *initiating incident*. It is an event from which all else follows. Cinderella's father dies (initiating incident), which creates her problem—she's left with a stepfamily that despises her. That leads to her need—to get the hell out of her stepmother's house into a better life.

In the story that Russell Baker eventually told in *Growing Up*, his father died, too. He was left with a strong-willed mother who wanted to make

Russell into the man she believed he should be: "To make something of myself. . . . Oh how I hated those words."

The initiating incident of Baker being left in his mother's sole custody gives him a problem; it's not his nature to be the person his mother would like to mold him into. Actually, Baker has skewed the usual chronology: the scene of initiating incident of his father's death doesn't occur until almost halfway through the book; nevertheless, his problem is established at the very beginning. It leads directly to his need/desire—to get through childhood as his own person rather than who his mother wants him to be.

The problem and need established at the beginning is resolved at the end of a story, not necessarily by being solved, though that could be an ending, but, at least, by being understood in a transformative way. Your problem in a story could be a character weakness as innocuous as immaturity or ignorance, or it could be a flaw as serious as compulsive lying or uncontrollable rage. It could be that you were living with the wrong person or following a false set of beliefs. Whatever the problem you establish, it needs to lead to a desire.

DESIRE LINE

By establishing in the beginning your problem and need, you start a *desire line,* which should continue through the rest of the work. The key to doing this in autobiographic narrative is to include not only the account of "what was"—the events in your life—but also what you wished, what might have been, and even what still might be. Too often, writers forget that fantasies, hopes, and dreams belong in autobiographic works as much as events do. It is especially effective to give us your hope—what you desired—at or near the beginning of any story because then you and your readers can follow that desire line through your work, to see if you get what you wanted, rooting for you when you succeed, aching with you when you fail.

Your desire is the engine of your story and your desire line is the track it runs on. Establishing a strong desire line is the key to dramatic story construction. It gets us interested. That's a beginning. But it wouldn't be a story if your desire were immediately gratified.

The Middle—What You Got

The middle of a story is a struggle because the desire, which started in the beginning, is still running forward unsatisfied. When you have a desire, you generally will develop some sort of plan to fulfill it. The dramatic conflict in a story comes from the friction between your plan to fulfill your desire and the frustration that results from an adversary or adversaries foiling that plan.

⌒Struggle with Adversary

In giving us a problem you faced, you have probably also given us an *adversary,* someone or something that stands in the way of getting what it is you want or need. It could be a person like Baker's strong-willed mother, or persons like Cinderella's wicked stepfamily. An adversary need not be an enemy. It could be the person you love most. In a love story your desire might be for your lover to love you the way you want to be loved. Because he loves you his way instead, he is the one opposing your getting what you want; he's your adversary.

Stories that have human adversaries are the easiest to write, but your adversary could also be a thing, like a small town's provincial prejudices or crippling poverty. In Oliver Sacks's *A Leg to Stand On,* the adversary is his own injured leg! He wants it to heal quickly, but it foils his desire by taking the body's own slow, sweet time, healing in its own enigmatic way. Sacks comes to realize that as a doctor and a scientist he has a great deal to learn from the mysterious wisdom of his adversary.

Your adversary in an autobiographic story could also be a competing need or desire within you. For example, you wanted to be a trial attorney, but you also wanted to be loved and approved of as a sweet and feminine young woman. In autobiographic stories, the adversary can be a person, an external or internal force, all of those obstacles, or a series of them. Cinderella's desire for a better life is impeded by her stepfamily, but also by her economic powerlessness and her resulting lack of self-confidence.

The middle section of your story, then, is the struggle between your desire and the opposition of your adversaries, through which you have certain insights leading to a final realization at the conclusion. Now here's the tricky part. Your desire line, which should run with the power of a hungry tiger from the beginning through the middle, right on through to the conclusion of your story, doesn't necessarily go in a straight line. A story is not just "I want X, and I get (or I don't get) X." If it is, you have either a very short story or a predictable one.

While the desire line in a story should never be broken or abandoned, it may turn in a different direction; that is, it may be transformed into a new but related desire. A story is more like, "I want X, but that is turning out to be frustrating, so now I want Y, but then I see Z, which is closer to what I really want, but in the end I get X after all, and don't want it any more, or I get X and I'm happy, or I don't get X but I get Z and I'm happy, or I don't get X or Y or Z and I realize that I never will unless I change." This suggests only a few of the possible variations of how a desire line can bend and lead to your conclusion.

For Cinderella, the turns and escalations in her desire line are especially clear. Her overall need is to get out of her bottom-dog position as unpaid scullery maid and find a better life. However, the first desire she is conscious of is simply to go to the ball. It's not such a large desire, not out of line; she works all day trying to please her stepfamily, the least they could do is let her go along to the big dance with the rest of the town. Of course, it wouldn't be a story if her adversaries just said sure, you can go.

As you know, thanks to her fairy godmother, Cinderella gets to go after all. However, once she gets to the ball and sees the prince, her desire just to go to the ball is forgotten; all she wants now is for that gorgeous guy to dance with her. It's human nature. As soon as one desire is fulfilled, the ante is upped and another takes its place. She is still pursuing her basic desire to get a better life, but now it has escalated to a new object. After the prince dances with her, her desire intensifies again. Now what she wants is him, and then all she wants is to marry him. So, you see, her desire line at certain crucial points bends and intensifies.

The desire line in *Growing Up* also bends. Russell Baker first wants to impress and please his mother by being the best paperboy in Belleville, New Jersey, and later he proves his independence by marrying Mimi against his mother's wishes. To want to be a top paperboy to prove his worth to his mother and to want to marry a woman his mother dislikes are quite different desires, but both are part of Baker's overall need to come to terms with his strong-willed mother.

INTERIM PIVOTAL EVENTS

Each time the desire line in a story bends or intensifies, the juncture is marked by a *pivotal event*. When Cinderella lays eyes on the prince, it is a pivotal event because it causes her desire to escalate from just wanting to go to the ball to wanting to dance with him. When the clock strikes, warning her it's almost midnight, it's another pivotal event because her desire turns to getting home before everyone finds out she's not who she seems to be. One way to plot a story is by first setting in place your pivotal events. It's like planning a trip to the Grand Canyon: First you plot your course to the Salton Sea, then you will hit Kingman, and from there you'll go to Flagstaff. If you first plan what scenes will be your pivotal events, you can write up to and away from these markers.

Writing a story is easy, I've heard it said, just figure out your ending and your beginning and then fill in the middle. That's true, except that the wasteland of the middle remains the problem. If it's just a flat highway through Kansas, a reader as passenger may have a hard time staying awake. You don't want everything to be of equal value or predictable, which is why the turns caused by pivotal events are desirable in stories.

Fortunately for the sake of memoirs, things in life rarely go in a straight line from desire to outcome—though that may not feel so fortunate at the time. When in a horrendously frustrating or embarrassing situation, you say, "Someday this'll make a good story," you're right. It makes a good story because you experienced an unexpected turn in the road. You were going down your desire line and suddenly there was a brick wall ahead and you had to swerve, or you took a more inviting road on impulse, or you got waylaid by picking up a beautiful hitchhiker. Actually, Aristotle said it best: In a story you want actions that (1) happen contrary to expectation, and (2) are brought about one by the other.

A short story is built around only one major pivotal event (consisting of the crisis and climax at the conclusion), but book-length memoirs may have many interim pivotal events that lead to the final and major one of crisis and climax. In the classic three-act structure, there are three pivotal events, but your story may have any number, five or more, or only two. The turns created by interim pivotal events keep the middle of book-length stories interesting. They are the lesser climaxes on the way to the big one.

⌒ PRECIPITATING EVENT

The *precipitating event* is the pivotal event that marks the end of the middle section of your story. If the beginning, middle, and conclusion of a story were of equal length, it would mean the precipitating event would happen two thirds of the way through a work. Generally, the precipitating event is much closer to the end than that, because the end of a story is much more condensed than the middle.

The precipitating event is a turn of fate and usually a surprise. The prince announces he will marry the woman whose foot fits the slipper found after the ball. This unexpected event kicks off everything that happens until the end. In *Growing Up*, Russell Baker calls Mimi on New Year's Eve expecting her to be sitting by the phone. When at 2 A.M. she is still not answering, Baker is surprised. It is a precipitating event because it precipitates his crisis. It forces him into awareness that he is going to have to marry Mimi or lose her.

A story's precipitating event can be anticipated as long as it forces a crisis. For example, your terminally ill father dies, an anticipated event, which forces you decide what to do about his wacky wish to have his ashes divided and sent to each of his former law school colleagues. Here the anticipated event forces a crisis: You must choose between your father's flamboyant desires and your own sense of proportion.

The Conclusion—What You Realized

The three major components of a story's conclusion are crisis, climax, and final realization. Usually these elements occur sequentially, but occasionally some of them appear to happen simultaneously.

CRISIS

The precipitating event pushes everything to a critical juncture; it narrows your options so that you finally have to make a choice. In other words, it causes a *crisis*, a crossroads, a dilemma that can take you to a higher or a lower moral place depending on how you deal with it. "Crisis" can be understood by the two symbols that make up the Chinese ideogram for the word "crisis": "danger" and "opportunity." At a dramatic crisis, you often hit a low point, are tempted to despair, or find another escape from facing the self-defining choice demanded of you. This is the danger. At the same time, a crisis presents the opportunity for you to rise to the occasion. By narrowing your options, the crisis (though you don't realize it at the time) is exactly what was needed to force the problem and desire initiated in the beginning of your story to a resolution. It crystallizes the polarity between you and your adversary that has run through the story. It necessitates a climactic choice.

For example, Mimi's actions made Russell Baker know he must choose to become his own person by marrying her against his mother's wishes or lose the opportunity to define himself and be with the woman he loved. That was his crisis.

In "Cinderella," the precipitating event was the prince's announcement that he would marry the woman whose foot fit the tiny slipper left at the ball. As a result of this precipitating event, Cinderella faces a crisis. The prince's emissary comes to her house, and when the stepsisters can't force their big feet into that impossibly small shoe, he looks around for other takers. This is Cinderella's chance: She can step forward, claim the slipper, and endure her stepfamily's anger, or remain silent and lose the prince. Today Cinderella would have taken assertiveness training and claimed that slipper. She would have behaved like a male hero in a story and gone after what she wanted. She would do what dramatists say a protagonist in a story should do—be active, make the choices that affect one's life. But Cinderella isn't a modern heroine and she isn't assertive. She sits in that corner wishing with all her might that her life would change, but she doesn't do a thing or say a word on her own behalf. The fairy tale wasn't meant to teach girls to be courageous or inventive; it teaches them to be patient and passive. The prince's emissary says, "What about her over there in the corner?" For the sake of thoroughness he insists that even the girl in rags try on the slipper.

Here I must pause in the moment between Cinderella's crisis and her story's climax. Here is where dramatists say a hero makes a choice, as Russell Baker did to marry Mimi. But Cinderella, true to her character, refuses to throw herself on her own side. She lets someone else do it. That is a dramatic flaw as well as a character deficit. And here is what you need to know. It doesn't matter that a piece of the story structure is missing or broken or backwards. The story still works. Works like an unstoppable nuclear chain reaction, like a spell that puts you to sleep for centuries, like a fatal passion. Works in the Golden Book, the Disney animated movie, the Rodgers and Hammerstein musical, in the film *Pretty Woman*. For even if some element of the expanded story structure set out here is absent, the story can still work if the basic tripartite structure (desire, struggle, and conclusion) is strong. In the case of "Cinderella" the myth is so strong that it endures like the pyramids—or like toxic waste you can't get rid of.

Now, back to the story. Cinderella doesn't face her crisis, but you could say she makes a decision by refusing to act like a hero and make a decision. She chooses to be meek and patient and keep her mouth shut, and in the story it pays off in spades. Shazaam! She turns into a princess. That life-altering change is the climax of her story.

CLIMAX

In teaching story, I find that people have more confusion about the difference between a crisis and a climax at the end of a story than about any other aspect of the storyteller's craft. If you think of the crisis as a dam which forces all the tension in the story into a narrow space and the climax as the explosion of water that shoots forth from the dam all at once, you'll never forget the difference between crises and climax.

The climax within the conclusion of a story is a big deal. It's the payoff, the final and major pivotal event. So, like any major event—the opening of a new shopping mall or a presidential inaugural—elements of preparation build up the excitement before the climax. That is the function of the precipitating event and the crisis in a story—to build the tension so the climax is explosive.

Now, as I did with crises, let me slow down to try to explain what a climax is in an autobiographic story. The definition of a dramatic *climax* that I find most helpful to autobiographic writers is: *the scene in the conclusion where something dies so something can live.* At the climax of "Cinderella," a revolution takes place internally as well as externally. Cinderella's sense of unworthiness as a poor wretch dies so that she may be reborn as a princess.

In a drama, the transformative climax takes place within a single scene. For example, in the film *Schindler's List,* there is a climactic scene where Schindler decides to spend his own money to save the lives of his Jewish workers. Something dies—Schindler's future affluence—so something can live—the Jews who work for him. In the climactic scene of Jane Campion's film *The Piano,* the heroine pushes her piano off a boat on which it is being transported, then tries to drown herself with it. The scene tangibly signifies her internal transformation. The heroine's private aesthetic life dies, is literally sacrificed through the destruction of her piano, so that she can be reborn into the natural world of human communion. She is symbolically reborn when she rises to the water's surface and is pulled out by the people on the boat.

However, and here's the sticking point, in life, transformative climaxes don't usually happen in a definite scene, at a particular moment. Real life is no movie. Unlike a constructed drama, real life is disorderly; there are too many characters and competing themes going on at once, and no apparent stairs of rising conflict to a single climactic scene.

Nevertheless, in life, transformative climaxes do happen. We all, at times, experience a death and rebirth of the spirit—at every important crossroad in our lives. Each important stepping-stone of our life is a turning point where something must die so something else can live. Often, life-turning points are preceded by a crisis, despair, the confusion of self-doubt and blinding birth-pain, and followed by unanticipated renewal. However, it is generally only in retrospect that we can see life climaxes because they are part of an ongoing passage that may stretch over weeks and months, even years.

This difference between life and drama causes a lot of confusion about writing about crises and climaxes in autobiographic works. In attempting to write her memoirs, Virginia Woolf complained that life did not have the tightening of dramatic crisis. So, although she was an accomplished novelist, Woolf could not see how her real life could be given a dramatic structure. Consequently, she approached her autobiographic writing as simply the setting down of memorable moments of being. It is not surprising that without the impetus of story she tired of the task and ultimately abandoned her memoir writing.

Other writers who do not have Woolf's commitment to interior truth but are similarly unable to find crises and climaxes within their lives take an opposite tack. They plow forward, and then, knowing that they need some sort of climactic moment to accomplish an ending, think they have to add something dramatic that didn't really happen—a fight, a demolition, or a physical birth—believing that a climax has to be physical. But finding crises and climaxes in autobiographic writing is not a matter of adding on. It is a matter of going deeper.

If you learn to plumb your soul for its epiphanies, you will discover that your life is full of dramatic crises and climaxes. They don't usually happen within an instant or in neat sequential scenes as in a movie, but by writing your life stepping-stones, you can identify transformations that led you in a new direction. After these turning points you were different, perceived something differently, or lived differently in the world.

In all likelihood, any of life's stepping-stones could serve as the final crisis and climax for a story. I'll bet that if Russell Baker were to write his life stepping-stones, "married Mimi" would appear on his list. "Married Mimi" is the pivotal event that serves as the climax of *Growing Up.* When he decided to marry her, something died for Baker so that something could be born. His obligation to his mother died so that he could become a husband to his wife.

Modern lives, which are longer, more mobile, and more apt to include abrupt changes in personal relationships or work than the lives of our predecessors, also contain more climactic pivotal events—every time we make a moral decision, come to a new awareness, or leave one life passage and enter the next. Each of these turning points can be the dramatic climax of a story, the spot where something in you dies—your selfishness, your pride, your faith—so something can live—your love, your understanding, your self-protectiveness. The possibilities are nearly endless. If you embark upon the task of finding story in your life by first identifying an important turning point as your climax, you will be able to write to a dramatic ending. You will be bringing the power of myth to the events of your life.

However, in order to create a dramatic climax from a real life change, you need to marry imagination to memory. Sometimes life does provide the perfect scene for your story's climax and all you have to do is remember it. More often, though, you cannot recall the exact scene in which a transformative life climax took place. You need to imagine the time and place where it *could* have taken place, or you need to find an equivalent for your interior change, what poet T. S. Eliot called an *objective correlative*. He defined the objective correlative as "a set of objects, a situation, a chain of events which shall be the formula of that *particular* emotion." In other words, you need to find a tangible expression for an intangible interior event.

Let us say that about a year after your lover left you, you finally experienced a turning, an interior change, where you accepted the fluidity of life and no longer clutched at the thought of your beloved being with someone else. Where you were and what you were doing when this happened you cannot recall, but you know that you often took the Staten Island ferry back and forth to work at that time. So you imagine a scene in which that interior change took place on a particular evening on the ferry. In the scene, you make the image of the water streaming by as you looked down from the railing the objective correlative of the feeling of release and flow you felt.

So the climax of a story need not be a huge dramatic event like your house burning down. It could be a quiet scene of a person standing on a ferry watching the water as obsession at last slips away. Just remember, however, that a story's climax is not something residing only in the mind, but something felt deeply throughout the body as well. The climax contains a burst of feeling that accompanies the shattering of an old self or old way of being and the simultaneous eruption of the new. Out of the eruption springs a new awareness, the story's realization.

REALIZATION

At the end of a story, your desire, which has been running through the story, is satisfied, disappointed, or transformed with an accompanying final *realization*. The final realization as readily comes out of the disappointment of an initial desire as its satisfaction. Further, the satisfaction of an initial desire does not guarantee a happy ending, any more than the disappointment of it necessarily means a tragic ending. Your initial desire may have been to become a concert pianist, a goal you never achieved, yet the craving is resolved when you realize that family has been your greatest satisfaction and a shared enjoyment of music has been a joyful part of your family's bond. Not an unhappy ending, yet it contains the disappointment of your initial desire.

In an autobiographic story, your personal final realization is generally the same as the point of the story. In crude terms, its lesson. It's the bottom line, the reason you tell the story, what you want someone to get out of it. This final realization completes the climax and results from having lived through the story (or having written it).

This might seem too obvious to warrant mention, but you would be surprised how many people forget that a story is supposed to be the embodiment of a human truth that we finally understand at the end. It might be a lesson about a different way of behaving or relating to others or the world. In literary works it is usually more subtle than that. The final realization might be a small new perception, a slight shift in values, or a single moment of insight.

Russell Baker doesn't teach a moral lesson at the end of *Growing Up,* but he has a final realization that makes his point. He realizes that in achieving independence from his mother, he can finally appreciate what a remarkable woman she was.

Cinderella's final realization is more problematic. Though Jungians may read into it a woman's need to be united with her *animus,* her own male side, on face value the lesson "Cinderella" teaches is the one little girls take from it: If you are beautiful, sweet, and patient enough, a prince will marry you and transform your life from rags to riches so that you may live happily ever after. It's a false realization in that it is misleading, just as Mother's well-intentioned advice "It's as easy to marry a rich man as a poor one" is a downright lie. The point of "Cinderella" is not relevant to or predictive of contemporary women's lives. Deceptive as it is, though, no one can deny that it makes a strong and seductive point.

What drives me crazy is stories that go on and on and never make a point, never have a satisfying conclusion at all. I have a neighbor who loves to bend the ear of anyone who makes the mistake of coming within ten feet of him. He's a kind man and well informed. The anecdotes he insists on telling you are full of specific and accurate details, one characteristic of a good story-teller. So for the longest time I couldn't figure out why listening to him bored me to distraction. Then I finally realized that it was because there is no point to his stories. They are just talk, talk, talk. I feel like screaming at him, "Will you get to the point!" But he never does.

The point of this unkind anecdote is that you don't have a story unless it has a meaning. You can have a story without an initiating incident or without a precipitating event. But unless it makes a point, you don't have a story. It doesn't have to be a moral point; it could be emotional, spiritual, or aesthetic. But there needs to be a reason for telling the story.

This is so important that I believe it is worth thinking about at the very beginning. Very often the point that your story will make when it is finished will be different from what you assumed it would be when you began. The realization you have as a result of writing the story is likely to be deeper and more original than the one you started with. Nevertheless, if you begin your journey without a destination, you're likely to wander all over the place and get lost. With a tentative destination in mind, you will certainly go somewhere; you will end up with a truth to tell even if it has changed.

So with some temerity I am offering you a formula I have developed for structuring a story before you begin writing it. I know it may appear presumptuous of me to present a formula to fit all life stories; no formula could do that. Yet after much internal debate, I've decided to offer this one for three reasons. First, to provide a way for people with limited time to outline their life stories. Second, because of the problem of emotional flooding many people experience when doing autobiographic writing. Emotions from the past well up and become so intense that it becomes impossible to continue. The solution is containment, to write in small segments, one page at a time. But you can only do that if you have a plan for your writing.

The third reason I've created this formula is that everyone, at some point, even if only when they rewrite, needs some help in structuring story. The formula is not meant to replace your own creativity, but to stimulate it. There is much to learn about storytelling that no formula can contain. This series of question prompts for creating story from your life refers to the nine essential story elements I have defined for you: initiating incident, problem, desire line, struggle with adversary, interim pivotal events, precipitating event, crisis, climax, and realization.

Formula for Structuring Your Life as Story

The following formula will allow you to create a plan for your story with sites to hit, like an actor's predetermined marks on stage. Your markers are key scenes that, if included in sequence, will guarantee that your story will have a dramatic beginning, middle, and conclusion. Don't worry if you can't answer all the question prompts right away. Allow them to spark your memory and imagination and put down whatever comes to mind, even if that is only another question or an answer that doesn't seem to fit, or several different answers to the same prompt.

Keep your responses to the following question prompts in your creative journal. You may find that as you get into the writing of the work, you will have different or differently nuanced answers to the same question prompts. Prompts for which you had no answers the first time through will later be filled in by your natural instincts as a storyteller.

It is valuable to create a preliminary structure for your work using this process before you begin writing, and then periodically to redo it. This allows you to play with the shape of your story without having to write the whole thing. Creating a preliminary structure helps you learn to think of your story in broad strokes, as progressive beats—that is, as the units of your changing states of being. The texture of detail is a major pleasure in autobiographic narrative, but details can disguise your story's shape if you don't have a way to see its essential parts.

It is important to maintain an openness to self-discovery throughout the writing process and, especially in these early stages, allow whatever you set down to be provisional.

STEP ONE: IDENTIFY YOUR STORY'S FINAL PIVOTAL EVENT

The most difficult part of writing a story, especially an autobiographic story, is to find a satisfying ending. Therefore, in looking for the essential parts of your story, the conclusion is where you are going to begin. Once you can answer this first question prompt, the rest will be easy.

T. S. Eliot's lines from the fourth movement of *Four Quartets,* "to make an end is to make a beginning. / The end is where we start from," applies to conceiving story. By determining the final pivotal event of your story (its ending), you will be able to find your initiating incident (its beginning). To identify your final pivotal event ask yourself, *Is there a turning point that could be the end of my story where something in me died so something could live or be born?* This could be a stepping-stone you have already identified from doing Exercise 4: "Pivotal Events" in Chapter 4.

STEP TWO: IDENTIFY YOUR THEMATIC CONFLICT

After the final pivotal event, what conflict in you was resolved? It need not have been resolved permanently, but it should have been resolved for the moment. Another way to determine your thematic conflict is to ask yourself, *What conflict in me led to this final pivotal event?*

STEP THREE: THE INITIATING INCIDENT

Ask yourself, *When was the first time I was aware of the conflict resolved at the pivotal event? Where did this thematic conflict begin for me?* or, *Was there an event that incited the problem and desire that led eventually to the final pivotal event?* The initiating incident is the event that gets the motor of your story going.

Try to backtrack in your memory—if this hadn't happened, then this wouldn't have happened—all the way to the incident that caused or greatly intensified your problem and desire. Although the initiating incident may not turn out to be on your first page or even in your first chapter, it is the real beginning of your story.

STEP FOUR: YOUR PROBLEM

Ask yourself, *What was my problem, whether I was aware of it or not, incited by the initiating incident?* Your problem could be external or internal or both. It could be that you lost your physical sight in an industrial accident or that you became blinded by adopting the vision of a corrupt guru. Whatever your problem is, it will be compounded into other related problems as your story progresses.

STEP FIVE: YOUR DESIRE

Ask yourself, *What did I want in response to my problem at the beginning of the story?*

STEP SIX: YOUR ADVERSARY OR ADVERSARIES

Ask yourself, *Was there a person, people, or power that stood in the way of the satisfaction of my desire?* (Remember, an adversary is not necessarily an enemy.) List all the people or things with whom you played out your central conflict as identified in Step Two. In the most dramatic stories, the adversarial force is focused into one or a few key people, but may include a number of secondary adversaries. Identify your key adversaries.

STEP SEVEN: INTERIM PIVOTAL EVENTS

Did the desire which got the story going bend or intensify at any point or points? What events caused my desire to go in a slightly different direction? For example, your initial desire was to get married and then you met a particular person and your desire turned to wanting to marry *that* person and no other, and then you met another person you irrationally fell in love with, so then your desire was to figure out which one you wanted to be with and what love really is. In this case, meeting the first person and meeting the second person are each pivotal events that provide the twists and turns to keep the middle of your story exciting. *Make a list of your interim pivotal events.* Each will be a key scene you will likely want to include in your work.

STEP EIGHT: EMOTIONAL BEATS (OPTIONAL)

Along with the pivotal events of your story, list each of your major changes in feeling or attitude. You can think of these as movements in a symphony. Each musical movement is distinguished by a different tempo: allegro, lento, etc. So in autobiographic writing, you want to think of a progression of feeling states and, whenever possible, tie them to events.

In life, emotional states of anger, calculation, relief, regret may seem to be a chaotic jumble, but to make this feelings outline, you need to slow down the pace to distinguish one from another. In writing a work, you will want to express many nuances of feelings, but for the sake of this preliminary list you are only trying to distinguish your predominant feelings.

Once you have a chronological list of events and related emotions, you will have a rough outline of your story. You can play with event/emotion items on your list like pieces of a jigsaw puzzle until you find a picture of your life that makes a coherent story. You can rearrange, add, or subtract items.

STEP NINE: PRECIPITATING EVENT

Was there an unexpected event that forced you into a crisis, that narrowed your options? Or was there an event that you anticipated that put you into a crisis? Identify the precipitating event that propelled you to a final turning point or choice of some sort.

STEP TEN: CRISIS

Did you hit a low point? Did you almost despair or come into danger? What was the danger or low point? *How did the thematic conflict between you and your adversary crystallize and reach its greatest polarity?*

STEP ELEVEN: CLIMAX

Was there a moment of transformation when something in you or in your life changed? Was there a point where something in you died so something else could be born? Was it a belief, a need, a feeling, or a person that died in you? Did it involve a choice, even if not a fully conscious one?

Identify a moment when that transformation *could* have taken place. *Where would you have been? What would you have been doing?*

STEP TWELVE: REALIZATION

What did you realize at the moment of transformation that made the transformation possible? What did you realize or perceive when the stage of your life in this story came to an end? Or what do you realize now about this stage in your life?

Is this the point of your story—the insight you want to convey?

STEP THIRTEEN: RESOLUTION (OPTIONAL)

Did something in your behavior change as a result of the realization? Did you join AA? Did you take the teaching job you'd been offered? Was there an action that followed your final realization? The *resolution* has become optional in modern stories. Many times, writers will simply end with the realization, or what James Joyce called the epiphany, a new level of awareness. There is a satisfaction, though, in seeing characters complete the turn of the final pivotal event by taking action in their new direction.

With an understanding of the nine essential story elements and the formula for structuring your life as story, you may now have a sense of your story's shape. If you don't yet, stay open. There is more than one way to find story in your life. Just as in *The New Diary* there were many devices through which to reach the same self-knowledge, so with finding story in your life: if one door doesn't work, enter through another. You may have to write your heart out and then search as in a child's puzzle for the figure hidden within the trees. You may find your story by developing your central characters as recommended in Chapter 10 or through working with your thematic conflict as described in Chapter 15.

It doesn't matter how you put your story together, whether you imagine the pattern in advance or discover it within your completed first draft, as long as you eventually include and order the basic components. As surely as a stone arch will endure if the right pieces have been assembled in the right arrangement, so a story arc that has its essential parts in sequence will hold strong, will feel sure, will share the quality of myth—perpetuity.

6

Genres of the Self

Sometimes, as with dreams, life stories fall into recognizable genres. Think about it; don't some of your dreams seem like genre films? Horror dreams, slapstick, action-adventure, gothic, romance, thriller, or X-rated? Dramatic genres must have evolved from dreams and situations in life with characteristics recognizable enough to develop names. And now we use those genre names to describe our lives. We say, "My life is a soap opera," when our relationships become overblown and complex, or, "It's a tragedy," when a friend dies of AIDS.

Although it happens rarely, I occasionally find myself working with a student whose true story falls into a fictional genre, and then we have the fun of seeing how far we can follow the conventions of that genre in developing the story. For instance, Marlena Fontenay was writing about her mutually exploitative relationship with Harry, a Hollywood hanger-on, and it became apparent that what she was writing was a vampire story—Harry had been sucking away her life spirit. The advantage of seeing this was that we could then discuss the essential elements in all vampire stories: the initial attraction, the first "kiss," illness and fear, the encounter with death, the final struggle to escape the vampire's control, and ultimately the need to put a stake through his heart.

When Marlena was reshaping her story in a second draft, we drew on some of these elements. I don't mean that she turned her real story into a vampire story. If you are to flirt with genre devices in autobiographic writing, the key is to keep them subtle and oblique. So Marlena would never call

Harry a vampire or refer to his sucking her blood. Instead she would use the genre's structural conventions as scaffolding and suggest its imagery without ever overtly making the analogy between Harry and a vampire.

This is Marlena's "stake through the heart" scene:

I took the contract. Tore it up into little pieces, and sent them floating out over the edge of the terrace. I stood there and watched them fall. Like bits of confetti. Shimmering white in the moonlight . . .

The night air was sweet with the smell of lilacs. My granny had a big white lilac bush in her garden and I used to sit under it when I was little and pretend that nobody would ever find me. Now, when I smell lilacs, it makes me cry. And that night, when the tears came, I cried for what I'd let Harry do to me. I cried out all the sadness. . . . I cried until I felt clean inside.

A reader without being told would never think of this as a "stake through the heart" scene. It functions as such within the story because in tearing up the music contract that would have bound her to Harry indefinitely, Marlena killed the relationship. When she cried herself clean, he, at last, died for her. This scene had not been in her first draft and something had felt missing—the story didn't have a climax. It was by comparing her story's structure to that of a vampire story that we could see what sort of scene the climax should be—a stake in the heart, a scene where Marlena decisively took the offensive.

It's beyond the scope of this book to break down the conventions of every fictional genre that might enhance an autobiographic work. If you see that your story is also a haunted house story or a retelling of "Beauty and the Beast," you can look for what conventions are repeated in different versions of this type of story and then ask yourself what elements in your life might correspond.

As I said, though, personal stories rarely suggest fictional genres. They do, however, commonly participate in one or more of the established types of autobiographic writing, the genres of the self. It is worth contemplating which genre of the self suits the story you decide to write. Do you have a thematic autobiography which illuminates a particular profession, social problem, or place? Or a memoir of a specific period in your life? Is it a family history not meant for publication, or do you have a publishable personal essay, thrilling memoir, short story, or other type of autobiographic writing?

When Dan Wakefield wrote *Returning*, he followed the form of the tra-

ditional confession, beginning with his having sunk into a slough of alco-
holism as a Hollywood screenwriter and ending with his redemption in returning to the Episcopal church in which he'd been raised. Wakefield, one
of the early New Journalists, selected the most traditional form of autobiographic writing, the confession, because it best suited the story he had to
tell. Having found that a preexisting container fit his story, all he had to do
was modernize it.

However, not every story will so easily find a ready-made form. Just as
some people cannot go back to the religion of their childhood, so you may
find that you cannot express your story within a traditional autobiographic
form. You may have to customize one, perhaps by expropriating parts from
several. When Maya Angelou's editor asked her to write her autobiography,
she at first refused, but then embraced it as a challenge to recreate the genre.
What she ended up with in *I Know Why the Caged Bird Sings* pulls from the
written genres of the "coming of age" childhood memoir, the realistic novel,
black protest literature, and African-American oral traditions of folklore, sermons, spirituals, tales of exaggeration, ghost stories, and children's rhymes.
She combined numerous traditional types of expression with which she was
familiar to create a memoir which, while truly original, gave a collective voice
to her community and culture.

To expand your ideas of what autobiography can be, I'll describe the various types of first person writing here, though you need not choose up front
which type is for you. Be aware that this list is limited; the types of autobiographic writing are so vast and various that literary critics have simply
thrown up their hands in exasperation, protesting that autobiography isn't a
proper genre at all. Consequently, it has remained uncharted, and my attempt
to map what one critic called "the dark continent of literature" is bound to
need refinement. Also be warned there are no clear distinctions between
many forms of autobiographic writing. Sometimes I have put the same work
as an example in several different categories, because a book can be both a
memoir and a portrait, or a confession and a work of humor, or even all four
at the same time.

Types of Autobiographic Writing

FULL AUTOBIOGRAPHY

A FULL AUTOBIOGRAPHY covers an entire life from birth to the present. There are three good reasons for choosing this traditional form. (1) You

are writing for yourself to discover the meaning of your life by setting it down. (2) You are writing your life story for your offspring so that they can know you as a person, not just as a parent or grandparent. (3) You are famous, distinguished in your field, or infamous so you know people are interested in the story of your entire life and that a full autobiography by you would be published.

If your goal is publication but you are not famous, the full autobiography is probably not your best choice.

Examples of published full autobiographies are Benjamin Franklin, *Autobiography;* Elia Kazan, *A Life;* ceramicist Beatrice Wood, *I Shock Myself;* and John Houseman's three volumes, *Run-Through, Front and Center,* and *Final Dress.*

⌒ MEMOIR

✍ *A MEMOIR* puts a frame onto life by limiting what is included. A memoir may be publishable even if you are not a name if it focuses on a topic of significant popular interest or if it is so well written that it can be considered literature.

The limiting frame may be determined by *A PARTICULAR PERIOD IN YOUR LIFE*, for example, your childhood, your adolescence, or your fabulous fifties. Willie Morris's *New York Days* is restricted to the period when he was editor of *Harper's*. Lillian Hellman's *Scoundrel Time* is about the McCarthy era of the 1950s.

THE COMING-OF-AGE MEMOIR, restricted to childhood, has become a distinct literary genre in its own right, with some outstanding examples, including A. E. Hotchner, *King of the Hill;* Frank Conroy, *Stop-Time;* Mary McCarthy, *Memories of a Catholic Girlhood;* Russell Baker, *Growing Up;* Maya Angelou, *I Know Why the Caged Bird Sings;* and Tobias Wolff, *This Boy's Life*. James Joyce's *A Portrait of the Artist as a Young Man* and Dorothy Allison's *Bastard Out of Carolina* are somewhat fictionalized coming-of-age memoirs. You don't need to be "a name" to publish this literary genre, but the writing has to be superb.

A memoir's frame may also be limited by *A PARTICULAR SETTING* as with Annie Dillard's *Pilgrim at Tinker Creek,* Isak Dinesen's *Out of Africa,* Alfred Kazin's *A Walker in the City,* Joan Didion's *Slouching Towards Bethlehem,* and Phyllis Barber's *How I Got Cultured: A Nevada Memoir*. Memoirs of place from a multitude of regional voices have become very popular in contemporary American literature.

The *ECOLOGICAL MEMOIR* combines a sense of place with a spiritual theme that dissolves distinctions between the self and the earth. The American tradition descends from Henry David Thoreau's *Walden*. The new ecological memoir carries the sense that there is a place on the planet that is right for each person and expresses one's true self. Like Georgia O'-Keeffe, whose style as a painter was tied to the New Mexican landscape, some memoirists are transplants who find their voice only when they find their spot. Memoirist Terry Tempest Williams, though, realizes she was born to the land she loves. In *Refuge: An Unnatural History of Family and Place*, Williams writes that she does not crave travel because she finds greater depths to explore within Salt Lake City, where her Mormon family has lived and died for a hundred and fifty years.

A memoir can also be limited by the author's RELATIONSHIP WITH A CERTAIN INDIVIDUAL OR GROUP. Colette's *Sido* is about the author's relationship with her beloved mother. Simone de Beauvoir's *Adieux: A Farewell to Sartre* is about her affair and friendship with the existentialist philosopher. Ernest Hemingway's *A Moveable Feast* is restricted by place (Paris), period (1920s and '30s), and his social relationships with an interrelated group of American expatriate artists and writers.

In addition to the frame focusing on a particular time, place, or person, memoirs may focus on A PARTICULAR THEME. There are as many possible thematic topics for narrative memoirs as for novels, and new thematic memoirs bear close resemblance to contemporary novels. However, some thematic areas have a tradition of their own.

VOCATIONAL and OCCUPATIONAL MEMOIRS are among the oldest types of thematic memoir. The vocational memoir may cover the subject's entire life, but is limited to those parts that relate the recognition and fulfillment of a particular "calling." The earliest examples are religious. Saint Teresa of Avila's *The Way of Perfection*, though fragmented by euphoric accounts of her visions, focuses on her struggle to be taken seriously by the church fathers and her eventual success in founding her own religious order. Malcolm X's *The Autobiography of Malcolm X* as told to Alex Haley, and Mahatma K. Gandhi's *Autobiography: The Story of My Experiments with Truth* are later examples of autobiographies unified by the story of a "calling."

Nurses, oil rig operators, hookers, and cops have published OCCUPATIONAL MEMOIRS, as have many others whose line of work is unusual or whose approach is fresh. Melvin Konner's *Becoming a Doctor: A Journey of Initiation in Medical School* and Oliver Sacks's *The Man Who Mistook His Wife for a Hat* are examples of medical memoirs. Joy Sterling's *A Cultivated Life:*

A Year in a California Vineyard is a celebration of her life and work as a vintner. Mikhail Baryshnikov's *Baryshnikov at Work* and Gelsey Kirkland's *Dancing on My Grave* are among the many memoirs by dancers. And, of course, memoirs by famous film actors and directors are de rigueur.

In *PHILOSOPHIC MEMOIRS*, a worldview is demonstrated through the writer's own story. Jean-Paul Sartre's *Nausea* and Robert Pirsig's *Zen and the Art of Motorcycle Maintenance* are influential twentieth-century examples. Closely related is the *RELIGIOUS AUTOBIOGRAPHY*, which is used as a means of founding or promoting a particular faith. Paramhansa Yogananda's *Autobiography of a Yogi* also fulfills the didactic function of most religious memoirs. A *NEW SPIRITUAL AUTOBIOGRAPHY* has also emerged, which is written as self-discovery rather than edification, each person finding a different spiritual myth or meaning that cannot be a model for anyone else except as the demonstration of process. The spiritual journey turns out to be the most individual dimension of a life.

Another theme traditional in memoirs is *ADVENTURE*, as in *THRILLING MEMOIRS*, *WAR STORIES*, and *NEAR DEATH* encounters. The thrilling memoir requires the dramatic structure of a struggle and a physical crisis, climax, and resolution. While many such stories are authentic, be aware that those that appear in male-appeal, *Soldier of Fortune* magazine and female-appeal, *True Confession* periodicals are not real memoirs at all, but fictional pieces written in the first person, or "pseudo memoirs."

The *HISTORICAL MEMOIR* is the one form of thematic autobiographic writing in which the importance of factual accuracy and chronology supersedes the creative imperatives of inner truth. Heavily influenced by journalism and reportage, historical memoirs are often authenticated by quotes from newspapers, letters, and other verifiable, external records. The historical memoir is written not only to tell the subject's own story, but also to document the story of his or her times. Yet even with the most conscious commitment to objectivity, the historical memoir is really a settling of accounts, a selective statement of how the author wishes to be remembered in history. Examples of historical memoirs abound, including *The Education of Henry Adams; The Autobiography of W. E. B. Du Bois;* Ida B. Wells, *Crusade for Justice;* and Margaret Thatcher, *The Downing Street Years.*

It is possible for people who are not architects of history to publish historical memoirs if they have been close observers of the events of their times, for example, Holocaust survivors or Vietnam vets, although the market has been glutted with these. It is also possible to write historical memoir as New Autobiography using fictional devices. Melissa Fay Greene's firsthand historic account of racial changes in the South, *Praying for Sheetrock,* focuses on a few ordinary citizens in a small town and reads like a novel.

DEALING WITH ADVERSITY is in some ways the theme of all narrative autobiography, but there is a particularly rich tradition about struggles with a particular medical or physical malady, such as blindness, cancer, or paralysis. Originally, this type nearly always took the form of the INSPIRATIONAL, a struggle against the odds in which the courage of the subject brings about a triumph, at least of spirit, in the end. More recently, a new LITERATURE OF ADVERSITY has evolved, which does not depend upon the "final triumph," but which derives its value from the depth and frankness of its discussion. Nancy Mairs, an author who has multiple sclerosis and has written of it in several memoirs, said in an interview that the clichéd story of overcoming illness does a disservice to people with disabilities. It sets up the belief that if one just wants to get up and walk badly enough, they should be able to. This message does "a real injustice to people with disabilities and to the general population in making them not experience genuine human suffering and loss and discovering the dimensions of those experiences that are transcendent." Thematic explorations of illness include Norman Cousins, *Anatomy of an Illness;* Betty Rollin, *First, You Cry;* and Caroline Knapp, *Drinking: A Love Story.*

PSYCHOLOGICAL ILLNESS is another adversity theme common in New Autobiography. Hannah Green's *I Never Promised You a Rose Garden* offers a firsthand view of schizophrenia. Barbara Gordon's *I'm Dancing as Fast as I Can* dramatizes the horror of one woman's addiction to tranquilizers. William Styron's *Darkness Visible* recounts his bout with suicidal depression; Elizabeth Wurtzel's *Prozac Nation: Young and Depressed in America* also explores that illness. And Donna Williams's extraordinary autobiography, *Nobody Nowhere,* allows us inside the mind of the autistic child for the first time, contributing to the understanding of autism as no outside psychological study ever could.

The theme of the INDIVIDUAL IN OPPOSITION TO SOCIETY, pervasive in the American novel, also fuels a broad range of memoirs, including a rich body of gay and lesbian coming-out stories, the autobiographic works of Beat poets such as Lawrence Ferlinghetti and Jack Kerouac, and a burgeoning, diverse literature that explores social themes of race, class, sex, ethnic, or age discrimination. Recently, Mark Matousek's *Sex, Death, Enlightenment: A True Story* combined the bravado of this type of memoir—memorializing his decadent life as a male hustler and member of Andy Warhol's Factory—with the redemptive ending of the confession.

THE CONFESSION

The spiritual *CONFESSION* begun by Augustine follows a clear plan: the recounting of one's sins, followed by the mending of one's ways. The key is to detail for a reader's enjoyment all your naughtiness (this should be the bulk of the work) and then tell why you aren't that way anymore. There are many secular examples of the form, among them Thomas De Quincey's *Confessions of an English Opium Eater;* Julia Phillips's *You'll Never Eat Lunch in This Town Again,* a confession of crack cocaine addiction; and Pete Hamill's *A Drinking Life,* an alcoholic's confession.

THE SPIRITUAL QUEST

Unlike the spiritual confession, the *SPIRITUAL QUEST* does not depend upon the sinner redeemed formula. It has the episodic structure of a journey in search of spiritual perfection. John Bunyan's *The Pilgrim's Progress* is the earliest example. Carlos Castaneda's *The Teachings of Don Juan* could be considered a pop example of the spiritual quest.

REMINISCENCE, REFLECTION, MEDITATION, AND REVERIE

These kinds of memoirs proceed by free association rather than chronology. They tend to be the least commercial type of autobiographic writing because they don't offer the reader a story and characters to hold on to. Carl Jung's autobiography, *Memories, Dreams, Reflections,* is a reverie that concentrates on the inner life of the subconscious rather than on the outer life of events. His work demonstrates that within the inner world, one can find specific images and details—necessary to keep such writing from becoming too abstract.

THE PERSONAL ESSAY

The *PERSONAL ESSAY* is undergoing a contemporary renaissance, nurtured by magazines such as *Harper's, The New Yorker,* and the "His" and "Hers" sections of *The New York Times Magazine.* In his introduction to the fine anthology he edited, *The Art of the Personal Essay,* Phillip Lopate traces the form back to Seneca and Plutarch, but attributes the source of its democratic informality to Michel de Montaigne, who wrote, "Every man has within himself the entire human condition."

The new personal essay is nothing like those little torture chambers of rhetoric and logical argument you had to write in English 101. Freed by public indifference, it has evolved into a meditation that explores how individual minds work, how they move by free association through thoughts and feelings to small, often subtle, realizations. Structurally, it is the most accepting form, allowing digressions, contradictions, mental journeys, and apparent shapelessness. Like poetry, it depends less on story than on motif and asks for precision and economy of language, though in a conversational, intimate style. Unlike autobiographic narrative, the personal essay need not have the dramatic shape of a story. According to Lopate, it is structured by the progression toward personal truth, "the 'plot' of a personal essay, its drama, its suspense, consists in watching how far the essayist can drop past his or her psychic defenses toward deeper levels of honesty."

An important key in writing the personal essay is to choose a very narrow frame, a limited, small subject, which you enlarge by exploring in detail and depth. The personal essay is a tiny aspect of a life under a microscope. Outstanding examples of collections of personal essays are Bernard Cooper, *Maps to Anywhere;* Phillip Lopate, *Against Joie de Vivre* and *Bachelorhood;* Sallie Tisdale, *Lot's Wife: Salt and the Human Condition;* Diane Ackerman, *A Natural History of the Senses;* and Barbara Kingsolver, *High Tide in Tucson.* Each year you may find wonderful examples collected in *The Best American Essays* edited by Robert Atwan.

The personal essay is short enough to be manageable even by those with limited time, and it can be published in a variety of periodicals. Those who distinguish themselves by consistently publishing essays in respected periodicals may overcome publishers' reluctance to publish books of collected essays.

THE TRAVELOG

The TRAVEL MEMOIR of a journey can be a particularly entertaining form of autobiographic writing if it doesn't fall into simply describing "what you saw" in dutiful chronological order. The form is at least as old as Margery Kempe's fifteenth century "as told to" account of her travels through England as an eccentric single older woman. In our time, Paul Theroux's *The Great Railway Bazaar, The Old Patagonian Express,* and *Riding the Iron Rooster,* and Peter Mayle's *A Year in Provence* demonstrate that it is not so much the journey or place, but the character, feelings, and reactions of the author that hold our interest. Irascible narrators seem to write the most compelling travel memoirs, probably because their exacting personalities put them into constant conflict with their foreign surroundings.

THE AUTOBIOGRAPHIC SHORT STORY

As it appears in magazines, the *AUTOBIOGRAPHIC SHORT STORY* is often indistinguishable from first person short fiction. In writing an autobiographic short story, you take a single, small turning point in your life as the epiphany of the story. Sometimes episodes in your life may suggest a particular literary style or genre, so there can be autobiographic ghost stories, autobiographic comedies of manners, autobiographic magical realism. Ray Bradbury's collection of short stories about his charmed childhood, *Dandelion Wine,* although memoir, reads like his science fiction.

Autobiographic short stories can be written piecemeal, published individually in different magazines, and later collected in a book. Nearly all the stories in Pam Houston's *Cowboys Are My Weakness* were first published in women's or literary magazines as short fiction. Yet, assembled, they can be read as the memoir of a woman who keeps finding herself in relationships with guys "whose favorite song is 'Desperado.' " An earlier example of this appealing "two for one" form is Christopher Isherwood's *Berlin Stories.* Each of his autobiographic stories is complete in itself, and together they make a coherent memoir of Isherwood's life in Berlin in the late 1920s and early '30s.

THE AUTOBIOGRAPHICAL NOVEL

THE AUTOBIOGRAPHICAL NOVEL differs from the thematic memoir in the degree to which it fictionalizes the author's experiences. Pat Conroy wrote two autobiographic novels, *The Great Santini* and *The Prince of Tides,* about a boy's childhood dominated by a father who, like his own, was overbearing and abusive. In both books, names and identifying details are fictionalized, but the characters have the problems of Conroy's actual family members. In *The Great Santini,* the father is a marine lieutenant, in *The Prince of Tides,* he is a shrimper, but in both novels he instills the same fear in his sons.

The autobiographic novel is a solution for those who have a whopper of a story to tell, but cannot for various reasons publish it as memoir. In calling a work a novel, the author makes a claim to its artistic merit. In some cases it is easier to publish an autobiographic novel than a memoir, but the writing must be of higher literary quality than is required of most memoirs. For instance, Sylvia Plath's *The Bell Jar*, about a teenage girl's nervous breakdown, closely follows the events of Plath's early life, but is called a novel because of its literary quality.

THE PORTRAIT

THE PORTRAIT closely resembles a thematic memoir that focuses on a relationship, except that the portrait emphasizes the subject rather than the author. In Patrick O'Higgins's *Madame: An Intimate Biography of Helena Rubinstein,* O'Higgins is present as protégé to the cosmetics queen, but his concentration is on Rubinstein's life rather than his own. Geoffrey Wolff's *The Duke of Deception* is simultaneously a coming-of-age memoir and a portrait of his father, a con artist par excellence. Depending on popular interest in your subject or your ability to tell the story of a fascinating character, portraits may be publishable.

THE COMPLAINT

THE COMPLAINT differs from autobiographic protest literature because the author does not find his or her oppression in social causes but in the misdeeds of a particular person. It is a very publishable form of portrait if the author's subject is famous. Examples include Christina Crawford, *Mommie Dearest,* Patti Davis, *The Way I See It: An Autobiography,* and Barbara Davis Hyman, *My Mother's Keeper.*

It is a natural fantasy to imagine getting even with people by exposing them in your memoirs, and revenge can fuel great writing; but for the most part, complaints suffer, like bad novels, from one-dimensional characterizations and an overly simplified, Manichean vision of the world.

THE CONCEPTUAL AUTOBIOGRAPHY

CONCEPTUAL AUTOBIOGRAPHY is a twentieth-century innovation, akin to New Journalism. To create it, the author goes out and does something outrageous or puts himself into an unusual situation in order to write about the experience. The earliest example may be George Orwell's *Down and Out in Paris and London,* written in 1933. Orwell intentionally allowed himself to fall into miserable poverty so he could report how men live on the bottom rung of society.

In order to experience racial discrimination firsthand and write *Black Like Me,* John Howard Griffin dyed his white skin to make himself appear to be an African-American. Cameron Crowe pretended to be a high school student to write *Fast Times at Ridgemont High.* Nancy Weber put an ad in the *Village Voice* offering to swap her home, job, friends, and lover with another woman in order to write *The Life Swap.*

For a writer who is not well known, conceptual autobiography may be the most publishable type if you can come up with a fresh concept, live through it, and write about it with insight. Such life experiments can be dangerous, though, and they are essentially artificial. Sue Estroff, a social anthropologist, wrote about her attempt to live among the street "crazies" in Madison, Wisconsin's flop houses to study their culture. She wrote a profoundly moving account, *Making It Crazy*, demonstrating that how we treat the mentally ill makes them more crazy. In the process of living like them and taking their medication, Estroff nearly lost her own sanity.

The best writers who have tried to become someone else in order to write about it have learned that you cannot really know another's life experience. You can gain insights, you can observe other people's reactions to how you appear, but still you are yourself assuming a costume and a role.

HUMOR

Autobiographic WORKS OF HUMOR range from vanilla soufflés to black bitters. Erma Bombeck wrote autobiographic personal essays and books about the ridiculousness of domestic life, such as *The Grass Is Always Green over the Septic Tank* and *If Life Is a Bowl of Cherries, What Am I Doing in the Pits?* S. J. Perelman showed the humor in cultural misunderstandings in *The Swiss Family Perelman,* about his family's temporary relocation to Thailand in the 1940s. Art Buchwald mixes his practiced wit with painful childhood memories in *Leaving Home.* Comedian Rick Reynolds developed a successful one-man show, "Only the Truth Is Funny," based on the professional and personal failures of his life. Whether or not they are works of humor, all memoirs need to include humor.

FAMILY HISTORY

THE FAMILY HISTORY or SAGA is often considered a form of autobiographic narrative because it is one person's exploration of self-identity, but it is not "I" writing about "I." I have noticed that writers who try to record the stories of ancestors along with their own life often end up with two works instead of one. Family histories can fall into the dutiful and often laborious tracing of the family tree and the telling of disconnected anecdotes, unless enlivened with fictional devices and an ever-present narrator's voice.

If you wish to publish a work about ancestors, you will have to write it like a novel with all the devices and drama of fiction. The most famous published example is Alex Haley's *Roots.*

SCRIPTS

DRAMAS and *FILM SCRIPTS* can be autobiographic works. Eugene O'Neill's and Tennessee Williams's powerful dramas are based on their experiences. Solo showcases based on a writer/actor's own life are currently the rage. Dennis Palumbo wrote the script of the film *My Favorite Year* about his initiation into the television business, but autobiographic film scripts are rare. To fit your story into the structural requirements of a multicharacter play or film demands a distance and objectivity about your material that few autobiographic writers have or should have. However, if you choose to try these forms, you'll find the story structure guidelines in the previous chapters indispensable.

OTHER FORMS

Autobiographic writing can also include some *LITERATURE FOR CHILDREN OR YOUNG ADULTS*, *PERSONAL NEWSPAPER OR MAGAZINE COLUMNS* such as those by Anna Quindlen, Ellen Goodman, and Ellen Snortland, and *PERSONAL MAGAZINE ARTICLES* such as those in *Reader's Digest* and *Reminisce* magazines.

ORIGINAL FORMS AND HYBRIDS

The most exciting examples of New Autobiography are new forms which are hybrids of older forms. Laura Esquivel's *Like Water for Chocolate* is simultaneously a memoir, a novel, and a cookbook. Each chapter of Susanna Kaysen's *Girl, Interrupted* is a personal essay and a short story. And altogether the work reads like a novel that follows a small group of characters and completes each of their stories. Like a historic memoir the book includes validating documents, such as photocopies of hospital forms completed by Kaysen's psychiatrists and nurses.

Having Our Say, a surprise best-seller adapted as a Broadway play, is experimental in form because two sisters in their eighties, Sarah Delany and Elizabeth Delany, collaborated to write one memoir. But perhaps the most original form of New Autobiography to date is Art Spiegelman's *Maus: A Survivor's Tale.* A comic strip in which Jews are mice and Nazis are cats, it is at the same time a memoir of Spiegelman's relationship with his father, and a saga of the father's escape from the Nazis.

AMERICAN AUTOBIOGRAPHIC TRADITIONS

In addition to the many types of autobiographic writing, there are some important American traditions. Within the *AFRICAN-AMERICAN TRADI-*

TION can be found some of our most outstanding examples of autobiography, memoir, and the autobiographical novel. The tradition begins with slave narratives told to white writers, but freed African-Americans quickly recognized the need to write their own stories. Early on, their quest for freedom was linked with their quest for literacy. The critic Robert Stepto traces the primary African-American archetype of the *articulate hero,* who discovers the links among freedom, struggle, and literacy, to the 1845 *Narrative of the Life of Frederick Douglass, An American Slave.* Later works that play variations on this traditional theme include Richard Wright, *Black Boy*; James Baldwin, *Nobody Knows My Name*; Claude Brown, *Manchild in the Promised Land*; Gordon Parks, *A Choice of Weapons*; Eldridge Cleaver, *Soul on Ice*; and Cecil Brown, *Coming Up Down Home.*

AFRICAN-AMERICAN WOMEN have created their own tradition, with its own archetypes. Critic Joanne Braxton points out that articulateness is important for the African-American female hero, too, and she identifies two common figures—the sassy female "trickster" and the outraged mother, both of whom rely on invective, impertinence, and ritual invocation for protection. In contrast to the solitary black male hero, she participates in a collective wisdom of courage, ingenuity, and love handed down from a beloved female figure, often her grandmother. In almost all examples of African-American women's autobiography, there is a period of perilous adolescence in which the heroine becomes aware of gender difference as well as racial prejudice. Often it is motherhood, no matter how early or difficult, that opens the pathway to her greater self-awareness and self-respect.

The African-American tradition of female autobiographic writing includes Harriet "Linda Brent" Jacobs's 1861 account, *Incidents in the Life of a Slave Girl: Written by Herself*; Elizabeth Keckley, *Behind the Scenes, or, Thirty Years a Slave and Four Years in the White House* (1868); the spiritual autobiographies of black women preachers, notably *The Life and Religious Experience of Jarena Lee* and *The Writings of Rebecca Cox Jackson*; a host of modern political memoirs such as Angela Davis's *An Autobiography*; and the back-to-Africa memoir, such as Marita Golden's *Migrations of the Heart.* Maya Angelou's *I Know Why the Caged Bird Sings* and Alice Walker's *The Color Purple* both derive from the powerful traditions of African-American memoir that precede them.

I have wondered why it is that in the arena of American autobiography, African-American women's contributions have been more outstanding than that of their white sisters. I believe it is because white women had more to risk by articulating their lives. Until recently, they have not been willing to risk their privilege; now they, too, are becoming fierce with the truth.

The *ASIAN-AMERICAN TRADITION* is indebted to the African-American tradition in recognizing the need to own anger in order to find an authentic voice. But issues of conditioned passivity and ingrained respect for parents and one's heritage are particular to the Asian-American tradition. Probably because they have been in the United States longer, Chinese-Americans have made a stronger contribution to autobiographic writing than other Asian-American groups to date.

The *LATINO-AMERICAN TRADITION*, like that of other ethnic minorities, concerns finding one's voice, but with a particular conflict between the narrator's self perceived in Spanish versus in English. Richard Rodriguez's *Hunger of Memory: The Education of Richard Rodriguez* is a thematic memoir that explores the conflict between Spanish as the personal language of home and intimacy versus English, a public language of commerce and achievement. His *Days of Obligation: An Argument with My Mexican Father* participates simultaneously in the Mexican-American tradition of autobiographic writing and in the tradition of gay coming-out literature. Sandra Cisneros's memoir, *The House on Mango Street,* shows the influence of Latin American literature on Latino-American memoir writing.

The first generation of *JEWISH-AMERICAN* autobiographic writers dealt with immigrant experience and the Holocaust; later generations are dealing with assimilation. Examples include Alfred Kazin, *New York Jew;* Vivian Gornick, *Fierce Attachments*; and Mary Gordon, *The Shadow Man.*

The *NATIVE AMERICAN TRADITION* is so different from the Euro-American tradition of individuation through written memoir that it stands in reproachful contrast to the underlying assumptions of this book. Native Americans have a strong oral tradition of autobiographic storytelling that conveys the values of the community and creates continuity between past and future generations. Such stories are autobiographic in that they tell wisdom learned from life experience, but most do not have identified authors; they are the tribe's stories. I've suggested that to find a story in your life, you decide where it begins and ends. From a Native American perspective, stories have no beginnings or endings. They are fluid, recycled, and acquire new meaning each time they are told. They are a sort of Rorschach test whereby the listener comes to understand the meaning later, through his or her life experience.

In addition to the oral tradition, there are over six hundred published works that are called Native American autobiography, but over three quarters of them were written by Caucasian anthropologists who imposed their own meanings and values on the lives they recorded. This has established a kind of collaborative tradition of its own that is quite controversial.

Combining both the native oral tradition and the written collaborative tradition, Greg Sarris wrote a portrait of his grandmother, *Mabel McKay: Weaving the Dream.* Mabel, a Pomo Indian medicinewoman and basket weaver, could not understand why her grandson, a professor at UCLA, kept worrying about finding a theme to tie together all her stories for his book. "Why would you need to tie them together?" Mabel asked—another example of how differently Native Americans view autobiography. Sarris says that he never did succeed in giving his work conventional thematic unity, but he did, in writing it, succeed in unifying himself. Born Native American and Filipino on his father's side, and white and Jewish on his mother's, Sarris grew up feeling illegitimate about his identity until, like his basket-weaver grandmother, he was able to make a whole from the fragments. In order to be true to who he is, Sarris had to create a composite form, and in doing so, participated in the evolution of the Native American tradition of autobiographic writing.

It may become apparent to you that the story you wish to write fits one of the types of autobiographic writing I have described in this chapter. If so, you are fortunate, because you can read examples of that form for inspiration. In addition to the ones I've suggested, your librarian will be able to direct you to others. Don't read them passively. Think about their structure as you read.

You needn't worry that to follow an established form is less creative than combining forms or inventing one. Your voice and your life are as individual as you are, and the way you adapt an established genre can be as creative as experimenting with hybrids or trying to come up with a new form.

However, just as it is sometimes impossible to know what your story really is until you have written it, so it is sometimes difficult to determine whether your work is a memoir or an autobiographic novel, a personal essay or a short story, until you have worked with it for a while. For instance, one young man I worked with wrote a childhood memoir without effort; it just poured out of him. He described movingly how his all-American *Leave It to Beaver* family had been altered profoundly by the expected death of his nine-year-old younger brother, who had been born with a weak heart, and then the unexpected death of his twenty-nine-year-old older brother from

cancer. The memoir turned out to be novella length; as such it made a trea-
sured gift to his sister and parents. Yet writing it had given the author the
desire to share with a wider audience what his family had learned. Unfortunately, the fact that he was not famous, along with the novella length of
his work, made publishing it difficult. Besides, when our class had read his
memoir, we had been left wanting more. We felt that, as in many first drafts
of memoirs, he had not included enough about himself. We wanted to know
more about this young man who so early had been surrounded by mortal-
ity.

One day in a flash he realized that he could intercut the memoir he had
already written with another work he had been contemplating about his experiences as a production manager on Robert Redford's film adaptation of
A River Runs Through It, Norman Maclean's autobiographical novel about
the death of a brother. Since the two pieces of time—childhood when he'd
lost his brothers, and young adulthood when he'd worked on a film about
a brother's death—were thematically related, they could be one work. This
would solve his problem of length and his foreseeable difficulty in getting a
memoir published as a "no-name." A publisher, perhaps, could use Robert
Redford's name to help market the book.

This young man did not come to his solution by calculating in the beginning how he could get his book published. He set down what he had to
write. Then he stood back, looked at it, and asked a few trusted others to
do the same. It was only by completing his original plan that he or they could
have discovered that his work was not yet complete. He could not have imagined when he first plunged in that his book might evolve into a hybrid of
half memoir and half personal journalism.

The process of autobiographic writing is like that of the painter who puts
down some colors, steps back to look at them, senses a shape emerging, and
with that shape in mind, paints some more. Your awareness of the genres of
self can help you recognize your work's shape as it evolves. Nonetheless, you
need to tolerate being in an uneasy state of unknowing, remain open for the
unexpected to enter, and trust the process. You may have many false starts,
but they aren't really false; they are necessary steps along the way. As you daub
colors before you have any idea what you are writing, you dip in and stir
your memory.

7

Tricks Memory Plays on You and Tricks You Can Play on It

In *Everybody's Autobiography,* Gertrude Stein writes:

> That is really the trouble with an autobiography you do not of course
> you do not really believe yourself why should you, you know so well
> so very well that it is not yourself, it could not be yourself, it could
> not be yourself because you cannot remember right and if you do re-
> member right it does not sound right and of course it does not sound
> right because it is not right. You are of course never yourself.

Memory versus Reminiscence

You are never yourself in autobiography, because it is not you; it is not
even the experience you had, no matter how conscientiously recorded,
because it is really words on a page. The more magic you can make the words
do, the closer they come to recreating the essence of an experience. But even
then, it is only what you remember of the experience, and that is itself un-
reliable.

We have all experienced how relative memory can be depending upon
our emotional state or point of view in the present moment. For example,
when my former husband and I began contemplating divorce, my memories of our relationship kept changing depending on the story I tried to make
from them, and that story kept changing depending on which friend I had
just spoken to or how my most recent phone conversation with my husband
had ended. In one version of our history, he was a controlling oppressor; I

was fortunate to finally be free of him. In another version, he was the one steady sun in my volatile, shifting universe; it had been my own failures that had brought about this painful ending. In yet another version, there was no fault; we had just grown apart, as the cliché goes. In the moment that I believed each version, it felt completely true; no matter that I had believed an entirely different one two hours before.

This was an extreme experience of the relativity of memory that occurred within a limited period of emotional confusion, but it illustrates a memory problem that extends over one's entire life. The past is gone; all we have of it is our memories, and they are not only faded, they also change shape depending upon both our position in time and the lens through which we look. The story you write about your first kiss when you are seventeen will be an entirely different story from the one you would write at age thirty about the same event, and both would be very different from the story about that kiss you would write at fifty.

Heisenberg's uncertainty principle demonstrated that the method a physicist used to observe a phenomenon altered the subject. In a similar way, our past is altered by both our position in time and the emotional and intellectual lens through which we view it. This is what any ideology does, whether religious, political, psychological, feminist, or mythological. Honesty in remembering depends on recognizing that the lens, by necessity, brings certain aspects of the past into focus and eliminates others. Actually, you want this selectivity of memory because it helps you to shape the randomness of experience into story—and because your lens interests a reader as much as your past.

Looking through a lens or set of lenses is unavoidable and desirable, but you can and should eliminate some of the distortions and blind spots. A common correctable distortion can be expressed through the old saw about the glass being half full or half empty. Cognitive research demonstrates what we know from personal observation—that some people tend to recall positive experiences, while for others unpleasant memories are stronger. Frank Conroy writes *Stop-Time* and Mary Karr writes *The Liar's Club,* both memoirs about brutally abusive childhoods; his is a complaint of unrelieved bitterness; hers is suffused with love and humor.

You have the power in the present to affect the past by how you remember it. That doesn't mean that you seek to distort the past. It means that you can more accurately recall it if you examine your temperamental bias and try to correct your lens. If you tend toward the bright memory clichés of a Pollyanna, it means going deeper and being more honest about negative feelings. If you tend toward melancholia, it means looking for pleasant memories to mix with the dark.

Amazingly, the point of view you assume when writing a memory actually changes the way you will remember it from then on. The way you remember in writing will become your history. As a writer and producer of television movies based on life stories, I noticed that after I'd scripted someone's past and let him read it, he would remember his life the way I'd written it! I would overhear him repeat an anecdote about his life with the dialog and twist I'd invented. The same replacement happens with autobiographic writing, as Annie Dillard spells out in her essay, "To Fashion a Text."

> Don't hope in a memoir to preserve your memories. If you prize your memories as they are, by all means avoid—eschew—writing a memoir. Because it is a certain way to lose them. . . . After you've written, you can no longer remember anything but the writing. However true you make that writing, you've created a monster. This has happened to me many, many times, because I'm willing to turn events into pieces of paper. After I've written about any experience, my memories—those elusive, fragmentary patches of color and feeling—are gone; they've been replaced by the work.

Roger Schank, a scientist who is trying to teach computers how to store and retrieve stories intelligently, has a theory that would explain why writing a memory transforms and replaces it from then on. In his book *Tell Me a Story*, he posits that we humans file and store our personal experiences in our memory banks as concentrated or partial stories; he calls these story "gists." He defines gists as "structured sets of events that function as a single unit in memory that can be transformed by a variety of processes into actual stories." The image I get is of a tight little memory pellet, like a concentrated golf ball core. There's a lot of material condensed inside that at first you can't see.

Schank goes on to explain that the accuracy of what is contained in our memory gists is approximate at best because memory is not static; it changes over time. On each occasion when we access a particular gist, we may retell its contents to ourselves or others in a different way. It may expand as new thoughts, details, or images attach themselves to the gist that were not actually part of the original memory. On the other hand, if memory gists are not accessed, not pulled out of memory with some frequency, they shrink, losing much of their content and detail, until they give only a vague impression that you went to the senior prom with the school rebel. What happened at the dance, where you went afterward, what you ate, drank, and said, has vanished completely.

Aristotle divided remembrance into two types. The first, "simple memory," he said was a lesser function shared with animals, and the second he called "reminiscence," a superior function possessed exclusively by humans. According to Aristotle, my yard dog Lucy has the first kind of memory. She remembers that I throw kibble on the porch to distract her from barging inside—which is why, whenever I open the door, she automatically tries to barge inside. Aristotle would say she has memory, but not reminiscence. He'd say she doesn't sentimentalize the night I gave her meatloaf and a bed after she'd survived without food for three weeks, drinking rainwater and sleeping in the gutter.

I find it hard to agree that Lucy does not reminisce like me about the night we met, though I have no proof because she won't write her memoir. I do agree with Aristotle, however, that reminiscence is superior to plain old memory. Too bad they didn't have PCs in ancient Greece, so Aristotle could have used them instead of animals to make his point about the difference between memory and reminiscence. My computer has perfect memory, but most certainly does not reminisce.

Some people, believing that memory is morally superior to the transformation of reminiscence, try to write with the accuracy of computers. What they get is a narrative of flat factuality where everything is of equal value. The state of reminiscence necessary to write memoir is the opposite of straining to remember as many facts as possible. Reminiscence is closer to the process of poetry, which William Wordsworth defined as "emotion recollected in tranquillity." Tranquillity here doesn't mean stripping memories of their emotional charge, but being relaxed enough to allow emotion from the past to flow through you again. Wordsworth understood that an experience can never be recaptured in its original intensity; the best you can do is stretch language imaginatively to achieve an *equivalent*.

As a poet, he also knew that evoking a past experience with language required sensate details. But here's the rub. The sensate details you need to recreate an experience are the very details you are likely to have forgotten. The distillation process through which events are stored in memory leaves out the details of place as well as the words and ideas of the participants. Like the fortieth generation of a photocopy, a general impression remains, but all definition has been lost. I remember that my mother, father, and I went for Sunday drives, but which songs played on the radio, what I wore, what we ate, and what we said, I cannot recall. Nor am I able to distinguish our many outings one from another. In my memory they have all merged into one typical Sunday drive.

So if you can't remember the details you need to recreate past experiences, how do you write effectively? In some cases you can find the details you need from research, by looking at old photos, videos, or diaries. But many times you won't find there what you wish to recall. In her autobiography, *An Unfinished Woman,* Lillian Hellman writes of her stay in Moscow in 1944.

In those five months I kept diaries of greater detail and length than I have ever done before or since, but when I read them last year, and again last week, they did not include what had been most important to me, or *what the passing years have made important. [Italics mine.]*

She gives a number of examples that demonstrate that the diarist, no matter how conscientious, cannot know what will be important to the memoirist.

. . . my notebooks tell what people I saw, what the usually glum dinner conversation at Spasso was about, the bad plays that the Russians were convinced I wanted to see, my impatience with the foreign colony's ill-humored complaints. . . . but nowhere is there a record of how much I came to love, still love Raya, the remarkable young girl who was my translator-guide. . . . And I know the name, because it is written down, of the three-year-old fat, blond orphan who threw himself at me the first time I ever saw him and who, when I went to see him twice every week, would sit on my lap and feel my face because the lady at the orphan school said I looked like a picture of his mother, but I couldn't know then that I would think about him for years afterwards, and dream as recently as last month that I was riding with him on a toboggan.

The passage illustrates what I think Aristotle was trying to say about reminiscence: It is richer, more complex, poignant, and resonant than memory. Reminiscence is the truth of now and then, not strictly the truth of then.

So if the details you need to write effectively have been swept away by the broom of time, and research proves inadequate, what choice do you have but to use your imagination? And what is reminiscence, after all, but memory mixed with imagination?

Reverie

The mode of achieving reminiscence is reverie, a dreamlike state of relaxation in which you start with the memory fragment you have and, by mixing memory with imagination, dream your past. Every time you become aware of a detail you do not remember, you guide yourself to imagine it with self-directed questions. It's as if you were an actor onstage, and at the same time the director giving instructions offstage. Whenever you hesitate because you've forgotten the script, the director prompts, "Improvise! Make it up!"

I'm teaching you this technique as a form of prewriting, as an exercise to practice in your creative journal to gather details you will need to write scenes. Once comfortable with the technique, when you are writing your work you won't have to do a complete reverie. Instead, when you come to a spot where you can't recall the detail you need, you'll just prompt yourself to:

TOUCHSTONE 2
Make it up.

This is your touchstone whenever you can't recall sights, sounds, textures, objects, tastes, or aromas.

The paradox is that only by letting go of your fear of not being able to remember accurately can you remember the sensate details you need to make your writing come alive. By letting go of your fear of inaccuracy, you free yourself actually to remember.

The first time you try this powerful technique, start with the memory of a special place in your childhood. This should be a place where you felt safe, completely yourself, where you had your best times, did what you most enjoyed, where you played alone or with other kids, daydreamed or read, or where you spent time with a beloved relative or friend. For now, just think of what that place might be.

EXERCISE 8: *Writing a Reverie*

Sit in a comfortable chair with your pen and your creative journal at hand, at a time and in a spot where you won't be interrupted. If it's your office, turn off the phone. Begin by relaxing your body and mind. Systematically tighten and relax all your muscles, then take a deep breath, hold it—then release it completely, releasing all tension.

Close your eyes and take another deep breath. Release the tension. And again. Allow your breathing to become deep and regular. When you feel relaxed, allow that special place to come to mind, where as a child you were most yourself. Is it a wide open expanse or is it confined in some way? Sense the size and strength of your body at the age you were when you enjoyed this place. Are you moving, sitting, standing? Are you alone or with another?

Now begin to accumulate more information by asking yourself questions. Each time you think "I can't remember," relax and invent an answer. Don't worry if you are fantasizing rather than really remembering, as long as the answer feels plausible.

Ask yourself and imagine:

- *What do I see?*
- *What do I feel on my skin?*
- *What do I hear?*
- *What do I smell?*
- *What do I taste?*
- *What is the light like?*
- *What do I want?*
- *What do I think?*
- *What feelings do I have?*

Write in the present tense what comes to you. Allow your imagination to take over where memory stops as you write.

So far, the scene you are describing is probably like a slide, full of detail but without movement. Now add movement. Turn it into a film. See and feel yourself move a part of your body. If you can, actually move as you would have then.

- *And then what happens?*
- *What do you do?*
- *What do you think or say?*
- *What changes?*

Write whatever comes without censoring it.

~ Making Up the Truth

If you have done this exercise correctly, it will feel as if you have just written fiction, but reread what you have written. Can you be sure the details you imagined weren't remembered? Perhaps it was actual memory that provided the images. Mary Jane Moffat, who published a childhood memoir, admits, "I confess that I am a lazy researcher. When I found I couldn't remember certain details, I felt free to invent. I rationalized that I wasn't writing factual history, but what I hoped might approach artistic truth." After her mother's death, in sorting through her papers, Moffat says, "I found scads of material I was relieved not to have known of when I was writing *City of Roses*. I might have been tempted to include burdensome facts that wouldn't have added to the ultimate meaning of the stories. As well, I was startled to discover that details I'd thought I'd invented turned out to be uncannily correct."

I tried the exercise I have just given you. The gist I began with was only a general impression of sitting in the back seat of the car when my parents went for Sunday drives and a feeling of yearning to leap inside the heads of pedestrians we passed. As I wrote the passage, I knew I was making up the details rather than really remembering.

In the early 1950s, people used to go for Sunday drives in Los Angeles for pleasure. My father at the wheel, my mother wearing white gloves and a black sheath dress, we would cruise the neighborhoods of Los Angeles. Over the hill from North Hollywood, we would wend our way downtown, past Angel's Flight and Olvera Street, past the courthouse at Hill and Temple, past Pershing Square where poorly dressed men gave impassioned speeches, past rundown resident hotels and old apartment houses. Then we would follow Wilshire Boulevard all the way to Beverly Hills and, gliding in my father's Lincoln, ogle the estates and mansions on Rodeo and Maple and the elegant apartment houses on Lindbrook and Camden. We never got out of the car, but at noon ate the sandwiches my mother had packed for our outing as we drove back toward home through West Hollywood. That was my cue to start begging to see the "stone house," a peculiar house made all of large smooth rocks that sat on the corner of an otherwise completely average block of tract houses. As the finale of the trip my father would finally drive to the modest street where it sat, so I could stare and dream about it to my heart's content.

Throughout these car trips, I'd sit alone in the back seat listening to my father's music on the radio, Count Basie or Frank Sinatra, pressing my face to the window, wondering, longing to know, how do people live in that colonial house? Who is the woman hanging her laundry out that apartment window, what is her story? Who lives in the room of that old hotel with the shade drawn? How did his life lead him there? Who built the stone house and why? Who lives in it? Do they have children? Who would I be if I lived in that stone house? As other children wish for magical abilities to fly or to speak to animals, I wished I could leap into the minds of other people, to see through their eyes, to feel their feelings and know their stories.

I decided that I would test if there was any validity to what I'd made up here by asking my father, who has a remarkably good memory, to read the passage and tell me if I had gotten any of it right.

On the sunlit patio of the Tivoli Café, I sipped my coffee as he read this, the first of many scenes I would write exploring our relationship. Even though I had made the situation safe for myself by asking him only to comment on the factual accuracy of the writing, during the interminable three minutes while his eyes were on my page, I forgot to breathe. Finally, he laid down the pages.

"I like it. No one could be offended by this." I understood his subtext— *I'm relieved you didn't write about the unsettling stuff we don't talk about.*

"But did I get it right? Are those the places we drove to?"

"Yes. Absolutely. I can't find any mistakes except the make of the car." He showed me he had penciled in "Pontiac" where I had written "Lincoln," then added, "You have a remarkably good memory."

This amused me, because actually I have a rather poor memory inherited from my mother, a weakness that has, I suspect, contributed to my interest in diary and autobiographic writing. I pressed further.

"Did we really drive to Beverly Hills? I thought I made that up."

"Well, I don't remember that. I mostly remember driving out of town to go on long drives in the country. In those days, you could get out of the city in twenty minutes."

For a moment we were both silent in a shared reverie of those country drives, my father's fingers on the steering wheel and my small foot in midair keeping the beat to Count Basie on the radio. Like the flicker of a silent movie, sunlight shoots between and disappears behind the dark sycamores that line the road. Where the trees stop, furrows in the planted fields replace one another like escalator steps, creating a hypnotic illusion. If ever so briefly, this little writing experiment has transported us, allowed us the fulfillment of every parent and child's dream—to return together to the time when we were both young, and all there was between us yet was love.

"I hadn't remembered those drives," my father said, "but now that I read this, it's all coming back to me."

When pressed further, he admitted he remembered the sandwiches and deviled eggs my mother packed in waxed paper and the trips downtown and into Beverly Hills only because I'd written it that way. Neither of us really knew if that's what we ate or if we'd actually driven to those places at all. My writing it down had made it real—for him as well as for me.

In doing the exercise, I hadn't been trying to write something that wasn't true. I was trying to write what was true and allowing my imagination to provide plausible possibilities. Once selected and written down, these imagined memories began to feel true to me—and, amazingly, to others. It is by using this technique of making up the truth that even people with faded memories can do autobiographic writing.

And certainly nobody cares whether what my mother packed was deviled eggs rather than fruit salad. The truth one seeks in autobiographic writing is not so much literal truth as emotional truth. As autobiographic novelist Toni Morrison has said, making things up and fact are two different things, but you may need some of both to get to the truth.

A Note of Caution

Obviously, I chose a completely innocuous example of making up a memory, one that, as my father said, no one could be offended by. I did so intentionally, and to begin with so should you. Mixing imagination with memory is a powerful technique, perhaps the most important secret of autobiographic writing I will teach you.

What concerns me is that I have heard a popular phone-in psychologist use a technique similar to making up memories to retrieve actual events, without recognizing that some memories that come are only poetic. That is, they represent feelings in a metaphoric way, but they may not be real memory. Experienced creative writers know that using the imagination to remember will bring up some actual buried memories and some inaccurate ones that convey emotion rather than fact.

Any technique that is so powerful—like hypnosis, or the free association of traditional psychoanalysis, or writing with the nondominant hand, or making up memories—must be used responsibly. Using this technique to imagine a memory that your father molested you and consider it proof would obviously be irresponsible. The writing could contain a poetic truth, or for some people might represent an actual memory, but to consider it *evidence* of actual events would be unwitting and dangerous.

I mention this because I have noticed in my classes an increased number of students who have a need to write about early traumatic abuse before they can go on to other stories. Autobiographic writing is a powerful way to retrieve such a memory and can be therapeutic, but if one is dealing with any severe trauma for the first time, it is best not to do it alone; it is best explored initially with a carefully chosen, reputable therapist.

At this stage in your writing, I suggest that you use reverie to gather concrete details, descriptions of people and places, dialog, and forgotten thoughts and feelings. When you begin to make up events—your own and other people's actions—you move into the area of fiction rather than creative non-fiction.

～ Repressed Memories

You will find that once you are engaged in an autobiographic work, the process starts a memory chain reaction. You will be taking a shower, driving the car, putting stamps on your bills, when suddenly an incident you thought you had completely forgotten will come to mind. One of the uses of your creative journal is to capture these moments as they come, nonchronologically, often for reasons that are not at first clear.

Most often they are memories forgotten from disuse; but sometimes, as Freud discovered, they may be memories that were hidden from consciousness because of some larger unresolved emotional issue. Freud gave the simple example of a case in which a patient mislaid a book, a gift from his wife with whom the patient had been at odds for some time. Six months after he'd lost the book, the patient and his wife reconciled, and he promptly remembered where he'd placed the book.

Repressed memories, unlike memories lost through disuse, generate emotion that has gotten misplaced or is misunderstood. They aren't lost memories at all; they are buried secrets that we are keeping from ourselves. Sometimes they are negative memories, events so painful that the conscious mind has shut them off. However, not all repressed memories are negative; they are repressed any time we cannot allow ourselves to experience and accept all our feelings.

For example, in her memoir, *The Lover,* Marguerite Duras recalls a positive emotion of love that she had repressed. Writing from the point of view of her mature self, she remembers the sensual affair she had with a wealthy Chinese man in Vietnam when she was only fifteen and a half. At the time, she told herself she was sleeping with him for her family's sake; they were poor and her lover gave her money. It is only when she reaches the conclusion of her story, the end of the affair and her departure for France, that the repressed memory comes through and functions as the emotional climax of the work. She recalls what she had not allowed, could not allow herself to know as a girl, could not tell her lover—that she loved him, that he was the love of her life. It is only through her autobiographic writing that the narrator can finally feel what she could not let herself feel as a girl.

Traumatic, negative memories, too, have been the basis of powerful contemporary literary works, such as in Pat Conroy's autobiographic novel, *The Prince of Tides*, which uncovers at the climax a memory of a violent attack on the narrator and his family when he was a child. In addition to being an outstanding example of literary New Autobiography, *The Prince of Tides* was undoubtedly therapeutic for Conroy to write. But the key to its literary success and its ability to heal lies in craft, in its structure and use of language.

Writing dark and repressed memories is like the art of glass-blowing. Out of grains of pain you can create exquisitely beautiful shapes and objects. But you must approach the work with respect for its danger; only when you are armed with tools and technique can you work with the flame rather than be consumed by it.

I'd like you to keep this caveat in mind as you try here another technique for retrieving lost and repressed memories, the technique called "free association" in Freudian psychoanalysis and "stream of consciousness" when used by modern autobiographic novelists such as James Joyce, Virginia Woolf, and Marcel Proust. (I refer to it as "free intuitive writing" in *The New Diary*.)

Here the technique is used to unravel a resistant memory. The key is to write so fast that your own internal censor can't keep up with you. You can't even keep up with yourself. It's as if your hand is doing the writing, as if the ink were flowing from the back of your head, down your arm, and pouring out your fingers onto the page without your effort or control.

EXERCISE 9: *Free-Writing a Memory*

Choose a moment that you don't remember well and free-write about it in the present tense. Any memory fragment will do. Here are a few memory sparkers if you don't have one in mind:

- *Your earliest memory*
- *An embarrassing moment*
- *An experience that took your breath away*
- *Your first kiss*
- *A time you felt what it was to be a woman/a man*

You can do free-writing without a time limit, but I suggest you give yourself five minutes the first time. Set a timer and write the entire five minutes without lifting your pen from the page. If you get stuck or stop, that's fine, just wait and write the first thing that comes to mind in the stillness, even if it makes no sense, is ungrammatical, wrong, or embarrassing. You want to surprise yourself, so don't plan or think about what you are writing; just let your pen do the writing, fluidly—as fast as you possibly can. Faster.

A man who had undiagnosed myopia as a boy chose to free-write his feelings at being forced to play baseball at school.

He hits the ball my way it isn't supposed to come back here that's why they put me here I'm afraid of it a meteor it comes so fast what if it hits my face before I can catch it let it fall then it will be over then it won't come this way again . . .

His free-writing expanded a single moment and allowed him to recall the thoughts and feelings that took place within a span of seconds forty years before. Until writing this experiment, he had forgotten that he had willed himself to miss the catch.

Keep this technique in your arsenal. It will be especially helpful for blasting through memory blocks as you are writing.

Give Your Memories a Last Chance

Here's another memory trick, an adaptation of an exercise offered by Deena Metzger in her book *Writing for Your Life*. It is a form of list-making combined with timed writing. Metzger calls it "The Dream Police" and asks you to imagine:

Suddenly there is a knock at your door. A trusted friend enters to warn you that the Dream Police will arrive in twenty minutes. Everything, everything in your life, that you have not written down will evaporate upon their arrival. You have a short time—twenty minutes—to preserve what is most precious in your life, what has formed you, what sustains you. Whatever you forget, whatever you have no time to record, will disappear. Everything you want must be acknowledged in its particularity. Everything, to be saved, must be named. Not trees, but oak. Not animal, but wolf. Not people, but Alicia. As in reality, what has no name, no specificity, vanishes.

When the mind knows it only has a certain amount of time to deliver, it goes into high gear and performs. Everything you list need not be positive, Metzger says, "In this exercise we select what is essential to us, what has formed us, what we cannot live without; this as often includes grief, losses, and failures as it does joy and triumph."

Once you get your memory process going, it is like unraveling yarn; if you catch an end and pull, the rest will unwind. As in a "last chance" speed-writing exercise, Hellman, in this passage from *An Unfinished Woman*, in a rush names with specificity all she cannot bear to lose from her life with Dashiell Hammett, as it had been before they were blacklisted and lost their financial and emotional security. She first recalls the turtle traps they set on their property, and the rest spills out.

> ... the memory of the turtle traps brought back the first snapping turtles Hammett and I had caught, the nights spent reading about how to make the traps, how to kill the turtles, how to clean them, how to make the soup; and the soup brought back the sausage making and the ham curing, and the planting of a thousand twelve-inch pines that must now be a small forest; and the discovery of the beaver dam, and the boiled skunk cabbage and pickerelweed for dinner, in imitation of American Indians, that had made everybody sick but me; and working late into the night—I had written four plays at the farm and four or five movies—and then running, always with a dog and sometimes four, in the early summer light to the lake for a swim, pretending I was somebody else in some other land, some other century. And then back again to that last day: I had carried the turtle traps back to the house, forgetting until I got to the tree nursery along the lake road, that I didn't own the house anymore. I stopped there to look at the hundred French lilac trees in the nursery, the rosebushes waiting for the transplant place they would never get, the two extravagant acres of blanched asparagus, and standing there by the road that May afternoon of 1952, I finally realized that I would never have any of this beautiful, hardscrabble land again.

Hellman wrote this passage, she tells us, in a Moscow hotel room, at a time when she had no intention of digging up frozen roots of memory. Nevertheless, that is when she was ready for them. In autobiographic writing as in journal writing, there seems to be an internal wisdom at work that guides us to write what we are ready to understand. Different memories will ask to be written at different times, and this is an instinct we generally can trust. For the most part, people's natural defenses protect them from memories they are not ready to face.

For this reason, unlike other writing instructors, I do not give a lot of exercises that prescribe subjects to write about. My goal is to teach you the deep structures, skills, and devices you will need in order to write about any aspect of your life when you are ready to do so.

Therefore I'd like to offer you a selection of additional tricks you can use to retrieve memories. Put them into your tool bag and use them when and if they are helpful and appropriate for the work you choose to write.

Photos as Memory Sparkers

A favorite photo from the period you wish to write about can be the starting point for reverie. Ask yourself questions such as:

- Why was I wearing that dress/that suit?
- What were my feelings toward the other people in the photo?
- What was I thinking that I looked so sad/so happy/so surprised?
- What does the composition of the photo reveal?
- What does the photo hide?

Susan Golant began her memoir of being the child of Holocaust survivors by writing a reverie on a photo of herself at age two and a half. It led her into the theme of her book.

The portrait was taken in 1950 or '51 by a professional photographer, a great luxury in the days when my parent, grandparents, sister and I still crammed into a tiny fifth-floor walk-up in the Bronx.

I am sitting on a bench, up against a wall, holding a small toy bird, the photographer's prop. In this picture I was portrayed as a beautiful child. I had very large brown eyes—my mother was fond of saying they were "as big as saucers," in the expression of the day— and the retoucher's brush reddened my cherubic cheeks and full lower lip and mascaraed in thick lashes. I am wearing a yellow and chartreuse striped dress with puffy short sleeves and white embroidered yoke. My arms, crooked at the elbows, are plump and pinchable.

... This is a picture of me as a little girl—no, it is *my* little girl—

the child who resides within the woman. And, as such, it is a re-markable portrait of my childhood.

For what draws me to the photo is not how cute it is but rather the look in those saucer-eyes: the look of fear, even terror, and utter sad-ness. A look that ought not to have ever occurred. A look that tells it all.

My parents had been among the few to have survived the Nazi persecution of Jews during World War II. This picture was taken a scant five or six years after their liberation from torture, starvation, slavery, and disease. And although I imagine there was great joy at my birth—joy that they actually *could* bear children after all they had endured, joy at adding another child to the community that had been so ter-ribly destroyed—it is also clear to me that I absorbed with my mother's milk, with her love and affection, a sense of the horror and abyss that was their lives for more than six years.

Photos can help you reenter the feelings of the person you once were. They can also help you remember others at the period of time you are try-ing to recapture. In *The Lover,* Marguerite Duras inserts a reverie on a photo of her mother, which takes the writer to a disclosure it would have been dif-ficult to make without the objective medium of the photo.

It's the courtyard of a house by the Small Lake in Hanoi. We're to-gether, she and us, her children. I'm four years old. My mother's in the middle of the picture. I recognize the awkward way she holds her-self, the way she doesn't smile, the way she waits for the photo to be over and done with. By her drawn face, by a certain untidiness in her dress, by her drowsy expression, I can tell that it's hot, that she's tired, that she's bored. But it's by the way we're dressed, us children, all any-how, that I recognize a mood my mother sometimes used to fall into, and of which already, at the age we were in the photo, we knew the warning signs—the way she'd suddenly be unable to wash us, dress us, or sometimes even feed us. Every day my mother experienced this deep despondency about living. Sometimes it lasted, sometimes it would vanish with the dark. I had the luck to have a mother desper-ate with despair so unalloyed that sometimes even life's happiness, at its most poignant, couldn't quite make her forget it.

I must suggest restraint here. Though one's family pictures may be fasci-nating to oneself, there is always the chance their analysis will bore a reader if overused. The examples I've cited are from books that contain only two or three photo reveries. The exercise is best used for prewriting, though sometimes, as in the examples cited, it can be incorporated effectively into a work.

Writing a family history around a set of photos to be included in the final work can be a charming arrangement for an autobiography written for descendants. However, a random selection of old family photos cannot provide a narrative structure. If you wish to use this device to organize a book-length work, you must select your photos carefully, so that by sequence and changes seen within the pictured characters, they tell a coherent story. A better plan might be to write your work and then see if you have any photos that complement it. An overabundance of photos can be more a hindrance than a help if they divert you from focusing your themes and shaping a meaningful story.

⌒MUSIC

Pete Hamill admits that in writing his memoir, *A Drinking Life,* he could remember more about being eleven than being thirty-two, because at eleven he wasn't yet drinking. So he used a memory trick you may find useful. He bought a book that listed the top hit songs of 1943, and then he bought CDs of those songs. He says that listening to Cole Porter's worst song brought back memories of where he was the year the song was popular, whom he was with, and what he was doing—even memories of streets he had driven while listening to "Don't Fence Me In."

We have all experienced how a certain song brings back the feeling of a particular time in our life. When you are writing about that time, play the song and allow yourself to make up specific, detailed memories as you listen.

⌒OBJECTS

Objects seem to hold the energy of the past. As anyone who has lost mementos to fire, earthquake, or hurricane knows, certain objects are irreplaceable because of the memories they contain.

Having found that meditating on certain photos led her into reverie, Susan Golant also tried meditating on chosen objects. In contemplating "soap," she recalled how her mother had hoarded bars and boxes of soap when she was growing up, and she realized that she, too, hoarded it.

I thought about the two baby blue bars of I. Magnin lanolin-enriched jasmine
soap that have been languishing in a bathroom drawer at my house for the last

several years. "I use them for sachet," I told myself, "yes, for sachet," even though
time has nearly sucked all of the fragrance out of them.

    . . . I thought about the concept of deserving. Many of my "American"
friends grew up with a profound sense of entitlement—as my mother would
say, "They think everything is coming to them." . . . My parents, on the other
hand, exhibited a profound sense of what I have come to think of as disenti-
tlement. Whereas others deserved whatever they wanted, my parents—and my
mother especially—acted as if they deserved nothing. My mother's Yiddish
phrase, "sis meir a shued," echoed throughout my childhood "Eh, what do I
need it for?"

Susan had no idea when she began writing about a bar of soap that it would
lead her to issues of entitlement and disentitlement. The chapter expanded
like a personal essay from the contemplation of something small and com-
monplace to larger insights not seen before.

Indeed, the contemplation of an object works especially well for the personal essayist. Sallie Tisdale wrote a whole collection of essays, *Lot's Wife:*
Salt and the Human Condition, all having to do with different aspects of salt—
salt in tears, salt in the ocean, the chemical composition of salt, salt in
mythology. Diane Ackerman writes personal essays that explore the senses
in her intoxicating book, *A Natural History of the Senses,* focusing on particular objects such as sweat, violets, roses, hair, tattoos, vanilla, ginger, and
chocolate.

Thomas Mallon wrote a personal essay that appeared in *Harper's,* which
is a reverie on his father's checkbooks that Mallon found when settling his
deceased father's affairs. Through a contemplation of the register, whom his
father wrote checks to and the amounts, Mallon creates a profile of his father and a short memoir of his relationship with him.

⌒FLOOR PLANS

Perhaps because the memory is embedded through our primary senses of
direction and movement, we can recall the floor plan of the homes we have
lived in even when no other memory remains. Gaston Bachelard writes in
The Poetics of Space:

    . . . the house we were born in is physically inscribed in us. It is a group
    of organic habits. After twenty years, in spite of all the other anony-
    mous stairways, we would recapture the reflexes of the "first stairway,"
    we would not stumble on that first high step. The house's entire being

would open up, faithful to our own being. We would push the door that creaks with the same gesture, we would find our way in the dark to the distant attic. . . . The word habit is too worn a word to express this passionate liaison of our bodies, which do not forget, with an unforgettable house.

If you are having difficulty remembering how you lived at some period in the past, the way to reconstruct your life could be from the foundation up.

EXERCISE 10: *Building a Memory House*

On a large piece of paper draw the floor plan of the house or apartment you wish to remember, including the hallways, bathrooms, bedrooms, back and front yards. After you have completed it with as much detail as you can, put it aside and find a quiet place to write a reverie in your creative journal. Imagine yourself approaching this house the way you had to get there, from a freeway off-ramp, on a country road, into a horseshoe driveway, up three steps to the door—however you entered. Once inside, walk through and enter a room of your choice.

Now, imagine the details, furnish the room—where is the bed or table, is there a fireplace or cupboards, are there rugs or carpets on the floor? Is it day or night? Are there lamps or overhead lights?

Place yourself inside this room and allow your writing to go where it will, exploring your feelings and thoughts at the age you were when you lived there, concentrating on your interaction with other people in the house.

Floor plans can provide a safe foundation to build memory upon if you have the opportunity to interview parents or siblings about their memories of the past. As I've mentioned, my mother had a frighteningly bad memory; I believe she willed herself to forget her life. Yet when I once asked her to draw the floor plan of the first apartment and houses we lived in when we moved to L.A.—telling her that the exercise was a game so she wouldn't associate it with memory—she cheerfully drew floormaps, including a sunporch and blackbird-infested apricot tree I'd forgotten.

RESEARCH THE PAST

Just as you induce reminiscence by looking at photos or listening to music of a particular period, so you can aid your memory by looking in guidebooks for geographic reminders, and in almanacs, periodicals, or films of the period for details about the times. Chronological compilations of hit songs, popular films, and historic events, such as the Time/Life series *This Fabulous Century*, are particularly helpful. Sometimes you can visit places you lived or worked. If you can't recall what it was like to work in a print shop, go visit one, smell the tart ink again. Your skill will be in weaving the details you glean from such research into your text so that no one can tell it came from a source other than your amazing memory.

THE BODY'S MEMORY

Another way to remember is through repeating body movements. For example, if you worked in an ice cream parlor, stand up from your desk and, like a mime, bend over and stretch your arm down to scoop the hard ice cream at the bottom of a cardboard container and feel the refrigerator frostbite your nose and cheeks.

Imagining a Missing Past

Sometimes despite all these tricks, you find memory blanks of months or even years where there isn't even a thread to pull at. Doris Lessing comments in *Under My Skin,* the first volume of her autobiography, "As you start to write at once the question begins to insist: Why do you remember this and not that? Why do you remember in every detail a whole week, month, more, of a long ago year, but then complete dark, a blank? *How do you know that what you remember is more important than what you don't?"*

In *Writing for Your Life,* Deena Metzger tells the story of a woman whose father had died and whose mother was a reclusive alcoholic. This writer, who had herself lived a severely curtailed life, felt she had no "usable history" as the basis for autobiographic writing. Metzger recommended that the writer take the fragment of a memory she possessed about an aunt she had met only once and from it imagine in great detail the personality and life of this daring, artistic woman the student never really knew.

Having written the imaginary portrait, the student went one step further. She "re-remembered" her adolescence *as if* this aunt had visited her often, become her mentor, and invited her to come live with her in Manhattan. With the painstaking detail of a novelist, the student wrote about an imagined year when she lived with the aunt and how it had changed her. She literally created for herself a usable history, and according to Metzger, the writer was transformed and became more courageous in her current life as a result.

The notion of imaginary memories functioning like real ones is tantalizing. Freud observed that mistaken memories functioned as a source for neurosis as truly as real ones. At the August 1992 meeting of the American

Psychological Association, Michael Nash, an associate professor of psychology at the University of Tennessee, suggested that there may be no structural difference in the brain between how a fantasy about the past and a viable memory function. He presented the clinical case of a patient who had come to him with all the signs of someone suffering from previously repressed traumatic memory, including symptoms of sleeplessness, flashbacks, and withdrawal from social engagement. The man "remembered" having been abducted by aliens, and seemed to get better as he was able to elaborate on the report of trauma and integrate it into his view of the world. Even though he never gave up his fantasy of aliens from another planet, he left therapy fully functioning and cured of his symptoms!

If there is no structural difference in how imagined memories and actual memories function in the psyche, then we all need to maintain a certain skepticism about memory even as we freely use it to rewrite our past. At the same time, the tantalizing healing potential of working with imagined memories takes us into the far reaches of New Autobiography.

In the past several years women have been meeting in workshops across the country to use autobiographic writing to recapture their lost "herstory." Women have been silenced for so long that we have not inherited from our grandmothers and great-grandmothers the knowledge of their lives we crave. We feel newly hatched, without the benefit of a feminine collective wisdom. Especially in the United States, where assimilation, geographic separation, and the drive for upward mobility have demolished family continuity, many women—and men—find themselves bereft of a knowledge of their roots.

As their autobiographic writings suggest, African-American women have a stronger oral and written tradition of feminine wisdom handed down through a matriarchal grandmother than do most Americans. For those of us without knowledge of our female ancestors, Dorothy Randall Gray, an African-American, teaches a workshop on how to find one's ancestors within. She uses ritual and invocation to bring up the name of a great-grandmother and asks that through imagination you "remember" this forgotten woman's life. If you want to try doing this, you could allow yourself to "hear" a woman's name come to you in silence, the name of a forgotten ancestor. When you hear a name calling to you from within, you can make up the memory of what it must have been like to be in her life. You can begin with imagining where she lives, in what landscape, what kind of housing. You can imagine a room she occupies and ask yourself the prompting questions: What do I see? What do I hear? What do I smell? What am I thinking and feeling? In this way you can give a voice to the silenced, forgotten women who came before you.

Rediscovering ancestors through imagination is useful for self-discovery and to mend the broken connection to your roots, but generally has little use in nonfiction. However, in *The Woman Warrior,* Maxine Hong Kingston invents fictional ancestors as a literary device within a nonfiction memoir. *The Woman Warrior* is written in three parts, each with a subject and style distinct from the other. The second and third parts are recognizable traditional memoir. The second part tells the story of Kingston's mother and aunt, how they were diminished and defeated by their immigrant experience in the United States. The third part tells of Kingston's childhood, how she escaped the restrictions her culture had put on her as a proper Chinese-American little girl—how she found her anger and strength in her (previously silenced) voice. But it is the first section of *The Woman Warrior* that is the most inventive and radical. It records the fantasies Kingston has made up about powerful, warrior women ancestors whose blood fills her veins. These are the ancestors she needs in order to achieve her liberation in the third part of the book. It is truly a new kind of autobiography, which allows you to see the writer reinventing her personal mythology.

MAKING UP MEMORIES IN WRITING A FAMILY HISTORY

Kingston's memoir pushes the boundaries of autobiographic experimentation and would seem not to be relevant to people writing a family history for their descendants. Family members generally don't want you to invent fantasies; they want to know who did what and why. Yet to write an interesting narrative, one does need to *imagine* what life was like for those earlier family members.

One of the most common mistakes that first-time autobiographic writers make comes from their fear of not being completely truthful. They avoid mentioning details at all because they do not know them. Consequently they end up with vague, generalized and often clichéd writing. Such writing cannot capture the truth of human experience, which is specific and individualized. Paradoxically, if you imagine details, your writing seems more authentic than if you restrict your imagination.

Take Roberta, an athletic, white-haired grandmother, who took my class in order to get pointers on writing a family history and autobiography for her grandchildren. The first chapter she showed us about her own adolescence was full of sensual detail and funny dialog. Then she brought in a chapter she had written about the courtship and marriage of her grandparents. The writing was dutiful, factual, and, frankly, boring. Here was the potential of romance within the gaslit world of women in bustles and salesmen who rode the rails, but she couldn't fill it in with enough detail to make it come alive.

"I only know what my mother told me," Roberta explained. "I can't know what my grandparents felt or what their first apartment looked like. I wasn't there."

"You know what it might have looked like from your knowledge of that era, and you can research by looking at photos of that period or reading books about daily life then," I suggested.

"That would be cheating," Roberta said.

And another student chimed in, "She's writing for her grandchildren. She just wants to give them the truth."

"All the more reason to make this long-past world come alive for them by using fictional devices." I held my ground. "Children love the magic of traveling in their imaginations to another time and place."

I saw a look of recognition brighten Roberta's face. Of course! She was telling stories to her grandchildren; she had to embellish as she did when she tucked them in bed and delighted them with anecdotes about their mother as a girl. If she enhanced her knowledge of the past by researching a little and adding details from her imagination—what could it hurt?

8

Finding Your Voice

Voice, your particular style of expressing yourself, is more important in autobiographic writing than in any other literary form. In experiential writing, you cannot take on someone else's writing style; you must find your own. This one time Mama was right: Just be yourself, darling, and everyone will love you, pimples, uneven hem, gap teeth and all. Just be yourself, compassionate or ironic, flirtatious or embarrassed, imperfect and real, your style, your tone, and your sense of humor. Write as you would to that little group of admirers who is really interested in what you have to say and laughs at your jokes. Loosen up, improvise, relish the sensuality of words.

Often I read a published memoir not for its story at all but to hear the author's voice and through it to enter his or her world. The principal appeal of memoirs such as Elia Kazan's *A Life,* or Anne Lamott's *Operating Instructions* is in the writer's distinctive voice. Producer Julia Phillips's autobiography, *You'll Never Eat Lunch in This Town Again,* has no wisdom to impart; it is sustained through the wanton energy of Phillips's voice. Listen to it in this scene when, having fallen from Academy Award winning producer to an unemployed crack addict, she receives a visit from Hollywood mogul Ray Stark come to offer her a job.

When Ray arrives promptly at two forty-five the next day, I keep him waiting, not out of power games, but because I am still taking that one last hit for the road in my bathroom. When I finally make my entrance, I find him seated in the cramped little anteroom between the kitchen and my bedroom on a far too cute and small wicker sofa. He is dressed a decade behind the times: plaid shirt, jeans, a cowboy belt with a huge turquoise buckle. He looks like a sad old queen.

Further, his jeans are too blue. I fixate on them for a moment, communing with the tightly woven blue-and-white threads. They start to separate and slink around on his thighs. Little snakes on Big Daddy Snake. I close my eyes and take a deep breath and wave them away in my mind. When I open my eyes, they wave back. I sit next to him on the matching wicker rocking chair. As he talks, I start to rock.

"Miss making movies?" Always . . .

"I make them in my mind . . ." Ray permits himself an imperceptible upturning of his mouth. I notice all these things, because my brain is goin' ninety.

"I'll get right to the point . . ." Busy busy Ray. Places to go, people to see.

Now listen to the voice of Sandra Cisneros in *The House on Mango Street,* a memoir told in a series of vignettes, this one titled "Those Who Don't."

Those who don't know any better come into our neighborhood scared. They think we're dangerous. They think we will attack them with shiny knives. They are stupid people who are lost and got here by mistake.

But we aren't afraid. We know the guy with the crooked eye is Davey the Baby's brother, and the tall one next to him in the straw brim, that's Rosa's Eddie V, and the big one that looks like a dumb grown man, he's Fat Boy, though he's not fat anymore nor a boy.

All brown all around, we are safe. But watch us drive into a neighborhood of another color and our knees go shakity-shake and our car windows get rolled up tight and our eyes look straight. Yeah. That is how it goes and goes.

In vocabulary, imagery, tone, and rhythms, Cisneros's voice is distinct, as yours will be when you find it.

Hearing Your Own Voice

The term "finding your voice" suggests it has been lost. And I suppose for many educated people it has been. They have learned to write the King's English, but since they aren't the king, it's a kind of ventriloquism.

Maybe you have never written in your natural voice but only in what Tom Wolfe called the beige voice, used in business letters, legal briefs, newspaper journalism, academic and instructional writing. Unlettered people who have distinct speaking voices can end up writing in beige, too, if they try to alter their style out of self-consciousness. But overeducated or undereducated, the same prescriptions work:

• Follow the advice Gore Vidal once gave, which could be taken as an antidote to the beige voice: Know what you want to say, say it, and don't give a damn.

• Join a writing group where you read your work aloud to others who can say to you, *"This* is your voice. Here, in this portion!" Once you have identified the parts of your work in which others hear your voice, return to those sections. Read them aloud and use them to put yourself in tune, or . . .

• Try listening to your speaking voice on tape. Some people who can't get comfortable sitting at a computer dictate their work into a tape recorder and transcribe it or have it transcribed, then rewrite from the transcription. If you can afford an amanuensis or simply someone to talk at while a tape recorder runs, the results are even better. I'm serious. Hire a kid in high school or college or your grandchild or a neighbor, anyone who is a good listener. Tell them to nod now and then like a shrink, and occasionally ask a pertinent question, only instead of paying them $120 an hour to do it, pay them ten dollars an hour. Give them this book to read so they can help you create and stick to a chapter and scene outline. Instruct them to elicit from you the sensate details that make a work come alive. Writing is lonely and the hardest part seems to be to get your bottom in the chair. So if you can afford it, why not hire yourself an audience who will show up at a set hour? Even if you are only paying them minimum wage, you will find that you won't want to waste the time.

Though I think hiring a listener is a great plan, I don't know anyone who has done it. Most people believe they can't afford it or don't deserve it, though many of them would hire a secretary for dictating business letters. So I have one more suggestion for finding your voice.

• Write a diary for yourself alone.

The diary process of writing spontaneously and rereading allows you to hear your voice, sort of like singing in the shower. In a diary, you develop your unique voice over time, but keep in mind that it is over time. The voice you used in early volumes of a journal will not fit easily with your voice in the present.

Daniel Harris, in a personal essay, "Biography of a Prose Style," published in *Salmagundi,* explored the difference between his voice "then" as it appears in old diaries and his voice "now." Harris is embarrassed by his early un-trained voice, yet, as a professional writer, knows how indebted he is to it.

The scathing fractiousness of my early letters to my family mellowed into the deadly earnestness of the diaries I kept between the ages of seventeen and twenty-two. Comprising some 500 to 600 pages of dense prose poems written in biblical cadences, these vapid medita-tions give us direct access to the mind of an irrepressibly verbose poseur in the throes of an act that is seldom documented, the psy-chologically complex process of teenage self-invention. Here is a typ-ical entry:

> September 10, 1975
> I am sitting by the window writing words that hold
> my sadness in their hands, that touch me like a breeze. I
> am thinking of the kiss I gave my mother and the kiss
> that she returned, and both were soft as a petal that fell
> from its flower to my hand, soft as a blade of grass and
> both so lonely. . . .

Although it is central to the theater of my notebooks that the reader believes he is eavesdropping on an act of solitude, it is obvious that I am convening a kind of literary open house, a salon in which a vast assembly of admirers are huddling around my desk . . . as I whirl about, clutching my brow. Far from being spontaneous, I am engaging in an entirely disingenuous sort of writing: the creation of an apocryphal biography of the artist as a young man. . . .

Writers as a tribe loathe the paper trail that has led each of us to our present position. . . . In fact, writers are, ironically the worst book burners around, systematically effacing our traces, burning our diaries, obliterating the record—all in an effort to pretend that we have not changed, have not developed, were always exactly as you find us now. . . . We attempt to deceive others into believing that there was no self-experimentation, no posing, no lying, no insincerity, that we were born with a fully evolved style.

Harris is able to integrate diary material into his essay by pointing out the stylistic differences between his present autobiographic prose and his earlier journal writing. The problem with using earlier writings comes when one tries indiscriminately to marry different points of view and style. Many people think because they have trunkloads of old diaries and letters, their task of writing autobiography will be easier; all they need to do is self-plagiarize. In some ways the opposite is true. You must resist the temptation to put undigested excerpts into your work that break its coherence and narrative flow.

You should read through such source material to jog your memory and help ensure the accuracy of what you recall, but do not rely on it. You may find sense impressions and details you wish to use. My advice is to mark these or copy them out and set them aside. Then write from memory and imagination independent of journals and letters, allowing the present self to confer coherence and meaning on the past.

Those who have not kept journals and letters should take heart that they aren't at a disadvantage. For a memoirist the greatest benefits of writing a diary are in acquiring a personal language for feelings, developing a facility for writing dialog, and saying what it is you thought you dare not say; you can acquire these skills by beginning to experiment in a diary now.

The Value of the Vernacular

While it is true that written language needs to be more condensed and precise than spoken language, in autobiographic writing, you want to use the diction you speak. Flowery or abstract words, too many modifiers, and long sentences don't work well in autobiographic narrative. Avoid unnatural, academic, or consciously literary language. It will distance the reader, and in autobiographic writing, a reader wants to be as close as the narrator will allow.

Whereas in school you are taught to eliminate the cant and slang that you and others speak, in autobiographic narrative the spoken language of your time and place allows a reader to experience your way of life. In his book *Makes Me Wanna Holler, Washington Post* journalist Nathan McCall recreates in part through street slang his experience as a teenager holding up a McDonald's with his buddies and keeping guard over the store manager.

I aimed the piece at his face, tightened my grip on the trigger, and tried to decide in that split second what to do. I swear I didn't want to blow him away. All I wanted was to get the cash and dash. But I made up my mind that if he moved again, I had to smoke him. I hated him for putting that pressure on me. I didn't even know him, and I hated the hell out of him. Intuitively, I sensed he was an Uncle Tom, one of those head scratching niggers, willing to put his devalued life on the line to protect the white man's property. I looked him in the eye and warned, "Move again, and I'm gonna bust your ass."

McCall strikes a balance between clarity and flavor, between the self now who knows how to write for a mass audience and the self then who spoke and thought in the language of the street. In comparison, listen to Josette Dermody Wingo, whose memoir of being a Wave in World War II, *Mother Was a Gunner's Mate,* was published by the Naval Institute Press. Wingo uses the slang of the 1940s without much concern for a present day reader. In this passage she and her girlfriends are on liberty for the night.

We are so busy talking that we don't see the shore patrol guy unwind himself from the wall he was holding up by the prophylactic station. (We Waves are not supposed to know about prophylactic stations so we play dumb with our eyes in the middle distance as we walk by them.) This guy is so big he fills the whole sidewalk. I feel his truculence before I see him. He plants himself in front of us, his legs enclosed in white gaiters, his white hat drawn down over his eyebrows. He's blocking our way, so we stop, bewildered. He slaps his truncheon, splat, into his gloved palm, hard. "Where ya goin', mates?" he snarls, looking dangerous. Nobody answers, it's none of his business. He pushes his gob hat to the back of his head, allowing his springy ginger hair to fall over his forehead. He leans toward me. I quail a little, not understanding. You can never let them know you are afraid, only way, so I suck in my breath and stand my ground, looking him straight in the eye, my face blank and innocent. "I ast youse a question, din't I? You're out of uniform, Sister." Splat! the truncheon hits his palm again in punctuation.

Wingo has chosen flavor over clarity, and for some readers she has gone too far. In addition to changing spelling in the dialog to duplicate pronunciation, she does not explain lingo a modern reader might not understand. I have no idea what a prophylactic station would have looked like, though I'd like to. Is it a guy hanging out at the corner like a dope dealer or is it a condom dispenser machine?

Wingo's work is at first difficult to follow for another reason. She has chosen to write it in the "historical present" tense, which means that we are right there with her in the moment as events happen. Because her past self is speaking in the present tense, her present self can't have a voice. This restricted point of view of the historical present has a cinematic immediacy, but in confining the narrative voice to the past self, Wingo has sacrificed the memoirist's privilege of composite vision, the self now reflecting on the self then.

The Composite Voice of Autobiographic Writing

Most commonly, the voice in autobiographic narrative is a combination of your younger self as protagonist in the past and your older self as narrator in the present. Generally it is the best choice because it creates dramatic tension. As protagonist/hero (the main character in the past), you give us beat by beat your feelings and observations as they were at the time. As narrator (the teller of the tale), you are the self who has survived the experience and is now able to recall it as story. As narrator, you also include your emotions and reflections as you see things now. You are the present self who can weep for the unknowing cruelty of the person you were and know that there is another way to be than the behavior then. You are the self, now crippled and lonely, who can reexperience the skip in your stride swinging hands with a young husband. You are the one who, looking back, sees your weakness but also the courage of which you were unaware at the time. The dramatic engagement between the self now and the self then can sustain reader interest even when a work lacks the mechanics of a forward-driving plot.

Using your present self as narrator looking back at your past self as protagonist allows you the most flexibility as a storyteller. The "I now" is a sprite who can fly anywhere, into the past, present, or future, address the reader, toy with the reader, lie to the reader, abuse the reader, flirt with the reader, or surprise the reader.

Here is an example of the self now recalling the self then from Carolyn See's memoir, *Dreaming: Hard Luck and Good Times in America*. She begins with a sort of apology to the reader from the narrator.

The second most boring thing in the world after people bending your ear about dreams is people bending your ear about their acid trips. Nevertheless! I saw immediately that everything, not just the refrigerator, was alive. The chair I sat in was holding me up, with great consideration. The trees outside Marina's open door waved and said hello. The bedspread on the single bed next to the wooden wall stretched and wrinkled and said hi. . . .

I saw the walls breathing, shallowly and quietly. After a while—and I saw that time was an illusion, that we were spinning in eternity—Marina suggested that I might like to lie down. It was getting dark, and I did. Marina put on the Beatles: "Revolver" had just come out. And after straining and straining all through the fifties to hear the chord changes underneath the hectic fluttering of Lee Konitz, Wayne Marsh, Charlie Parker, now effortlessly—and with such joy!—I heard every single note, and the breaths of those sweet boys as they inhaled, and sang a line, inhaled and sang a line. I put out my hand to the wall, the breathing wood, and felt it was not solid, that nothing in the universe was solid.

If I can't feel that right now, it's because my senses are too dull. I can remember it, though, and I date that evening and night to the most important personal discovery in my own life: that I wasn't a desperately unhappy person faking cheer in an abominable world, I was part of a wide, free, joyous universe.

See moves from the discerning voice of her narrator to the ecstatic voice of her protagonist/self in the past on acid, back to the circumspect, present self who, unexpectedly, confirms the validity of what the past self was discovering.

Some literary pundits hold that the novel is superior to memoir because the novel can contain the diverse points of view of many characters, whereas a memoir is limited to the subjective point of view of one person, "I." However, New Autobiographers can achieve a complexity of vision equivalent to that of the novel through diverse points of view of the same person. The beliefs of your younger self as protagonist in the past, your older self as narrator in the present, and your yet older self as you may be in the future, may each be different and equally valid. Useful phrases for the autobiographic writer are: "Before then I had felt," "Later I imagined," "Then I thought," "Now I realize," "Sometime I may decide."

Marguerite Duras experimented with the multiplicity of self as protagonist and narrator in her novelistic memoirs. Here in *The Lover,* she recalls, "the only image of myself I like, the only one in which I recognize myself, in which I delight." It is of herself as a girl of fifteen taking a ferry from Sadec across the Mekong River and meeting a twenty-five-year-old man with whom she will have an affair.

The elegant man has got out of the limousine and is smoking an English cigarette. He looks at the girl in the man's fedora and the gold shoes. He slowly comes over to her. He's obviously nervous. He doesn't smile to begin with. To begin with he offers her a cigarette. His hand is trembling. There's the difference of race, he's not white, he has to get the better of it, that's why he's trembling. She says she doesn't smoke, no thanks. She doesn't say anything else, doesn't say, Leave me alone. So he's less afraid. He tells her he must be dreaming. She doesn't answer. There's no point in answering, what would she say? . . . He says the hat suits her, suits her extremely well, that it's very . . . original . . . a man's hat, and why not? She's so pretty she can do anything she likes.

She looks at him. Asks him who he is. He says he's just back from Paris where he was a student, that he lives in Sadec too, on this same river, the big house with the big terraces with blue-tiled balustrades. She asks him what he is. He says he's Chinese, that his family's from North China, from Sushun. Will you allow me to drive you where you want to go in Saigon? She says she will. He tells the chauffeur to get the girl's luggage. . . .

She gets into the black car. The door shuts. A barely discernible distress suddenly seizes her, a weariness, the light over the river dims, but only slightly. Everywhere, too, there's a very slight deafness, or fog.

Never again shall I travel in a native bus. From now on I'll have a limousine to take me to the high school and back from there to the boarding school. I shall dine in the most elegant places in town. And I'll always have regrets for everything I do, everything I've gained, everything I've lost, good and bad, the bus, the bus driver I used to laugh with, the old women chewing betel in the back seats, the children on the luggage racks, the family in Sadec, the awfulness of the family in Sadec, its inspired silence.

He talked. Said he missed Paris, the marvelous girls there, the riotous living, the binges, ooh la la, the Coupôle, the Rotonde, personally I prefer the Rotonde, the nightclubs, the "wonderful" life he'd led for two years. She listened, watching out for anything to do with his wealth, for indications as to how many millions he had. He went on. His own mother was dead, he was an only child. All he had left was his father, the one who owned the money. But you know how it is, for the last ten years he's been sitting staring at the river, glued to his opium pipe, he manages his money from his little iron cot. She says she sees. He won't let his son marry the little white whore from Sadec.

In *The Lover,* Duras alternates between referring to herself as "I" (sometimes as narrator in the present, sometimes as protagonist in the past) and referring to herself as "she," also her protagonist self in the past. When other writers attempt this it never seems to work well, but in Duras's work one can follow her rifts in point of view, along with her nonchronological time jumps because they are never haphazard. Duras is an original stylist because she is simply attempting to be clear about what is very complicated, the workings of memory. When she writes about herself as "she," Duras the writer is consciously turning her life into fiction. It is a process some of us do in our heads all the time, moving "I" into "she" or "he," seeing ourselves as our own protagonist in each situation we encounter.

I always thought it was something that everyone did until I read this in Nancy Mairs's *Voice Lessons.*

Recently, another introverted writer and I were getting through a cocktail party by trying to figure out how we'd come to be the way we are. Neither of us could remember not writing, in the sense that from our earlier memories we had watched and narrated to ourselves the stories of ourselves, translating every experience even as it happened into language, or perhaps having no experience at all unless it was translated into language: "and then Nancy . . ."; "and then Barbara. . . ." I'd always assumed that all children consciously make up their lives this way as they go along, but apparently, she'd found recently, they do not.

(However, I suspect that if you have read this far in a book about writing your life as story, it is something you have always done.)

Yet, even though you think of yourself as the protagonist in a story in autobiographic writing, you probably should not refer to yourself in the third person, "he" or "she," as Duras does. The use of "I" in referring to yourself, past, present, and future, is your natural voice. It permits maximum intimacy with yourself and with a reader. Duras's shifts in perspective from "I" to "she" illustrate the freedom of voice possible within autobiographic narrative, but won't suit the purposes of most writers.

Occasionally, very occasionally, it can be the right choice to sacrifice the perspective of the first person point of view. In Douglas Hobbie's account of his daughter's death, *Being Brett,* he refers to himself as "he," perhaps because he could only have written it with the distance of the third person. It is also occasionally appropriate to sacrifice the double perspective of the first person, to eliminate the self now. For example, one of my students, Lianne Clenard, instinctively and correctly chose to make her narrator her past self in the present tense in her book *Why I'm Glad I'm Not a Boy.* It is a collection of short vignettes, which together tell the story of how Lianne, reared in the 1950s, learned the feminine virtues of self-sacrifice and self-effacement—but not how much self-effacement was too much. Now, as an adult, she has gone back and given the unassertive girl and young woman she was center stage. The adult Lianne stays out of it. The voice in each vignette is the age Lianne was at the time. For example, in this short piece, "Plaid Pants," she is four years old.

I hate them! I hate them! I'm never *ever* going to wear them *ever* again!

Mom said get dressed but when she came in my room I was still playing and she said hurry up so I opened up my playclothes drawer but she started getting mad when she looked inside and she started saying, "Look at your clothes! They're so old they're falling apart! Look at this! They're threadbare!" and I didn't know that I wasn't supposed to have clothes falling apart so I started crying, "No they're not!" but she got madder and her voice got louder and she said, "Yes they are! Just look at this!" and she picked up the plaid flannel pants and yelled, "These are so threadbare all you have to do is *this* . . . !" and she pulled on them to make them rip but they didn't rip and then she tried it again, "like *this* . . . !" but still they didn't rip so she threw them on the floor and picked up the other pair and yelled, "Like *this* . . . !" but they didn't rip either and she threw them on the desk and she pointed at them and yelled, "You can see right through the knees! The next time you wear them they'll fall apart!" and then she picked up the pants from the desk and threw them across the room and I saw them headed straight for the mirror and I saw her reflection behind them big and white and scary and I saw myself next to her with my mouth hanging open and crying and I looked dark and strange like a dwarf next to her and the desk was brown Formica and the wall was blue with turquoise gingham curtains but everything looked flat and tight in the mirror and she screamed, "Oooooh, this makes me so mad!" and then she left and I was still crying because I hadn't known my clothes were bad I hadn't known I was supposed to keep them from getting old I just thought they were my pants I would have figured out a way if only she had told me before I would have figured out a way to make sure my clothes were good I would never have old clothes to make her mad I would have figured out a way if I had known and then I picked up my plaid pants that were lying on the floor and I folded them up and put them away in the drawer but now I don't know what to do because I don't want to stay here in my room anymore but I don't know what clothes it's OK to put on.

One of Lianne's major themes is how the child is ensnared in catch-22 dilemmas, so, appropriately, her protagonist-child is entrapped within a narrowly limited point of view. Lianne's self now is in the background crafting the child's experience with a gently satiric hand, but never speaks.

In contrast, Mikal Gilmore's present self as narrator is very much in the foreground in *Shot in the Heart*. In this passage, in which he recalls the only time he saw his parents hold hands, just before his father's death, it is the thoughts and realizations of Mikal in the present that predominate.

I remember the look on my father's face as he sat and held my mother's hand that night I found them in the kitchen. I remember my mother hearing the news of his death, and crying out from such an astonishing place of loss and loneliness. Yes, those two people loved each other. It is plainer now in retrospect than it ever was when they were alive. Or maybe I can just see it a little better now, having learned for myself what a bittersweet thing love can be. From my vantage, love—no matter how deep or desperate it may be—is not reason enough to stay in a bad relationship, especially when the badness of it all is damaging or malforming other people. But I didn't get to make that choice for my parents, any more than I get to make it for you.

It would be hard to say who is the protagonist in *Shot in the Heart*. The memoir is about the entire Gilmore family, Mikal's parents and his brothers, including executed murderer Gary Gilmore. It is a tragic postmodern family saga, but for me the protagonist is Mikal now, the narrator, because it is his adult desire to know his family's secrets and make peace with his ghosts that drives the story.

Fortunately the majority of even beginning writers instinctively choose the right combination of the "I" now and the "I" then for their work. They only get into trouble if they think about it too much and try to be literary.

Here, in her memoir (*Dance to the Piper*), is Agnes de Mille, a dancer/choreographer who was only incidentally a writer. She moves seamlessly from the perspective of the protagonist self in the past to the narrator self in the present and back. It is easy to follow and easy to write this way because it is how we think and speak about past and present.

> Once when my ballet was unnecessarily interrupted . . . during a run-through, I gave a scream of anguish and hurled myself on Oscar Hammerstein's bosom. He was taken quite unaware and looked down startled at the hysteria on his waistcoat, but it was the comment from the rear rows that really surprised him. "Agnes," said Mother peremptorily, "control yourself."
>
> I snapped up as though a ruler had been applied to my hand. I trust Oscar got over his surprise. I've continued to hurl myself on the same spot for years now. His is the largest and most receptive bosom in the Western Hemisphere.
>
> All the dances in the show were set within two weeks.

Besides leaping gracefully from past to present, de Mille does something else in this passage worth noting. She gives you the experience of perceiving her world as she does—the essence of having a distinct voice. You feel you are experiencing life as a choreographer-artiste through the intensity and physicality of her prose. Her verbs are precise and full of the body's motion: "hurled," "snapped up." Her imagery for her emotions is idiosyncratic: Hammerstein "looked down startled at the hysteria on his waistcoat" and "I snapped up as though a ruler had been applied to my hand."

By using her own unique imagery for her feelings, Agnes de Mille conveyed what it felt like to be Agnes de Mille. She avoided the trap of using clichés to express emotions, "Tears fell from my eyes" or "My heart sank" or "My heart leapt to my throat" or "My heart—[almost anything]." Instead, de Mille invented a prose that, like her dances, bore her signature.

Write Your World

W e are each authorities on our worlds, and it is by observing its de-tails—how people dress and decorate their houses, what they eat, how they speak, how they spend their money and their leisure time—that we convey it. Natalie Goldberg in *Writing Down the Bones* says it well.

> This is what it is to be a writer: to be the carrier of details that make up history, to care about the orange booths in the coffee shop in Owatonna.... Our task is to say a holy yes to the real things of our life as they exist—the real truth of who we are: several pounds overweight, the gray, cold street outside, the Christmas tinsel in the showcase, the Jewish writer in the orange booth across from her blond friend who has black children. We must become writers who accept things as they are, come to love the details.

Your work will have a consistency of voice if in addition to observing details, you draw your similes from your world. When you reach for figurative language outside your own time and place, no matter how exotic, it is not as effective as creating similes and metaphors from images and experiences familiar in your own life. Listen to Maya Angelou's ripe, resonant voice in *I Know Why the Caged Bird Sings* and notice how her details and imagery allow you to taste a world she has preserved with language.

> On Sunday mornings Momma served a breakfast that was geared to hold us quiet from 9:30 A.M. to 3 P.M. She fried thick pink slabs of home-cured ham and poured the grease over sliced red tomatoes. Eggs over easy, fried potatoes and onions, yellow hominy and crisp perch fried so hard we would pop them in our mouths and chew bones, fins and all. Her cathead biscuits were at least three inches in diameter and two inches thick. The trick to eating catheads was to get the butter on them before they got cold—then they were delicious. When, un-luckily, they were allowed to get cold, they tended to a gooeyness, not unlike a wad of tired gum.
>
> We were able to reaffirm our findings on the catheads each Sun-day that Reverend Thomas spent with us. Naturally enough, he was asked to bless the table. We would all stand; my uncle, leaning his walk-ing stick against the wall, would lean his weight on the table. Then

Reverend Thomas would begin. "Blessed Father, we thank you this morning . . ." and on and on and on. I'd stop listening after a while until Bailey kicked me and then I cracked my lids to see what had promised to be a meal that would make any Sunday proud. But as the Reverend droned on and on and on to a God who I thought must be bored to hear the same things over and over again, I saw that the ham grease had turned white on the tomatoes. The eggs had withdrawn from the edge of the platter to bunch in the center like children left out in the cold. And the catheads had sat down on themselves with the conclusiveness of a fat woman sitting in an easy chair. And still he talked on. When he finally stopped, our appetites were gone, but he feasted on the cold food with a non-talking but still noisy relish.

Her images are poetic but never take you out of the range of her experience as a little girl from Stamps, Arkansas. The eggs bunched in the center of the platter "like children left out in the cold" and the cathead biscuits "sat down on themselves with the conclusiveness of a fat woman sitting in an easy chair." The word choice "conclusiveness" belongs to the adult narrator, lettered in English literature, but the image of a fat woman settling into a comfortable chair is one the protagonist/child could have observed at home. Maya Angelou's *voice* combines all she *is* as a learned poet and all that she *has been,* including the African-American traditions from which she draws. Her voice contains the music of her roots, the rhythms of gospels, spirituals, and the Blues, and the oral traditions of African folktales, ghost stories, Brer Rabbit trickster yarns, and revivalist church sermons, along with the eighteenth- and nineteenth-century novelistic devices of Swift, Defoe, and Dickens. Her voice is black, female, literate, and *inclusive.* She writes as herself, but, to paraphrase Walt Whitman, she is large, she contains multitudes.

Even when not conscious of it, we all write our lives not only as individuals but also as male or female, Asian, black, white, Hispanic, Christian, Jew, Muslim, or Buddhist, as part of the baby boom generation, as a midwesterner, an expatriate, a Texan, a Canadian. We are part of a group of rape victims, or revolutionaries, male nurses, or World War II pilots. All of us have been formed either through opposition to or assimilation into the era, place, and culture in which we have lived our lives. Beneath our idiosyncrasies lie vast strata of commonality. By consciously recognizing how the personal in your life is also cultural, you expand your voice. Eldridge Cleaver, like almost every other male African-American memoirist from Frederick Douglass on, wrote about his life as a political act. Maxine Hong Kingston broke silence for other Asian-Americans, and to do so, invented a brand-new voice for memoir. Carolyn See consciously wrote her thematic autobiography, *Dreaming,* as a southern Californian, who defines through her own family life a postwar culture of drinkers and dopers.

In part we acquire an identifiable voice by reading other authors whose voices speak our language. I hear Joan Didion in Carolyn See, and in both of them the southern California landscape. It's a voice created by sparseness, cynicism, and attention to banal details that become, through selection, cultural artifacts. In Joan Didion's celebrated book of personal essays, *Slouching Towards Bethlehem,* we hear in her arid prose the "hot wind whining down through the Cajon Pass." Because Didion selects "Cajon Pass" rather than "the canyon" we are convinced that she is an authority on her world, that she speaks for it. When Carolyn See describes having waitressed at Van de Kamp's restaurant, she observes her own world as precisely as Margaret Mead studying the rites of Samoan adolescent girls.

> I decided to work five to two in the morning, instead of tame five to eleven. At eleven the vast majority of good girls went home. As the lights went down, we became an after-the-movies hangout for a predominantly Jewish clientele who prompted racist slurs from us because all they ever wanted to order was a "vaffle vell done," and there were only five waffle irons to accommodate the rush to two hundred people.
>
> After the vaffle people went home, kids lounged around and planned parties and went to them, so that because of Teresa you found yourself sitting at three in the morning with gay guys in love. English movie actors failing in Hollywood. Giddy girls, physically exhausted, emotionally serene. We passed joints around—and this was 1952,3,4. We listened to jazz. Once, late at night, Teresa, who wore Shalimar perfume and silken clothes with metal threads, said, "Laws doesn't know anything, do you, Laws?" And leaned forward and kissed me.

See's writing is alive because it is so full of perfectly chosen details, and it is through her details that she best makes her case that Marx got it wrong: "Could he have overlooked the obvious: Opium is the opium of the people? Alcohol is the opium of the people? You can't engineer a revolution with a hangover." When she, very rarely, sums up in abstract language, it is inevitably less convincing than when she reports from her own experience.

Can it be that the system is totally rigged? That when they repealed Prohibition, they did it for tax purposes? That California's biggest cash crop, marijuana, is there for a reason? That kids are killing each other in unspeakable slums so that guys on the golf course don't have to be bothered? Has America become the old country again, and all in a few hundred years? Is the American Dream, to put it bluntly, nothing more than a sham and a crock?

See takes the onus off this lecture by making it rhetorical and then, as if she realizes how ineffective such generalizations are anyway, answers herself, "Oh, no no no no no," and goes into a riff of specifics that unquestionably do make her case.

The point is, no one can write effectively solely as a progressive, or as an African-American woman, or as a Native American man, or as a member of Generation X, or as a representative of addictive personalities. Trying to do so forces you into generalizations. You can only write convincingly as a unique individual with your specific history and cultural experiences. As you individualize your voice, you will speak for others through your inclusion of racial, political, historic, geographic, spiritual, or cultural themes. The slogan of the women's movement in the early 1970s was right, the personal *is* political. When writing about the secret parts of your life, you inevitably illuminate how the private life derives from and in turn gives meaning to your situation in society.

So there is a great deal that others learn about you from your voice—and a great deal you can learn about yourself. After you have been writing for a while, listen to yourself. Is your voice solitary or do you speak for others? Is it ironic, up-beat, funny, philosophic, or all of these? Is your voice layered like that of Marguerite Duras, or deceptively simple like Lianne's voice of her four-year-old self? Hearing your voice is like seeing yourself in the mirror for the first time . . . aah, so that is who I am. As the fashion magazines tell anxious girls, all you need to do now is learn some tricks to bring out your good features and fix your bad ones. If you write good dialog, write more of it. If you're funny, let 'er rip. If you use too many adjectives, stop that. Instead of trying to change yourself, though, your goal, once you've recognized your authentic voice, is to see how much more like yourself you can become.

9

Portraying Yourself: You Are Your Hero

Here's a riddle:

In New Autobiographic writing, you are a character, a fiction, but at the same time, the most real "you" you can be.

You are a fiction because the person on the page is only words. On the other hand, the person you present as yourself in New Autobiography is the most real "you" you can be, because the process is one of taking off masks that have hidden your true self. The process is one of discovering your true feelings, of recognizing your true abilities and weaknesses, even if you were not, could not, be aware of them in the past. New Autobiography demands an emotional authenticity and level of intimacy that many people have never before experienced.

So in writing New Autobiography, you need to do a balancing act, remembering that at one and the same time you are seeking to uncover your truest self and you are portraying yourself as a character. As the main character in an autobiographic work, you need to treat yourself as you would the hero of a story. You are the character whose feelings and thoughts need to be tracked beat by beat. "I" is in every scene, and in every scene we must know what I wanted and, moment to moment, how I reacted and felt, what I said and did. Probably the most common feedback I give students is, "You forgot to include yourself as the central character. That's why the writing feels flat. You need to put in your reactions, your reflections, and your feelings beat by beat by beat." When you include your feelings and reactions, especially when you allow yourself to be vulnerable, a reader will be on your side even if what you reveal is immoral, illegal, heartless, or degrading. This is especially true when you are writing about yourself as a child. A reader will accept all of a child's selfish thoughts and impulses as normal.

Out of curiosity I once read Charles Manson's "as told to" autobiography. It recounts from his point of view his awful childhood in and out of reform schools, rejected by a mother who didn't want him. The writer was careful to include Manson's feelings and reactions as a child. I was stunned, not by the content, but by the power of the first person to put a reader on the side of the narrator. I found myself feeling sympathy for a man who is an abhorrent murderer! That is the potential power of the first person.

I've noticed that journalists have a particularly difficult time including their feelings and thoughts because they have been trained to exclude them. I have to go to considerable lengths to distinguish the difference in reader expectations between memoir and journalism. In journalism the author is writing about a protagonist other than himself or herself. For example, John Berendt's best-seller set in Savannah, Georgia, *Midnight in the Garden of Good and Evil,* is crafted like New Autobiography with fictional techniques and written in the first person, but it is New Journalism because the protagonist is not the author. The protagonist whose drama we follow is Jim Williams, a Savannah antiques dealer. Berendt is present as himself, but only as an observer, not as a leading character.

The fact that you make *yourself* the protagonist in an autobiographic narrative has profound implications. By definition the protagonist is the character who drives the story, whose desires, conflicts, and choices *are* the story. That is what is meant in dramaturgy when it's said that your protagonist should be active rather than merely reactive. Seeing yourself as the protagonist of your life, you look for your responsibility in the story your life makes, rather than seeing it as having "happened to you." For women, especially, this can be a radical shift in perception.

As the hero of your story, you, like any dramatic hero, are a flawed personality, but one who can learn from your life and have a final realization. Before you begin writing an autobiographic narrative, ask yourself, "What were my weaknesses as a character at the time of this story or chapter? How did those weaknesses affect events?" Accept responsibility, but don't get bogged down in regrets or recrimination. Every flawed hero also needs to have positive traits that make us care about her—whether it be her sense of humor, her energy, her vulnerability, or simply her ability to change. Just as you will want to look for your Achilles heel, you will also want to recognize your heroic qualities.

In order to get a sense of yourself as the protagonist of a story, you need to see yourself from the outside as others might, as well as from the inside. In one of my classes we played a game to recognize what others find most interesting about us and would like to read about. I asked the question, "What is it that people always ask you?" and we went around the room as each person in our large circle answered. The question was not helpful for everyone. (One woman said, "People always ask me where I get my hair cut.") It was very helpful for others. One thing became clear. Generally what people want to know about someone is what is most unique or different in their experience. Responses included:

- How could you not know your fiancé was gay?
- How did you make a marriage work for thirty-five years?
- How did you recover from cancer?
- What is it like being the hearing child of deaf parents?

You can see how each of these questions could evoke an interesting story. Try it. Ask yourself, "What is it that people always ask me?" and "What are they really asking?" There may be a clue in your answer to what other people would find most interesting to read about your life. If you get an evocative answer, it could be a way to begin. Even if you later decide to open in another way, it will start you on the right track, especially if you are interested in publication.

Here is how Susanna Kaysen begins *Girl, Interrupted,* a memoir about her two-year stay in a mental institution:

> People ask, How did you get in there? What they really want to know is if they are likely to end up in there as well. I can't answer the real question. All I can tell them is, It's easy.

Kaysen's friends and acquaintances probably often asked her, "How did you get into a mental hospital and what was it like?" Her literary memoir answers both questions.

A student of mine, Hanh Hoang, begins her memoir similarly, with a surprise in store for the reader.

> I left Vietnam to come to study in America in 1974, five months before the civil war ended back home. Only a few of my compatriots were here then, and being Vietnamese invariably aroused curiosity in

my American acquaintances. One of the first questions they asked me was, "What was it like in Vietnam?"

"Normal," I should have answered them, because that's how I felt my life was. I think people grow accustomed to almost any environment, no matter how unusual it may seem to others, and come to see their lives as ordinary. Like the protagonist in Camus's *The Stranger*, Meursault, who believed that he would have gotten used to living in the trunk of a dead tree if he had had to, with nothing to do but look at the sky and wait for birds and clouds to flow by.

I have come to the same conclusion after having thought a lot about the fate of frogs. Yes, frogs. You see, some of my compatriots like to eat frogs, and they have a very particular way of concocting this food. Unlike the French, who perhaps have given them the taste for the amphibians, our villagers prepare the dish long in advance, when the animals are still in their tadpole stage. The live larval creatures are first inserted in a coconut, then the entrance hole is sealed. As the animals grow in the shell, they eat the coconut flesh and their own droppings. This method of raising frogs, I was told, is to ensure the tastiness and purity of their meat. In the process the animals become blind and discolored.

The thought of pale and sightless frogs used to revolt me. "How cruel! What a terrible way for these frogs to live!" I thought, as if the poor amphibians could feel unhappiness and wish for a different life.

I do not think in any way that my life was that of a person confined in a dead tree, or a frog in a coconut shell. But although I see my childhood as normal, I realize that not everyone has grown up, like us, in a place where epidemics of medieval maladies such as cholera and bubonic plague broke out almost yearly; where gunshots and bombs were so much a part of the familiar daily sounds that I now miss them in my life in Southern California. I was often unaware of this form of homesickness until a shrill whistle of bullets in drive-by shootings, or the rattling rumble of an earthquake, suddenly made me feel euphoric. At home.

During the riots in Los Angeles, I ventured out while others cowered, drunk with my childhood excitement of billowy smoke and flames. I had lived through coups d'etat and frequent fires that were started by accident rather than by the war. Anything now that breaks the monotony and is reminiscent of the past brings out the child in me.

One of the benefits of being in a memoir group is that you get imme-diate feedback on what interests others. Listen carefully when readers say, "I wish you would write more about . . ." or "I didn't really understand this part." In writing about yourself as your central character, you repeatedly need to ask yourself: *Am I so far inside myself that I have forgotten to give necessary information? Am I taking for granted that a reader knows everything I do?* Appro-priate readers can help you answer these questions.

In my classes the students speak about the "I" in each other's work as "this character," rather than as "you." It is because readers see only the character on the page that they can help you see yourself as the character presented there. Though they may not be able to tell you what is important for you to write, they can point out what you mistakenly assumed they would know, understand, or accept.

Other people can also help you perceive what about your life is of in-terest that you don't even realize. During lunch one day, Jeremy Tarcher, the initial editor of this book, said that while he might write personal essays, his life could not make an interesting narrative.

"I bet it could," I said.

"No, I've been surrounded in my life by self-made women who have ac-complished enormous success. My mother, my sister [novelist Judith Krantz], my wife [entertainer Shari Lewis]. I'm a cheerleader on the sidelines."

"But that's a wonderful story," I said, and meant it. "And it's very funny. You've had huge success as a West Coast publisher, the only individual to re-ally make a go of it. The irony is you can't see it because you are surrounded by these towering women. No matter what you accomplish, you can't see it because you're in their shadow."

Leaving aside that having a successful life is a nineteenth-century con-cept of what is required to write autobiography and has nothing to do with what makes a worthwhile narrative, Jeremy's difficulty in seeing what is fas-cinating about his life is common. Like psychics who say they can see other people's futures but are blind to their own, so some of us, I think, can see other peoples' stories, but cannot see how our own lives make an interest-ing story.

Several years before I'd decided to write this book, I complained to my friend Renate Druks, who had already begun her memoir, "I can see a story in everybody else's life, but I don't see how my life makes a story."

"Are you crazy?" she said with her precise Viennese inflection.

Knowing that Renate never leaves any question unanswered, I asked her to tell me my story. She said, "Once there was a young woman who liked to put on costumes like an actress. She tried out one role after another, as a political activist, a professor, a filmmaker, an author, a wife, a producer. Whatever was the fashion of the moment she assumed. Finally she looked at herself naked in the mirror, but even then she saw only a façade, because as the Vedantists say, mirror-gazing only shows the mortal body, the corpse. One day in turning around she will catch a glimpse of her real self, and she will be struck down by seeing a very large soul. She will know that like Kali, the many-armed goddess, she needed all those faces to become herself."

Now while the story Renate told is *her* story of me—*she* is a Vedantist—and while I don't think I could write that story, I am very glad she is the person of whom I asked the question, rather than one of several people who might have said, "I see the story of a talented woman who wasted most of her life because she could not focus and commit to one thing." I could write that story, but it would imprison me in regret. It is not a story seen through eyes of love as is Renate's story.

Asking someone you trust to tell you your story can be amazingly illuminating about you and them, but please be sure you only ask someone who truly cares about you. The job of a good therapist is to help us find a healing story out of our life experience. My job as a writing consultant is similar: to reflect back to my writers the stories I hear them trying to tell and help them transform them into art. Such work must be done with love or it can be destructive.

However, even if someone else helps you see your story, you must also develop it from inside. As important as it is to get feedback only from those who have your well-being at heart, it is even more vital that you care about yourself. It is an axiom that a writer cannot make a reader care about the protagonist in a story if the writer does not care about and sympathize with that protagonist. This is all the more true when the main character is yourself. *You must be on your own side.* The touchstone to repeat when portraying yourself is:

TOUCHSTONE 3:
Tell the whole truth with love.

When you look at your life as story and portray yourself, it must be done with love, you must be rooting for yourself. Sometimes when I tell students that they need to be on their own side, they mistake that for self-justification. That is why the touchstone says "tell the whole truth," including your sins and flaws, but with compassion toward yourself.

There can be a temptation to use autobiographic writing for the wrong reasons, to create a persona that you would like to have seen and remembered, to argue your own case, to compensate. This is *not* what I mean by being on your own side. You have to be on your own side, but in a genuine way; not in self-justification or self-accusation, but with enough security to tell even the uncomfortable truths.

Sarah Snow, a student I worked with, was writing an autobiographic novel about the difficulties of having chosen to build a large multiracial family. When she and her husband married in the 1960s, they had idealistic intentions. They added to their biological children three adopted children with special needs, having faith that the financial means and inner strength would be there to deal with whatever problems might come. Sarah later realized she had been reckless in building such a large and needful brood. She tried to control the damage that came with a schizophrenic boy; she tried to escape into romanticism as was her nature. Eventually she came back from her attempts to escape, to do the best she could to love all her children.

She wrote the first two-thirds of her novel in the present tense, which kept her at the center of the story as its protagonist. But when she got to the most difficult material to write about, she decided it would be more literary to have another perspective of her protagonist, someone who could see her with love. She chose the point of view of her older daughter.

Sometimes multiple points of view are the best way to tell a story, but in Sarah's autobiographic novel it became confusing because she had used the first person for most of the book and then suddenly switched to her daughter's point of view. When we talked about it, Sarah admitted that the daughter's story was a separate work, that it didn't belong in this book. She realized that she had chosen the daughter's point of view because the daughter understood and accepted her in the most difficult time of her life. Her daughter saw her faults, yet was the only one who was completely on her side.

I suggested to Sarah that she go back and, instead of taking a detour away from it, stay in her own point of view. She needed to see her weaknesses but to write as if she were on her own side. To do this would be transformative. Perhaps through her life, she had never been on her own side. Perhaps she had done things or let things be done that were bad for her and others. But now she was going to remember and rewrite her life—the same life, the same events—only this time she was going to give herself the understanding and sympathy she would have to give to any literary heroine. In so doing she would not only be achieving the literary unity her work needed, she would be altering her relationship to herself and to her own history. Even if she never published this novel—which she was reluctant to do for fear her children would see themselves in it and never forgive her—she would have done for herself what the most intensive psychotherapy *might* be able to do.

In the best writing, there are no purely good or bad characters. Instead there is a protagonist and the protagonist's allies and adversaries. The adversary may be as good a person as the protagonist, even a better person; nevertheless, we are on the side of the protagonist. In autobiographic writing, you are the protagonist, so you must give yourself sympathy and keep the reader on your side, and you can only do this through self-acceptance. That is why autobiographic writing has such great power to change the writer.

Fear of Bragging

Occasionally, when I say that you must be on your own side, a writer will object that he is afraid he will sound like a braggart. This was the concern of a student, a retired engineer who wanted to write about having designed with his brother during the Depression the first remote-controlled aircraft to fly across the continental United States. He was right to feel proud about their accomplishment, but it was true, the account sounded like he was tooting his own horn.

The problem was in his voice as narrator. In his attempt to appear objective, to simply give the facts and stay impersonal, we got no sense of this man's personality, so we could not warm to him. Later in the class he brought in a short piece about shaving in the mirror and observing what had happened to his face with age. It was full of self-deprecating humor. "This is your voice!" we said. What was needed was to go back to the first piece and rewrite it in this same voice. The antidote to sounding like you are bragging is to include your embarrassing moments, self-doubts, and vulnerability. This was the secret to Ronald Reagan's likeability. If he had a pimple on his nose, he never failed to draw it to your attention. Russell Baker has this ability to use self-directed humor to season autobiographic accounts of his considerable accomplishments.

If only Anaïs Nin had known the trick of humorous self-deprecation, she would have saved herself the wrath of many a critic who called her a narcissist for describing her own beauty and talent. She was trying to give herself the approval she did not get from the world, but she neglected to include her self-doubt.

The more one has accomplished, the more attractive modesty becomes in autobiographic writing. For example, look at the genuine humility in this passage from the opening of James Ingebretsen's memoir. He is a businessman whose life followed the American dream of self-made material success until, at age forty-five, he had an epiphany after which he committed his resources to spiritual development and service to others. His spiritual autobiography, *Apprentice to the Dawn,* is careful not to set himself up as anyone's guide, and he generously acknowledges those from whom he has learned.

> In my life I am not a road builder, but a climber. . . . Not able to see ahead, I can only reach up and find the handholds carved by those before me. I have found a great sense of community in others' words. It seems you never know when you're going to be affected by some idea caught in print or paint, no matter how far removed in origin it may be. We are forever finding ourselves in another—thousands of miles or thousands of years, we are the same. There is something indescribably magical in discovering pieces of what you feared was unique to your own soul in other people's lives, other people's times, other people's dreams.

Avoiding Self-Pity

When I say that in autobiographic narrative you need to treat yourself as your own hero and sympathize with yourself, some students articulate their fear of bragging, but others protest that they dislike the voice of self-pity they would then assume. I have occasionally read autobiographic pieces that did make me feel that the writer was feeling sorry for herself. It was not because the writer had described wrongs done to her or had reentered painful memories; it was my sense that these experiences had not yet been understood in terms of a meaningful story and had not been expressed in their full complexity. The writer was still reluctant to enter the depth of her own pain and confusion. The somewhat shallow writing that resulted often had an accusatory, angry tone, like a legal brief making a case and pointing the finger at a bad parent or other enemy.

What a reader perceives as self-pity is really a lack of genuine and courageous self-love—a lack of assuming responsibility. Even if you have been an innocent victim of a violating experience, you have a responsibility to yourself and the world to heal or use the wound. Writing about such a wound with total honesty from a safe place is an act of self-affirmation.

You do need to be able to recognize when it is too early for you to plumb the terrible mystery of an injury. Sometimes when I read an account full of angry judgments and generalizations, I recommend that the writer seek a good therapist to help him or her achieve sufficient peace of mind to be able to "recollect in tranquillity."

This is not to say that people cannot write movingly about injustices and pain in their lives without having had psychotherapy. Here is where attention to craft can come to the rescue—remembering that you are creating a text, a character on a page who exists only through your selection of words. One technique for avoiding a tone of self-pity, for example, is to avoid general statements altogether, to write the specifics of an event rather than your opinion about it. A small detail can evoke identification from a reader better than many emotional words. When you want to avoid bragging, you need to include more of your vulnerable feelings, but when you are afraid of self-pity, remember *Dragnet's* Sergeant Joe: "Just the facts, ma'am. Just the facts."

A related trick to avoid a self-sorry voice is the use of understatement. I had the problem of self-pity when writing about being abandoned by my father, when he lived in Mexico for several years after leaving my mother. As a child of eleven, I had not let myself feel the sorrow and hurt; I told myself that it was a good thing because I wouldn't have to listen to my parents fight anymore. Yet repeatedly in my life I go back to inspect the wound and suspect that, like the licking of a dog, the habit appears offensive.

So how to write in a personal essay about a topic so pitiable yet so tired for me? I had to remember to select what was specific and concrete in my recollections and leave it at that.

> One morning most of my father's clothes were gone and only his old set of golf clubs were in the hall closet. Two months later my sister and I got a postcard of a donkey wearing a sombrero. It said my father had decided to live in Mexico City and practice law there. He promised to send us some Mexican fiesta dolls, but they must have gotten lost in the mail.

I used an ambiguous statement, that the dolls must have gotten lost in the mail, rather than a more accusatory phrase such as "but my father neglected to send them." This way the reader may sense the child's attempt to put a good face on things and, I hope, feel more for her than if I had exaggerated my father's negligence.

Lack of genuine self-love in autobiographic writing can cause a self-sorry voice, but it can also be responsible for a judgmental coldness to self. If you censor yourself as you write, a reader won't necessarily detect it as such, but will unconsciously disengage from the writing. You risk losing a reader's involvement if you neglect to track the feelings and thoughts of the person you were.

Even if you could not be fully aware of your feelings and reactions at the time, you must, as the writer, discover them now. For example, Hanh Hoang, the student writing a memoir about growing up in Vietnam during the American occupation, movingly portrayed her parents' hardships. Yet when Hanh came to a chapter in which the war began to decimate her own life, as a reader I felt distanced. She used understatement and concrete detail in her prose beautifully, but that alone could not carry the magnitude of her experience. We realized that she was not slowing down the pace sufficiently to track each of her own emotional beats. She had endured that time by not feeling, so she did not readily recall her reactions. Now, as an adult, she would have to give the stoic child she had been the understanding that her mother, crushed with the exigencies of survival, had not been able to give her. Hanh would have to warm to herself and her own condition so that her readers could, too.

You need to slow down the pace of the writing to track your emotional beats—even if you now disapprove of the thoughts and feelings you had. For example, Nathan McCall writes his blistering memoir, *Makes Me Wanna Holler,* as an adult who has straightened out his life and is now a respected journalist for the *Washington Post.* He makes no self-judgments in writing about the brutal street punk he was in high school. Rather, he lets us inside the feelings and thoughts of the adolescent as they were—which is much more terrifying to contemplate.

For me, guns were life's great equalizer. When I was armed, the older hoods who had once seemed so intimidating didn't faze me anymore, and I no longer feared going across town or being double banked by two, or even twenty, guys, because I had the equalizer. Even grown-ups like my stepfather began to look more vulnerable to me when I had that piece nestled in my belt.

My faith in the power of guns shot up a few notches more one night, a few months after I was jumped. I was walking home by myself from a girl's house when the Cherry Boys and some others spotted me and came charging my way.

Normally, I would have had to dash or take another head-thumping. But I had the loaded .25 tucked into my coat. I had the equalizer, and I wasn't scared. I waited until they got within twenty yards of me, drew the gun, aimed, and fired several shots into the crowd, bam! bam! bam! bam! They dove to the ground and then scattered like flies. It made me feel powerful to be able to scatter a crowd like that. I stood there for a moment, full of the sense of what I'd done. I just stood there and took it in. Then I turned and calmly walked home.

When you feel ashamed of your actions in the past, it can be frightening to recall and reexperience who you once were—and even more frightening to expose it to others. So while one side of being your own hero is to treat yourself as the protagonist of a story, the other side is courage. Not that you need to have been a courageous character in the past, but that you the writer need to have courage now. Courage to remember. Courage to feel. Courage to be ruthlessly honest. Courage to be the most real "you" you can be. Accepting your past through love is half of portraying yourself; the other half is telling the whole truth.

"And what will people think of me if I tell how screwed up I was?" you worry. How venal, petty, angry, fearful, jealous, mistaken? They will accept you. It is the admission of human weakness, not its denial, that inspires sympathy from a reader. Remember, you are your hero in autobiographic writing, and if you have the courage to tell the whole truth, you will be ours.

10

Portraying Others: Casting Your Story from Life

Unlike a novelist, who invents characters, you as an autobiographic writer choose from the thousands of people you have known, a few main characters and a slightly larger number of minor ones. As in other aspects of autobiographic narrative, the problem is life's multiplicity. With what criteria do you select your cast?

One guideline is that the most powerful autobiographic stories are about emotionally compelling relationships. While that could mean an encounter with a stranger that prompted a turning point for you, most often it means a primary relationship: mother, father, sister, brother, lover, spouse, child, close friend, or occasionally a mentor or professional peer. These are the characters you know best, their weaknesses and strengths.

Family relationships are the gold of autobiographic writing, whether they be nuclear families or self-created families, such as families of friends. Notice that I say *relationships* are the gold, not colorful characters (those might be the bronze). Unless you are writing a portrait, where your subject is the protagonist, the key to casting characters is *their* relationship to *you*. You are the protagonist of the story, its most important character. The second most important character is your antagonist.

Beloved Antagonists

The word "antagonist" is misleading because of its secondary meaning of enemy or hostile person. Dramatically, an antagonist is simply the person whose desire is in opposition to yours. Parents make great antagonists, especially strong-willed ones like Russell Baker's mother. Spouses and lovers are my favorite antagonists. Children are good antagonists, especially when they are teenagers. Siblings are born antagonists, except when they become allies in opposition to parent antagonists. All are beloved antagonists, and each could qualify for a leading role in an intimate autobiographic story.

～Using Your Antagonist to Generate Story

Let's hatch a story about you and a mate to demonstrate how story can be generated simply from identifying your main antagonist. Let's say that at a critical stage in your marriage your spouse wanted to have another child and you didn't. That doesn't make your spouse a villain; on the contrary, you may have loved (let's say him) then and love him now more than anyone else on earth. The questions that could generate story from this situation might be:

• How did you both grow and change as a result of this conflict?
• Was there a turning point?
• Is there a larger thematic opposition that you wish to explore through this relationship?
• What do you realize about it now in retrospect?

Through answering these questions, you may sense a story emerging. You can develop it further through my favorite way to generate story: starting with just two characters, you and your main antagonist.

EXERCISE 11: *Relationship Beats*

This exercise could not be simpler, yet goes to the heart of making story. It can give you an outline for a long or short work. After considering the preceding questions, all you do is list the stepping-stones (the main emotional beats) of your relationship with your antagonist. In other words, what were the micro stages that your relationship went through?

Here is an example of a list of relationship beats using the situation of a disagreement over having a second child:

1. Richard told me when we were dating that he wanted a big family. I wanted him and that sounded romantic to me.

2. We were both overjoyed when I delivered Egon.

3. Richard was supportive when I went back to work because we needed the money.

4. I got a promotion. Now I was making more than Richard. It made me feel in control of my own life for the first time. Richard was silent about it, except he made jokes about my being head of the family.

5. Egon started begging to have a little brother or sister. I knew Richard had been encouraging him. Richard reminded me that our plan was to have a big family. I said it wasn't the right time.

6. I saw there was a chance to become director of the arts center and I knew I wanted this and I would be devastated if I didn't get it.

7. Richard joined a Christian church and started taking Egon on Sundays. I used the time to catch up on work. I felt their disapproval.

8. Richard got a promotion at his job. It made him more confident and fun at home.

9. We took a long-planned trip to Europe without Egon. Unexpectedly it was like a second honeymoon.

10. The director of the arts center announced his resignation.

11. I discovered I was pregnant. I wept.

12. I knew if I told Richard I was pregnant he would never forgive me for not having the child.

13. I became irritable and started to have morning sickness, which I tried to hide.

14. Richard was more kind than ever, which made me feel guilty. I almost told him I was pregnant, but I lost my courage.

15. My friend took me to get an abortion.

16. If Richard ever suspected, he didn't say anything. But something had died between us. Trust.

17. I got the directorship. I knew I had made the right choice. I loved my position and the power that came with it. This was all my life, what I was meant to do.

18. Richard and I began to live very busy and independent lives, and he never again mentioned having another child.

19. Now so many years later when Egon himself has three children and Richard and I are comfortably retired, but not really close. I still believe I made the right choice for me, but I often wish I'd had the courage to tell Richard and we'd fought it out, instead of each of us taking a solitary, silent road.

You will notice that this list of relationship beats already feels like a story. There is an ongoing thematic opposition between the narrator's individual desires and the desires of her family. There are three turning points of increasing intensity: the promotion at work, the discovery she was pregnant, the decision to have an abortion.

Having generated such a list of relationship beats, you could convert each beat into a scene and link them together with narrative transition. You would have a rough first draft of a work.

⁓Choosing Supporting Characters

Of course the story would feel more realistic if it were peopled with a world beyond the narrator. One way to select supporting characters for your story is to ask yourself, "Who else in my life was affected by the opposition between myself and my antagonist(s)?" Audition supporting characters and cast only those who enrich your main thematic conflict.

For the sake of illustration, let's say you state your central conflict to yourself as "Your right to professional self-fulfillment versus commitment to family life." The first thing to understand before character sorting is that no one embodies just one side of a thematic opposition all of the time. Probably you felt *within yourself* a conflict between the right to professional self-fulfillment versus commitment to family life, and in all likelihood your spouse did, too. On occasion you both may have even flip-flopped. On some issues—say, helping your son with homework—you were the one more dedicated to family obligations. These variations on your theme make your story and characters real, *not just receptacles for ideas.*

EXERCISE 12: *Character Sorting*

In your creative journal ask yourself which person or people in your life during the period of your story represent the opposing sides of your theme. Make two lists, placing characters where you believe they belong given the thesis and antithesis of your theme. (Some characters may appear on both lists.)

Given the thematic opposition of professional self-fulfillment versus family commitment, the list might look like this:

SELF-FULFILLMENT	COMMITMENT TO FAMILY
My single journalist friend	My son, Egon
My selfish sister	My self-sacrificing mother
My co-worker who wanted to have an affair with me (he wasn't committed to his family)	Egon's third-grade teacher (asked for family meeting)

My therapist (she encouraged my professional self-fulfillment)	*My therapist (she encouraged me to be open with Richard)*
The recurrent figure of Amelia Earhart in my night dreams (flying as freedom)	*The minister of the church Richard attended*

No matter how interesting or ubiquitous other people in your life may have been during the time of your story, you have to be a ruthless casting director. If they don't contribute to the progression of your story along your thematic line, forget 'em. They don't belong in this story.

"But what about my grandfather Leo?" you say. "I have to tell my grandchildren about him!" Well, of course, if you're writing a full autobiography for descendants, thematic economy isn't required.

"But what about my eccentric neighbor Dora, the one who raised the geese that attacked our German shepherd? Dora is so interesting."

Absolutely not. With each character you add, your story becomes more episodic and less compelling. You don't want too many characters.

"Oh, please," you beg, "I just have to write about her."

Then write another story, I say. Make her the antagonist in a different story about your relationship with her.

"No, really, I feel she could fit in this story," you insist. So I try to respect your instincts, even if she hasn't appeared on either of your thematic lists. Maybe, I concede, your instincts are telling you that she belongs in a subplot intertwined with your main story, in which her conflict sheds light on yours. For example, let's say your neighbors organized to rezone the block so that Dora could no longer raise her geese, which were attacking everyone's dogs. Dora's right to do what she loved (raise geese) was in opposition to the good of the collective, which is related to and expands your thematic opposition—your individual self-fulfillment versus the family's well-being.

I'm warning you, though, if you want to include a subplot, you need to make sure that its outcome influences the outcome of your main story. Otherwise it will seem extraneous. For example, let's say the neighbors succeeded in getting the block rezoned, and Dora had to get rid of all her geese. She became so depressed that she attempted suicide. Seeing how not being able to have what she loved destroyed Dora, you decided that wouldn't happen to you. This impelled your decision to get an abortion. You see how the main story is dependent on the subplot? One would not have happened without the other.

But in this story you don't need that silly subplot to catapult the outcome of your main story, and that Dora character ruins the tone of what could have been a realistic, domestic drama. So I still say give her the boot.

⌇ALLIES AND ANTAGONISTS

Now that we have gotten rid of Dora, let's discuss the characters already on your list. Some may be allies, people who help you pursue your desire of professional self-fulfillment, and some may be antagonists who, along with your spouse, in the example given, frustrate it. You'll want some of each. Allies and antagonists either help you achieve your desires or impede them, which usually, but does not always, correspond to which side of your thematic opposition they fell on when you made your character sorting list. Know also that an ally can become an antagonist and vice versa, which adds interest to a story. When I was a teenager, my major antagonist was—surprise!—my mother. Later she became a major ally. She was just as good a person and just as well-meaning when I was a teen as she was later on, but her relationship to me changed when I became an adult. We still stood on different sides of many thematic issues, but the fact that my desires were such that she could support me in achieving them, rather than stand in my way, turned her into an ally.

⌇Villains

Autobiographic works do not need to have villains. Ordinary adversaries do quite nicely. Miscommunication, moral muddles, wrongheadedness, and incompatible goals provide enough conflict in true life stories without needing an outright immoral, ill-intentioned character. Yet perhaps because they are so rare, villains can make autobiographic stories absolutely compelling. I am thinking of Joan Kite's memoir in progress about her adulterous relationship with a homicide detective who shot and killed his wife in what he explained was a bizarre accident. For two years the Miami police brought no charges against the sergeant, and Joan, believing he was innocent, moved into his house and became a surrogate mother to his young sons—until faced with evidence that he had, indeed, executed his wife. He was a sociopath and, as a jury eventually decided, guilty of first degree murder. Wounded though she was by this experience, Joan does not seek in her writing to condemn the man. Study him, yes; reveal his heartlessness and selfishness through recording his words and deeds, yes; reveal her own self-delusion, most definitely; judge—no. Judgments stop the unlayering of character and block our engagement with life's mystery, including the mystery of evil.

This is what Anaïs Nin, in *Novel of the Future,* said she learned from her favorite crime novelist, Georges Simenon: "Simenon would study almost scientifically the most complex and perverse character formation leading to its downfall or crime, destruction or self-destruction. He went so deep, and without judging, in quest of the truth, that one forgot to judge in the process. Almost always, by knowing all the facts, one ceased to condemn."

Not condemn a villain, someone who has done you irreparable harm? Why not? Out of self-interest. Readers want to make their own judgments; that is how they participate in the writing. Sticking pins in a character you intend to hurt boomerangs. If you have no compassion, no psychological insight, no ethics in your written portraits of others, it will show, and then a reader won't like you. You need to treat with humanity those very people who have caused you outrageous pain. In the writing, that is. If in life you want to tell them to go take a flying fall into a pile of glass shards, I'm all with you.

Occasionally in my classes there is a student who has not gotten past the fantasy of publishing a memoir to get even with someone, usually a bad parent or a former spouse who done 'em wrong. Once it was a young woman who wanted to write vengeance on a man whose dog bit her. Unfair as it may be, the class reading her angry prose disliked the writer. Sure, celebrities and those related to them can get Mommie Dearest exposés published. But the fun of seeing the defects behind a celebrity's glossy public image doesn't necessarily extend to the exposure of unknown scoundrels.

You can learn a great deal about successful character portrayal by reading literary memoirs that contain villains, such as Tobias Wolff's violent stepfather in *This Boy's Life,* Dorothy Allison's violent stepfather in *Bastard Out of Carolina,* or Mary McCarthy's violent legal guardian in *Memories of a Catholic Girlhood.* Each of these cowardly, vulgar brutes is treated as a human being whose depravity has resulted from social, economic, and emotional strains too great for their weak moral characters. They aren't excused, but they are understood.

Being Fair

Most autobiographic writers do not have villains to portray, just plain disagreeable people. And generally writers are more concerned about the injustice they may do their antagonists than in getting even with them.

I've encouraged you to write about the people closest to you and to make them your antagonists. At some point, you are going to protest, as my students do, "I can't say that about him! It would disrespect his memory." "I can't say my mother whipped me with a belt; she's going to read this!" I'll tell you what I tell them. Use the same touchstone you use to portray yourself.

TOUCHSTONE 4:

If you tell the whole truth with love, you cannot be unfair.

If you tell the whole truth, the complete picture, if you include all sides of a person, the dark and the light, then it is possible to tell even ugly truths about someone without committing character assassination—*if your motive is not to condemn but to understand.* It is not the objectivity of the reporter you should strive for, but a human treatment of the truth, a feeling for the vulnerability of human beings.

Before publishing *Growing Up,* Russell Baker worried that showing his mother's impatience and exposing her secret prenuptial pregnancy might be exploitive. He was deeply relieved when a *Wall Street Journal* review began, "Russell Baker's mother, a miraculous woman . . ." Baker's unrelenting mother comes across as a miraculous woman not through idealization, but because he shows all sides of her.

A fair portrait is achieved by addition, the accumulation of different and contrasting shades of a character. Baker attains balance and complexity through his technique of presenting dark tones in his mother's personality followed by lighter ones. His harsh pictures of her are juxtaposed with affectionate glimpses.

For example, he portrays her as strident in a scene that occurs before his father's death. His father had come home later than usual with a present for Russell's little sister. (So that the reader will not condemn his father in this scene, Baker precedes it by informing us that because his father was diabetic, he couldn't handle alcohol—a condition no one then realized.)

. . . He was smiling and holding something behind his back.

"Where have you been?" my mother asked.

"I bought a present for Doris."

"Do you know what time it is? Supper's been over for hours."
All this in a shout.

Holding his smile in place, trying to ignore her anger, he spoke to Doris. "You want to see what Daddy brought you?"

Doris started toward him. My mother pulled her back.

"Leave that child alone. You're drunk."

Well—and he kept smiling—actually he had taken a drink along the way, but just one—

"Don't lie about it. You're stinking drunk. I can smell it on you."

—had been in town looking for a present for Doris, and run into a man he knew—

"Aren't you ashamed of yourself? Letting your children see you like this? What kind of father are you?"

His smile went now, and he didn't try to answer her. Instead he looked at Doris and held the present in front of him for her to take. It was a box with top folded back to display a set of miniature toy dishes made of tin, little tin plates, little tin saucers, little tin teacups.

"Daddy brought you a set of dishes."

Delighted, Doris reached for the box, but my mother was quicker. Seizing his peace offering, she spoke to him in words awful to me. It wasn't bad enough that he wasted what little money he had on the poison he drank, not bad enough that he was killing himself with liquor, not bad enough that he let his children see him so drunk he could hardly stand up. He had to squander our precious money on a box of tin junk.

In a rage she ran to the kitchen screen door, opened it wide, and flung Doris's present into the darkening twilight. My father dropped onto a chair while I watched this unbelievable waste of brand-new toys. When I turned back to see if he intended to rescue the dishes, I saw that he was just sitting there helplessly.

Doris and I ran out into the gloaming to recover the scattered dishes. While we scrambled on hands and knees groping for tiny cups and saucers, the sounds of my mother's anger poured from the kitchen. When the shouting subsided, I crept back to the door. My father was slumped on the chair, shoulders sagging, head bowed, his forearms resting lifelessly on his thighs in a posture of abject surrender. My mother was still talking, though quietly now.

"For two cents," I heard her say, "I'd take my children out of here tomorrow and go back to my own people."

I sneaked back into the darkness and found Doris and tried to interest myself in the dishes for a while. The screen door banged. My father was silhouetted against the light for an instant, then he came down the steps, walked toward the pear tree, and started vomiting.

Baker does several things here worth noting. First, he relies on his mother's own words and behavior to portray her. Second, although she seems shrill and hurtful, he gives sufficient information to make her reactions understandable. Third, this scene is only one of many about his mother that show different aspects of her personality. The scene that immediately follows takes the curse off by offering a much gentler side of both parents.

There were also sweet times in that house. On breathless summer nights my parents brought blankets down from the steamy upstairs bedroom to make a bed on the living room floor. The summer I was four years old my mother bought me my first book and started teaching me to read.

As the scene continues, Baker recalls that his father helped him read a sentence, then complimented his mother.

"You're doing good with him. Maybe we ought to send him to college." Pleased, my mother reached across me and kissed him on the cheek. Smiling down at me, he said, "You want to go to college?" They both laughed a little at this. Maybe he liked the extravagance of the idea as much as she did. Then he turned off the kerosene lamp. That night they let me sleep between them.

Baker presents contrasting facets of his mother's personality sequentially. As in life, we learn about her cumulatively, a little at a time, first one color, then another. This is one way to be fair: consciously pull from memory the positive, not just the negative, about a character. Another strategy is to allow yourself to enter the perspective of another. How can you do that if you are writing in the first person? The answer is that you can finesse perspectives other than those of "I." The most common way autobiographic writers include the point of view of others is through the use of the conditional: "She must have felt," "He may have realized," "Maybe she thought." A skillful writer can even *imply* the conditional—that he has good reason to believe such were another person's thoughts without explaining the sources of the knowledge and without stating a conditional phrase "must have," "may have," "might have," "could have."

Hanh Hoang puts us inside her mother's perspective in a scene in which Hanh was not even present to observe her mother's reactions. Hanh's mother, desperate for money, having lost her job with the withdrawal of the American troops from Saigon, had fallen for a Ponzi scheme. When she realized that Tham Hoa, to whom she had given her last piasters, had duped her, Hanh's mother went to the woman's house, taking along Hanh's sister, but not Hanh.

... She had wanted me to come along, but I refused to.

My mother knocked. It took a long while before the maid answered.

"My mistress is not home," the maid said, her face expressionless. She blocked the entrance to the living room, her right hand held the door slightly open while her leg pressed against the frame. "I don't know when she will be here."

"Could we wait for her?"

"No, the family is going to bed now," the maid said, slamming the door shut.

Perhaps Tham Hoa would come back soon, my mother thought. She stood outside, in the rain, clinging for hours to her dreams, with a plastic bag covering her hair. There, breathing in the warm sour smell of the rain drops and damp garbage, the metallic odor of the wet earth, my mother must have thought once in a while of her life, what it amounted to, all these hours of waiting, and despaired.

In this scene, Hanh has allowed us into her mother's feelings. The narrator lets us sympathize with her mother, from whom at the time a teenage Hanh withheld any sympathy. A reader does not think about how the narrator can describe her mother's perspective so intimately. If pressed, a reader might say Hanh evidently knew about her mother's reactions from her sister's report. As long as there is a plausible explanation, it does not have to be spelled out.

The Telling Detail

Another way to refrain from passing judgments on your characters while portraying them with precision is through the use of telling details rather than adjectives. If you call a guy pretentious and uptight, it's an open and shut case, but if you give details about him, as Pam Houston does about Richard in her story "Highwater," a reader can come to that conclusion.

> Casey has known Chuck exactly as long as I've known Richard. . . . This is what I told her about Richard: He put marinated asparagus into the salad, he used the expression "laissez-faire capitalist" three times, once in a description of himself, he played a tape called "The Best of One Hundred and One Strings," and as far as I could tell, he'd never had oral sex.
>
> "You're kidding, right?" Casey said.

Notice that you get a strong sense of who Richard is even though Houston gives no physical description of him. Here's an exercise that will help you use choice details and avoid judgmental adjectives.

EXERCISE 13: *The Telling Detail*

Choose a character you wish to portray. Make a list of all the details you can think of that help define this character. No generalizations and no descriptive adjectives allowed. If you find yourself wanting to write the word "selfish," you must stop and find a detail that proves it—say, "When a vagrant asks her for a quarter, she'll say, 'If you give me a dollar.'" You can include the person's possessions, how his house is decorated, a favorite item of clothing, pets, hobbies. Find the details that distinguish this person from all others. Then, when you are writing, try to fit some of these details into your portrait.

Introducing Characters

The first time you introduce a character, it's good to give him an attribute that will help your reader remember him. A reader will more easily remember the man with thick russet eyebrows than that his name is Michael, so mention those eyebrows when you introduce Michael and refer to them again if you bring him back into your story after a considerable absence.

Unless a physical feature is for some reason memorable, it isn't the facts that go on a driver's license that matter—the color of someone's hair or eyes, their height or weight. The details you mention should suggest the person's singularity and temperament, and the effect of those attributes on you. Here is a character introduction from Hanh Hoang's memoir that tells us as much about the narrator as it does about Luu.

I envied Luu although she wasn't what you would consider pretty. Her face, like her mother's, was ungracefully flat. Because such a feature was considered unattractive in our culture, we even had a special name for it in our language: Mat phen phet. The adjective, "phen phet," wasn't used in any other context.

On top of flatness, Luu had a protruding chin, which gave her an air of toothlessness. Yet, unlike her mother, Luu could flash the sweetest of smiles, and then she was all grace and charm.

I also loved her freckles, round and brown like the spots on a banana skin. I had not seen them on any other Vietnamese. With the dots on her upturned nose, she seemed Western, exotic, even distinguished.

If you are going to give us physical details in introducing a character, be selective; instead of giving ten, choose one or a few that best distinguish that person. And you don't need to lay out all your description at the beginning or in any one place within a work. Rather, you can parcel out one or two descriptive elements at a time spread through a work. For example, Hanh introduces "Sister Sophie of sallow face and equine teeth," but does not add any other description of her until there is a logical place to do so. Several paragraphs later, where Sister Sophie is addressing the narrator, Hanh works in another descriptive detail: " 'You are free to choose whomever you want to be friends with, there is no way to stop you,' she said, gesticulating with her long, awkward fingers."

In life, rather than receiving knowledge of a person all at once, we acquire it gradually. You have one impression of the person from what others say before you meet; another from his appearance and behavior at an initial meeting; and you amplify or revise your first impression at subsequent encounters. Further, the characters you portray are not static; like you, they change. Major supporting characters make a discernible pattern as they move through time. Just as it is valuable for you to track your own character arc, it is worth contemplating theirs.

The Importance of Gesture

A few select physical details can be valuable when you first introduce a character, but an individual's gestures, especially habitual behaviors, are a more effective way to show personality. It's a technique used by our best contemporary novelists. For example, Barbara Kingsolver defines a character with one phrase at the opening of her novel *Pigs in Heaven:* "His idea of marriage is to spray WD-40 on anything that squeaks." As memoirists we have it easier than novelists because we need only recall the actual gestures of our subjects.

Russell Baker's first description of his mother in *Growing Up* relies on gesture and gives a much stronger sense of character than if he had identified the color of his mother's eyes or the texture of her hair.

> In that time when I had known her best, my mother had hurled herself at life with chin thrust forward, eyes blazing, and an energy that made her seem always on the run.
>
> She ran after squawking chickens, an ax in her hand, determined on a beheading that would put dinner in the pot. She ran when she made the beds, ran when she set the table. One Thanksgiving she burned herself badly when, running up from the cellar oven with the ceremonial turkey, she tripped on the stairs and tumbled back down, ending at the bottom in the debris of giblets, hot gravy, and battered turkey. Life was combat, and victory was not to the lazy, the timid, the slugabed, the drugstore cowboy, the libertine, the mushmouth afraid to tell people exactly what was on his mind whether people liked it or not. She ran.

Maya Angelou captures Mrs. Flowers in *I Know Why the Caged Bird Sings* with the simple gesture of her smile.

> I don't think I ever saw Mrs. Flowers laugh, but she smiled often. A slow widening of her thin black lips to show even, small white teeth, then the slow effortless closing. When she chose to smile on me, I always wanted to thank her. The action was so graceful and inclusively benign.

Specific gestures and behaviors are the essence of character, yet many writers neglect to use them. Here is an exercise that is great fun to do and a terrific way to find gestures to define character.

EXERCISE 14: *How to be . . .*

In your creative notebook, make a list of gestures and indicative behaviors as if you were writing a how-to guide for the impersonation of the character you wish to describe. When you have completed the list, choose the items you like best and incorporate them into a portrait of the person.

The first time I tried this exercise, I wrote a "how to be" portrait of my daughter.

How to be Jamie:
Giggle
Grow your legs long
Twist your perfect hair into a perfect knot at your neck
Burp the alphabet
Get a dog and don't walk him
Get a cat and don't play with it
Say, "Com'on let's talk about me."
Tell your mom you love her
Hold her hand except when other kids can see
Eat five popsicles a day
Eat spaghetti every other day
Eat pizza on the days you don't eat spaghetti
Wash and cut your new Barbie's hair the hour you get her
Look like Grace Kelly, talk like Butthead

Delighted with the portrait achieved simply through making a list, I turned it into a greeting card for Jamie, where the cover page said "How to be Jamie" with the list inside. It was such a hit that now I make these custom cards for my friends, withholding my business from Hallmark.

More relevantly, my students and I find the exercise a superb way to write better portraits. After a while, the practice of defining character by habitual behavior becomes habitual, so you automatically go through a list of possible characteristic actions in your mind as you are writing. I seriously doubt whether Mary McCarthy did a "How to be . . ." list before writing this passage in *Memories of a Catholic Girlhood* about her guardian, Uncle Myers, but that is essentially what it is.

Myers was the perfect type of rootless municipalized man who finds his pleasures in the handouts or overflow of an industrial civilization. He enjoyed standing on a curbstone, watching parades, the more nondescript the better, the Labor Day parade being his favorite, the next to that a military parade, followed by the commercial parades with floats and girls dressed in costumes; he would even go to Lake Calhoun or Lake Harriet for doll-carriage parades and competitions of children dressed as Indians. He liked bandstands, band concerts, public parks devoid of grass; skywriting attracted him; he was quick to hear of a department-store demonstration where colored bubbles were blown, advertising a soap. . . . He collected coupons and tin-foil, . . . free samples of cheese at Donaldson's, free tickets given out by a neighborhood movie house to the first installment of a serial—in all the years we lived with him, we never saw a full-length movie but only those truncated beginnings. . . . He was always weighing himself on penny weighing machines. He seldom left the house except on one of these purposeless errands, or else to go to a ball game, by himself. . . .

Despite Myers' quite justified hatred of the intellect, of reading and education (for he was right—it was an escape from him), my uncle, like all dictators, had one book that he enjoyed. It was Uncle Remus, in a red cover—a book I detested—which he read aloud to us in his den over and over again in the evenings. It seemed to me that this re-duction of human life to the level of talking animals and this cor-ruption of language to dialect gave my uncle some very personal relish. He knew I hated it and he rubbed it in, trotting my brother Sheridan on his knee as he dwelt on some exploit of Br'er Fox's with many chuckles and repetitions. In Uncle Remus, he had his hour, and to this day I cannot read anything in dialect or any fable without some degree of repugnance.

Using Humor and Understatement in Portraying Others

The idea of Mary McCarthy, member of America's lofty literary elite, being raised by the churlish Myers and forced to listen to him read *Uncle Remus* strikes me as deeply funny. It is humor that arises from the ironies of true life, the kind that works best in autobiographic writing. Though I dis-approve of Myers for beating and cheating McCarthy and her brothers, I can't help but relish any character that makes me laugh.

You can tell us devastating details about someone, yet if they are suffi-ciently entertaining, you will make us feel fond of that character. If you give us a character who becomes as familiar and ridiculous as members of our own family, then we will love you and that character. Just as humor is in-valuable in portraying yourself appealingly, so it can take the venom out of what would otherwise be a virulent portrait.

Mary McCarthy was a master at turning people who were dishonorable in life into delightfully Dickensian characters. Through understatement and irony, she allows a reader to fill in what she has implied or left unstated. I love her portrait of her wealthy, stingy grandmother who upon their parents' death disposed of Mary and her brothers by sending them to live with cruel Myers, whom the grandmother herself could not stand.

> She did not visit our ménage or inquire into its practices, and though hypersensitive to a squint or dental irregularity . . . she appeared not to notice the darns and patches of our clothing, our raw hands and scarecrow arms, our silence and our elderly faces. She imagined us as surrounded by certain playthings she had once bestowed on us. . . . Like many egoistic people (I have noticed this trait in myself) she was capable of making a handsome outlay, but the act affected her so powerfully that her generosity was still lively in her memory when its practical effects had long vanished. . . .
>
> . . . For my grandmother, the death of my parents had become, in retrospect, an eventful occasion upon which she looked back with pleasure and a certain self-satisfaction. . . . The housekeeping details of the tragedy, in fact, were to her of paramount interest. "I turned my house into a hospital," she used to say, particularly when visitors were present. "Nurses were as scarce as hen's teeth, and high—you can hardly imagine what those girls were charging an hour. . . ."
>
> My parents had, it seemed by dying on her premises, become in a lively sense her property, and she dispensed them to us now, little by little, with a genuine sense of bounty, just as, later on, when I returned to her a grown-up young lady, she conceded me a diamond lavaliere of my mother's as if the trinket were an inheritance to which she had the prior claim. But her generosity with her memories appeared to us, as children, an act of the greatest indulgence. We begged her for more of these mortuary reminiscences as we might have begged for candy, and since ordinarily we not only had no candy we were permitted no friendships, no movies, and little reading beyond what our teachers prescribed for us, and were kept in quarantine, like carriers of social contagion, among the rhubarb plants of our neglected yard, these memories doled out by our grandmother became our secret treasure . . . these crumbs from the rich man's table were a banquet indeed to us. We did not even mind going back to our guardians, for we now felt superior to them, and besides, as we well knew, we had no choice. It was only by accepting our situation as a just and unal-

terable arrangement that we could be allowed to transcend it and feel ourselves united to our grandparents in a love that was the more miraculous for breeding no practical results.

Such indirect poking is a wonderful technique for portraying difficult people, but you need to be careful that it is humor intended to make us laugh at human foibles, rather than vicious humor. It can be sarcastic and tongue-in-cheek, but if it becomes too directly humiliating, it won't be enjoyable. Sure you can get a snicker out of humiliating another person, but you have to be prepared that a reader will begin to distrust you for it.

Tribute Portraits

A folk art of the written portrait is flowering in our daily lives, unrecognized as such. In contemporary memorial rituals, friends and family find solace in writing and reading portraits of the deceased. One young widow I knew asked each of the people who loved her husband to give her a written portrait of him. She assembled them into a book for their infant daughter, who never knew her father. Many of us write portraits in our diaries trying to arrest in words the people streaming through our lives. The portrait is a human triumph over transience, preserving those we love on paper as well as in our hearts.

When I was forced in parochial school to learn the Eight Beatitudes, I always stumbled over the third one, "Blessed are the meek, for they shall inherit the earth." How absurd. The meek, from my observation, ended up with the chicken neck rather than the breast, the giver rather than receiver of nice birthday gifts, the one at home on New Year's, the one to care for ancient relatives and disabled pets no one else would keep, forgotten in the will, passed up for promotions, living in later years on Social Security in a trailer. I might buy "for theirs is the kingdom of heaven," but inherit the earth? Look around.

I get it now, though; for as I grow older I find that it is the meek I cannot forget. Long after I can no longer remember the ruthless, machinelike ones, I remember the gentlest souls. They are the ones I must celebrate, the ones whose portraits I find myself trying to write again and again, my mother, my dear Aunt Anne, my fifth and sixth grade teacher, Mr. Grekle. When I write the portraits of those who have loved me best, I understand how it is they inherit the earth, for they are the ones who have taken possession of me.

How to be Mr. Grekle:
  Take off your wire-rimmed glasses and silently wipe away your
    pique
  Never talk down to children
  Find the talent in each student and praise it
  Play baseball with the grace of Mickey Mantle
  After lunch give your urban students the scent of Canadian pine
    forests and the thrill of black bears by having them close their
    eyes, heads on desks, as you read aloud from *Tippecanoe and
    Canada Too*
  Always speak with respect and pride about Mrs. Grekle even
    though she's a bitch
  Beam as your students recite the American poetry you love
  Find your Christian Scientist god in nature, in the present moment,
    and in the children you teach

After my father left her, my mother invested her alimony money in the
Doris Grekle School of Encino in exchange for free tuition for my sister
and me. When after four years the tiny private school failed, and Morris and
Doris Grekle moved to Arrowhead to sell real estate, I think my mother felt
she had been conned, but only about the money.

My mother described Mr. Grekle as a small, homely man, but I remember him as tall and Gary Cooper handsome behind his wire-rimmed glasses.
The first day of the school year he stood authoritatively in front of the classroom in his beige, wrinkled suit. After attendance he unsealed cardboard
boxes that contained our new texts. As he removed each volume he caressed
it, putting it to his nose like a sommelier to inhale its aroma of faraway forests
and iron sheets. He turned each book over in his hands, then ran his index
finger down the smooth margin of inviolate pages. Finally he walked to the
desk of each student to present us ceremoniously with our own book, carefully, as though it were a gift box containing fragile treasures.

How I longed to open my new text, but I sat, impatient and obedient,
hands in my lap, until he would give permission. "If you read your book before seasoning it, the binding will crack and one day the pages will fall out,"
Mr. Grekle warned. I imagined my pristine book lying on the sidewalk,
derelict, the loosened pages tattered as detached moth wings. When Mr.
Grekle finally announced, "Now open! Exactly in the middle," I followed
his instructions eagerly, sliding my finger down the center seam, lifting the
pages on either side, finding the seam again, and with both fingers now, press-

ing apart the pages at the binding, again and again, so that when at last I would be allowed to read my text, each page would turn easily, responding to my touch.

But what was this? This book, my sixth grade history text, had something wrong with it. The pages were uncut at the beginning! I raised my hand.

"My pages need to be cut. May I use the scissors?"

"No, read what it says in front of the uncut pages," Mr. Grekle said. He had a remarkable ability to be firm while remaining gentle.

It said: "Not for children. These pages are to be read by adults only, your parents or any other old people, that is people twenty, thirty, or older." I was offended. I could read better than most of the adults I knew. How dare the author put a message to my mother inside *my* book! She had to work; she had no time to read. I was sure Mr. Grekle would let me open those forbidden pages. But he insisted they remain uncut.

As soon as I got home that afternoon and had eaten my ice cream sandwich from the freezer, I pulled the book out of my bag and set it on the kitchen table. I pushed the uncut edge to force a pocket between the pages and laid my head sideways on the table. I could make out the bottom and top sentences this way, but not a whole paragraph. I couldn't understand what was being said there without cutting the pages.

It is a testament of how much I respected Mr. Grekle that I didn't cut those pages until the semester was over and we were allowed to take our textbooks home to keep. During the summer I was alone in the house all day, and try as I might to resist, I was drawn to that book. Finally I could stand it no longer, and recklessly I cut the pages with my mother's sewing shears, wondering what horrible plagues would come down on my head. I sped through what was written there with horrified fascination and understood why children were not supposed to read it. In compound sentences and multisyllabic words, the author described his approach to history and to writing a world history for children. He explained that children were prone to fantastic misinterpretations unless the author were very precise. For example, if he were to write that Rome was built on the River Tiber, a child might imagine a city built on stilts over the water. He also referred to two other fantasies a child might have. He said a nine-year-old child might still believe in Santa Claus or that God was a white-haired gentleman in the sky. I already knew there was no Santa but I had not realized that God, too, was only an imaginary old man.

I became aware of the hiss of our neighbor's sprinklers and the jingle of a Good Humor truck down the street. The sounds were remote but seemed terribly important in a world without a father.

The portrait has a unique place in autobiographic writing. It can be part of any genre of self, from the personal essay to the full autobiography; it can be an autonomous work; and it can be the seed for something unexpected, as my portrait of Mr. Grekle transformed itself into a piece about an event in my childhood. Yet whether it is a discrete work or part of another story, the same touchstone you use when portraying yourself holds when portraying others: Tell the whole truth with love.

This is unequivocally so when writing about family, no matter how dysfunctional. Mary Karr, author of *The Liar's Club*, says that when she went on her book tour, she did so with dread that she and her hard-drinking, often neglectful and violent parents would be seen as grotesques. Instead she came away stunned that so many people identified. "After eight weeks of travel, I ginned up this working definition for a dysfunctional family," she says, "any family with more than one person in it." Despite the oft-decried dissolution of the family, Karr concluded that families—divorced, violated, secretive, or scattered—are surviving in new forms, and the popularity of memoir derives in part from our need to know how. "People go on birthing babies and burying dead and loving those with whom they've shared deeply wretched patches of history," Karr says. "We do this partly by telling stories, in voices that seek neither to deny family struggles nor to make demons of our beloveds."

11

Truth in
Autobiographic Writing

Truth, like light, must be in motion. Though we believe it exists and seek it, it is impossible to pin down. Its elusiveness tortures some memoirists—how much may you shape reality and call it nonfiction?

Several years ago I tried to option the film rights to a thrilling memoir, *O Rugged Land of Gold,* in which writer Martha Martin recounted her survival through the winter on a remote Alaskan island, alone, injured, and pregnant. At the climax of the story, Martin delivered her baby by herself and laid the child on an otter's skin.

Martin wrote her memoir as if it were a diary, but I could tell by how effectively the material had been crafted into a drama that this was not a natural diary. Clearly the author had edited, rewritten, and shaped the material at a later date. I recognized it could be a film precisely because the author had imposed a powerful dramatic structure upon actual events. Here was a true Robinson Crusoe story of a self-sufficient woman adjusting to primitive conditions and reuniting with nature, free of man's aegis.

In tracking down the rights I learned that Martha Martin was the pen name for Helen Bolyan, the wife of a gold prospector. Her son, Clyde Bolyan, had had quite a few inquiries from producers over the years. He referred me to his attorney, but before he did so, he felt compelled to confess to me that while his mother had certainly survived in the Alaskan wilderness totally by her own wits and all the details she'd recounted of her ingenuity in providing for herself were authentic, she had actually delivered her girl child, who subsequently died, at another time and not without assistance. So what I liked best about the story, the incident of a modern woman giving birth unaided in the wilderness, wasn't really true. Martin had taken two separate incidents, the childbirth and her isolation in the wilderness, and merged them. "Do you think it makes a difference?" Clyde asked me. "Would you still want to do it even if it isn't completely true?" Forty years after his deceased mother had heightened the drama of her story at the request of an editor, her son was tortured by the belief that mom had perpetrated a fraud.

What should I have told him? I said it didn't really present a problem for me because most television movies and films take license with the truth anyway. Television movies even have terms that help the audience understand the degree of license taken. "Based on a true story" allows the fusion of two different time periods or the use of composite characters in a fact-based story. "Inspired by a true story" goes further in permitting even the creation of events and characters that never existed. Nevertheless, there was still concern in Clyde's voice when he said, "Well, if it doesn't bother *you* that it isn't all true . . ."

I confess it did bother me a little. I was so in love with the idea of Martha Martin bearing her baby as the ice of winter was just beginning to crack and awakening from exhaustion to cut the birth cord with her sewing scissors, that I wanted it to be true. Poetically it was so true. It completed the theme of woman as autonomous survivor that had run through the entire book.

I didn't option the story for other reasons, but continued for years to ponder the puzzle of how the author could have presented her material more truthfully without ruining her story. I thought perhaps Martin should have informed us in a preface that she had created a composite story, but if I had known when I read the book that it was partly contrived, I would not have enjoyed it half so much. The thrill of reading thrilling memoirs is in believing they are what really happened. Does that mean I enjoy being conned, like the readers of the *National Enquirer,* who know that much of what they read is false?

Perhaps Martin should not have shaped her material. Perhaps she should have recorded all the events chronologically exactly as they had happened. I would have been saved my let-down upon learning that the story had been devised, not lived as such. But then I probably would not have read the book through. It would not have been as readable, meaningful, or as universally true as the book she did write, and certainly I would not have imagined it as a film.

Perhaps Martin should have called the book a novel instead of a memoir to indicate that she had used fictional devices. However, though it makes a fascinating memoir, it would make a poor novel. If she had taken that course, it probably would never have been published at all.

I go over this question as I would a Zen koan, trying to figure out the answer, and I realize that there is no right answer. Nevertheless, it presented a practical problem when new editors decided to republish Martin's out-of-print book. They were aware of how Martin had condensed and shaped her story. Their solution was to place an editor's note at the end of the book explaining that during the period in which Helen Bolyan set her story, many of the events in the memoir did occur, such as the time Helen was injured and stranded alone while her husband was marooned on another island. "The birth of her child was based on an earlier incident in her life," the editors wrote. "Helen chose several experiences and wove them together into one complete story. This technique raises a few questions, but there is now no way to answer them accurately. It is important to remember that although some facts were changed by author or editor to create a smoothly flowing story, Helen wrote straight from her heart, just as she lived her life."

The editors soft-pedaled the issue with careful language. Of the various options, they have, I believe, chosen the best one.

If Martha Martin had been the Japanese author of an "I" novel, her son would likely have been proud of her ability to poeticize and enhance her experience, not embarrassed. To combine realities of life with truths of the spirit is not considered fraudulent within the Japanese tradition of autobiographic writing. Perhaps it is a form of art for which we in the West simply do not have a tradition and name, but toward which we are groping. In the past two decades, thinkers such as Joseph Campbell, Robert A. Johnson, and Clarissa Pinkola Estés have asserted that the most important truths of our lives are on the invisible plane of myth. The woman who finds that her life can be understood through the myth of Persephone is discovering a truth that has little to do with objective fact. If she were to try to express this subjective truth by writing the story of her life following the myth, she might have to alter certain facts of chronology to make the story fit. She would be sacrificing one kind of truth, objective fact, for the sake of another kind, poetic or mythic truth.

Many people still assume that the autobiographic writer should have little choice when she begins to write about her life, that she is chained to circumstances, and it is her job simply to set down as accurately as possible everything that happened to her, "just as it really happened." The trouble with such an understanding is its reduction of the writer to a mere recorder. The results would be the equivalent of C-Span.

Instead, what readers really want from an autobiographic writer is her vision of reality. Memoir, at its best, ought to reveal what it feels like to be the person writing. From that perspective, Martha Martin has told us more of what it feels like to be Helen Bolyan by organizing her story around the central metaphor of her giving birth alone at the onset of spring, than if she had related the actual chronology of events. Through her artistry we as readers feel Helen Bolyan's profound identification with nature. We are inside her vision of the truth. Martha Martin was creating personal myth out of the raw material of her life. In that sense, she was writing New Autobiography fifty years ago.

Because autobiography is in transition from writing meant to preserve history into a form that explores the mythic stories in each individual's life, there are no set rules as to how strictly factual it must be. Each writer makes his or her own decisions about how much poetic license to take. In part it depends on who your audience is. In writing for yourself or for family, you may wish to take less poetic license. If writing for publication, you may need to take more.

While you are free to make up the truth in New Autobiography, a reader is trusting you not to make up lies, not to lie about what really matters: your perceptions, feelings, motivations, your actions and those of others. Lying requires the intent to deceive. With the possible exception of famous accused felons who write quick-money memoirs, most people intend to write the truth.

If you plan to alter names and identities, change chronology, or make up details, you can maintain frankness with a reader by writing a disclaimer. It's part of the contract with a reader that you set up in the beginning what is called the writer's *donnée*, French for "given."

EXERCISE 15: *Your Disclaimer*

Compose a few sentences or paragraphs that explain your donnée, your intended method in writing your autobiographic work. It could be as simple as "I wish to preserve and make sense out of this time in my life. Where I have been unable to remember fully, I have allowed my imagination to fill in." Or "To protect the privacy of certain individuals I have in many ways disguised their identities. Sometimes I have taken poetic license with the order of events for the sake of the narrative."

After writing your disclaimer or apology or note to the reader in your creative journal, you may wish to place it at the front of your manuscript. Later you might revise and keep it as part of your final draft, or ultimately dispense with it. Whether or not your disclaimer ends up as part of your final work, its value at this point is to give yourself permission to write creatively.

Disclaimers often appear in works of New Autobiography because it is still an emerging form. Old assumptions about what memoir should be co-exist side by side along with new realizations of what it can be, causing confusion for both writers and readers. Inevitably, writers sometimes feel illegitimate, that somehow it is cheating to take liberties with details of chronology or identification. They feel constrained from shaping their inner myth, even if it is the vehicle through which they can tell the most essential truths. Mary McCarthy writes in her introduction to *Memories of a Catholic Girlhood:*

> Many a time, in the course of doing these memoirs, I have wished that I were writing fiction. The temptation to invent has been very strong, particularly where recollection is hazy and I remember the substance of an event but not the details. . . . There are cases where I am not sure myself whether I am making something up. I think I remember but I am not positive.

Writing in 1957, McCarthy is uneasy about having made up the truth, which is why she follows each well-constructed chapter with a rundown of how she altered details.

> Miss Gowrie was always reporting her favorites for breaking the rules. She did report me for smoking, but I don't think this happened the day after "Marcus Tullius." This is an example of "storytelling," I arranged actual events so as to make "a good story" out of them.

Today's writers are not so apologetic, and keep their explanations brief. Richard Rodriguez in *Days of Obligation, An Argument with My Mexican Father* inserts a page after the dedication and before the acknowledgments that reads:

> Apology
> Some names and biographical details in this book have been altered.

Rodriguez writes an apology but doesn't sound apologetic. Neither does Julia Phillips in her disclaimer to *You'll Never Eat Lunch in This Town Again.*

> Some names have been changed to protect the privacy of, and me from, guilty people, places, and things . . . the truth remains substantially intact.

Janet Frame begins her autobiography, *To the Is-Land*, with an overt commitment to writing the myth in her life, not a literal record.

From the first place of liquid darkness, within the second place of air and light, I set down the following record with its mixture of fact and truths and memories of truths and its direction always toward the Third place, where the starting point is myth.

Nancy Mairs, in *Remembering the Bone House*, places a simple note on a single page before her preface.

In order to protect the privacy of certain individuals who appear in this book, names and other identifying characteristics have been changed.

Yet in the preface itself, Mairs goes on at some length about how intimate her writing is. Here one does detect a note of self-consciousness, if not apology.

In writing a memoir, I have found, the temptation to censor material can grow enormous. Sometimes I have put pressure on myself to omit or prettify details in order to disguise truths about myself I didn't want to face up to or speak aloud. I've been drilled in the rules of polite discourse. I know that talking openly about certain matters— "telling the truth about my own experiences as a body," as Virginia Woolf put it—isn't "nice," especially for a woman. Time and again I've felt myself shrink from the task, and probably I've yielded in ways I don't even recognize. I believe, however, that the proscriptions traditionally placed on a woman's speech foster feelings of shame that lead her to trivialize her own experience and prevent her from discovering the depth and complexity of her life. In defiance of the conventions of polite silence, I've spoken as plainly and truthfully as the squirms and wriggles of the human psyche will permit.

New Autobiographers have become increasingly comfortable with creating disguises to tell the truth, but still worry about how their naked human truths will be received. Though it may be less factual than the old, New Autobiography is characterized by far greater personal openness. It's like the witness who comes on *60 Minutes* wearing a fake nose, a beard, and with his voice electronically altered in order to tell you something shockingly honest. In New Autobiography the writer may disguise characters, alter chronology, and embellish descriptions, but does so to reveal truths of personal experience formerly hidden.

⌒New Autobiography Guidelines

Whether or not you add a disclaimer up front, you have made an implied contract with your reader by presenting your work as nonfiction. The implied contract commits you to genuineness, authenticity, and believability, just as the presentation of one's work as science fiction implies on the part of both author and reader a suspension of disbelief. Nevertheless, the kind of truth you are dealing with differs from that of other nonfiction writers. It need not be journalistic or historical; it may be emotional and spiritual.

The most exciting examples of New Autobiography push against the boundary between fiction and nonfiction and play on its edges. However, as in all nonfiction, you must never go so far that you lose credibility with the reader. Credibility has to do with perception rather than intent. Some liars come across as credible if they are clever about it, and some sincere people lose credibility because they do not understand how they are being perceived. Here are some guidelines to help you maintain credibility and remain truthful while giving yourself the freedom you need to turn your life into story.

• If you are citing publicly verifiable facts, make sure they are accurate. If you are writing a personal essay about having attended Woodstock in 1972, but the reader was there and, despite all the drugs, knows it was 1969, you will have lost credibility.

One piece of advice here. Do your fact-checking on your second draft. Otherwise your work may never recover from what Oscar Hammerstein called "research poison." Besides, if you stop to get the details right on your first draft, it will slow you down and you may waste time researching a date, place, or name for a passage that in a later draft you will toss. It is helpful in first drafts to give the facts as best you can from memory and add in the text a note to yourself such as "check this" or "right date?"

While you maintain an earnest effort to achieve factual accuracy, remember that it is not the most important level of truthfulness. Memoir is a human document, and as such will contain errors. Autobiographic writers are to be forgiven; they are not under oath.

• To preserve credibility, you occasionally have to alter facts, because the truth is confusing or sounds unbelievable. If, for example, four of the most important characters of your story are all named Barbara, and that fact is not important to the story, you might be better off simply changing some of the names to keep your reader from being confused. The best way to deal with facts that are essential to your story but stretch believability is to address a reader's incredulity. If, for example, you had three brothers all named John, and the fact that your parents gave all three boys the same name *is* relevant to the story, you can tell your reader that you realize it is hard to believe, directly addressing their disbelief and thereby dispensing with it. For example, "It was certainly a bizarre thing to do and it caused no end of confusion, but my parents named all three of my brothers 'John.' "

Using this technique of addressing the strangeness of fact, Lillian Hellman, in *An Unfinished Woman,* tells the reader she realizes her father's behavior was eccentric before describing his behavior.

My father had, among other eccentricities, an inability to travel from one place to another in a conventional line; if it was possible to change trains or make a detour, he arranged it.

• Do not invent major events that never happened. To do so will break the implied contract that your work is nonfiction. You may, however, rearrange facts in the following ways for the sake of narrative interest and artistic economy:

• *Changes in actual chronology.* Such as Martha Martin changing the time of her daughter's birth to the winter she was stranded.
• *The creation of representative composite scenes.* On three different occasions you and your lover went Christmas caroling. You combine memories that may have occurred at different Christmases into one dramatic scene.
• *The creation of composite characters.* During the six years you lived in Belize you employed three different gardeners. In your narrative you combine them into one character because to introduce and characterize each would distract from your story, which is not about them.

The practice of creating composite characters is most often used for minor characters.

• You can and probably should alter the names and identities of people who could be hurt by what you say about them. This is a thorny matter and will be dealt with in detail in Chapter 21. Of course, you cannot disguise familial relationships, such as a father, mother, or brother, and since family relationships are the most interesting and dramatic subject matter for autobiographic writing, this presents a real dilemma (also addressed in Chapter 21).

• "I imagine" is an instant disclaimer you can give yourself at any point within a work, two magic words that many autobiographic writers forget they can use. While writing "I can't really remember" or "maybe he was wearing a fedora. I don't know, some kind of hat" is irritating—no one is interested in what you don't remember—the words "I imagine" are a positive assertion that pulls the reader in and allows you to be concrete rather than vague.

Take, for example, this passage from a short essay by Phillip Lopate, "My Drawer." The essay begins with an inventory of the top drawer of his dresser, "the way station" in which he keeps the miscellanea he cannot yet bear to throw away. It moves—jumps—as essays may, back to the memory of his parents' drawer.

> What was so fascinating about rifling through their drawer? I used to find nothing very unusual: some objects of obscure masculine power, like my father's leather traveling case, a shaving brush, a pair of suspenders, a wallet with photos of us, the children. Then I would go over to my mother's side of the drawer, and visit her bloomers and her gypsy scarves. I would pick up each item and smell the perfume: Arabia! Then back to my father's side, for some clues into his stolid, remote, Stakhanovite personality. In the middle section was no-man's-land, with elastic bands, garters, pipe cleaners. Once, it seems to me, I found a deck of pornographic playing cards. Am I imagining this? Isn't this rather what I kept looking for and *not* finding?

Within the text, Lopate puts us on notice that he may be imagining this detail.

"I imagine" can also provide a way to include scenes in your autobiographic work that never really happened, but which you need in order to create a dramatic ending for a piece or to provide a crucial dramatic scene. For example, in writing a personal essay about my relationship with a childhood playmate whose mother had shot his father, and who later in life was imprisoned for having shot his homosexual lover, I found that I needed a scene between the two of us as adults to give the piece an ending. In reality I had not seen my friend since we were both in high school. "I imagine" gave me the freedom to include the necessary scene while remaining within the arena of creative nonfiction.

> I had an impulse to try to find Timmy. I wanted to comfort him the way we had done for each other as kids when one stubbed a toe or skinned a knee. I wanted him to know that I understood the dark place inside him, that I could see that it had been his mother's finger on the trigger of his gun not his, that I loved him still.
>
> But I was a married woman with a kid in grade school and everyday distractions being what they are, I didn't try to find him. I just kept returning to him in my mind.
>
> Though he probably is out of prison by now, perhaps even practicing psychiatry again, in my imagination I find him in his cell. I move from the door to sit on the cot next to him and we hold hands. Together we go back, talking into the night as we did as children side by side in bed in the dark.

As the essay continued, "I imagine" allowed me to make up a scene that never really took place, yet was completely true. No one can argue with the fact that I imagined it. If ultimately I were to turn this essay into a fictional story, I could drop the use of the "imagine" words and keep the scene.

Sometimes within a memoir, "I imagine" can be implied; you don't need the words. For example, student Brason Lee needed a climactic scene in which he gave up his emotional dependency on a young therapist who had supported him through rehab for brain injury. Brason knew that the correct place for the scene with his former therapist was at his college graduation ceremony. But she had not come to the ceremony. In fact, although he had thought about her constantly, he hadn't had any actual interaction with the young woman for over a year. In the commencement scene he wrote, Brason saw her amidst a crowd of well-wishers, and he was flooded with gratitude toward her for unexpectedly attending. Then Brason's jubilance was dashed because he realized he had been mistaken; it was not she, after all.

In life, Brason had not mis-seen the young woman, but he did experience the same sequence of emotions: hope, disappointment, and, finally acceptance. In writing the scene, he created a dramatic equivalent for those emotions. This is what is meant by creative nonfiction.

If you strive for emotional honesty and permit yourself the vulnerability it requires, your reader will in all likelihood forgive your factual alteration, omission, or embellishment of details. On the other hand, writers who alter events to create a false happy ending or leave out the most negative parts of their own motivations or present their behavior in a better (or worse) light than actually occurred are running the risk of losing credibility. It's very difficult to fool a reader when it comes to the essential stuff. Readers have an uncanny radar for emotional inauthenticity. By the same token, they intuitively know when you have hit the mark. Just as you gasp with recognition when you read truly honest writing, so a reader will have that response to your work if you risk the truth.

12

How to Write
What You Dare Not Say

If memory is a fiction and our identity the result of the stories we tell ourselves, how can we ever know the truth of our own lives? Whatever philosophers surmise, for autobiographic writers the answer is in our gut. You know you've hit the truth when it gives you heart palpitations, when you think, I can't be writing this, when you feel exposed and vulnerable as a shucked oyster. There is a self-recognition and sudden release of emotional tension when you have gone as far as you can go, reached ground zero, been completely honest with self. Such emotional honesty, though, is the most difficult part of autobiographic writing to achieve.

All writers have times when they feel afraid, when the writing stops or becomes dull and merely informational, when they want to give up. The "B" word, though, the Block, is worst for autobiographic writers because we can't hide behind the guise of fiction or poetry. Fortunately, most B——problems are at the beginning of a work. I find that once my autobiographic writers get past their one-third mark they are unstoppable. By then they've arrested their fear demons, the ones that send you thoughts like "If I write this, my father will roll over in his grave," or "If I write this, everyone will know what a screw-up I really am," or "Who am I kidding? I'm not a writer and this is a waste of time that will never make me wealthy."

You would be wise to get the jump on such inner bullies before even starting your work. You will find that all of the techniques for overcoming writing blocks mentioned in *The New Diary* will be useful, especially that of writing dialogs with inner voices that try to scare you.

In journal dialogs, let internal voices know that you want to hear what they have to say. Listen, remain polite, open, and reasonable, but stand your ground. You, the writer, are in charge. Try to find a creative solution that will allow you to proceed with your work. It is particularly effective to ask carping inner voices to be constructive and to help you, to leave you alone on the first draft, for instance, but to make editing recommendations on your second draft.

Sometimes, internal negative voices are so uncivil that at first you will not be able to reach a point of successful negotiation. Then you must deal with them as you would with any difficult or abusive person in your life. You stop the dialog and tell them that if they want to speak again they are going to have to be respectful. When internal voices learn that you mean business, they begin to dialog more constructively.

Yet even if you get a jump on inner critical voices by identifying them before you begin writing, they may fool you once you are engaged in the work. You may find yourself detouring from the heart of the story's conflict, or feeling discouraged before you even have a first draft, or changing your mind repeatedly about which story to write, or rewriting the first two pages twenty times, unable to go further. Who do you think is giving you these bad directions? None other than those same internal voices, yammering away like a car full of back-seat drivers. At first you may not be aware that they are internalized voices, you just feel too tired or too insecure to do anything. But turn around fast. Name all those presences you feel looking over your shoulder as you write, and give them another talking to in your journal. Bribe, negotiate, flatter, or threaten, but never let them have the upper hand. After a dialog with any negative inner voice and before you return to the work, complete in your journal the sentence, "In order for me to feel comfortable writing this work I need to . . ."

The First Draft Is for You

No matter what your concern—fear of hurting others, fear of humiliating yourself, fear of being judged a poor writer, fear of inaccuracy (the list goes on)—there is one piece of advice I give all writers: Write your first draft for your own eyes only. If you do, your final work will have an emotional authenticity and integrity at center no matter how much you edit, omit, and disguise later. Whether you ultimately decide to throw caution to the wind and publish all, to ask permission of a loved one, to try to bring them along gradually, to fictionalize, or to cut out certain people or certain hurtful details from your text, you cannot and should not make these decisions while writing your first draft.

You need to treat your first draft very much the way you treat diary writing, withholding self-judgments, allowing the unexpected to happen, and feeling safe to say anything, knowing that no one else need ever read it. To accomplish this you may have to keep the work secure from family members just as you would a diary. If you work on computer, you can establish a code that makes your personal writing inaccessible; paper copies can be locked in a file. In your first draft, you should include everything you think you will have to take out later. If you need to keep reminding yourself of your personal freedom, write at the top of every page: *This is for my eyes only.*

If your perfectionism still gets in your way, I pass on one more piece of advice, given me by Phil Stutz, the only therapist I ever got my money's worth from. "When you sit down to write," he said, "tell yourself, 'My goal is to complete a really shitty first draft.' " Phil went on to explain that perfectionism was death, a rejection of life. "You think," he said in his New York street voice, "that if you make something perfect it will save you. But it won't. Everything, everything in life has a piece of shit in it. Nothing will save you from the imperfection of life but death." So now I repeat this little mantra when I start a new project—"My goal is to complete a really shitty first draft." And you know what? This little sentence, not years of trying to understand why my father wanted me to be a bank teller, or why I thought I was too ugly to be an actress, or why I changed careers whenever I got successful, this stupid little sentence was the most valuable thing I got out of thousands of dollars of therapy, and I'm giving it to you at a fraction of the price.

Anne Lamott has a chapter on writing shitty first drafts in *Bird by Bird, Some Instructions on Writing and Life* (did she go to Phil, too?). She is advising fiction writers, but memoirists need the advice even more. We have to strip naked, expose our stretch marks and inadequate pecs, in addition to dealing with our revulsion at the way we write. Lamott says:

> For me and most of the other writers I know, writing is not rapturous. In fact, the only way I can get anything written at all is to write really, really shitty first drafts.
>
> The first draft is the child's draft, where you let it all pour out and then let it romp all over the place, knowing that no one is going to see it and that you can shape it later. . . . If the kid wants to get into really sentimental, weepy, emotional territory, you let him. Just get it all down on paper, because there may be something great in those six crazy pages that you would never have gotten to by more rational, grown-up means.

If you judge your writing in your first draft, not only will you miss the something great in those six crazy pages, you'll arrest your memory. Memory releases memory in a chain reaction. If any part is censored, the process is broken, and you will never get to some of your best material—some of which would be unrelated to emotional or legal concerns and would never have had to be cut.

Contagious Courage

Among the autobiographic writing classes I've taught, there is one that stands out. The level of writing was extraordinary; the excitement of each meeting palpable; the honesty and intimacy of the work unmatched in other classes. The source of this energy was the delicate sprite Marlena Fontenay, who said she had been a street person, a minstrel, a torch singer. On a chilly southern California night, she brought in a stack of stapled photocopies of her autobiographic short story, "Feeding Time in L.A." It recounted her mutually exploitative relationship with Harry, a bankruptcy lawyer she'd met while working as a waitress at NaNa's in Beverly Hills. In the story, the narrator convinces herself to sleep with Harry because he promises to back her dream of becoming a recording artist. The portrait she gives of him is about as appealing as a swollen tick. She portrays herself as fairly grasping, desperate, and sleazy, too. This passage is from the scene of their first date.

"What's it take to make a record?" he asked. "Let's make one. Your life's gonna change, with me. I'm telling you. You got no idea what I can do for you. So, what's it take to make a record?"

That was all I needed to hear. I was his. Harry had found the password. R-E-C-O-R-D. I was spread-eagled on the table, offering myself, body and soul to Harry. He could've done it to me, right there in the pasta. The champagne flowed. We drank to my future.

I asked Harry about the redhead I'd often seen him with at NaNa's. Personally, I thought she wasn't anything to write home about. She'd sort of erased herself. She never talked. All I ever heard her say was, "I'll have what he's having." I wanted to shake her, to make her laugh or react or something, just to prove she was alive. Anyway, Harry said she was history because she hadn't treated him good, even after he'd given her an apartment building. And he was one of those people who could never forgive someone who betrayed him. I wondered what she'd done, just what Harry meant by "betrayed," but he didn't volunteer the information, and I didn't want to pry. Besides, I had the feeling Harry was just trying to let me know he could be real generous, but that I shouldn't cross him.

During dinner I was thinking about whether or not I should do it with Harry that night. Should I wait till the second date? I mean, in the grand scheme of things, what difference does it really make? First date, second date . . .

We hit Nickie's Lair on Sunset for after-dinner drinks. It's a trendy watering hole for yuppie singles. A bunch of lonely people, scoping each other out, trying to get laid. Not my kind of place, but Harry was obviously a regular.

What the hell, I figured, let's get this show on the road, so I brought Harry back to my little studio in West Hollywood. Just around the corner from the SEVENTH VEIL, LIVE NUDES 'TIL 2. Harry was plowed. He rummaged through the trunk of his car and managed to pull out a garment bag, which he dragged up the stairs to my apartment, muttering, "I'm dead! I'm dead!" Only it came out more like, "I'm 'ed! I'm 'ed!" because he was so drunk, his speech was slurred. And when he took off his clothes and plopped down onto my futon, looking like a beached whale in cowboy boots, I started to wonder about Harry. About what I'd gotten myself into.

There he was, on the bed, mumbling, "S . . . sh . . . uck my 'ick! S . . . sh . . . uck my 'ick!" over and over again. I was glad when he passed out, a few minutes later.

First thing in the morning, Harry was ready for action, which I would find out later was an event. Harry being one of those men who needs to be wired back together again. They drink because they can't get it up. They can't get it up because they drink. . . .

Harry wasn't much into foreplay. He went for the brass ring. The orgasm. And he didn't care about the ride it took to get there. That morning, he just pulled me over on top of him, bounced me up and down a few times, remarked on how great my pussy was (so tight it could open a beer bottle, he said) and he came. I'd have to teach Harry a few things about enjoying the ride.

But what Harry didn't put out in foreplay, he sure made up for in flattery. I had the body of a twenty year old, he said. Legs that wouldn't quit, flawless skin, and the greatest ass in the world. Just watching me walk from the bed to the bathroom, Harry said, was the highlight of his week. That stuff's pretty addictive and guys like Harry can smell out a woman who needs to hear it.

"I'll give you a grand to shave your pussy," Harry said as he put on his shirt from the night before, after he'd sprayed it with cologne.

"For your birthday," I said to him, laughing. "I'll give it to you, for your birthday! And here's a copy of my demo tape, so you don't forget me."

"Forget you?! Not likely. Not likely at all!"

Harry left that morning, a happy man.

"I'm your future!" he called back to me, as he walked down the stairs. "And don't you forget it!"

Marlena didn't sleep the night before bringing the story into class. She anticipated scorn for exposing how she had let herself be used and degraded in pursuit of an illusion. She was not prepared for the reaction of the class members. When she finished reading the story, there was silence for an uncomfortably long time. Marlena twisted her hands, staring at them to keep the water in her eyes from spilling out. Finally, to break the stillness, she began to apologize. It was only then that members of the class spoke. They thanked her for her honesty. They said they wished they could write that way. It wasn't their words that surprised Marlena; it was their attitude toward her, the protective warmth and appreciation she suddenly felt from them. These eighteen people and I had been taken with something like love for Marlena. It *was* love, that which happens between people in the closeness of intimacy, that which happens when you read a writer who opens a naked heart to you.

We all wanted to learn from Marlena. How had she been able to go back and face that time? Where did she get the confidence to present her blemishes instead of trying to hide them? Hadn't the story been painful to write? How had she been able to reenter the feelings of that time without being swallowed up by them? Marlena paused before she spoke. She closed her eyes. It was terribly painful to recall, she said. We saw a shadow of anguish darken her face. "I think it was possible," she offered, "because while I was remembering and reliving that time, there was a part of me sort of floating above that knows I can be and I have been in a better state I could return to."

Marlena was speaking of the double state of being that characterizes autobiographic writing, the self now looking at the self then. In writing the story, Marlena returned to the perspective of a lesser self while maintaining in the present her awareness of a better way of being. It is this double awareness through which you can encourage yourself to tell the whole truth. Encourage. Give yourself courage.

After Marlena read her story, other women in the class—this class had only one man in it—began to write like the devil. I read them a quote from a review Nathaniel Hawthorne wrote about one of columnist Fanny Fern's novels: "The woman writes as if the devil was in her; and that is the only condition under which a woman can ever write anything worth reading. Generally women write like emasculated men . . . but when they throw off the restraints of decency, and come before the public stark naked, as it were—then their books are sure to possess character and value." Hawthorne was sexist, but there is a valuable lesson in this quote. Writing worth reading is that in which the author has taken the risk to bare all. Marlena was the leader in a skinny dip. After she plunged, other women stripped and dove in too.

You can catch courage from reading published autobiographic writers who take risks you admire. I point to the works of many in this book. Or perhaps you can bring someone who writes like the devil into your memoir group. Or you can simply encourage yourself by listening to your heart. The word "courage" comes from the Latin *cor,* which means "heart." When you encourage yourself, you ask your heart to say all that is there.

How do you know when your heart needs encouragement? When you feel afraid, when you want to stop writing. Then you seize those feelings as if they were exactly what you have been looking for. They are your golden opportunity. *That frisson of fear is a marker pointing to the very door you want to open.*

To blast through the door, the technique I like best is your next touchstone.

TOUCHSTONE 5:

Write What You Dare Not Say.

When you're afraid to write the next sentence, ask yourself, "What is it I dare not say?" Write the question on the page and then answer it right there on the page. Write so fast that you don't know what will come next. Write as *if* you were crazy and uninhibited. Set a timer for five minutes and don't stop until it goes off. You will have written what you don't dare write, and you will have survived.

In writing *Memoirs of a Nun on Fire* about her years in a convent, poet Philomene Long put the question in her text and left it there.

Five years within this cloister. An enclosure of silence. Latin. Eyes fixed on the floor. Black robes, medieval gestures. In the most secret recesses, a thousand daily deaths.

But I hide behind these images. What is it I am afraid to say? I have spoken of this to no one. I was told not to. I have obeyed . . . until this moment. Suddenly I wish to escape the shame.

The shame: flagellation. That we did it to ourselves. That I took the metal chain with its hard edges, the "discipline," from the hands of the postulant mistress, that I brought it to my lips and with great affection, kissed it.

Every Saturday night. The flogging. The chains . . .

Ask yourself, "What is it I am afraid to say?" or "What am I hiding from myself?" right on the page when you, like Philomene, recognize that you are poeticizing words or trying to give an impression rather than revealing what would be embarrassing to you. If you cannot write what it is you have been hiding from yourself in your manuscript, move into your journal and free-write it there or write it on a piece of paper you promise yourself you can destroy.

Eventually, taking risks in response to fear will become habitual. You will go for the surprise without needing to write the question, "What is it that I dare not say?" You will courageously tell the whole truth, because you will love what it does for your writing.

13

Dealing with Your Dark Side

There is not always a benefit in revisiting trauma. Remembering a painful incident, even one that has been repressed, will not in itself guarantee release. To think it will is a popular misconception and a misinterpretation of Freud, who himself recognized that it was by helping the patient make a meaningful story out of buried memories that his cure was effected.

In fact, by intentionally recalling a traumatic or painful experience, you may simply reinjure yourself—unless it is as part of a larger healing story. It is by making *meaning* out of memory that one is healed, whether through therapy, life, journal writing, or autobiographic writing. That meaning need not be religious, spiritual, or psychological; it can be philosophic or aesthetic. Sometimes the only meaning one can find in certain events is aesthetic, the ability to make something beautifully crafted out of what in life was arbitrary, ugly, or painful.

Autobiographic narrative is more than simply remembering on paper. It is a second chance, a chance to get it right. Not that you change events, not that you don't write about helplessly watching your sister drown with all the pain and guilt you experienced, but that this time you are on your own side, even in pain and failure. Now you can tell the story with insight and find the meaning of the single experience within the context of your whole life. Remembering one's suffering from the perspective of acquired wisdom is different from simply replaying it.

Yet even if the process is ultimately healing, it can still hurt mercilessly. Humiliation, self-recrimination, self-loathing, regret, self-pity, resentment, and murderous rage are only some of the demons with which autobiographic writers grapple.

Even with the students I work with most closely, I have to stand aside, helpless, when they write about their most painful experiences. I see how they suffer in reentering the pain, sometimes more intensely than during the original experience. Some of them weep as they write; some get somatic ailments—sore throats and painful hands. All I can do is assure them that the way out of the suffering is by going through to the end, by staying in the writing and ultimately finishing the narrative. All I can do is witness and applaud their courage and assure them that the works that most deeply touch others go to the edge, reach into dark, unexplored territory.

I recall a particularly painful and lonely period just before my husband and I articulated to each other our hopelessness about our marriage. The greatest comfort I found during that time was reading before bed Mikal Gilmore's blistering memoir *Shot in the Heart,* about the brutal childhood the author shared with his brothers, one of whom was executed murderer Gary Gilmore. I couldn't wait for the end of the day when I could enter the sordid American landscape of Gilmore's childhood. It wasn't that the horrible wounds his family members inflicted on each other made mine seem a scratch. It was that I felt strengthened by the courage it must have taken Mikal Gilmore to articulate the hopeless cycle of family violence from which he alone survived. His memoir gave me a shot in the heart to embrace—even when most difficult—the drama of my life.

Plenty of people quit writing with the decision that it is not worth it to open old wounds, but I am grateful to those who battle through to the end. Not only is it healing for them, I know it has value for others, and not just others with the same life problem, but for all those in the community of pain. At the prewriting stage, I have intentionally asked you not to do reveries on your most painful memories. They may well belong in your autobiographic work, but before entering them, you need to be prepared with the guidelines offered in this chapter and a knowledge of craft presented in subsequent chapters.

⌒ Protect Your Light Colors

Since you define yourself through autobiographic writing, if you were to include only negative memories, it could harm your mental health. If you have a particularly dark or painful story to tell, you would do well to build for yourself a nest of some positive memories to sustain you when you plan to plunge into the dark. Here's an exercise that will demonstrate how to find the positive memories you need in order to write about the darkest times.

EXERCISE 16: *Spots of Light*

Choose a period in your life that seems to you the most painful. Now list twelve moments during that period when you experienced joy as human warmth, as nature's endurance, as a sense of inner quiet, or as an observation of beauty or character—even if you were not fully aware of them at the time.

Take one of these moments and expand it in detail by writing a reverie.

If you choose to write about a very dark period, you may need to use every one of your spots of light. From an artistic as well as a mental health point of view, you need light with dark memories. In autobiographic writing as in painting, you need to protect your light colors, because if you use only dark colors and mix them indiscriminately, you will end up with a muddy, gloomy mire. Periods of painful struggle make for the most dramatic stories, but drama cannot be achieved without contrast, including the contrast between dark and light.

Take, for example, the use of light colors in Susan Golant's memoir in progress about growing up as the child of Holocaust survivors. Although her childhood was filled with the wounds of her parents' traumatic experiences, notice how she juxtaposes positive memories against dark ones, making both more effective.

> . . . my mother did describe how, in January of 1945, when she and a transport of women arrived at Bergen-Belsen, they were stripped naked, paraded on a selection line, and sent to the showers where they stood under a deluge of scalding water, after which they were chased barefoot and naked into the frozen winter night. She told this story on many a morning, in our warm kitchen, while feeding me my daily dose of Cream of Wheat, as I prepared to go off to school.

The contrast of the warm kitchen and Cream of Wheat with the terrified naked women in the frozen winter night intensifies the images and maintains the opposition inherent in Golant's overall theme: that although evil exists, so does goodness.

⁓The Importance of Story

Though Susan writes spontaneously—beginning each chapter of her memoir with an image, a photo, or an object, and allowing reverie to take her where it will—she does have a sense of the story she wants to tell, or, at least, the realization she wants to reach at the end. She knows that the problem her childhood has presented is the difficulty of believing in a God who could allow the Holocaust to happen, and that she wants to conclude with her adult realization of an equivalent mystery, the inexplicable acts of goodness beyond self-interest of which some people are capable. This is not just the ending to her story, it is also her point of view, which permeates every scene in the work.

When reentering the most painful moments, it is well to know that they are points along the way in a story that will give them meaning in the end. The structure of narrative is one of intensification of drive through to a climactic release followed by a relaxation. It may take years to complete some autobiographic works, but if you keep writing, you will eventually come to a place of liberation, and it is well to keep that in mind. Autobiographic stories don't require happy endings, but they do require a reason for being, a purpose. Knowing the end of the story means that even if a painful memory temporarily casts a pall over your present while you are writing it—and it well may—it is only a point in the story, not the entire story.

The phenomenon of how the end of a story colors the entire content intrigued Jan Oxenberg, an experimental autobiographic filmmaker, in *Thank-You and Good-Night,* an imaginative documentary about her family's reaction to her grandmother's death. In one scene, Jan's brother, a philosopher who still lives at home with mom, speculates whether Grandma's life was happy or unhappy. He says,

> You can't tell if you have had a happy life until the end of the life. If it turns out to have a purpose, then what you thought made you unhappy ends up having made you happy.
> If there is no purpose then you are unhappy.

He decides that Grandma's life was happy even though she griped all the time because her purpose in life was to procreate, and that in having had grandchildren, her life fulfilled its purpose. It's a way of saying that the end of the story changes how we see each part of it. You can demonstrate this for yourself by trying the following exercise. It is a variation of the "Once Upon a Time . . ." fairy tale exercise in Chapter 3.

EXERCISE 17: *The Original Wound*

You are again going to tell a fairy tale that begins "Once upon a time there was a little girl who, a woman who, a little boy who, or a man who . . . ," but this time it is going to be a specific type of fairy tale, the type that begins with a wound. Since, as Jungian James Hillman says, "the wound is the place where the myth and the real life meet," you write in this exercise about a real event in symbolic terms. For example, "Once upon a time there was a little girl whose father cut off her hands . . ." is the fairy tale language I used for exploring how my father's fears silenced my creativity. "Once upon a time there was a boy who was told he must be perfect in order to be loved," is a more direct beginning, but still has the condensation of myth and fairy tale.

You will know what your "original wound" is.

After writing about how it came to be for a paragraph or so, you will, as in all fairy tales, tell the middle part. "As a result of this wound . . ."

The last section, the conclusion, "And in the end . . . ," contains a change and a realization. Most often, a destiny is discovered that could not have been found without the initiating incident of the wound.

If you take yourself, even briefly, through the story process of finding a meaningful inner myth before writing about your deepest wounds, you will be able to write about your bloody amputated hands using your artfully made healing hands of gold. You will be able to write about your despair from the outlook of one who has survived to tell the tale. You will carry the entire narrative within you as you write, and it will give you the perspective you need so that you can use your memories, instead of your memories using—and overwhelming—you.

Be forewarned that there are times when you cannot find that ending. You try to write the story, but you meet repeatedly with frustration. If you are unable to finish the fairy tale or feel that your conclusion is only wishful thinking, let me recommend an additional step I add when I use this exercise in workshops.

After you have written the fairy tale as far as you can—to take it farther would feel inauthentic or forced—make a list of the earth's wounds that bother you the most. For some people it is homeless children, for others it's pollution of the ocean, over-population, abuse of women, economic corruption, needless physical pain, or another societal, political, or human problem.

After you have made your list, read it and circle which of the earth's wounds you have put down has the most resonance for you. Then ask yourself and reflect in your journal: Is there a destiny for me in the path between my original wound and this earth wound?

For some people the answer to this question suggests a destiny that is still unfolding, still ahead.

There are stories that have to wait to be written because the insight that will give the story meaning has not yet come. Perhaps you have not lived it yet. For example, there was a story I had wanted to write for ten years about my relationship with Judy, a friend and business associate who had betrayed me. I knew that dramatically it was a good story because it had a clear adversary and plenty of conflict and passion. I also knew that it would be cathartic for me to write because I had carried my anger toward Judy for ten years, despite writing about her in my journals, my spiritual practices, hours of discussing in therapy how she functioned as my shadow, and my conscious desire to forgive. I could not end my anger toward her, perhaps because I could not find an ending to the story I could live with.

Then, unexpectedly, a film director whom I'd worked with went into business with Judy. He phoned me to request that he be allowed to implement a reconciliation. It gave me a crisis, a decision to make. Now that there was an opportunity to end the years of enmity, I was forced to realize that I did not want to end my anger. When I asked myself why, I came to know the secret that I had been keeping from myself: that I had loved hating Judy, that losing the thrill of that drama would for me be a loss akin to losing the passion of love for someone. Though I chose not to accept the opportunity for reconciliation, my realization gave me a way finally to give the story an ending. I knew it was authentic because I felt a release of long-held tension and, finally, of my anger.

Unfortunately, it can be hard to distinguish between the wrong time to write a story and your reluctance to face certain realizations. If I had not pushed myself by asking myself, "Why don't I want to give up my anger toward Judy?" and "What is the secret I am keeping from myself?" I wouldn't have found the realization I needed, even though the time was right.

So how do you know which it is—not yet time to write the story, or your resistance to going deeper? There is no easy answer. If you try repeatedly and you can't get an ending, you may have to wait. But you need to develop an ear for your own authenticity, and reflect in your journal—Am I refusing an invitation to courage that would pay off? Sometimes the members of your memoir group can give you help with the answer.

Autobiographic writing is full of extremes to eschew. You have to avoid self-delusion on the one side and self-recrimination on the other. You have to enter your pain and stay in it to achieve the best writing, yet, at the same time, keep yourself detached enough not to be overwhelmed.

Emotions from the past can flood autobiographic writers and disable them from writing altogether. Neurologists explain that neurons which transfer experience into memory use receptors which are binding sites for chemicals that affect mood and behavior. The body doesn't necessarily recognize whether its feelings are from present circumstances or from the past. Memories accompanied by a charge of feeling promise a story worth telling, but can threaten emotional flooding. The best writers seem to hold a balance bar over a tightrope; on one end is passion, and on the other, attention to language.

⌒Attention to Language

New Autobiography pushes the boundaries into unexplored areas of human experience, some of them very dark—schizophrenia, autism, depression, self-sabotage. Writers who explore new territory must simultaneously search for a language capable of containing and transforming what might otherwise be impossible to look at. Learning the craft of writing not only enables you to communicate more effectively; it also allows you to explore areas of personal experience you could not otherwise reach.

Writer Nancy Mairs has referred to herself as "the Connoisseur of Catastrophe" and once wrote an essay for *The New York Times* that she only half facetiously titled "The Literature of Personal Disaster." In her memoir *Ordinary Times,* she writes about her own degenerative multiple sclerosis as well as her bouts of agoraphobia and suicidal depression. She begins the memoir at a time when her husband is undergoing chemotherapy for cancer. You might think that such subject matter would make her memoir difficult to read. Yet look at how inviting she has made these devastating opening pages, through precision of language and light memories mixed with dark.

> "You will love me?" my husband asks, and at something in his tone my consciousness rouses like a startled cat, ears pricked, pupils round and onyx-black.
>
> Never voluble, he has been unusually subdued this evening. Thinking him depressed about the mysterious symptoms that have plagued him for months and that we know in our heart of hearts signal a re-

currence of cancer, although the tests won't confirm it for several more days, I pressed up against him on the couch and whispered against his neck, "This may be the most troublesome time of our lives, but I'm so happy." This awareness of joy, though it's been growing for several years now, has recently expanded in response to my own failing health. A few weeks ago, pondering the possibility that I might die at any time, I posed myself a new question: *If I died at this very moment, would I die happy?* And the answer burst out without hesitation. Yes! Since then, in spite of my fears, I've felt a new contentment. What more could I ever ask than to give an unequivocal response to such a question?

His silence persisted. "Scared?" I asked him after a few moments, thinking of the doctor's appointment that morning, the CAT scan scheduled for later in the week. Head resting on the back of the couch, eyes closed, he nodded. More silence. Finally I said, "George, you know how I love words. I need words?"

And now, words: "You will love me?" Behind his glasses, his eyes have the startled look I associate, incongruously, with the moment of orgasm.

"Yes," I tell him, alert, icy all over. "I can safely promise you that. I will always love you."

"You asked the other day whether my illness could be AIDS," he says unevenly. "I'm pretty sure it isn't because I had the test for HIV some time ago, after I had an affair for a couple of years with another woman."

The sensation is absolutely nonverbal, but everybody knows it even without words: the stunned breathlessness that follows a jab to the solar plexus. What will astonish me in the days to come is that this sensation can sustain itself long after one would expect to be dead of asphyxiation. I have often wished myself dead. If it were possible to die of grief, I would die at this moment. But it's not, and I don't.

Asked in an interview what she believes separates good literature about personal suffering from voyeuristic or sentimental books of this kind, Mairs replied, "For me it has a lot to do with language and the capacity to use language in ways that distinguish one's experience from other people's, so that you get a kind of combination going of identification . . . because all readers have sorrows and pain of their own, and yet the reader is excited by the very individuality of the voice talking about these common experiences."

For Mairs, transcendence is found through accuracy of perception and language. Her work demonstrates that the transformation of memory, no matter how ugly or painful, into something beautifully crafted offers mastery over experience and a liberation that is very different from the easy happy ending of a cliché.

Emotional Flooding

Nevertheless, there are times when your language is as precise and faceted as a cut ruby and you are writing to a healing realization, when still the pain bleeds into the present so that you feel you will expire. For the remainder of this chapter, I am going to suggest techniques that are external to the writing itself. Each is a way to take a break and nurture yourself if you begin to drown in your emotions.

• Make a practice of doing meditation or repeating self-created affirmations before and after writing sessions.

• Spill your feelings in your journal. Dialog with your figure of inner wisdom for advice or with your inner adult for protective guidance.

• Discuss your feelings with members of your memoir group.

• Look for humor in the situation you are remembering or in your present reaction to it.

• Contain your writing. This is in the category of one-day-at-a-time, baby steps, assembly work, and war rations. It means you divide your work into small sections, and when you have completed a section, you stop and don't let yourself write any more.

(I suggested this plan to Clarissa, an intense young woman who lived alone and feared having another nervous breakdown as she had had seven years before. She was a romantic who would isolate herself for days of nonstop writing and sometimes produce amazingly passionate, original work. But too often she would become so overwrought by her emotions that she could not write and instead went into a dangerous depression. By containing her writing to seven pages a day, she was forced to maintain a healthier balance in her life. She consciously instructed herself not to allow her emotions to spill over into the rest of her day, which she was to fill with constructive activities. The plan kept her attentive to the craft of writing, and what she produced was better than her uncontrolled outpourings.)

• Get off your butt and get some exercise—walking, running, dancing, yoga, whatever works for you to discharge pent-up energy. I take gardening breaks; there's nothing better than pulling weeds or transplanting a gardenia bush. But you may prefer an aerobics tape.

• Make lists of moments of joy that happened within the period you are writing about—and in your present life. You will find that almost all such moments come from your senses.

14

Writing the Body

The body does not lie. If you can articulate the feelings in your body, present or past, you can generally reach your own complex truth. Even if you did not know your feelings at the time, they were recorded by your body, so that if you can consult the sensations you felt and identify them now, you can uncover what is, what was, real. In one of the personal essays in *Voice Lessons,* Nancy Mairs writes, "Fortunately one cannot *be* without being a body. One simply *is* blood, thud of heart, lick of tongue, brain humped and folded into skull. And it is as a body that one inhabits the past and it inhabits one's body...." Even if one has lived within a mind cut off from the body, the body has been there all along, a seismograph recording every emotional temblor.

I have lived most of my life in a guillotined head, but I have learned to recover my feelings by consciously interrogating my body. Let me demonstrate. Some time ago I submitted a business proposal to someone who rejected it over the phone. When I put down the receiver, I felt restless and confused, my nerves on edge as when the dog whines unceasingly at the door. To understand what I was feeling, I needed to consult the sensations in my body. There was that elevator plunge in the stomach that goes with failure, but something else. My breathing had slowed and my shoulders had not slumped so much as relaxed. Relief. I had felt relief as well as disappointment. Now I had to ask myself, why had I felt relief? Because the success of the proposal would have curtailed my own writing. I could only get to that complex mixture of frustration and relief peculiar to that moment through examining the feelings in my body.

Because feelings are intangible, we must rely on figurative language to express what otherwise could not be conveyed. The good news is that in finding imagery to express bodily sensations, we can know and express our true feelings. The bad news is the difficulty of finding fresh language to communicate the poetry of nerves. Here we fall into a cliché pit. We are assailed by phrases from other writers who realized the importance of finding imagery for feelings, but could not come up with something new: "My head swam," "It was with a heavy heart," "I blushed crimson," "My soul [where is that?] lifted."

The surest way *not* to find one's true feelings, past or present, is to write in clichés. Deny yourself the old chestnuts, and you will be forced to come up with your own imagery and language. Admittedly it is work; you may have to dig. Here is an exercise that will help.

EXERCISE 18: *Free-Write a Feeling*
Let us say you want to describe your feelings upon meeting the gaze of a person for whom you felt a compelling physical attraction. Immediately all the clichés come to mind. "Our eyes locked and I felt a bolt of electricity go through me." You reject that cliché and all the others that follow. Instead, you direct yourself to do some "free intuitive writing" on the sensations you recall. Let it be nonsense written at 90 mph. Embrace rubbish and absurdity in the attempt to find fresh imagery for your feelings.

I found myself grinning whooey! black hair, blue eyes, that Elvis, po' white trash mouth. He must have seen my pupils diffuse like spilled ink he flashed no his smile pulled me in like a flounder in a net, shimmying, gleaming, arcing as if in ecstasy. He wore army fatigues and thick-soled boots, dressed for dangerous adventure. It was December but my limbs felt light and free as when I wear a sleeveless sundress in July.

Now I might use none of this, and try again another time, or I might find a usable phrase or image. The only one I like here is "His smile pulled me in like a flounder in a net." The point is that while the exercise allows clichés to enter as they will, "black hair, blue eyes," "dangerous adventure," it also enables you to swerve away, using the clichés as a signal to take another route, "he flashed no his smile pulled me in like a flounder . . ."

A Fresh Language for the Senses

Autobiographic writing explores the secret dark places of human experience, but it also celebrates the joy of being human, of being a creature of the natural world. The pleasure of reading experiential writing is not only to enter into how another person thinks and feels, but to know what it is like to perceive through their senses. Reading Diane Ackerman's *A Natural History of the Senses* allows me to live within her keenly tuned body for a time, and later I am more alive to my own body. She writes:

> I woke one morning this winter after a sudden heavy snowfall to see the evergreens in front of my house bent in half under a burden of snow and ice. Unless I freed them, they would snap under their own weight, so I took a shovel and started bashing the branches to shake the snow down. Suddenly one of the heaviest branches let fly, and snow burned my face like sunlight, iced and clung and kept on pouring as I stood, chin tilted toward the dam-burst, pillar-calm, with my every sense alert. But what a puzzle for the neighbor boy, jarred from his play by that basso whump!, to see a madwoman gripped by her own storm. Out of the corner of my eye, I saw him wrinkle his face, then ravel his sled-tow and tramp away. For me, time did a lazy soft-shoe; long minutes seemed to pass, and I thought of mammoths, goose down, Ice-Age cunning, the long white drawl of a glacier on the move, snow avalanching down a polar chasm. For him, the same moment fled like a gnat.

The gift of writers like Ackerman is to slow time to a lazy soft-shoe for the rest of us who have been racing through, inattentive to the wonder of being a body alive in a world of infinite pleasures. We are creatures who originally came from the sea and should exist in an unceasing tide of sensations. Instead, we die slowly from sensual asphyxiation. Some autobiographic writers remind us how to breath in the world through all our senses.

Other writers perceive the world most intensely through one sense, and teach us its range. For example, Sandra Cisneros uses the sense of smell exquisitely in her autobiographic short-story collections, *Woman Hollering Creek* and *The House on Mango Street*. Here she is describing an abandoned garden.

. . . Thorn roses and thistle and pears. Weeds like so many squinty-eyed stars and brush that made your ankles itch and itch until you washed with soap and water. There were big green apples hard as knees. And everywhere the sleepy smell of rotting wood, damp earth and dusty hollyhocks thick and perfumy like the blue-blond hair of the dead.

⌒ Writing about True Sex

Although many autobiographic writers can be specific about places they've seen, dinners they've consumed, and shirts they've stained, they lose their voice when writing about sex. If writing in your natural voice is like talking on the page, there's a rub. Most people do not talk expressively about their sexuality, and can't write about it either.

If they don't avoid the topic altogether, writing about sex takes many writers to a Neverland. They use descriptions so generic they could be about anyone. This doesn't present a problem if sexuality is thematically irrelevant in your work. It does if you are writing about intimate, sexual relationships and all you can do is coyly fade to black when it comes to a consummation scene. I recall working with a writer who turned out the lights so often on such scenes that it drew attention to his sudden loss of candor. I encouraged him to take a less Victorian approach. The next time we met, he had expanded an eighteen-page chapter to forty, and all the additional pages were one sex scene. When I read it, I felt as if I had entered another book, a pornographic paperback. The writer's voice had disappeared and an impersonal description of lovemaking moves and positions had usurped it. Not having a personal language for sexuality, the writer had borrowed the general, clichéd language of pornography. We went back to turning out the lights.

Anaïs Nin and Henry Miller were the first autobiographic writers to give sexuality a personal voice in English; she in her published *Diaries* and he in his autobiographic novels, *Tropic of Cancer* and *Tropic of Capricorn*. They were lovers, and their books and correspondence suggest the power of writing to intensify passion and the power of passion to intensify writing. Here from their exchanged letters about the same meeting, collected in *A Literate Passion,* they recreate each other's bodies with words.

From Miller to Nin:

Fragments race through my mind—I can't think anything through. Your saying once that the Spanish woman liked her man to come to her with the smell of wine on his lips. . . . Description of yourself walking through Paris and the tips of your breasts taut and tingling. Feeling, as I read your book, that for the first time I was going to know what are a woman's sensations in love. . . . Asking myself over and over, does she look at men always with those steady eyes? . . . And then, invitation to walk through the country—to walk, not through the country, but to some obscure inn, to waylay you with wine, smell out your arab blood. Your blood—I want a smear of it to put under the microscope. Once you came within a foot of me, face to face, the back of a chair between us—how did I ever restrain myself?

From Nin to Miller:

Aware of you, chaotically. I love this strange, treacherous softness of you which always turns to hatred. How did I single you out? I saw you with that intense selective way—I saw a mouth that was at once intelligent, animal, and soft . . . strange mixture—a human man, sensitively aware of everything . . . a man, I told you, whom life made drunk. Your laughter was not a laughter which could hurt, it was mellow and rich. I felt warm, dizzy, and I sang within myself. You always said the truest and deepest things—slowly—and you have a way of saying, like a southerner—hem, hem—trailingly, while off on your own introspective journey—which touched me.

This autobiographic writing is effective as seduction because it is specific, not generic.

Today's personal essayists, such as Phillip Lopate, Nancy Mairs, and Bernard Cooper, explore the wild zone of eroticism with greater realism and craft than Miller or Nin. Here is Cooper describing the first time he slept with a girl. It's from an essay titled "Truth Serum," which first appeared in *Harper's*, about his relationships with women before he'd professed his homosexuality.

. . . Alison showed up at my Brooklyn dormitory wearing a skimpy white dress. . . . She'd been visiting her cousins on Long Island and wanted to surprise me. "You're hilarious," she said when I suggested she stay in the guest room at the end of the hallway. She flopped onto my bed. Kicked off her shoes. Fixed me in her bright green gaze. Flipped her hair to and fro like a flag.

We batted her overnight bag off the bed, and it skidded across the floor. Articles of clothing arced through the air. I tried, with brusque adjustments of my hips, to disguise any tentativeness when I entered her. It's now or never, I remember thinking. Her vagina was silky, warm, and capacious. It struck me that my penis might be too small to fill her in the way she wanted, and just when I thought that this tightening knot of self-consciousness might make the act impossible, she let out a yelp of unabashed pleasure. I plunged in deeper, single-minded as a salmon swimming upstream. My hands swept the slope of Alison's shoulders, the rise of her breasts. I didn't realize it until afterward, but I had sucked her neck the entire time, fastened by my lips to a bucking girl. Alison's climax was so protracted, her moans so operatic, her nails so sharp as they raked my back, that when she sat up and felt her neck I thought she was checking her pulse. Suddenly, she rose and ran to the bathroom, a swath of bed sheet trailing in her wake. "I told you," she shrieked, her voice resounding off the tile walls. She appeared in the doorway, legs in a wide, defiant stance, nipples erect. "I told you, no hickies!"

"No, you didn't."

"I said it right at the beginning."

"Then I didn't hear you, Alison."

She held her hand to her neck, Cleopatra bitten by an asp. "What am I going to do?" Her voice was about to break. "What am I going to tell my cousins?"

It was preposterous; she had come to Brooklyn to seduce me, and now Alison was mortified by the small, sanguine badge of our abandon. I said I was sorry.

" 'Sorry' isn't going to take it away."

"What about this," I said, turning to show her the marks I could feel scored into my back.

"Oh, great," she said. "Let's compare war wounds." She bent down and scooped up her white dress; it lay on the floor like a monstrous corsage. "You men," she said bitterly.

Forgive me, I was flattered. Placed at last in a class from which I'd felt barred.

As this passage illustrates, the keys to writing about sexuality are the same as for all good autobiographic writing: be specific and vulnerable, say what you dare not say, and avoid clichés altogether. It is *intimacy* that makes personal writing sexy. That means a willingness to use precise language about our bodies and to explore *all* our feelings, even if we fear they are not all appropriate to the situation.

Knowing that women in particular have been proscribed from knowing and writing their bodies, and that it has caused them to trivialize this enormously important aspect of their experience, Nancy Mairs consciously set out to write the autobiography of her body in *Remembering the Bone House*. She regrets that women have not claimed their own bodies and quotes the French feminist Helene Cixous: "Women haven't had eyes for themselves. They haven't gone exploring in their house. Their sex still frightens them. Their bodies, which they haven't dared enjoy, have been colonized." So Mairs reclaims her body by writing it, her specific body crippled by multiple sclerosis and other assorted ailments. In her words, "I can write only from this body as it is now: female, white, well-educated, moderately prosperous, crippled, a Roman Catholic convert, heterosexual."

By the end of *Remembering the Bone House,* Mairs has achieved her goal of writing her body and has been changed by having done so. At a conference where she is to address the National Multiple Sclerosis Society, she realizes that at last she feels like some*body,* not because she is a celebrity (she isn't) but because *through writing her body she has become it,* "A difficult body, to be sure, almost too weak now to stand, increasingly deformed, wracked still by gut spasms and headaches and menstrual miseries. But some body. Mine. Me." The last sexual encounter described in the memoir follows her newly found sense of self-assurance and her husband's recent surgery for melanoma. It is specific to those aspects of their life and has the intimacy of sex between people who have been married and loved each other, less and more, for over twenty-five years. This is the intimacy possible in autobiographic writing.

I press my breasts and belly against George's back, my pubis against his buttocks, my knees against the backs of his knees. Reaching over his hips, I take his limp cock in my hand and rub the tip with my thumb. This must be why I love to wear silk above all other fabrics, its slip against my skin the nearest I can come to this softness.

We've been trying to have intercourse. No use. Stroking, squirming, tongue-thrusting, murmuring. But he couldn't get hard. "I want you," he whispered against my face. Twice he rolled between my legs and tried to coax his cock into me, but it flopped in his fingers. Usually it pops up hard at the first caress, but today he's had an upset stomach and no amount of willpower has overcome the effects of queasiness. I climbed into bed planning on a quick good-night kiss and sleep, but he reached for me and held on.

I've caressed him with my fingers, my tongue, my words: "I wish I weren't crippled." Murmuring, "I wish I were still strong enough to kiss you starting at the top, all the way down, then up the other side." Nothing. He laughed a little at himself, but his gestures felt impatient.

"Roll over," I said to him finally. He turned his back to me and curled up. Now I have his recalcitrant cock cradled in my palm. It moves a little at my touch, and the tension of desire his stroking and sucking have aroused starts beating between my legs.

"Oh God, I'm coming just by touching you," I breathe. He reaches back and slides his finger into the slit between my legs and I push at it hard. Tonight, wouldn't you know, I want his erection inside me, pushing through the tunnel and against the arch of my vagina. This is the image of my insides I get during lovemaking: a tunnel through a dark and reddish arch. Like some street in Casablanca, maybe, though of course I've never been there. But I'm not going to get that. Still, I'm getting a lot.

His cock is stiffening. I feel for the drop of fluid at the tip and smooth it all over the silky swelling head. I stroke his foreskin forward, pull it back. Forward. Back. His breathing thickens. His buttocks thrust back into my pelvis. I keep coming in sporadic soft bursts, stroking, squeezing, stroking. All of a sudden I know he's made it.

"Here I come again," I gasp. Fluid wells out of his cock and I catch it in my palm to lubricate the whole shaft. Shudder. Shudder. Sweet slippery semen. Breath trembling, slowing.

"For once I've got the wet spot on my side," he laughs.

"Oh, it's not so bad." I stroke his buttock with my wet hand. "Actually, come feels kind of nice, see?"

"Till it gets cold."

Explicit as this passage is, it is completely unlike pornography, which severs sexuality from the rest of human experience. The scene Mairs writes is specific to its unique moment and to everything else going on in the couple's lives, physically, emotionally, spiritually. Ironically, Puritanism's prohibition of the erotic side of life tends to create what it abhors. In banishing the sexual from the rest of human experience, sexuality becomes separated out as pornography.

Our body's other senses, too, have been isolated from the natural world. Shut up in concrete buildings, breathing AC air, touching only synthetic surfaces, the body is starved. Lured constantly by media images of sex, food, and violence, it is no wonder people seem obsessed with only these experiences of the body.

In consciously exploring her body in all its dimensions, Nancy Mairs, like many people who come alive to their bodies, discovered that eroticism has a more global meaning for her than language usually permits.

> I lie in bed, run across a playground, eat favorite foods, listen to the radio, tease my sister, roll in new snow. All these acts, happening to me as a body, shaping my awareness of my embodied self, form my erotic being. It is that process I seek in all my writing to capture and comprehend: how living itself takes on an erotic tone.

Living itself takes on an erotic tone when we use writing to conjoin body, mind, and soul divided by puritan tradition.

⁓The Expanded Body

A new "ecological memoir" has arisen from a desire to reintegrate the body with the soul and the natural world. The new ecological memoir manifests the concept of Gaia, all parts of the earth interlinked as one organism. Terry Tempest Williams's ecological memoir, *Refuge: An Unnatural History of Family and Place,* contains an expanded concept of self that extends to the world she lives in. The memoir relates her mother's death from cancer (both mother and daughter had been exposed to atomic testing) with the decline of Tempest Williams's personal refuge, an endangered bird sanctuary on the eastern shore of Great Salt Lake. Each chapter is named for a different bird, and the writer's voice is their song as much as her own. In Tempest Williams's writing, the boundary between the self and nature dissolves.

> ... The lake is like steel. I wrap my alpaca shawl tight around my face until only my eyes are exposed. I must keep walking to stay warm. Even the land is frozen. There is no give beneath my feet.
>
> I want to see the lake as Woman, as myself, in her refusal to be tamed. The State of Utah may try to dike her, divert her waters, build roads across her shores, but ultimately, it won't matter. She will sur-

vive us. I recognize her as a wilderness, raw and self-defined. Great Salt Lake strips me of contrivances and conditioning, saying, "I am not what you see. Question me. Stand by your own impressions."

We are taught not to trust our own experiences. Great Salt Lake teaches me experience is all we have.

Experience is all we have, and it is only through our bodies that we have it, and only through our senses that we can know and convey it.

15

Theme: String for Your Pearls

Theme" is the conceptual string that runs through and holds a work together; loosen it or break it, and the work tends to fall apart. Whereas story is the growth of character, theme is the development of an idea. Story provides the mythic and emotional skeleton for autobiographic writings; theme provides conceptual coherence. Knowing your theme helps you include only those incidents, characters, and scenes that can be hung on it. It is your premise for deciding what to put in your work and what to leave out.

Thornton Wilder said, "A good story is life without the bla bla." Autobiographic writing is the easiest form of narrative, except for this problem: you have the most bla bla. Russell Baker advises from his own experience, "Anything that is autobiographical is the opposite of biography. The biographer's problem is that he never knows enough. The autobiographer's problem is that he knows much too much. He knows absolutely everything; he knows the whole iceberg, not just the tip. . . . So when you're writing about yourself, the problem is what to leave out." You know more about yourself than you would ever have time to write.

Annie Dillard concurs. Speaking about writing her memoir, *An American Childhood,* Dillard offers, "I leave out many things that were important to my life but of no concern for the present book, like the summer I spent in Wyoming when I was fifteen. I keep the action in Pittsburgh; I see no reason to drag everybody off to Wyoming just because I want to tell them about my summer vacation. You have to take pains in a memoir not to hang on the reader's

arm, like a drunk, and say, 'And then I did this and it was so interesting.' "
You have to be ruthless in deciding what to leave in and what to leave out.

It is as simple as rummaging through a stuffed, long-ignored bureau and
deciding what to keep and what to toss—and as difficult. Janet Malcolm, in
an extended essay in *The New Yorker*, ponders the writer's housecleaning problem.

> Each person who sits down to write faces not a blank page but his
> own vastly overfilled mind. The problem is to clear out most of what
> is in it, to fill huge plastic garbage bags with the confused jumble of
> things that have accreted there over the days, months, years of being
> alive and taking things in through the eyes and ears and heart. The
> goal is to make a space where a few ideas and images and feelings may
> be so arranged that a reader will want to linger awhile among them,
> rather than to flee. . . . But this task of housecleaning (of narrating) is
> not merely arduous; it is dangerous. There is the danger of throwing
> the wrong things out and keeping the wrong things in; there is the
> danger of throwing too much out and being left with too bare a house;
> there is the danger of throwing everything out. Once one starts throw-
> ing out, it may become hard to stop. It may be better not to start. It
> may be better to hang on to everything.

But, as Malcolm goes on to realize, if you hang on to everything, you will
never write. The angst of ruthless selection creates the visceral nausea and
resistance that every writer knows. The fear of making the choices—right
or wrong—is "the fear felt by the writer who cannot risk beginning to
write."

Though Malcolm will likely chafe to have her metaphor pulled from its
literary context and adapted in a how-to book, her housecleaning analogy
irresistibly suggests an exercise to help isolate theme.

EXERCISE 19: *Life Sorting*

*Imagine you are filling two containers, one a box of what you want to put in your
work, the other a garbage bag of what you want to leave out. In your creative journal, make two lists, one labeled "In," the other "Out." Write quickly—you can always change your mind and pull something back out of either list. As Malcolm points
out, unlike living your life, writing about it provides abundant opportunities for revi-
sion.*

Since I am in this reckless mode of concocting illustrations from the literary hoi polloi, let me pull my example for this trash-sorting exercise from Annie Dillard. In talking about her process in writing *An American Childhood*, Dillard said she consciously decided what to leave in and what to leave out. I've reduced her choices to two lists.

What to leave in:

- *A child's interior life*
- *The child's growing awareness of the world*
- *The American landscape*
- *The sensation of time pelting me as if I were standing under a waterfall*
- *Pittsburgh, the Alleghenies*
- *River men*
- *Scotch-Irish Presbyterians*
- *Money, just to make trouble*
- *Books*
- *Rock collecting*
- *My parents*
- *Industry, wrought iron*
- *The influence of the great industrialists on Pittsburgh*

What to leave out:

- *Social history, lyrics or titles of popular songs, names of radio and TV programs*
- *Product names, clothing fashions*
- *Myself*
- *My private involvement with various young men*
- *Anything that might trouble my family*

An equally accomplished writer might decide to leave in everything that Annie Dillard decided to leave out. Dillard's decision to leave out "myself" and "anything that might trouble my family" makes her text—careful and poetic as it is—rarefied. It's not nearly as engaging as it would have been had she put herself in. But, as she says, she had decided to use *An American Childhood* to investigate a certain idea—how a child moves from an awareness of her interior landscape to an awareness of the American landscape around her. This idea was her theme, and she felt her individuality was not relevant to it. The result is that *An American Childhood,* though book length, is an extended personal essay about an idea, rather than a story about a person.

In the hands of a writer less skillful than Annie Dillard, this very long essay about an idea might have become abstract and ponderous. For that is what happens when one writes *directly* about an idea. Generations of students think they hate composition because we were told in school to write directly about ideas, to write "themes" on assigned topics. Writing was used to teach us to think logically, a very good use for language, but one that completely ignores all the other marvelous uses of words—to express passion or subtle, ambiguous feelings, to discover personal truths, to tell stories, to capture how the human mind works. The informational *formal* essays we were instructed to write leveled us all to the same flat style of expression.

Though Annie Dillard says she leaves herself out of *An American Childhood,* it is a *personal* essay because she writes with breathtaking specificity about her perceptions. As Phillip Lopate explains, "How the world comes at another person, the irritations, jubilations, aches and pains, humorous flashes—these are the classic building materials of the personal essay. We learn the rhythm by which the essayist receives, digests, and spits out the world, and we learn the shape of his or her privacy."

In other words, personal essays, like all autobiographic writing, proceed by beats of feelings and realizations rather than by the *logical* development of ideas. Annie Dillard says she was motivated to write *An American Childhood* in order to explore the concept of waking up in childhood and "noticing that you've been put down in a world that's already underway." However, she explores that concept through her senses rather than through the progression of logical argument.

> Whenever I stepped into the porcelain bathtub, the bath's hot water sent a shock traveling up my bones. The skin on my arms pricked up, and the hair rose on the back of my skull. I saw my own firm foot press the tub, and the pale shadows waver over it, as if I were looking down from the sky and remembering this scene forever. The skin on my face tightened, as it had always done whenever I stepped into the tub, and remembering it all drew a swinging line, loops connecting the dots, all the way back. You again.

Though she believes that a literary work exists in the service of an idea, Dillard knows better than to write directly about the idea. She advises:

It is especially helpful if the writer so fully expresses the idea in materials that only a trained technician can find it. Because the abstract structure of a given text, which is of great interest to the writer and serves to rouse him out of bed in the morning and impel him to the desk, is of little or no interest to the reader, and he'd better not forget it.

In formal essays, such as the themes we wrote at school, the thematic idea *is* the work; it is the surface as well as the structure. But in autobiographic writing, including narratives and personal essays, theme is best kept unseen, providing a structural girder, while what is visible is the casement of character, dialog, imagery, and scene.

However, this construction analogy is flawed, for with a building you must have the girder in place before you make your casement, whereas in autobiographic writing most of my students do just the opposite. Many are not aware that there is a thematic concept running within their work until after they have written a large portion of it. They dash from the starting block inspired by specific memories and may speed ahead for weeks or months. Inevitably they do become stymied when at some point they face a juncture where there are too many possible directions to go in and no way to choose.

You, too, may find a time where you hit a memory web site where the options are overwhelming, and you will slow to a halt. That is the time to retrace your steps to figure out your theme from what you have set down. Once you've discovered your thematic string, you can stretch it forward as a guideline for completing your work.

This inspired start and stop sudden pattern is like that of a recurrent flying dream I had as a child. I knew how to soar as long as I didn't think about how I was flying. Arms outstretched, feet kicking occasionally as when swimming, I swept over roads and trees, over swimming pools and lawn furniture, out over open fields of rye grass. I was exhilarated and confident; none of the wolves and demons that haunted my nightmares could get me up there. Then—why couldn't I learn?—I made the very mistake I had tried to remember not to repeat. I began to wonder, how could I be flying? I tried to study my own technique so I wouldn't crash, but by becoming self-conscious, I forfeited my buoyancy. My body lowered toward the ground like a balloon losing air until in despair I felt wet grass on my bare feet. Overcharged with the adrenaline of panic, I froze, as a wolf, mouth slavering as in a cartoon, charged out of the bushes. I had to force my little girl legs to move, until I could get them to run, run for my life, though I could not leave the ground.

As the wolf gained on me, I consciously replayed in my mind how it was I had been able to fly. I would analyze my technique again, even though it was that mistake that had grounded me in the first place. And mystery of mysteries, I would remember! The very intellectual effort that had lost me my flight in the first place was the only way I could retrieve it. As I felt the pressure of air beneath my stomach and angled my face to the sky, my confidence returned, tarnished now with wariness, but accompanied with knowledge.

Writing from inspiration is like dream flying; in the midst of it, it seems nothing can ever ground you. This is the transcendence that lures and addicts one to writing. Woe be to those who stop in the rush of inspiration to think about why the writing is working. They will crash as surely as I did in my dream. On the other hand, it is when you find yourself grounded, when you have lost your way and doubt yourself, that it is valuable to go back to search for the intellectual construct of theme in your work.

The intellectual construct I figured out in my dream about flying is similar in a way to what you must discern. I'd tried to propell myself off the ground by kicking; it didn't work. I'd tried getting wind resistance from stretching my arms; no go. What I realized, only in the nick of time, was that it wasn't just *one* thing that gave me forward motion, it was the friction of *two* things at once. And this is what you need to realize about theme: It isn't one idea—it is two opposing ideas together, a dialectic. To generate energy, a thematic string needs to have positive and negative strands entwined. To drive a work, a theme must contain conflict.

As Hegel explained in *The Science of Logic,* "It is only because a thing contains a contradiction within itself that it moves and acquires impulse and activity. That is the process of all motion and all development." Like the opposition between you and your antagonist, the conflict between two underlying concepts or values propels your work forward. So instead of thinking of theme as a single string running through your work, think of it as a twine, a black and a white strand coiled together.

⌒Thematic Conflict

"I don't like to think of my life as conflict. I prefer to say 'encounter,'" a man protested in one of my classes. I said he could use whatever word he liked, but that by using the word "conflict," I didn't mean to suggest arguments or fights, although they can be expressions of thematic conflict. I didn't necessarily mean negative experience, either. You can be so in love, so filled with the thrill of being alive that you are pained by life's brevity. That's a thematic conflict—two opposing ideas.

Annie Dillard's *An American Childhood* doesn't contain a single fight or argument, as I recall, yet it has thematic conflict. The theme isn't one idea; it's a dialectic of two opposing ideas: the child unconscious inside herself versus the child conscious of herself as part of the ongoing world. "Who could ever tire of this heart-stopping transition," she writes, "of this breakthrough shift between seeing and knowing you see, between being and knowing you be? . . . this surfacing to awareness and this deliberate plunging to oblivion— the theater curtain rising and falling?" No one could tire of it because this movement between polarities in her essay excites energy.

When you search for your theme in your work, notice where the writing has energy, where it feels alive. Look there for a recurrent and central conflict of values. Then see if you can express the conflict as two related ideas in opposition. For example, "With passion, jealousy is inevitable; yet jealousy kills love." Feel how stating your theme as a conflict invites you to think dramatically.

Often in a story, theme is created when the values inherent in your desire line come into conflict with values opposed to it. Your desire contains a thesis and the barrier to achieving the desire contains its antithesis. I asked several of my students to express the theme of their work as an opposition of ideas. Notice how in each statement of theme, what the writer desired suggests a value system in opposition to what impeded the desire.

ADRIANNA NERY: My desire to be part of the white world versus my need to know myself as a black woman.

HANH HOANG: Growing up in Vietnam I fantasized about and loved everything American, though my real experience of American culture was destructive.

BRASON LEE: My determination to overcome the problems inflicted by my head injury versus the reality of permanent damage I'd received.

Sometimes the dilemma inherent in a dramatic theme is expressed as a question.

Lois Henley: How did I keep the space I needed to grow as an individual, yet stay close enough to Clyde to keep love alive in our marriage?

Once you have a clear notion of your theme as a double strand running through your work, you will be able to use it to choose those elements—characters, images, scenes, and dialogs—that contribute to the development of your thematic conflict and exclude those that don't.

What do I mean by the development of your thematic conflict? I mean, forgive me, the dialectic of thesis and antithesis leading to a synthesis. Come again? I told you it's ponderous to write directly about ideas. My students' eyes glaze over when I quote that Hegelian construct, so let me demonstrate what I mean experientially with a fascinating exercise:

EXERCISE 20: *The Story You Were Told*
In your creative journal, intuitively answer the following questions in a paragraph or less:

1. *What was the story the world you grew up in told you that you should become? (By "world" I mean your environment, including your parents or whoever raised you, and the society, class, and culture in which you grew up. What was the message you got from them of who you should be?)*
2. *What was the story of who you should become that you told yourself?*
3. *What is the story life has told you of who you are?*

Read over your answers. Is what you told yourself the same or the opposite of what you were told? Is what life has told you a creative combination of your previous answers?

While there are some fortunate people for whom the story they told themselves is virtually the same as that told to them, for most their answer to the second question is in opposition to the first. What they were told is a thesis. What they told themselves is its antithesis (its opposite), and what they learned from life is a synthesis, a new idea that contains elements of both sides of the conflict.

Here are sample responses:

1. *I was told I should become a bank teller.*
2. *I told myself I would be a famous movie star.*
3. *Life has told me that I am a romantic who keeps my feet on the ground.*

1. I was told that boys are superior to girls; that they can become president of the United States or a famous physicist, but a girl could not. I was told that to succeed in life I would have to win the love of a successful man.

2. I told myself that though no one knew it, a mistake had been made and that I had a boy's brain inside a girl's body, so that I could do what other women could not do—I was different from all other women.

3. Life has told me that I am quite intelligent, but that emotionally I am just like other women, and I have not fulfilled my potential because most of my time and energy has been spent seeking the approval and acceptance of men.

Notice that in each case the story the writer told herself appears to be a reaction against what she had been told. It is humbling to realize that the story you told yourself is no more freely chosen or necessarily right than the story told to you. It was the inevitable antithesis to the first thesis. Notice, also, that the answer to the third question, which comes out of the writer's life experience, contains a new idea that merges parts of each earlier idea, a synthesis.

Probably unconsciously, Russell Baker used this very formula when he rewrote his initial draft of *Growing Up.* Thematically, you can look at *Growing Up* this way.

The story Russell's mother told him of who he should be: Ambitious, hard-working, someone who pulls himself up by the bootstraps and makes something of himself.

The story Russell told himself of who he should be: Someone who takes the easy way, gets the best of life without working too hard, maybe a novelist.

The story that life gave him: He became a journalist, one of his mother's ambitions for him, yet a journalist distinguished for his own easy-going style. It is a synthesis because as a newspaperman he combined the self-discipline drummed into him by his mother and his own independence of mind.

One of my students, Anne, a tall twenty-eight-year-old with the features of a *Vogue* model, had written two lively chapters of a memoir about growing up adopted. Then she came to a screeching halt and panicked that she didn't know what she was writing. I asked her to do the exercise above, "The Story You Were Told." Here is what she wrote.

The story I was told: Because you are adopted you are more loved than a natural child.

The story I told myself: Because I am adopted my parents do not really love me.

The story that life has given me: I am worthy of love and my parents loved me in their way, but I felt unloved because their way of perceiving and dealing with the world is so different from what is natural to me.

At first Anne was very excited. She realized that the thesis and antithesis she'd come up with would be perfect for her theme, and immediately she wrote an outline for her book. But by the next class she was again full of self-doubt. She was afraid she couldn't use this particular thematic formula, of the story you were told, the story you told yourself, and the story the world has told you, because it had been done before. It wasn't original. After all, I had demonstrated it to her in Russell Baker's memoir.

It took me nearly half an hour to convince Anne that themes are rarely original. While stories depend on specific events, themes are general life topics. Theme ensures that no matter how unique your personal experience, how unusual your story—or how ordinary—its essence will find resonance in others. By having an identifiable human dilemma at the heart of your story, you can concentrate on what makes you unique and on specific details in the writing. You can select what is surprising and unexpected in your experience without fear of losing the bond of commonality with a reader.

Themes are general life topics, but there are hundreds of them. The formula of "The Story You Were Told" may work for you if, like Anne, you are writing a memoir that includes your childhood. However, if you are writing about your experiences as an adult, it would be irrelevant. For instance, in Peter Mayle's *A Year in Provence,* a combination travelog and humorous memoir, the conflict lies in the opposition of French and British cultural values. This is a good example of how thematic conflict isn't necessarily negative. The fun of Mayle's memoir is in the conflict between the opposing value systems. You never want the conflict to end.

It's so in any autobiographic work. It's not the lesson at the conclusion that is spellbinding; it is the struggle. It seems the rules for living a good life and for writing a good story are in this respect inverted. In a good life, we may seek to avoid conflict or to resolve it as soon as possible. In writing a good story, we seek to find conflict and leave it unresolved as long as possible. So though you may want places where it rests, you don't want to remedy your thematic conflict too soon. You want it to build until one side forces the other into a conflagration. You want to withhold the synthesis of your thesis and antithesis until the very end of your story, or chapter, or book.

So after you have searched for your theme as a conflict of values in your work and expressed it as a dialectic, contemplate the most dramatic way that your dialectic could realistically come together at the end. Remember, and this is important, the coming together in a dramatic work doesn't have to be a compromise where both sides of the dialectic get equal shares. In a drama, unlike a calm negotiation, the ending is a battle of sorts where one side forces the other into submission and then absorbs it. The new idea is more than the addition of its parts.

Usually the synthesis of your thematic conflict coincides with the final resolution of the conflict between you and your antagonist. Story and theme are interconnected. At your conclusion, story and theme should become one, so that your final realization, which accompanies your emotional climax, *is* your synthesis, your new idea.

For example, in Brason Lee's memoir "Without My Helmet," his desire was to overcome the results of his brain injury. His antagonists were the people and situations that reminded him he had not overcome its effects. His thematic conflict was between an optimism so insistent it became denial, and the discouragement of reality. His story and theme came together at his final realization. A crisis was forced when Brason was confronted by the members of a veterans' discussion group he was leading. They demanded to know why he could not remember their names. What was wrong with him; didn't he care about them or his job? (Brason had never told them that he'd been brain injured.) Shaken by this interaction Brason, hitting a low point, retreated to the library where he read devastating articles about his condition.

> My family insisted I had no remaining problems, but reality painted another picture—an image that wouldn't stay away. . . .
>
> Most of the articles did not sound promising about the long-term prognosis. They talked about the drop in employability, the stop in educational advancement, the deficits with information processing. . . .
> Most of them arrived at the same conclusion; people with head injury face a complex range of long-standing social, emotional, mental, physical, and speech problems.
>
> I closed my eyes and began thinking about what I had read and

what I had gone through in my life. . . . I saw myself pushing each leg muscle to move, bouncing a ball with both hands, summarizing what I read in a short paragraph. . . .

I saw myself back at the classrooms at Mesa College, hiding from the laughter of others while sitting at my desk. I took humiliation because I had a goal to meet. . . . Then I saw myself standing on top of my chair at graduation six years later, claiming victory over a mountain that the studies said no one had ever climbed after traumatic head injury. . . .

Head injury was more than a condition I read about in journals. Head injury is about me, about my past, present, and future. I AM HEAD-INJURED! I'd been head-injured since 1981.

I began to see how my denial had released me from dwelling on my disability in order to pursue life's goals. . . . I then saw how the same denial that once worked so well had turned.

I'd pushed myself harder than I could have imagined. Through years of effort, I'd rediscovered the most important part of me, the self who knows that I can still be able and competent. I found that disability does not mean the end of embracing hopes. It does not mean the end of a sense of future. Even with certain impairments, I could still feel proud and accomplished, no matter how big or small the feat. No one can take that from me. I decided I would not take it from myself.

The new idea, the synthesis, is that while Brason acknowledged his residual damage from head injury, his remarkable recovery was possible only because he'd believed it to be possible. The positive value of faith in his abilities wins, but it is tempered with realism, a complex concept that contains both sides of his struggle.

There are writers, of course, who prefer to begin their process with theme. Some writers, and Annie Dillard seems to be one of them, fall in love with an idea and then find a narrative to bring it to life. So if you are having difficulty tracing story in your life, it doesn't mean you can't write autobiographically. Perhaps you will find you like writing personal essays, reflections, or meditations that depend more on theme and don't require a story. Or perhaps you will find that in identifying your theme, the story or stories that express it will emerge. Theme is only an abstract idea that, like a virus, by itself is lifeless, but warmed in flesh can perpetrate a story.

So if you are one of those writers who needs to find an intellectual door into your work, I offer you Exercises 20 and 21, which begin with theme and move you into story. They will also be helpful to writers who have completed a draft of a piece, but find it is blurred and unfocused.

The following exercise leads you to identify thematically coherent stories within your life. Frequently, though you may not be able to find an overall theme that runs through your life, you can find an opposition of values within a particular period.

EXERCISE 21: *Doing Story Splits*

1. *List the major conflicts within yourself.*
2. *Select the pair that has the most energy for you.*
3. *Cluster on each side of the conflict as in the illustration below. (In clustering, you put down a word or phrase, circle it, and link it to another circled word or phrase without worrying about connecting them linguistically. This form of nonlinear free association allows ideas to flow and bypasses self-censorship.) In this exercise you will have two cluster maps, one for each side of your selected conflict.*
4. *Ask yourself what experiences contributed to creating these clustered conflicts. Make a list.*
5. *What people in your life have represented different sides of this conflict? Make a list.*
6. *Finally, make a list of the times you have felt this conflict most acutely. Select one of these times to write as a story.*

Cheryl came into my autobiographic writing group as a latecomer. Already a stringer on medical issues for a West Coast newspaper, she wanted to supplement her income by writing autobiographic short stories for women's magazines. To get her up to speed, I asked her to do the exercise above. Here were her responses:

1. *List the conflicts within yourself.*
   - *Diet—eat what I want*
   - *Freedom—marriage/child*
   - *Religion—abandon*
   - *Money—desire not to work*
   - *City life—live in country*
2. *Select the pair that has the most energy for you.*
   - *Diet—eat what I want*
3. *Cluster on each side of this conflict.*

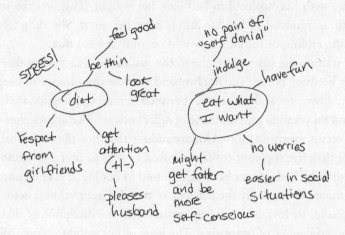

4. *Ask yourself what events or experiences may have contributed to creating this conflict. Make a list.*
   • *Peer pressure*
   • *Social life*
   • *Media messages*
   • *Parent messages—be thin/clean your plate*
   • *Husband*
   • *Health awareness*

5. *What people in your life have represented different sides of this split? Make a list.*

Pressure to Diet	Eat What I Want
Mother	*All are on the other side, too!*
Girlfriends	
Husband	
Co-workers	
Deb	

6. *Finally, make a list of the times you have most acutely felt this conflict. Select one of these times to write as a short story.*
   • *In bed with Bruce.*
   • *He says let's eat out then gets depressed about my weight.*
   • *Emotionally charged situations: work, home, Anna's health.*

Cheryl had brought to that first class a list of "nice" ideas for stories, but after doing this exercise, she abandoned them in favor of writing about her conflict with her husband in bed over her weight. This was the story that was still unresolved in her life and tearing her apart. She didn't yet know what the ending or resolution would be, only the conflict.

In writing the story, she came to the realization that the conflict was not simply between herself and her husband over the importance of keeping her weight down; it was also a conflict between her not wanting to face the problem and his wanting to, a thematic conflict between two approaches—avoidance versus confrontation. Understanding that her theme actually went deeper than the apparent conflict allowed Cheryl to find a resolution in the story that she had not yet been able to find in her life. It turned out that her main theme was actually the dialectic of two different value systems on how to preserve the love in a marriage, rather than the discipline of dieting versus the indulgence of overeating. The issue of her weight was actually a subtheme rather than her main theme. Always stay open to the possibility that the thematic thread you are following may lead you to a deeper theme you have not yet discovered.

In a book-length memoir, each chapter may focus on a subtheme that is an expression of your main theme. This next exercise will help you identify each chapter's theme before or after you write it. Usually if you have written a chapter that feels diffuse, it is because you have not reached the real meaning of what you wanted to say; you have not yet gone deeply enough into the experience; you have not found the chapter's true theme. When you finally understand your theme, you can rewrite with verve—and what you have been trying to say will come up like a Polaroid picture.

The following book chapter exercise is an adaptation of a journal meditation recommended by Ira Progoff for exploring a chapter of your life.

EXERCISE 22: *Finding a Chapter's Theme*

Relax, meditate on your breath, close your eyes, and allow yourself to enter the period in your life to be covered in this chapter. Feel the primary quality of your life at the time. In your creative notebook write the sentence stem, "It was a time when . . ." and record without judgment the tone and circumstances of that period, your hopes and frustrations, your attitude toward life, your beliefs and special relationships, the philosophy that guided your actions, and the events of the period that come to mind. Each time you find yourself hesitating, repeat the phrase "It was a time when . . ." and continue. Allow a metaphor or simile to come to mind that represents the period, "It was a time that was like . . ."

When you have finished, reread what you have written, asking yourself if there was a thematic conflict that seems to run through this period. Try to express that conflict as an opposition of values.

Ask yourself, Does this opposition ever find a synthesis? It could be in the chapter you are contemplating; it could be in a later chapter.

Finally, ask yourself, How does the thematic conflict in this chapter relate to the overall thematic conflict in my book? A chapter's theme may be identical to the book's general theme, or it may be a specific subtheme.

One subtheme contained in nearly every memoir concerns the author's process in writing autobiography. Mary Karr, in her childhood memoir *The Liar's Club*, brings in awareness of her autobiographic process stylistically. As the daughter of a teller of tall tales, she is always conscious that she is telling a tale.

> *My father comes into focus for me on a Liar's Club afternoon. He sits at a wobbly card table weighed down by a bottle. Even now the scene seems so real to me that I can't but write it in the present tense.*

As Karr writes, she allows us into her *process of remembering* and of transforming her memories into writing.

In her memoir, *Paula,* Isabel Allende watches over her comatose twenty-eight-year-old daughter who she fears will have amnesia, if she ever awakens. For Allende, the subtheme of her autobiographic process is inseparable from her main theme—wanting to give her self, her life, to her daughter.

> In the long silent hours, I am trampled by memories, all happening in one instant, as if my entire life were a single, unfathomable image. The child and girl I was, the woman I am, the old woman I shall be, are all water in the same rushing torrent. My memory is like a Mexican mural in which all times are simultaneous: the ships of the Conquistadors in one corner and an Inquisitor torturing Indians in another, galloping Liberators with blood-soaked flags and the Aztecs' Plumed Serpent facing a crucified Christ, all encircled by the billowing smoke-stacks of the industrial age. So it is with my life, a multilayered and ever-changing fresco that only I can decipher, whose secret is mine alone. The mind selects, enhances, and betrays; happenings fade from memory; people forget one another and, in the end, all that remains is the journey of the soul, those rare moments of spiritual revelation. . . . Until now, I have never shared my past; it is my innermost garden, a place not even my most intimate lover has glimpsed. Take

it, Paula, perhaps it will be of some use to you, because I fear that yours no longer exists, lost somewhere during your long sleep—and no one can live without memories.

In a very different way eighty-nine-year-old James Ingebretsen ties the subtheme of the autobiographic process to his main thematic conflict—the dichotomy between his values as a successful lawyer and man of his times versus the value he places on the feminine principle in his soul. It took him fifteen years to write his spiritual autobiography, during which time he recognized that his lawyerly, logical approach to writing would not serve.

Another way of thinking is required of me, a different sort of approach. So as I sit here now, I begin to wonder: In relation to all of the various ideas, intimations, relationships and activities of these eighty-odd years, is it I who am collecting and arranging and reminiscing about all this, or are these ideas and relationships simply using me as a convenient place to meet and mingle in order to go their separate ways toward new places and new meanings?

I see my life as having circumambulated around some kind of evolving core of personal, mythological, archetypal, or symbolic set of "truths," or essential ideas. The very nature of that core defies any simple linear description of the kind that is available to a lawyer logically arguing a conclusion from a given set of facts. . . .

So . . . I engage in this spiraling process of circumlocution over and through these many years of experiences and explorations. Even at this late date, I'm still finding it difficult to refine and clarify all the many threads in which I see the ever-growing interpenetration of relationships, ideas and archetypal images. I seem content to enjoy the ever-widening perspective as, like a soaring falcon, more and more of the terrain becomes visible and related.

. . . in the final analysis, perhaps it is justifiable that a life that takes 80-odd years to live should take 15 years to tell of. This prolonged reflection has granted me a whole new mode of vision, enabling me to experience the world through an imaginal eye. To see that timeless forms inhabit all. To understand that memory contains eternity, and finally to feel no separation between men or women in the realm of soul. I could have written the story of my life then, 15 years ago, but I would have known none of these things.

James Ingebretsen sponsored the work of Joseph Campbell and Ira Progoff, studied philosophy with Gerald Heard, sufism with Pir Vilayat, yoga with Khan Chuan, tai chi with Professor Wen-Shan Hwong, and Gnosticism with Stephan Hoeller. He approached writing memoir as the ultimate spiritual discipline. His experience confirms what I am suggesting to you here: that you can find within your life the timeless forms of myth and the core essential ideas of theme, but not through reason alone. Although I have offered you some formulas for discovering theme, I warn you not to become reductionist about fitting your life into what appears to be a mathematical equation. Far better to take James Ingebretsen's approach of wonder as you write, to leave your work open for the unexpected and as yet unknown to enter. For theme reveals itself as a spiritual mystery does, surfacing explicitly on rare occasions, usually remaining beneath the surface, veiled.

Once you have recognized your thematic conflict, it is something you can pretty much trust to be there. You need not worry about it unless you again become lost. As with a string of pearls, your attention—and your reader's—should be focused on the pearls (your scenes, images, details, and dialog), not the string holding them together. When Elia Kazan opens his full autobiography, *A Life,* he doesn't tell us in a declarative statement that his autobiography is about his lifelong compulsion to grasp whatever was beyond his reach and his inevitable dissatisfaction once he'd seized it. He begins with a "pearl," a dramatic scene that pulls us into his story.

"Why are you mad?"

My wife asks me that, seems like every morning. Usually at breakfast, when my face is still wrinkled from sleep.

"I'm not mad," I say. "It's just my face."

I've said that to her ten times. She's my third wife and I'm happy with her, but she has yet to learn that I don't like to talk in the morning. Which is tough on her, a decent person, full of lively chatter, like bright pebbles.

Confronting me where I'm sitting at my typewriter is a small round mirror, clamped in a pretty but rickety Mex-made stand. It frames my face neatly, and sometimes when I work, I study my image. I certainly look mad.

The fact is I am mad, most every morning, I wake up mad. Still.

This scene contains Kazan's central theme—a driven man frustrated by his inability to be satisfied—as does nearly every other scene in the 825 pages of this remarkably candid autobiography. The scene embodies the idea of Kazan's theme in flesh and blood.

Remember, you want your thematic twine, your coil of opposing black and white strands, to run through your entire work, to penetrate every scene. But you don't want your thematic twine to be noticed. It is there to hold together your pearls, your well-developed scenes. Only they glow; only they can enthrall.

16

Scenepearls

To imagine your story as a fairy tale, you took a sweeping view of your life from a great distance. At the other extreme, in your reverie of a particular memory, you zoomed in close on a single moment. You went from the abstract, overall view of God the Father in the sky, to the concrete, close-up view of God the Mother from inside life and inside the immediate moment. You went from viewing life through a telescope to observing it under a microscope, from the macrocosmic to the microcosmic.

Now I am going to teach you to write in summary and scenes, shifting from one way of perceiving your life to the other as readily as closing one eye and opening the other. A summary is a condensation of what happened, whereas a scene is an expanded moment set at a particular time and place. You are going to learn to use summary and scene alternately, as the novelist does.

Traditionally, autobiography, like journalism, was written in continuous blocks of narrative summary without dramatic scenes and dialog. But modern readers have been spoiled by the close-up immediacy and drama of movies and TV. So now contemporary readers have a hard time staying with continuous blocks of straight expositional prose. They prefer fiction, journalism, and now even biographies, autobiographies, and memoirs, that include the immediacy of dramatic scenes and dialog. Because New Autobiography is storytelling written with dramatic scenes, not just a report of what happened, it is far more engaging to read than old autobiography.

Here from Lois Henley's unpublished autobiography, *The Choice or the Privilege,* is a passage which consists of narrative summary (roman type), an extended scene with dialog (in italic typeface), and another summary section set in roman type.

We had moved in mid-1936 to Greencastle, Indiana, where Clyde was dervishly happy with his new job as salesman in his own district. He relished his opportunity to make good money ($3,000 a year then including salary and commission), to start new dealers, to learn more and ever more about what he then and now considered the best product in the world: Purina Chows for poultry and livestock.

I knew the kind of man I had married and I was glad that he had found a company he could believe in so energetically.

But I was not prepared for and I instinctively resisted the part I realized I was expected to play in the scenario which the Ralston Purina Company had drawn up for the involvement of a wife in her salesman-husband's work.

The first incident I clearly remember occurred in the early summer of 1938. Clyde was the epitome of energy and enthusiasm that evening when he came home "bright-eyed and bushy-tailed," as he and other salesmen were wont to describe themselves in those days. He was still high from a late sales meeting and bursting to tell me about a trip he ("we," he said) had won.

"Yo, ho, ho, have I got something for you!" he sang.

He swung me around and asked me if I could guess what we were going to do in two weeks.

I couldn't.

"We're going to take a trip!"

Oh, boy.

"Where?"

"I've—we've—won a trip, the first time I've gotten this kind of recognition, and it's going to be just wonderful. We're going to Camp Minniwanca in Michigan for a meeting. Isn't that great?"

"Isn't it though? What will we do? How did you win it?"

"I sold more than my quota of feed for this period and we'll go with the other salesmen who sold their quotas—and with their wives, of course—and we'll see Camp Minniwanca. I'm really excited about winning this. Aren't you?"

He could see the questions I was thinking.

"Yes, of course I'm glad. I'm as proud as can be of your success. I think

you certainly deserve the recognition. But this sounds a little far-fetched to me. How is this trip a reward? What is Camp Minniwanca, anyway?"

"It's a camp for underprivileged boys and girls that Mr. W. H. D. has established in Michigan. It has large meeting rooms and a lake and swimming facilities and we'll eat with the kids there and see what he's doing for them— and have a sales meeting."

Oh—a sales meeting.

That was the reward—another sales meeting.

"Well," I said, "I can see why they want the winners to go, to get them inspired to sell more feed. But maybe they should send the losers to be with those underprivileged kids so they will see what happens when you lose."

His face had lost its glow.

"Oh, come on," I said quickly, repentantly, "I'm only kidding. But really, it doesn't seem exactly like a vacation to me."

Clyde could not understand my reaction, then or later. He was hurt, almost offended by my cynicism and joking, although he tried to accept it in good humor. He really did feel rewarded. I felt trapped.

Having expressed my doubts about the real intentions of the company in offering us the Camp Minniwanca "trip," I could see that Clyde expected me to go and the company expected me to go. I asked for two days off from my job at DePauw University and we went to Camp Minniwanca as guests of the Ralston Purina Company.

Once there, I performed the role of Purina wife as I was expected to do, not even letting a serious telephone call from home interfere with our "vacation. . . ."

Notice how the first narrative summary passage enters the scene by funneling closer and closer to its precise time: "The first incident . . . occurred in the early summer of 1938. Clyde was the epitome of energy and enthusiasm that evening when he came home . . ." Notice how the scene is developed through dialog that expresses an opposition of values between husband and wife, and how the subsequent summary quickly covers a number of weeks and delivers you into what will be the next dramatic scene set at Camp Minniwanca.

Recalling an image from the previous chapter of a string of pearls, in which the string is your theme that holds everything together, you can now visualize your scenes as pearls anchored and separated by little knots. The knots are narrative summary binding the scenes one to another:

dramatic scene *narrative summary* *dramatic scene* *narrative summary*

O—x—O—x—O—x—O—x—O—x—O—x—O

As you are composing, you speed along your thematic string writing narrative summary, leaping over weeks or years in a few lines, skipping past dead time and thematically irrelevant events. When you get to a scenepearl—a relevant dramatic moment set at particular time and place—you slow down to develop in detail the world of that scene before hurrying on to the next one.

Through speeding up and slowing down with the gears of summary and scene, you replicate subjective, emotional time. Within emotional time, all memory moments are not equal. Some moments have the potential to be dramatic scenes, especially those that express the opposition of values and characters intrinsic to your story. These moments you slow down and develop like a little drama on a stage.

Because they are like little dramas, scenes are far more engaging to read than the condensed report of narrative summary. They come closer to real time and provide a truer imitation of life, making the past seem present again. A scene allows a reader to know where you were, hear what you and others said, observe your gestures, even feel your feelings and thoughts. Even though scenes take greater imaginative invention to write, readers "believe" the dramatized scene more than a narrative report, because they can see, smell, and hear the scene. With straight narrative summary, readers may feel lectured to with someone else's conclusions, whereas the immediacy and physicality of the scene allows them to believe their own eyes.

Even if you are writing for yourself alone, you will want to learn the skill of writing in scenes, for it is from within the specificity of the scene that your most unexpected revelations come. As Nancy Mairs says in her memoir *Ordinary Times,* "I always expect spiritual insights to shower like coins of light from on high. When instead they bubble up from the mire like will-o'-the-wisps, I am invariably startled." Mairs is referring to spiritual insights bubbling up from daily reality, but she is also implying her methodology as a writer—God *is* in the details. It is by writing specific scenes with visceral detail and dialog that one discovers wonder within moment-to-moment, ordinary life. Moreover, the specificity of scene writing requires you to engage imagination with memory, opening up poetic truths—and forgotten memories—you could never reach through generalized memory alone.

∽Two Ways to Start Writing with Scenes

∽LOOK FOR SENTENCES AND PHRASES THAT ARE "DOORS IN"

When beginning writers come to my classes, the first piece of work they present is almost invariably a narrative prose summary written without scenes. I have come to realize that this is exactly what they need to do before they can write in scenes. Screenwriters refer to such a condensed prose summary as a "treatment" and often write one before starting a screenplay to see whether their story works—whether it has a beginning, middle, and conclusion that develops a coherent theme. A benefit of writing a treatment is that you can recognize and anticipate story problems before, like Russell Baker, you write 450 pages without a story. Another benefit of writing a treatment is that you can present it to selected others for feedback before you complete a work.

A narrative summary treatment is easy to write because if you limit it in length to between two to ten pages, you can generally complete it in a day or two. It is much like the condensed plot summaries you wrote as book reports in grammar school. Here is student Marie Wyler's treatment for an autobiographic short story.

> Let me be the millionth mother to say it: a good baby-sitter is hard to find. *Discovering the exceptional sitter,* the one who will stay with your child and treat it as you would—or better—is like winning the lottery: for a while you're thrilled, then you wonder what you've gotten yourself into. I was so *happy to finally find someone like Lelia,* but after a while I felt like *she had* moved in and *taken over*—not just *my home,* but my baby as well. *I couldn't do anything right, and she subtly let me know it.* When *my baby began to prefer Lelia's care over mine, I started to question* if this working-mother-with-perfect-nanny was really worth *the toll* it was taking *on my self-esteem.*

You will notice that certain phrases are in roman type, which you can think of as "doors-in." They are places like on a computer screen that you can select to enter. What is only a small dot in the overall picture can be enhanced or blown up into a detailed scene or scenes of a particular place and time. Here is one of Marie's italicized doors-in magnified into two scenes.

"She had taken over my home."
 Scene 1
 Lelia came to my house and made herself at home. She had two English words in her vocabulary—chicken and beef—so we relied on my college Spanish to communicate. She was the same age as me but had married at 14, had five children and wet nursed four more.
 "I have kept nine children alive with my breasts alone," she declared to me, with a subtle intake of breath that lifted her chest. She did not approve of the formula I mixed every night, the temperature of my home or the fact that we had a dog.
 "Dogs breathe out bad air which will make your baby very sick," she said. "Plus, dog hair is everywhere, also very bad."

 Scene 2
 Once when she had not been with us very long, Lelia had found a huge kettle—one my mother used to steam lobsters in when I was a child—in the back of my kitchen cabinet, and it was in that kettle she made several home remedies, things my pediatrician would shake his head over, giving advice that I knew Lelia would shake her head over later.
 "Ancient Aztec medicine, passed down for hundreds of years," Lelia nodded at me, as I watched her bathe my daughter in the milky yellow water. Standing at the kitchen sink, sweaty and anxious in my suit and pumps, I had fled home in a mad rush of guilt for leaving my pink-eyed baby, who I then found sitting in a sinkful of this ancient remedy—cooled water in which all the pears I'd bought yesterday had been boiled.

Within your own narrative summary, you can mark potential doors. Or, if you are in a memoir club, you can ask others for their feedback on which sentences or phrases they would like to see expanded into scenes.

⁓IMAGINE YOUR LIFE AS A MOVIE
In the examples above, you write all in narrative summary and look for scene opportunities. To imagine your life as a movie, you take the opposite approach. You initially write no narrative summary; instead you simply *list* possible scenes by asking yourself to visualize your story as a film script. With this technique, whatever you wish to communicate can be expressed only

through events that a movie camera could film. You must tell your story through scenes set in a particular time and place in which something happened to you or in which you did or said something.

At first, a lot of your memories may seem too general to assume the specificity of a dramatized scene. You recall that you and your spouse often went to dinner parties given by another couple when you were first married, but just when you first began to suspect that they were drug smugglers, you cannot recall. In this exercise, you can't summarize "In time I began to wonder where they got their money." Rather, you choose one particular evening and one particular place where that suspicion could have arisen, and perhaps a specific sentence he said or action she took that led to it.

By asking yourself the questions where, when, and how, you can bring a scene to consciousness. Out of the inky darkness of memory suddenly a scene surfaces like the called-for answer to the top of a shake-it-up Magic Eight Ball. It floats, an island in the surrounding blackness. Generally a scene first appears in memoirs as a frozen moment, a single frame. This provides the one-sentence gist you put down on your list. Later you can develop the full scene by starting with this single image and, through reverie, run the film backward to the beginning of the scene and forward to its end.

If you simply cannot come up with a scene for a particular occurrence, you can finesse that item on the list because, unlike the screenwriter, you can fill in with narrative summary. This exercise works best, though, if you force yourself to imagine how you would have to dramatize your story for a film.

As you list your scenes, some incidents may come to you out of chronological order. Just put them down as they come. You can rearrange the list later. You could even, as screenwriters do, put each scene on an index card so that they can be sorted to create the most dramatic structure for your story. Another way to experiment with the sequencing of scenes is to type your list on a computer, then play with different chronologies to see which most clearly defines the shape of your story.

Making scene lists lets you anticipate structural mistakes before writing at length in the wrong direction. Making scene lists of what you have already written can help you analyze where you may have gone wrong. You want your scenes arranged so that they maximize your story's *goina*.

The *goina* is the first rule of dramaturgy. I learned it from the late screenwriter James Poe. The *goina* needs to be in every story, every chapter, every scene. So what *is* it, you want to know? I shouldn't tell you yet, because the *goina* is: What's *goina* happen?

Liesal Fleishenberg made a stepping-stone event list for a personal essay on how she and her husband changed their lives from from Washington, D.C., fast-trackers to Costa Rica pioneers. She also made a list of her desires that covered the same period of time. Finally, she folded her event list into the desires list. She made sure, as you may have if you completed Exercise 4, that on her combined list each of her event scenes was preceded by the desire scene that prompted it. She also made sure that her reader would *not* know whether a desire was satisfied—unless she had established a new, and related, desire to take its place. In this way she could keep her *goina* going.

LIST OF DESIRES AND SCENES:
First I craved a way to have more time with our children.

> *Scene 1. Looking at Impressionist exhibit at the museum, Dan floats the idea of our changing our life.*
> *Scene 2. He's startled that I pick up on the idea as we are preparing for a dinner party at home. I say if we are going to make a change, let's make a real change.*

Dan and I need to figure out a place that would satisfy our desires.

> *Scene 3. In bed Dan and I make a list of what we want.*
> *Scene 4. At a hurried breakfast I say what about Costa Rica. He says, Where?*
> *Scene 5. First arrival in San José at worst time of year.*
> *Scene 6. Disappointment in Tico cuisine.*
> *Scene 7. Falling in love with the rainforest.*

(Once she and her husband had decided on moving to Costa Rica that *goina* was answered, so another was needed.)

How would we find the right house?

> *Scene 8. Seeing our house for the first time.*

How would we make a living in our new home?

> *Scene 9. Meeting with government officials to set up film commission.*
> *Scene 10. Peace breaks out and funding for project development dries up. I tell Dan my discouragement.*

> *Scene 11. Phone call asking me to cater a dinner. I ask for time to de-*
> *cide. Realization that this is what I want to do, make my avoca-*
> *tion my vocation.*
> *Scene 12. Dan and I start "Flying Stars" catering in San José.*

In writing from such an outline of desires and events, you look for opportunities to create scenes that will set up each new desire. Some desires
can be introduced within narrative summary sections, but it is more powerful to set them up within scenes.

Making scene lists has several uses beyond helping you find the best
structure for your story. As mentioned, people who need to contain their
writing to avoid emotional flooding can create a scene list and consciously
limit themselves to writing only one scene a day. People with busy sched-
ules can use scene lists similarly to plan short writing sprints of one scene at
a sitting. And people who dictate their work can use scene lists to stay on
track. Scene lists are like a prescription drug that is good for several unrelated symptoms, say, seizures, cataracts, and arthritis.

Marie, the student who wrote the treatment about her child's nanny,
complained that between the demands of being a wife, the mother of an
infant with fragile health, and a full-time job doing public relations, she could
never get more than twenty minutes at a time to write. She loved writing
as much as the other parts of her life, but, as for most of us, it had to take
second or third or fourth position to more pressing economic and family
demands.

I recalled that I had developed a technique for Linda, another writer who
was in a different kind of situation. Linda had completed almost half of the
book she was writing on being an HIV positive woman. She knew she was
writing against the clock, trying to finish the book while she had the energy and clarity to do so. Suddenly she developed cytomegalovirus, which
made her vision so unsteady that she could no longer work at her computer.
We agreed that she could write the rest of her book by dictating into a tape
recorder. But the problem with dictating autobiographic narrative is that you
so easily get lost and wander off theme and into interesting memory bogs
where you get stuck and then can't find your way back.

Linda already had a chapter outline for her book, which she had developed by putting down the major pivotal events of her story. She knew in a
general way what would go in each chapter. So I suggested that as Linda
began each new chapter, she make a list much like the list she had made to
generate the chapter outline. Only here she would list the scenes within that

chapter's time frame. By following her scene list, she could each day dictate her scenes in order, with some narrative transition between them. If she wanted to rest, she wouldn't have to worry about where she was in the chapter because she would have her scene list to guide her.

It seemed to me that this technique might work well for Marie, who had no more than twenty minutes at a time to herself. First I had her create a structural outline for her short story following the section "Formula for Structuring Your Life as Story" in Chapter 5. Then I had her convert this into a list of scenes. With this scene list, she would know exactly what to do each time she could grab a quick writing sprint. The first day she would take the first scene and write a reverie on it, letting her mind roam freely, accumulating memories and images. The next day she could write a scene from this raw material. Spending an average of twenty minutes a day, she could write in sixteen days the eight scenes that made up her story. She could then create transitions between the scenes with narrative summary, stringing scenepearls one to another. Yes, what she would have as a first draft might feel a little like the scarecrow's patched coat in *The Wizard of Oz*. But she would have a first draft! Then she could spend her twenty minutes a day rewriting and polishing.

A Misleading Metaphor

To teach, I reduce complex structures into their simplest components and rely on similes to convey elusive, abstract ideas of form. Unfortunately, the pearls-on-a-string metaphor, useful as it is to teach writing in scenes and summary, is in one respect misleading. It suggests a completely regular alternation of scene/narrative summary/scene/narrative summary. Sometimes it does work out this way—you find a complete scene, then a paragraph or so of narrative summary, followed by the next scene, some more narrative summary, and so on. However, the two modes can be combined into many other variations.

Sometimes two or more scenes follow each other without transitional narrative between them. Scene and narrative summary also merge: A scene may contain some short narrative summary, or a long summary passage may contain a few lines of quoted conversation, creating a tiny scene. Take this passage from "Jackson Is Only One of My Dogs," from Pam Houston's collection of autobiographic stories, *Cowboys Are My Weakness*. I count three different scenes in it. It follows a descriptive scene of the narrator having been injured while training her horse.

After the operation, after the implanting of the two steel plates, the fourteen screws, the piece of cadaver from the bone bank, my lover, the one whose favorite song was "Desperado," dedicated himself to me like a husband, like a mother, like a best friend. He cooked and cleaned and read to me and washed my hair in the bathtub.

He said, "I wish it could always be this way."

"Of course he does," Debra said. "You're helpless and he's in control."

It didn't last. My arm improved, as it was bound to.

I said, "Is there anything I could do, outside of shattering bones, that would make you treat me like this again?"

Now, in order for you to recognize the three scenes in this excerpt, you need to understand that every scene conveys the following information:

WHO, WHERE, WHEN, AND WHAT.

Unlike a newspaper article where it must be explicit, this information may be implicit in a dramatic scene. *Who* is almost always implicit in autobiographic narrative; it's "I" and anyone else in the scene. *Where* is the scene's location, which can be as specific as "at 1435 Downey Street" or as vague as "at her place." *When* can be as specific as "at 3:12 that afternoon" and as general as "sometime later." *What* is an interaction, most often between yourself and another person or persons and less often between yourself and an aspect of yourself, the natural world, or an inanimate object. As a result of the interaction, something is altered in you or in the other person or entity.

Now let me show you how all this information, who, where, when, and what, can be inferred in the three scenes in the short passage above. The excerpt begins with narrative summary as transition into the first scene: "After the operation, after the implanting of the two steel plates, the fourteen screws, the piece of cadaver from the bone bank . . ." This narrative summary covers a great deal of time and many events in a flash. It channels us toward the exact moment of the scene. "He cooked and cleaned and read to me and washed my hair in the bathtub" is still not the specific time of the scene, but narrows it further, leading us right into the moment of the first scene: "He said, 'I wish it could always be this way.' "

This one line of dialog is the entire first scene. It is the "what" of the scene. Who, where, and when are all conveyed through context. The narrator doesn't have to tell us she was there, because we assume that in autobiographic narrative. She tells us her lover was there through "he said." We

242 • YOUR LIFE AS STORY

know from context "when" was sometime "after the operation." We assume "where" is the narrator's home. There is also an implied emotional beat in the scene because we presume the narrator enjoyed her lover's attentiveness.

Scene two also consists of only one line of dialog: " 'Of course he does,' Debra said. 'You're helpless and he's in control.' " It is an entirely new scene because who, what, where, and when are all different. Now the interaction is taking place between the narrator and Debra instead of the narrator and her lover. Where and when are only implied, but we know it's at a later time than the previous scene and that it must be in a place where the lover cannot overhear. Like the previous scene, this one line of dialog is also an emotional beat. We know what the narrator's reaction must have been from context, because of our own feeling of deflation in reading the line, "You're helpless and he's in control." This is a good example of less being more, of the writer allowing the reader to provide the emotion.

A line of narrative summary acts as a transition between scenes two and three: "It didn't last. My arm improved, as it was bound to." The narrative summary speeds through all the months it took for the narrator's arm to heal.

Scene three is also only a line of dialog: "I said, 'Is there anything I could do, outside of shattering bones, that would make you treat me like this again?' " Who is implicit: We know from context that the narrator is speaking to her lover. Where is implicit: probably at her house again. When is implicit: sometime after she improved. Part of the "what" is even implicit: We know from the line of dialog that it must have come as a reaction to the lover having stopped cooking, cleaning, and reading to her. Again it is an emotional beat because we assume the narrator's emotional state of disappointment. Moreover, this single final sentence of dialog is simultaneously the climax and realization for the dramatic build that was created by the first two scenes.

If you are feeling intimidated, you aren't alone. This is extraordinarily nimble writing, jumping from scene to narrative summary to scene with dazzling economy. Yet the reader never gets lost and stays right with the narrator's emotional beats. I think it's because the writer has the rhythm in her bones of alternating from the macrocosm of summary to the microcosm of scene. Like a jazz musician, Houston is so familiar with the basic chords that she can improvise new variations every time she sits down to write.

Those who really know and practice craft are writing autobiographic texts that we may not only enjoy, but also learn from. When you are reading a writer you admire, mark the places where she or he is able to do something you don't yet know how to do. Try to figure out, with writer friends if possible, why a certain passage or sentence or image works. Then try the technique yourself.

Always remember that autobiographic writing isn't a competition. Some people have better stories to tell, some have better technique, some have more time to write, but no one has your story. Besides, if you learn to write good description, internal responses, and dialog, and understand the dramatic structure of scenes, all of which I'll teach you in the next chapter, you'll know more about crafting great scenes than do many successful novelists.

17

Anatomy of a Scene: Description, Inner Responses, Dialog, and Structure

Now that you know how to string scenepearls, anchoring them in place with transitional narrative summary, let's concentrate on the quality of the pearls themselves. To do that we need to study separately each component part of a scene. I don't mean the information the scene conveys—who, when, where, and what. I mean the modes of expression you use to write a scene, what it is composed of, its anatomy if you will.

A scene has three basic components: description, internal responses, and dialog. You don't have to use all of them in every scene. A scene could be all description, for instance. But most scenes contain some of each, so you need to know how to write them all and how to put them together.

Description

Our senses carry us into the past, the thick aroma of pot roast simmering taking us instantly back to a yellow tiled kitchen and an aproned grandma. Through describing smells, shapes, colors, sounds, textures, light, touch, and movement, we give the experiences of our senses to others.

In a scene, description is usually used to introduce a place or a person or to reproduce action. Here, in an example from James Baldwin's *Nobody Knows My Name,* the first paragraph is all description of place. (The second paragraph adds reflection.)

There is a housing project standing now where the house in which we grew up once stood, and one of those stunted city trees is snarling where our doorway used to be. This is on the rehabilitated side of the avenue. The other side of the avenue—for progress takes time—has not been rehabilitated yet and it looks exactly as it looked in the days when we sat with our noses pressed against the windowpane, longing to be allowed to go "across the street." The grocery store which gave us credit is still there, and there can be no doubt that it is still giving credit. The people in the project certainly need it—far more, indeed, than they ever needed the project. The last time I passed by, the Jewish proprietor was still standing among his shelves looking sadder and heavier but scarcely any older. Farther down the block stands the shoe-repair store in which our shoes were repaired until reparation became impossible and in which, then, we bought all our "new" ones. The negro proprietor is still in the window, head down, working at the leather.

These two, I imagine, could tell a long tale if they would (perhaps they would be glad to if they could), having watched so many, for so long, struggling in the fishhooks, the barbed wire, of this avenue.

You'll notice that Baldwin's description of the street where he once lived is more than physical; it gives you a feeling about what it is to live there. When you write description in a scene, you are setting a stage. Just as when the curtain rises on a play, you immediately know from the scenery and lighting something of the drama to unfold. The elements you put into a good description are selected from all the possible details to give a coherent and intended impression. Everything in Baldwin's description gives you a sense of imprisonment in time and place. The old house is gone and a project has been built, yet nothing essential in people's lives has changed. There is a physical sense of constraint, no place to go except across the street where a proprietor bends, head down, within the confines of his shop.

As an autobiographic writer, you have an aid in selecting the details that will give the impression you want—the selectivity of emotional memory. When you first remember a scene, the gist will have an emotional charge of tone, mood, and feeling, and an absence of detail. When you do a reverie, you may well come up with more details that you can or should use. So from these many details, you consciously select the best combination of a few to recreate the tone, mood, and feeling that came with the gist. After all, it's impossible to say everything about everything and a mistake to try, so the guiding principle in writing description is that you are not trying to make the reader know the facts about something so much as trying to recreate through selected sense-impressions a feeling or attitude.

Take this example from Oliver Sacks's memoir of recovery from a broken limb, *A Leg to Stand On*. It would seem to be an unpromising topic for a memoir, the month he spent learning to walk again, but it is full of feelings, insights, and surprises that make it an exciting spiritual journey. In this scene, which is all description, Sacks is about to have his cast removed.

> The orderlies shifted me on to a raised block in the center—something between a catafalque and a butcher's block, I felt—and went out, shutting the door behind them. I was suddenly alone in this uncanny silent room.
>
> And then I realized that I was not alone. The Caster, in a white gown, was standing in a corner. I had somehow failed to notice him when I was wheeled in. Or, perhaps, he had come in without my noticing. For, in a curious way, he did not seem to move, but to materialize suddenly in different parts of the room. He was here, he was there, but I never caught him in transit. He had a strangely immobile, carven face, with features of a medieval drawing.

Clearly Sacks is not attempting to give you facts in this description. He is recreating with images his feelings at that moment. He never has to say "I was frightened and disoriented" because his descriptions of the room and the Caster say it.

A note of caution. In using description to convey your state of mind, you need to be subtle. Be careful not to push nonhuman subjects to take on human characteristics in what is called "pathetic fallacy." For example, "The sky wept" or "The flowers, listening to the thunder, cringed." Pathetic fallacies make a reader cringe.

Good descriptions can subtly suggest the narrator's feelings, but they are also used effectively as contrast to set off and thereby intensify the narrator's state of mind. For example, in this passage, Hanh Hoang writes about cutting classes in Saigon after the American occupation. Notice how in the last paragraph she uses the description of a carnival as contrast to her feelings of disconnectedness and sadness.

> My siblings and I started cutting classes at the National Conservatory. On those evenings, my older sister went on her separate way while Dung and I wandered aimlessly, silently, on the streets of downtown Saigon. It was no sense of freedom, but sadness, that overtook us. We

had failed our duties as obedient, hard-working daughters and students; still, our mother trusted us. She trusted us, yet she had no time for us. No adult had any time for us anymore. They were in turn distant and intense, never about us. Even people on the streets no longer greeted and chattered. They discussed politics and events and Diem and Madame Nhu and the Americans. We were alone, lonely.

In our sadness Dung and I had nothing to say to each other. I felt responsible for my younger sister's low spirits. Why did I play hooky and drag her into this and now I can't do anything to help her, I blamed myself. We meandered through the crowds then sat on the public benches, watching for hours the passers-by. For no reason we would stand up and walk again.

The most depressing were carnival nights. I could not reconcile my unhappiness with the merriment going on, could not reconcile the angry and violent faces of daylight with their carefree cheerfulness in the evening. From a dark corner I stared out at couples and families who sauntered, stopped, laughed, played in the gaudy lights and jingling music. They swirled and twirled with the giddy Ferris wheel and merry-go-round, their elation so alienating, of a world that had ceased to exist for me.

SELECTIVITY

Description becomes tiresome unless it furthers the story. Modern readers have little patience for long, poetic descriptions, and if you find yourself going on at length in establishing the setting of a scene, you may be running in place to avoid getting to its heart, the dramatic action or interaction. On the other hand, some writers need to overwrite descriptions as a means of exploring all the possibilities. That's fine as long as you select in later drafts only the most telling, concrete details from all you have written. In fact, spending some time brainstorming many possibilities before writing can help you create more concise and precise descriptions.

EXERCISE 23: *Casting Your Net*

Before writing a description in a scene, spend a few minutes in reverie bringing up all sorts of sensory impressions associated with the time, place, or people. Cast your net wide; then from all you have dredged, select a few of the best details. You'll have to sort through a lot of refuse, but you're likely to get a treasure or two with this method.

Precision

It is impossible to overemphasize the value of concrete, specific details in writing description. When you find yourself using an abstract or clichéd word or expression, ask yourself, What specific detail or details could better convey this idea? For example, a Native American woman in one of my classes wished to write about growing up on an isolated Alaskan island. In writing a description of her mother, she began, as we often do, with a general impression, "My mother was a strong, kind woman." There is nothing wrong with this, but what does it mean? Was she strong as a disciplinarian? Was she the dominant partner in her marriage? Did she lift weights? Strong can mean many things. The class wanted to see this particular mother, so I prompted the student, "What image of your mother would convey her strength and kindness?" The writer came up with, "My mother carried fifty pounds of mail on her back, yet she had a shy smile for each of our neighbors as she labored up the hill." Now you see the narrator's mother as an individual.

Often, beginning writers mistake the need for precise details with the overuse of modifiers, that is, adjectives and adverbs. It's best to heed poet John Ciardi's advice: "Never send an adjective on a noun's errand." The same holds true for verbs and adverbs. A precise, active verb is always preferable to a verb that needs an adverb. If the student had said her mother had "climbed with difficulty up our steep hill," using both the adverbial modifier "with difficulty" and the adjective "steep" to make her point, it would not be as effective as her choice of the more precise verb, "as she *labored* up our hill."

Sometimes modifiers are unavoidable. "Shy smile" in the previous example is more precise than "smile" alone and tells us something important about the writer's mother. There are nouns for specific types of smiles— smirk, grin, simper—but there isn't a noun that will do the errand of "shy" in "shy smile." In general, though, try to eliminate modifiers in favor of bold nouns and verbs.

Avoid Clichés

Because clichés are overused words and phrases, often they come to mind first. You may not recognize the stinkers until you rewrite. Then you can make a game of firing them and auditioning fresher, more specific words to replace them. If you are in a memoir club, you can start a list of Banned Words, including words each member tends to use too often. Here's an example of one group's list of Banned Words:

Agony, ecstasy, rainbow, little creatures, Heaven and Hell, mist, dew, amid, amidst, and surmised (sound like trying to be writerly), splendor, magnificent, wonderful, majestic, soul, heart, glow, chasm, abyss, rose, lust, lurk, and loom, phantom, demons, vampire, witch, angel, devil, truth, beauty, beautiful, love, always, never, challenging.

Here is their list of Banned Clichéd Phrases:

Nails tapping, eye-catching smile, life style, romantic rendezvous, forbidden fruit, crisp, white coats, overstuffed library, straight out of central casting, hopes and fears, round and round, over and over, dysfunctional family, co-dependent relationship, we bonded (and all other words and phrases from pop psychology).

Banning a word or phrase forces you to dig into your sense memory to find a more specific, individual choice.

⌒EXPLORE ALL YOUR SENSES

Even when you delve down to replace a cliché, you may find that you have to mine even farther to get beyond exclusively visual images. While an apt visual image is a treasure, we tend to neglect pulling from our other senses. At least as an exercise, try soliciting all your senses when searching to replace clichés and abstractions. Not only, What did I see, but also: What did I smell? What did I touch? What did I hear? What did I taste? What did I feel in my body?

One of the best ways to come up with fresh descriptions of sensations is to use one sense to describe another. "Violets smell like burnt sugar cubes that have been dipped in lemon and velvet" writes Diane Ackerman, and though you cannot dip sugar cubes in velvet, we know exactly what she means. Likewise we feel the aptness of Samuel Johnson's description when he said that the color scarlet "represented nothing so much as the clangour of a trumpet."

The French Symbolists believed that a sound can be translated through a perfume and a perfume through a vision, that all our senses correspond to each other. If you add to this concept the fact that each of us perceives through a specific body, you will find that the imagery you create through sense correspondences is unique and true to you.

EXERCISE 24: *Substituting One Sense for Another*

Take a sensation you want to describe, say the taste of your morning coffee. You could call it acrid or smooth, using common words associated with taste, but try instead to describe it through a different sense, say, "a cup of coffee harmonious as C major." It's more specific. Try it.

⌒ DESCRIPTION DOS AND DON'TS

Writing vivid descriptions is easy if you follow these simple guidelines. Do be:

- selective
- concise
- precise

Don't use:

- clichés
- abstract words
- many adverbs or adjectives

⌒ Inner Responses

Whereas description captures the outer world, inner responses in a scene give a reader access to your intangible thoughts and feelings. In an attempt to appear objective, many firsthand writers omit their inner responses, and their writing is spiritless. Emotions and insights are like the close-up shots in a film. Without them an audience feels disconnected, at too far a distance. As you are writing scenes you need to ask yourself, "How did I feel?", "What did I think?", "How did I react?", and include these inner responses.

This excerpt from Oliver Sacks's *A Leg to Stand On* is nearly all inner response. Sacks's expansive style tends to inflate what to others would be small inner responses. Sometimes he becomes excessive, but for the autobiographic writer it is better to err on the side of including too much of one's feelings, reflections, and reactions. (I have put numbers into this passage preceding each beat of inner response.)

The day before my transfer to Kenwood, the Convalescent Home in Hampstead, I was taken down to the little garden I had so yearningly gazed at—taken down in a wheelchair, dressed in hospital pajamas. [1] This was a great joy—to be out in the air—for I had not been outside in almost a month. A pure and intense joy, a blessing, to feel the sun on my face and with wind in my hair, to hear birds, to see, touch and fondle the living plants. [2] Some essential connection and communion with nature was re-established after the horrible isolation and alienation I had known. Some part of me came alive, when I was taken to the garden, which had been starved, and died, perhaps without my knowing it. [3] I suddenly felt what I have often felt intensely before, but never thought to apply to my own time in hospital: that one needs open-air hospitals with gardens, set in country and woods—like some of the Little Sisters' Homes I worked in in rural New York; a hospital like a home, not a fortress or "institution"; a hospital like a home—and perhaps like a village.

In memoir writing, as in life, sometimes you have a feeling without a thought to explain it, and sometimes you have a thought which in turn changes how you feel about a person or event. At other times, feelings and thoughts are inseparable, one and the same. In the Oliver Sacks quote above, we get (1) his *feelings* of joy, which cause (2) his *reflection* that some part of him had died in being confined to a hospital room, which leads to (3) his *feeling* and *thought merged* in his realization that hospitals should be like homes with gardens set in country and woods. Each numbered passage could be considered a *beat* within the passage.

In autobiographic narrative, a beat is the unit of your state of being, which leads to the next unit. If you studied composition in school, you were taught to write essays and papers by the logical development of ideas. You were taught to have a topic sentence at the beginning of each paragraph, to develop your main idea, paragraph by paragraph, and to draw a conclusion at the end. The basic unit of development was the concept of each paragraph.

That's not how you do it in autobiographic narrative. Yes, as in expositional writing, you want a development of your subject by units. You don't want everything to be a blur, a jumble. But in autobiographic narrative, the basic unit of development is the *beat*, not the paragraph. So you have chapters, scenes, and within the scenes, beats. Each beat is a microrealization of your state of awareness, of your feelings and thoughts, which evolve beat by beat by beat.

Oliver Sacks's doctors said his was an "uneventful recovery." Not to Sacks, for whom it consisted of hundreds of minievents, hundreds of discernible beats. By slowing down and sensitizing himself to the process of his physical recovery, Sacks sets out what he comes to realize is the *music* of healing. Here Sacks, himself a physician, describes both his process of recovery and of writing his memoir in beats.

"Uneventful recovery." What damned utter nonsense! Recovery . . . was a "pilgrimage," a journey, in which one moved, if one moved, stage by stage, or by stations. Every stage, every station, was a completely new advent, requiring a new start, a new birth or beginning. One had to begin, to be born, again and again. Recovery was an exercise in nothing short of birth, for as mortal man grows sick, and dies, by stages, so natal man grows well, and is quickened, by stages—radical stages, existence-stages, absolute and new: unexpected, unexpectable, incalculable and surprising. Recovery uneventful? It *consists* of events!

Writing in beats, you capture and delimit "existence-stages, absolute and new."

Some writers outline the beats of a scene before they write it. Others are able to sense the beats as they compose a scene like music in their heads. Still others have to free-write until they have some idea of what beats the scene might contain. In first drafts as in life, emotions are often a jumble. Fear, anticipation, love, embarrassment, and irritation may all be present and not in discrete units. In writing, you need to separate and order them. Take this passage from Nathan McCall's *Makes Me Wanna Holler.* McCall recounts his feelings as an adolescent street punk of his first "train" (gang rape). In all likelihood, his emotions wavered back and forth between sympathy for the girl who was the intended victim and fear of doing anything to show that sympathy. In the writing, though, each emotion is separated into its own beat.

> She looked so sad that I started to feel sorry for her. Something in me wanted to reach out and do what I knew was right—do what we all instinctively knew was right. Lean down, grab Vanessa's hand, and lead her from that room and out of that house; walk her home and apologize for our temporary lapse of sanity; tell her, "Try, as best as possible, to forget any of this ever happened."
>
> But I couldn't do that. It was too late. This was our first train together as a group. All the fellas were there and everybody was anxious to show everybody else how cool and worldly he was. If I jumped in on Vanessa's behalf, they would accuse me of falling in love. They would send word out on the block that when it came to girls, I was a wimp. Everybody would be talking at the basketball court about how I'd caved in and got soft for a bitch. There was no way I was gonna

put that pressure on myself. I thought, *Vanessa got her stupid self into this. She gonna have to get herself out.*

Turkey Buzzard put his hand on her shoulder and said, "What you gonna do, girl? You gonna let one of us do it?"

The first beat in this excerpt is the narrator's sympathy for Vanessa, the second his desire to help her get out of there, the third his awareness that he would embarrass himself with the guys if he showed his sympathy, the fourth his decision to turn off his feelings for her. A fifth beat is initiated by Turkey Buzzard's dialog.

Once you get the hang of composing in beats, it will make all your scene writing easier. All scenes are composed of beats, no matter which mode of expression is being used, description, inner response, or dialog. For instance, inner responses combine with dialog within beats and dialog by itself proceeds in beats.

Dialog

The use of dialog in scenes distinguishes New Autobiography from the old, and memoirs written by experienced contemporary writers from those of beginners. Beginners often assume that because they cannot recall conversations word for word, they cannot write dialog. They marvel at the memory of the writer who seems to quote conversations verbatim from fifteen years before.

Actually, no one recalls conversations in detail. If you do recall a significant line or exchange, by all means quote it, but more often you will remember that a conversation took place and not the words or their sequence. All the better. You will have to imagine the conversation as the novelist would, without all the uhs and ahs, digressions and repetitions people use when they talk.

You want dialog to sound natural by being informal—"I'll be back," not "I will be back"—and you want it to have the rhythms of real speech—"You go ahead and eat." The best way to achieve natural-sounding dialog is to read it aloud, trying variations until it sounds how the speaker would say it. But good written dialog isn't a transcript of everyday speech transmitted to the page. It is speech ordered and condensed, speech that moves in an intended structure instead of circling back on itself. In extended dialogs it is speech that has been ordered in beats that follow a dramatic structure and enhance the thematic conflict of the work.

Look at the dialog in this scene from Susanna Kaysen's *Girl, Interrupted.*

It takes place at the mental hospital when Jim Watson, who was reputed in the 1950s to have "discovered the secret of life," comes to visit the narrator.

"Jim!" I said.

He drifted toward me. He drifted and wobbled and faded out while he was supposed to be talking to people, and I'd always liked him for that.

"You look fine," he told me.

"What did you expect?" I asked.

He shook his head.

"What do they do to you in here?" He was whispering.

"Nothing," I said. "They don't do anything."

"It's terrible here," he said.

The living room was a particularly terrible part of our ward. It was huge and jammed with huge vinyl-covered armchairs that farted when anyone sat down.

"It's not really that bad," I said, but I was used to it and he wasn't.

He drifted toward the window again and looked out. After a while he beckoned me over with one of his long arms.

"Look." He pointed at something.

"At what?"

"That." He was pointing at a car. It was a red sports car, maybe an MG. "That's mine," he said. He'd won the Nobel Prize, so probably he'd bought this car with the money.

"Nice," I said. "Very nice."

Now he was whispering again. "We could leave," he whispered.

"Hunh?"

"You and me, we could leave."

"In the car, you mean?" I felt confused. Was this the secret of life? Running away was the secret of life?

"They'd come after me," I said.

"It's fast," he said. "I could get you out of here."

Suddenly I felt protective of him. "Thanks," I said. "Thanks for offering. It's sweet of you."

"Don't you want to go?" He leaned toward me. "We could go to England."

"England?" What did England have to do with anything? "I can't go to England," I said.

"You could be a governess," he said.

For ten seconds I imagined this other life, which began when I stepped into Jim Watson's red car and we sped out of the hospital and on to the airport. The governess part was hazy. The whole thing, in fact, was hazy. The vinyl chairs, the security screens, the buzzing of the nursing-station door. Those things were clear.

"I'm here now, Jim," I said. "I think I've got to stay here."

"Okay." He didn't seem miffed. He looked around the room one last time and shook his head.

I stayed at the window. After a few minutes I saw him get into his red car and drive off, leaving little puffs of sporty exhaust behind him. Then I went back to the TV room.

Jim Watson is not an important character in Kaysen's memoir. He does not appear in any other scene in the book. Why then does she develop this extended dialog with him? Because the opposition in this dialog, the opposing points of view of each of the characters, actualizes the main theme of the work: the narrator's conflict between needing to return to life outside the hospital, and her sense of security inside it. Situations that contain your central thematic conflict are scene opportunities not to be missed.

The dialog proceeds in alternate beats like a debate on Kaysen's central theme:

> him: *Yes, you should leave the hospital.*
> her: *No, I don't think so.*
> him: *There's the sports car (he's gaining).*
> her: *She says no, but feels protective of him.*
> him: *We could go to England (that makes no sense; he's lost ground).*
> her: *No, she decides (it's the pivotal turn, the climax of the dialog; the tension of opposition is resolved).*

Like stories, many scenes, especially those that contain extended dialog, have an orgasmic structure; there is an increase of tension as a result of an interaction until some moment of change or realization is reached; then the tension falls off. This falling off of tension—there is no further to go—gives the scene closure.

∿ USING DIALOG TO REVEAL CHARACTER

Rather than be told how to view a person, readers prefer to come to their own evaluation through observation of what brought you to your view. It is far better to reveal someone's character through dialog and actions than to tell us "He was a selfish jerk," "She was a goddamned liar," or "Yvonne was a saint."

Look at this passage from Mikal Gilmore's memoir of his family, *Shot in the Heart,* which reveals what kind of people his mother and father were, even though Mikal doesn't make a single evaluation. In fact, he isn't even present in the scene because it is set when his parents were first married, before Mikal, his brother, executed murderer Gary Gilmore, or his other brothers were yet born. Taking a novelistic liberty, the writer here puts you into his mother's point of view. Thus he avoids emotional flatness caused by a lack of inner responses—a common problem when writing about predecessors.

There is no way Mikal Gilmore could know what his mother's thoughts and feelings were or what words his parents actually exchanged. Like a novelist, he invents dialog and inner responses but with the memoirist's advantage: He knows the actual characters so well that it is second nature for him to express how they would have felt and spoken.

Halfway through Fall, after a six-week absence, Frank returned home. Bessie saw him coming up the walkway to Fay's and, despite all her agitation, something in her heart surged. He had a way that got to her, something that told her he was the only man she was ever going to really love. Still she had to let him know that she wasn't happy being left behind, and that she had learned a few details about his life. She told him that Fay had told her about his other wives and many names. She told him that she had figured out that Ehrich Weiss was his father.

Frank took all this in without showing much in return. Just like his mother, Bessie thought.

"What else did Fay tell you?" Frank asked.

"Nothing else. She told me that if I wanted to know any of your other secrets, I'd have to ask you."

Frank seemed relieved by that. He gave my mother a look that told her that revealing anything more was the last thing on his mind.

Bessie decided to push a little. "Frank, where did you go? What were you doing?"

"If I thought it was any of your damn business," Frank said, "I would have told you already. Maybe it's better if you not know everything. Think of it that way."

There was one thing, though, she had to know: Did he have other families in other places? Did he still see any of his other wives or support their children? "I can take a lot of things, but if you are still seeing other women, I'll leave you."

Frank laughed and lifted her chin tenderly. He looked into Bessie's green eyes and said: "Believe me, you're more than enough for me. Besides, a man would have to be a damn fool to have more than one wife at the same time. Hell, I'm not a Mormon. Don't worry, I don't see any of those other women anymore. Once in a while I get in touch and see one of the kids. That's about it."

Bessie didn't know why, but she believed him.

The dialog quickly establishes *a distinct point of view for each speaker.* Bessie believes that spouses should not have secrets from each other. Frank believes that his past is his business and none of Bessie's. As the dialog dramatizes the characters' opposing values, it also reveals their temperaments. When Frank says, "If I thought it was any of your damn business . . . I would have told you already. Maybe it's better if you not know everything," we get a foreshadowing of his abusiveness and his need to control those close to him, even the way they think. When Bessie says, "I can take a lot of things, but if you are still seeing other women, I'll leave you," we sense her mettle and spirit which eventually her husband and life will pound out of her.

As *Shot in the Heart* progresses, Frank is revealed to be a violent and abusive con man, the source of much of the family's tragedy. Yet Mikal, who both hates and loves his father, throughout the book presents the man's appeal along with his destructiveness by letting us hear how he speaks.

TYPES OF DIALOG

This single scene between Mikal Gilmore's parents contains examples of the three ways in which you can recreate conversation: through *summary dialog, indirect dialog,* and *direct dialog.*

SUMMARY DIALOG

is a brief report that suggests a longer conversation, but doesn't give specific words or texture: "She told him that Fay had told her about his other wives and many names. She told him that she had figured out that Ehrich Weiss was his father." Gilmore sums up the conversation here because he is repeating information that the reader has already learned in previous scenes. You want to avoid having characters repeat information, and summary dialog is a good way to condense what you do not wish to cover in detail.

INDIRECT DIALOG

reports more details of the conversation than summary dialog, but is more efficient than direct dialog. It renders the feeling of what was said without quoting it: "There was one thing, though, she had to know: Did he have other families in other places? Did he still see any of his other wives or support their children?" In this indirect dialog, we get the tone of the dialog—Bessie is suspicious and piqued—but not the actual words Bessie said.

DIRECT DIALOG

is contained within quotation marks and is the most dramatic and immediate type. When Bessie says, " 'I can take a lot of things, but if you are still seeing other women, I'll leave you,' " it's as if we are overhearing the conversation, the exact words and phrasing. The purpose of direct dialog is not to convey information (though it may do that incidentally). It is to express the dynamics of the relationship between characters.

Extended scenes of direct dialog can be understood as a transaction, a negotiation of sorts. Frank and Bessie start out, each with a clear intent: Bessie to find out the truth about his other marriages; Frank to appease her without telling her what she wants to know. Each line of dialog is like a move in a chess game. The words the characters say are far less important than the underlying power contest between them and how it shifts and progresses.

The dialog proceeds beat by beat until the stance of the characters at the end of the scene is different from their stance at its beginning. In this case, Bessie at the beginning of the scene is suspicious of her husband and geared up to confront him. Within the scene there is an interchange between the characters through dialog, so that by its end Frank has pacified Bessie, and she has let herself be seduced into believing him.

You may think that this Frank and Bessie scene is exceptional in demonstrating how people negotiate power through dialog. After all, theirs was a relationship in which Frank misused his power over Bessie as a matter of course. But all intimate relationships, if carefully observed, tell about power: power shared, power taken, power abdicated, power reversed, or power unrecognized. When my daughter negotiates with me what time she has to be home from a date, it's about power. When you make love with your mate, power is in the mix. When you sit down to dinner with family and friends, power flows around the table, or pools at certain chairs.

It is the storyteller's job to use dialog to recreate the flow of power, that is, how for each character some sort of energy is gained or lost or stays the same in a scene. As in more formal negotiations, the outcome of a dialog scene can be win/lose, lose/lose, or win/win.

SUBTEXT AS HIDDEN DIALOG

The context of conversations and the gestures characters make are a hidden form of dialog that contribute to the dance of power. For instance, in the scene between Mikal Gilmore's parents, Frank's personality is revealed through what he leaves unsaid as much as through what he does say. Frank never says, "Ask all you want, but I'll never tell you the whole truth," but you know that from reading between the lines. Bessie never says, "You win," but we understand it from the scene's structure. As is characteristic of good dialog, there is a subtext beneath the actual words of dialog, the text.

Subtext is often communicated through people's gestures, which sometimes correspond to what they are saying and sometimes give a counter-message. When Mikal Gilmore tells us that "Frank laughed and lifted her chin tenderly. He looked into Bessie's green eyes," Frank's gestures are an inseparable part of his asserting his power over Bessie. The writer doesn't need to have Frank say "I don't take your worries and concerns seriously." Frank's laugh says it.

In fact, the truism "actions speak louder than words" applies to dialog. Look at the following scene from "High-water," one of the autobiographic short stories in Pam Houston's collection *Cowboys Are My Weakness.* The narrator is spending the night at her boyfriend Richard's house. Certainly, Richard's actions communicate more directly than his words here.

> We'd been in the tub together and Richard's bathrobe was closest to me, so without even thinking I threw it around me and answered the door.
>
> Our eyes met and widened and held for a long minute, and she must have been as surprised as I was to see her hair, her eyes, her mouth, her build, her stance on a stranger wearing the bathrobe she must have worn, still dripping from the bathtub where she must have bathed. Except for the ten years she had on me, we were identical.
>
> "Hi," I said.
>
> She looked hard at my face and then headed for her car. Her tires shrieked. I shut the door.
>
> "Who was it?" Richard was behind me.

"I think it was Karen."

"What did she say?"

"Nothing at all."

"Did it look like Karen?"

"I don't know what Karen looks like," I said. "It looked like me."

He was putting on his coat. He was looking for his keys.

"Don't go now," I said.

"I'll be back."

"Dinner's almost ready."

"You go ahead and eat."

"I don't yell at you," I said.

"But you cry." And it was true. I was crying then.

"This is my night," I said.

He shut the door on my hand.

I suspect that when this scene, or one like it, happened in life, the real Richard never shut the door on the narrator's hand. But the gesture is so right as punctuation to the scene that we accept it as true—the unspoken truth of the relationship.

In another scene from the same short story, Richard's gestures give a subtext that directly contradicts his words.

He didn't talk the whole way out to the lake, but when we got close to the place where you turn off the highway he held my hand and I could feel his muscles, tight all the way to the back of his neck.

The lake was calm and it reflected headlights from the interstate halfway to Nevada. . . .

"So." His voice made me jump. "What do you think our potential is in the long-long run?" It sounded like stocks.

"In the long-long run," I said, "I think our potential is good." His free hand drummed the dashboard.

"Do you think I can satisfy you, sexually and otherwise, for a long time?"

I said, "I think you can satisfy me for a long time." The veins around his temples looked like they would burst.

"Does it bother you," he said, "that I'm a little older than you?"

"Not in the least," I said.

He drew in a breath. "Do you want to have children?"

I didn't know the answer.

"I think so," I said, "someday. Do you?"

"I never thought so," he said. "But now I do. The only question is . . ."

"With who?" I said.

"I know that sounds awful," he said, "but I had to know how you felt."

Never cry in front of him, Casey said, but I did, entirely too often.

"Now that I know how you feel I can get things settled with Karen, and then you and I will go on a trip."

For a minute the idea of a trip cheered me up, but then I started to think about how we never had a conversation about our future that didn't have Karen's name in it.

Richard's hand drumming on the dashboard, the veins standing out at his temples suggest the subtext that he is conflicted about his relationship with the narrator, as opposed to his words which are about commitment.

There are occasions when characters say exactly what they mean, where there is no hidden subtext, but most often this is in cathartic scenes that resolve a story line. When dialog between characters is filled with unrecognized or unstated emotions and suppressed information, it builds tension and interest. Once people are completely candid with each other, the tension is released, so scenes without a subtext are most useful near the end of a story when you no longer need to keep the reader impatient to know what will happen. For example, near the end of *I Know Why the Caged Bird Sings,* Maya Angelou writes a dialog between herself and her mother that begins to resolve the tension between them.

Daddy Clidell told Mother that I was "three weeks gone." Mother, regarding me as a woman for the first time, said indignantly, "She's more than any three weeks." They both accepted the fact that I was further along than they had first been told but found it nearly impossible to believe that I had carried a baby, eight months and one week, without their being any the wiser.

Mother asked, "Who is the boy?" I told her. She recalled him, faintly.

"Do you want to marry him?"

"No."

"Does he want to marry you?" The father had stopped speaking to me during my fourth month.

"No."

"Well, that's that. No use ruining three lives." There was no overt or subtle condemnation. She was Vivian Baxter Jackson. Hoping for the best, prepared for the worst, and unsurprised by anything in between.

Just in case the reader might suspect a subtext in the lines, "Well, that's that. No use ruining three lives," Angelou assures us there is none: "There was no overt or subtle condemnation." Generally, you would not need to tell the reader there is no hidden subtext; it should be apparent from the way the scene reads. (I suspect the line was inserted for Angelou's white readers. Commonly in white women's true confessions memoirs, maternity out of wedlock is a source of shame, whereas in the African-American autobiographic tradition it is seen as a passage to self-worth and maturity, even for young, unmarried mothers.)

∽I Said, He Said, She Said

Many beginning writers go through contortions to avoid repeating the simple attribution, *I said, he said,* or *she said.* Yet there is nothing wrong with repeating "said," which is so common that the reader's eye just skips over it, as with quotation marks, without really noticing them. On the other hand, variations on "said," such as "answered," "muttered," "snarled," "roared," "replied," "added," "commented," and "queried," call attention to themselves and should be used cautiously, while adverbs in speech tags such as "she said mockingly" or "he responded coyly" often sound overdone. It is best to let the words of dialog themselves suggest the tone. When Richard asks, "Did it look like Karen?" Houston doesn't need to say, "he asked warily" or "he said anxiously." We know that from the context.

Fiction writers have developed effective ways to attribute dialog other than by using "said," and you can learn them by studying scenes with dialog you like. A gesture is useful to identify the speaker instead of "he said"; for example, from Pam Houston's first scene above: " 'Who was it?' Richard was behind me." Or from a student's work, "She touched a finger to my lips. 'Liar.' " You can also tag a line of dialog with a thought or emotional state as another economical alternative to "I said," for example: " 'You're here!' I was surprised how glad I was to see her," or, "I felt my fingernails sharpen like claws. 'Over my dead body!' "

The convention of starting a new paragraph each time you change speakers often eliminates the need for speaker identification tags altogether.

"Who was it?" Richard was behind me.
"I think it was Karen."
"What did she say?"
"Nothing at all."
"Did it look like Karen?"

Without "he said" or "I said," we can keep track of who is speaking if short exchanges alternate—at least for three or four lines when there are only two speakers. Remember, though, there is nothing wrong with using "I said," "he said," and "she said." In fact, they need to be repeated every so often to keep a reader from getting confused.

⌒ DIALOG DOS AND DON'TS

Do:

• Establish the POV (point of view) of each character, i.e., his or her values and attitudes.
• Recreate the impression of natural speech.
• Use dramatic structure to shape the sequence of what is said.

Don't:

• Let characters make long speeches.
• Put in "dead" dialog that doesn't further the story line, e.g., "Hello, how are you?" "Fine, how are you?" "I'm fine."
• Write "on the nose" dialog, i.e., dialog in which nothing is left unspoken, in which there is no subtext.

If writing dialog is new for you, these guidelines may seem a lot to absorb. Once you get started, though, just letting your speakers run off at the mouth, you will find that much of what is studied here will come naturally. Diarists who write journal dialogs will likely find that, without realizing it, they have been practicing a dramatic structure in journal dialogs. Most dialogs between aspects of oneself or with others written to resolve a problem move from positioning opposing points of view, to an emotional negotiation and exchange, to a modification in perspective of one or both parties.

Conscious work in writing good dialog comes in editing it, taking out every word that is extraneous without ruining its naturalism. It's like building a pyramid of soda cans, then trying to take out as many as possible while keeping the structure standing.

⌒THE DRAMATIC STRUCTURE OF THE SCENE

Now that you know how to write the pieces of a scene, let's look at how you put them all together. First, let me tell you something that tickles me the way the thought of tiny atoms replicating the mammoth universe does (even if that's scientifically questionable). Complete scenes with dialog are minidramas that structurally replicate the nine essential elements of a story! The correspondences aren't any more exact than those between the atom and the universe—few scenes contain all nine steps—but the concept is instructive. Here is a complete scene with dialog that does replicate all the structural steps; it may serve as a model of dramatic construction. It's from the title story in Pam Houston's *Cowboys Are My Weakness* and concerns her live-in relationship with Homer, a wildlife specialist who studies whitetail deer.

One day when I got back from my walk with David, Homer was in the cabin in the middle of the day. He had on normal clothes and I could tell he'd shaved and showered. He took me into the bedroom and climbed on top of me frontwards, the way he did when we first met and I didn't even know what he did for a living.

Afterwards he said, "We didn't need a condom, did we?" I counted the days forward and backward and forward again. Homer always kept track of birth control and groceries and gas mileage and all the other things I couldn't keep my mind on. Still it appeared to be exactly ten days before my next period.

"Yes," I said, "I think we did."

Homer has never done an uncalculated thing in his life and for a moment I let myself entertain the possibility that his mistake meant that somewhere inside he wanted to have a baby with me, that he really wanted a family and love and security and the things I thought everybody wanted before I met Homer. On the other hand, I knew that one of the ways I had gotten in trouble with Homer, and with other men before him, was by inventing thoughts for them that they'd never had.

"Well," he said, "in that case we better get back to Colorado before they change the abortion laws."

Sometimes the most significant moments of your life reveal themselves to you even as they are happening, and I knew in that moment that I would never love Homer the same way again.

Let's break it down into its component parts, beginning, middle and end.

THE BEGINNING

The first paragraph conveys the essential information of a scene (though there is no rule that this has to be so).

Who: The narrator and Homer
Where: "The cabin in the middle of the day"
When: "One day when I got back from my walk"
What: "He took me into the bedroom and climbed on top of me"

Homer's action, "he took me into the bedroom and climbed on top of me," is the *initiating incident* as in a drama; from it everything else in the scene follows. It is also the first beat in the scene. We know from what has preceded this scene that the narrator's *problem* is that Homer doesn't want to be committed and her *desire* is to get him to love her.

THE MIDDLE

The beginning paragraph of the scene was all description. Now, in the middle section, we get a beat of dialog, "We didn't need a condom, did we?" with description, "I counted the days," and another beat, " 'Yes,' I said, 'I think we did.' " The narrator's reflection, "It appeared to be exactly ten days before my next period," functions as the *first minor pivotal event* in the scene.

Now we sense mounting tension as the narrator's desire comes up against the *desire of her antagonist*, Homer. In quick succession we get two more emotional beats: hope ("Homer has never done an uncalculated thing in his life...I let myself entertain the possibility that his mistake meant that somewhere inside he wanted to have a baby with me") followed by wariness ("On the other hand, I knew that one of the ways I had gotten in trouble with Homer, and with other men before him, was by inventing thoughts for them").

The middle section ends with a *precipitating event* when the unexpected happens, here as dialog. Homer says, "we better get back to Colorado before they change the abortion laws."

THE CONCLUSION

Having to respond to Homer's assumption that she should get an abortion gives the narrator a crisis, climax, and final realization. In this scene, they happen all at the same time. As in a story, the *crisis* is a narrowing of options. The narrator must now decide whether to continue loving a man who clearly does not want to have a family with her or to affirm her dissatisfaction. At the *climax*, something dies so something can be born. The narrator's love for Homer dies so that her love for herself can be born. The climax and *final realization* occur together in the sentence, "I knew in that moment that I would never love Homer the same way again." A transformation has taken place, and with it, the tension in the scene, created by the conflict between the narrator and Homer, falls off.

This one scene hits every roadmark of dramatic structure. You can't be expected to, nor would you want to, nor does Pam Houston try to write every scene in a story or longer work as a complete drama. (Doing so in this case actually gives the writer the problem of revving up the story again in the next scene, because this one is so complete, so resolved.)

I have presented this scene for you to study because it is classic in its form. I think it would be valuable for you to try to write a classic scene from a memory in your life, on the theory that you need to understand the rules before you can break them. Still I don't really believe that; plenty of wonderful writers break the rules all the time without knowing them. Plenty of autobiographic writers instinctively write complete scenes and partial scenes without ever studying scene structure or dramatic structure. But for those of you who need to disassemble the vacuum cleaner into its component parts to understand how it runs, this classic scene provides a diagram.

This one scene contains all three modes of expression, but remember that a scene can be all description or reflection or dialog, and still be a scene. A scene can be missing any of the components of dramatic structure and still be a scene, and not a damaged scene or a disabled scene, simply a different scene. Nevertheless, if you are rewriting a scene that doesn't seem to be working, try asking yourself how you might redo it by including the nine elements of classic dramatic structure.

Now you know how to write great scenes, with descriptions that set the stage, inner responses that keep your reader involved, and dialog that reveals character and divulges subtle exchanges of power. You're ready to learn other techniques that only the cleverest novelists know. In the next chapter, you'll learn how to leap nimbly from scene to scene and, within scenes, to jump around in time.

18

Jumping and
Leaping through Time

*There is a sense of levels in human experience, levels as well as linearity.
You are not born with a sense of levels, they are formed on second thought
looking back on yourself.*

PHILIP DAVIS, Memory and Writing

oo many memoirists practice a slavish allegiance to chronology. They
are straitjacketed, imprisoned by time and place because that's how
they assume it must be. They have not learned the *vertical* and *horizontal devices* to loose themselves from calendar time. The vertical devices
allow you to move up and down levels of memory and awareness. The
horizontal devices allow you to move through your plot at any speed you
wish.

VERTICAL TIME DEVICES	HORIZONTAL TIME DEVICES
Flashbacks	Stretching and Condensing
Flashforwards	Leaps
Grabbers	Bridges
Bookends	Foreshadowing
Brackets	Cliffhangers
	Suspense

Vertical Time

odern physics tells us that our linear perception of time as past, present, and future is illusory. Medical doctor Deepak Chopra speculates that nature has given human beings a linear sense of time to protect us
from being overwhelmed by the actual simultaneity of all time, and that at

certain moments, when falling in love, or gasping at stars in the night sky, we say "time stood still" because at those moments we perceive the unity of time. We also perceive a unity of time when in the present moment we remember the past as if it were here again, or anticipate the future as if it had arrived. This simultaneity creates a sense of levels on a ladder of awareness.

In autobiographic works, this vertical movement up and down a ladder of consciousness is as important—often more important—than the horizontal development of plot. The expression of multiple levels of awareness within the same individual allows dramatic tension and duplicates the breathtaking complexity of human experience. Novelists can use multiple points of view, the same events seen through the perspective of different characters, to explore the relativity of experience. You generally don't have that option in an autobiographic work, but you can achieve an equivalent complexity through the opposition of your own perspectives at different points in time—"Before then I had felt," "then I thought," "later I imagined," "now I realize," "sometime I may decide" may all be in opposition and equally valid, though at different stages along a line of consciousness. As mysterious as the human mind's engagement with time and awareness is, it is replicable in autobiographic writing through tricks of craft.

FLASHBACKS

A flashback is a jump into memory. While you are doodling along chronologically through your past, you can enter an earlier period as easily as saying something like, "earlier I had," "I recalled when," or simply "once." Since flashbacks are a natural way of thinking, entry points are easy to find.

But this is what you need to know about jumping backward with flashbacks: They have to move you forward.

Now you may say, You're getting a little cute for me—how does flashing back take me forward?

It doesn't always, so you have to be careful. Flashbacks can suck you into a black hole into which you dizzily tumble, unable to recall your place of entry. If you make it out, you may find you have stopped the forward movement of your story. Flashbacks move you forward only when they enhance your current emotional beat and take you to your next one.

Notice how Brason Lee's flashback to his childhood helps you understand what he is experiencing within his main chronological story as a young adult. Here he is coming home from the hospital for the first time since his motorcycle accident and subsequent paralysis.

Images of my neighborhood drifted past my mind as my sisters and I drove home from the hospital.

National City, a racially mixed community south of downtown San Diego where I'd grown up, was a rugged place covered with concrete and graffiti. Most fathers depended on the sweat of their muscled arms and thick hands for a living, hammering and hoisting hour after hour in auto shops, or assembly plants . Mothers tested the limits of their budget, raising their children, preparing the meals, and maintaining the home. On occasion, they played the role of the father. Some also worked in factories part-time, sewing clothing in overcrowded rooms to supplement the family's income. The older kids, mostly from high school, cruised the streets, displaying their customized cars, hanging out on street corners, and marking their turf with spray paint. Sometimes they got into fist fights in honor of their turf and pride.

As a young boy, the ruggedness of life had not permeated my skin yet. I played with the kids nearby. Sometimes older kids, such as Raoul who was about three years my senior, also joined in the activities. We built wooden clubhouses, made fresh lemonade and played basketball. . . .

Most kids I played with began cruising the streets in the fourth grade. That's when Mom enrolled me into a karate school—not for self-defense, but for fellowship with other kids in a supervised setting. I agreed with her because I didn't like the streets. I did not like seeing people taking turns on the bleeding face of another, hearing the thumping sounds of fists, or feeling wary in the heat of an angry crowd. Instead I wanted to jump and kick like the heroes in karate movies. With my new adventure, I began to grow apart from the neighborhood kids. Only memories of playing in our clubhouse kept us loyal over the years. The kids from the old neighborhood now greeted me on my return from the hospital. Five, six, seven of them swarmed around as I stepped out of the car.

"Hey, Brason," said one neighbor.

"What's up," echoed another from the background.

Raoul, now wearing khaki-colored pants, red bandanna and gold chain, stood at a cool distance from the crowd greeting me home. The streets had trained him to show no fear, to fight in gangs, and to carry knives. A tattoo of a tear drop near his right eye symbolized his acquired status on the streets: the crown of acceptance by prison inmates; the mark of reputation in having taken someone's life; the sign of gang membership. The tattoo had served only one meaning to me—as a sign warning me to stay clear. But, as I returned my attention to walking up the path to my house, that tear meant a sense of unity from his heart, a sympathy cheering me home.

The world around me faded from sight as I tried to move, focusing my eyes on one leg at a time.

There are actually two flashbacks in this example, and more as the chapter proceeds. The device of an ongoing physical task—here, driving home from the hospital, opening the car door, Brason walking from the car and into the house—provides opportunity for memory jumps without danger of a reader getting lost. A physical activity with customary steps supplies clear occasions for reentry as the narrator returns from thoughts of the past to each action that requires his attention. "The kids from the old neighborhood now greeted me on my return from the hospital. Five, six, seven of them swarmed around as *I stepped out of the car,*" and "The tattoo had served only one meaning to me—as a sign warning me to stay clear. But, as *I returned my attention to walking up the path to my house,* that tear meant a sense of unity from his heart."

Lee's flashbacks move his chronological story forward because this chapter is about his partial recovery of memory after his brain injury. The flashbacks make concrete what it means to Lee for the neighbor kids to be there welcoming him home. It is a way of being specific about feelings. His memories move the story forward because they deliver us from the first beat of recognition into his next emotional beat of unexpected gratitude toward his childhood friends.

In the case of Raoul, we get a whole ministory within the ongoing story: Raoul as an older kid who played basketball with the younger kids, Raoul as a gangbanger who has been to prison, Raoul as a man who understands pain and offers sympathy. The physical image of the tear-drop tattoo that changes meaning for Lee is a portal into the past that delivers him home with a new realization. So we have a whole story through flashback: In the beginning Brason liked Raoul but then feared him, and as a result he stayed away, but in the end he realized Raoul now considered him a brother in misfortune. This illustrates how within a larger story you may tell many small stories.

Going into a mental flashback gives you enormous freedom. You can recall an amazing amount in seconds, memories with the sharpest details, images and sensations separated by years, conversations begun in one decade and continued in another. You can tell stories within stories. A few paragraphs or pages of flashback can cover thirty years of your life in the time it takes you to pour a jar of spaghetti sauce into a pot.

Yet all this freedom must be used with caution. If you go on for too many pages meandering in the past, a reader may lose interest. Fortunately, you can keep from getting lost in an unending memory chain if you visualize the use of flashbacks as a game of Pong. Yes, Pong. In this interactive video game, Pong, that little round figure who is supposed to be you, periodically leaps up so he can come down on and smash a traveling mushroom. He lands virtually in the same spot from which he leapt and continues marching forward with increased power because of his successful vertical jumps:

Pong's horizontal progress depends on his doing these vertical leaps at the right time. The vertical leaps don't slow him down; rather they make it possible for him to move forward to his destination faster. (Though he is sexless, I always think of Pong as male, perhaps because of his steady goal orientation. He speeds through those pretty electronic gardens and never stops to appreciate them. I tell myself it's because I do that I've never won at Pong.)

Feminist scholars observe that women in their autobiographic writings tend to use more flashbacks and other vertical time devices and are less committed to the progression of a horizontal plot than are men. (I think that was so only before the twentieth century, because male writers of autobiographic novels, such as Marcel Proust in *Remembrance of Things Past* and Pat Conroy in *The Prince of Tides,* certainly use a lot of flashbacks.) What is true, I think, is that all autobiographic writers need a facility for both horizontal story development and vertical time layering. One gives the writing momentum; the other gives it texture. How much you want of each largely depends upon what genre of the self you are writing. If it's an adventure memoir of your attempt to beat a sailing record in subarctic waters, you'd want fewer flashbacks than if you were writing a humorous personal essay on failed relationships. But not necessarily.

FLASHFORWARDS

The rule for flashforwards is virtually the same as for flashbacks; a flashforward must enable the horizontal story to move forward to its next beat. The example here is from the first volume of Doris Lessing's autobiography, *Under*

My Skin. She is describing the unexpected hardships and primitive conditions her mother faced when Lessing's father, a British missionary, moved the family to Southern Rhodesia.

> . . . When a farmhouse took a step forward into electricity, running water, or an indoor lavatory, neighbors were invited over to inspect the triumph, which was felt to represent and fulfill all of us.
>
> My mother must have realized almost at once that nothing was going to happen as she had expected.
>
> Not long ago I was sent the unpublished memoirs of a young English woman, with small children, who found herself in the bush of old Rhodesia, without a house, for it was still to be built, no fields ready—nothing. And particularly no money. She too had to make do and contrive, face snakes and wild animals and bush fires, learn to cook bread in antheaps or cakes in petrol tins over open fires. She hated every second, feared and loathed the black people, could not cope with anything at all. Reading this, I had to compare her with my mother, who would be incapable of placing a vegetable garden where a rising river might flood it, who never ran from a snake or got hysterics over a bad storm.

Because the flashforward, the anecdote of an unpublished memoir sent to Lessing in the present day, is so integral to the horizontal narrative, it is barely noticeable. It functions as a transition between Lessing's mother's surprise at what she found in store for her in Rhodesia and her competence in dealing with it. It serves another function here, too: The flashforward helps keep Lessing present as narrator while she tells her mother's story, a tale not her own, always a problem for the conventional autobiographer who begins with an account of parents and grandparents.

The flashforward is an opportunity for the narrator to remind us that we are reading memoir, that we are within the consciousness of the self now, recollecting. Look at how integral Geoffrey Wolff's flashforwards are in this excerpt from his memoir, *The Duke of Deception.* In the ongoing horizontal story, he is visiting home for Christmas after his first semester at Choate.

> On the flight down I had thought much about the impression I wished to convey. Prosperity, control, worldliness. "You seemed quite worldly," my mother admits. "You let me know that you were no longer a virgin." My mother was indifferent to the significance of that fiction. "I didn't feel I had much part in your life. You had grown up indepen-

dent of me; I felt I had no responsibility for your diet, health, morals, anything. I had no right to care."

While Toby gawked at his wised-up brother on the drive from Tampa to Sarasota, I confessed my imaginary sins. I had exhausted the inventory by the time we were downtown.

Wolff jumps from his flight home in the past, to his mother's recollection in the present, to her reaction to his affected worldliness in the past, to her continued recollection in the present, to his younger brother's wonderment in the past—simply by jumping back and forth between past and present tense. Autobiographic writers who limit their consciousness to the past of their chronological story lose a very important device for adding knowledge and keeping a reader involved.

GRABBERS

A grabber is a scene of intense dramatic conflict that appears at the beginning of a work to get a reader's attention by grabbing 'em by the throat. Here is the grabber that opens *Run, Run, Run: The Lives of Abbie Hoffman,* a portrait by his brother Jack Hoffman and Daniel Simon.

> To really begin to understand my brother Abbie, you've got to try to picture Aunt Rose, our mother's sister, a diagnosed schizophrenic who has not been able to look after her own basic needs for most of her life. If Rose is crazy, Abbie was crazy like a fox; they had nothing in common on that score. But something happened to Rose that led her to spend the rest of her days without a purpose, lost in the futility of her life. And in Abbie, the same sense of futility became the source for his extraordinary optimism. Yet his deep optimism, that he carried with him from the cradle to the grave, held the same tragic seed as her despair. His vision for revolutionary change, for a better world to come, came naturally to him. No different from Rose, our parents, or me, Abbie too was caught. Every family has its madness.

As with this example, a grabber typically contains a flashforward, which builds anticipation and sets the thematic conflict. In conventional full autobiographies, it is customary to begin with a grabber that functions as an adrenaline rush and a promise of what is ahead so the reader can stay awake during the soporific ancestor stuff. Publishers like grabbers because if you pick up a memoir in a bookstore and read the first page, it gets you hooked.

For the same reason, some authors like to begin many of their book chapters nonsequentially with grabbers.

I like nonsequential grabbers, but there are other good ways to begin a work. You can swing your hips saucily and seduce your reader with your voice, you can promise a big surprise and make him wait, you can make him think you are talking about him; he likes that. Take this opening of an autobiographic magazine article, "Waiting for Dennis" by Richard Stayton, which appeared in the *Los Angeles Times Magazine*. The narrator/protagonist progresses in the story from his desire to ghostwrite Hopper's autobiography, to his disillusionment at finding after exhaustive interviews that he can't get Hopper to sign a contract, to his realization that he no longer wants to be "in" with Hopper, he wants out. Stayton doesn't grab you with a dramatic scene of one of Hopper's outrageous behaviors or with a scene of his own conflict with Hopper, though those would be good nonsequential grabbers. Rather, he grabs you by appearing to be talking about you.

> It happens to all of us. At a party, across a crowded room, stands your former life. The woman who betrayed you. The man who broke every promise he ever made. You, the co-dependent in recovery, see the Significant Other who tormented and manipulated and consigned you to hell. In a single glance, countless therapy sessions vanish—nothing since has approached that relationship's intensity or promise.

⌒ BOOKENDS

A grabber becomes a bookend when the end of the work matches the beginning. With bookends, the situation, scene, or image with which you begin a work is completed at the end of the work:

[   ]

When you open your work with a flashforward and close it with a flashback, you have bookends if, set side by side, they would fit like pieces of a jigsaw puzzle.

James Ingebretsen begins his autobiography with a flashforward to a dream he had at thirteen.

> I dream I am alone, ceaselessly climbing an invisible ladder in pitch blackness. No far off beacon summons. Only the dark, timeless space

surrounds me, stretching perpetually outward. Somehow, I know the
ladder I climb is as everlasting as this darkness, and I am scared.

After this flashforward, Ingebretsen follows the convention of full autobiographies and reverts to the time before he was born, when his parents first
met. From there he proceeds chronologically, through his birth, childhood,
adolescence, adulthood, and old age. He ends in the present time, when he
is eighty-nine, with a bookend flashback to the thirteen-year-old's ladder
dream.

> I view that dream differently now. There is light there. Something has
> descended from above to join me on my climb, and help light the way
> ahead. The boy, meanwhile, has learned to radiate something of his
> own light. I said at the beginning that "to find meaning in life is a task,
> not a birthright . . ." The search for meaning can be daunting, no
> doubt, but one cannot help but be humbled by the enormous quan-
> tity of assistance that is at hand in the undertaking of the task. Mean-
> ing, as if with arms outstretched, seems willing to meet us halfway.

Through understanding the story his life has made, Ingebretsen has revised
his ladder image. Bookends, like subplots, need to be intrinsically connected
to your main story. In this case the bookends are pertinent; they illustrate the
central character arc of the book: a boy in darkness, afraid of his destiny to
explore the eternal mysteries and his life's journey to enlightenment, which
comes from effort and fortuity.

BRACKETS

Brackets are situations, scenes, or images repeated intermittently through a
work, not just at the beginning and end. Brackets are like bookends with
additional shafts separating and punctuating the work.

[STORY]|[STORY]|[STORY]|[STORY]|[STORY]|[STORY]|[STORY]

It is an old-fashioned device in fiction, which predates its best-known
example, *The Arabian Nights*. In *A Thousand and One Nights* (the story collection's other name), the brackets take the form of an ongoing frame story
about a king, who having discovered that his wife was unfaithful, kills her,

and then, loathing all womankind, marries and kills a new wife each day until no more candidates can be found. However, his vizier has two daughters, and one of them, Scheherazade, having devised a scheme to save herself and others, insists that her father give her in marriage to the king. Each evening she tells her bridegroom a story (such as Aladdin, Ali Baba, or Sinbad the Sailor) and she leaves it incomplete, promising to finish it the following night. The king is so caught up in what's *goina* happen that he keeps putting off Scheherazade's execution and finally abandons his cruel arrangement. The brackets of Scheherazade's story hold in place all the unrelated tales she supposedly tells the king.

Using brackets is a good way to assemble different kinds of autobiographic stories under one title. Remember the street urchin Marlena Fontenay, who enchanted my writing class? She went on to complete a book, *Torch Songs*, which consists of autobiographic stories linked by brackets of herself as a narrator/chanteuse sitting on a stage in a smoky, dimly lit cabaret. She begins the book by setting up the frame story.

> The room is small and dimly lit. Twenty tables, perhaps. Each one with a candle casting a frail light and shadows on the faces of those who are regulars. The smoke from their cigarettes snakes upwards, like incense, to the ceiling. The ice in their glasses clinks. They speak to each other in hushed tones, as if conserving themselves for what is to come. For a woman who will hold them in her hands and with her eyes, on the edge of her voice. They have come to hear her moan, scream, cry, and laugh. To watch her be welded into song by a blue flame. . . .
>
> She has a burning need, this woman, to bridge the distance between herself and others. To touch everyone in the room. To be intimate with them. Her voice, like a blue laser, cuts through the air, reaching each one personally, as she begins:
>
> Women. Men. Young girls. Boys. Disembodied spirits. Angels. Fairies. Demons. All of you, welcome. . . .
>
> A torch song is said to be a ballad about unrequited love, usually sung by a woman.
>
> Ah, yes! The ever-suffering, tortured female, grieving for love lost, or never found. Carrying a torch for her mate. An entire lineage of women burning, in the name of love. . . .
>
> I say torch songs are more than the tales of woe, of a woman de-

feated. They're her life stories, welded in the fire. The fire that destroys. That brands the heart with "never again." The midnight fire, the exquisite thirst, that licks you clean. The fire of lessons learned. Of change. Lead into gold. The common fire, easy, that keeps you warm. The heavenly fire. And the raging fires of hell. And that long corridor of desire, like madness, stretched between the two. Yearning. Never satisfied.

These are my stories. My torch songs to Her. Life. La Vie.

My first song, "Seeing Only Blue," could only have been written for my French gypsy mother, who taught me to float above the world, always looking for the wonder in things. . . . She taught me that a woman can be big as silence. And that there are voices one must listen for. In the air and the water. In the earth.

A friend once asked me if my mother was a witch.

I thought about it for a while. And then I answered, "Yes. My mother's an enchantress."

Marlena's first short story in the collection follows this introductory bracket, and between subsequent stories, she reappears as the chanteuse who introduces each story/song, explaining how she came to write it. For instance, in one of the intermediate brackets:

Certain men I've known will find themselves in this song. Those men who carry a woman inside them. Who came to rest for a while inside of me because they could. Because I let them. Those men who, with the night in their eyes, are afraid of the dark. They're of a different race, with a different knowing. Exiles, maybe. And their wings are exquisite.

The bracketing device that Marlena uses is organic to her self-portrayal; she is, in fact, a professional torch singer. Sometimes, though, writers use bookends and frames just to make their work seem more literary, when in fact they would be better off without these devices. A swift beginning that catapults the reader onto the track of your ongoing chronological story is usually preferable. Sometimes if you are getting fancy with bookends, frames, flashbacks, or flashforwards, you are avoiding the work of shaping your primary, horizontal story. Then you need to use the army private's touchstone that often I have to tell myself:

TOUCHSTONE 6:

Keep it simple, stupid.

⌐Horizontal Time Devices

Vertical devices unleash you from chronological time as our aging bodies know it into the timelessness of memory and imagination. But most readers are not comfortable in that ether for long. Chronology is writer-friendly and reader-friendly, so don't abandon it without good reason. Readers like stories to be like life and become instantly upset in autobiographic narrative if you confound them about chronology. They don't like to be baffled about geographic layout, and they hate to have to guess—now, was this happening before you married Johnny Carson or after your affair with Prince Charles? They want you to guide them in a horizontal line. What they don't like are the boring parts. Which brings us to the first of the horizontal devices,

⌐STRETCHING AND CONDENSING

Without knowing your theme, it's hard for me to say what are the boring parts in your narrative. Driving to the airport to meet your sister might be a boring part, and the interesting part would be when she got off the plane wearing a suit of medieval armor. On the other hand, if on the drive to the airport you were rehearsing in your head how to tell your sister that you were marrying her ex-husband, and your thematic conflict was your desire to be a star like your sister versus your need to be yourself, that drive might be a very interesting part. In general, an interesting part is an emotional beat of the story that intensifies your thematic opposition and moves your story forward. Boring parts are irrelevant to your theme and plot or repeat beats you have already covered.

Fortunately, being faithful to chronology doesn't mean you have to treat all time as equal. Like Alice in Wonderland, you have the power to make things big and make things small. One of the simplest axioms in writing is that what is important to your story you want to expand, and what is unimportant you want to condense. In writing as in life, the rule is a thing or a person is as important as the time you give to it.

You are replicating emotional time, so you want to s-t-r-e-t-c-h thematic emotional beats no matter how little time they took in life; and those hours, years, or decades that don't qualify as interesting and relevant, you want to shrink. You can slow down time by developing for pages important moments as scenes with description and inner responses and sometimes dialog. You can speed up time by skipping over years in a single summary phrase such as "Eight years later," or "I was in my forties when . . ." Or you can simply leap.

HORIZONTAL LEAPS

The quickest way to get past irrelevant or boring parts is to leap. You don't write any narrative transition between scenes. You don't even waste time on a transitional phrase like "That afternoon" or even a teensy, weensy word like "then." You just leap to a new paragraph and a new scene.

Now, the trick—and these are tricks—is to leap over that big time chasm and not lose your audience. You have to hurdle to the other side in a whoosh while pulling that big, lumbering reader with you. You need to land lightly in your next scene, making sure the reader didn't get left behind so dizzy that he fell right out of your story.

Here are some leaping tricks.

BEGIN A NEW SCENE WITH DIALOG.

In *One Child* by Torey Hayden, the narrator, a special education teacher, uses the dialog "Ed?" to leap from a morning scene in her classroom to an afternoon scene set in the school office. In the classroom morning scene she's trying to decide which student to transfer out of her class to make room for a newcomer as her supervisor, Ed, ordered.

> . . . As we went through the day, I kept asking myself who should go . . . I looked at each one of them wondering where they would go and how they would make it. And how our room would be without them. I knew in my heart none of them would survive the rigors of a less-sheltered class. None of them was ready. Nor was I ready to give them up, nor give up on them.
>
> "Ed?" I clutched the receiver tightly because it kept slipping in my sweating hand, "I don't want to transfer any of my kids. We're doing so well together. I can't choose any one of them."
>
> "Torey, I told you we have to put that girl in there. I'm really sorry. I hate to do it to you, but there isn't any other place."
>
> I stared morosely at the bulletin board beside the phone with its proclamations of events my children could never attend.

BEGIN A NEW SCENE WITH AN ACTION.

Here, in *Days of Obligation,* Richard Rodriguez uses Huerta's action of driving the car to leap from an afternoon scene set at the Balboa Café to a scene in a different place on a different day. Father Huerta, sitting in the cafe, says,

"Someday I want people to read my work and say not that I was Mexican or American but that I lived in the shadow of the missions."

Here? In the Balboa Café? *In the shadow of the missions?* That phrase preoccupies him. . . .

Father Huerta believes in the power of memory. Californians are linked by memory—mainly unconscious—to a founding Hispanic culture. In homage to that memory, Huerta writes scholarly articles in Spanish and sends them off to Madrid to be published. It is not that he repudiates Anglo-California; it is rather this matter of shadows. . . .

Father Huerta is driving. We have just passed Stonestown, a section of San Francisco I don't know very well. We are going to meet a man named Sig Christopherson, "the Mexican Sigui." Surely an ironic sobriquet? Huerta says not.

The front door is wide open. We ring the bell. Sig Christopherson is a big man in his sixties. He welcomes me with a slap on the shoulder.

CHANGE THE SET WITH A DESCRIPTION OF A NEW PLACE.

Richard Rodriguez does this in the example above. He leaps from driving in the car with Father Huerta to their arrival at Christophersons' house with the description, "The front door is wide open."

In a different example from *High Tide in Tucson,* Barbara Kingsolver leaps into a new scene through a description of the historical background of the new setting, San Sebastian de La Gomera.

San Sebastian de La Gomera is the port from which Columbus set sail for the New World. Elsewhere on earth, the approaching quincentennial anniversary of that voyage had been raising a lot of fuss, but here at the point of origin all was quiet.

LAND IN A NEW SCENE WITH AN INNER RESPONSE:

In *New York in the Fifties,* Dan Wakefield leaps out of a long passage of narrative summary (I quote only from its last paragraph) and into a specific scene with his inner response, "I loved writing journalistic pieces . . ."

> . . . The New Journalism was part of a confluence of historic forces, a growing trend that probably would have sprung up sooner or later, but if it got its name and fame in the sixties, like so many other movements that shaped our time, it started in the fifties.
>
> I loved writing journalistic pieces and profiles for Harold Hayes and *Esquire,* but I hadn't given up on fiction. One night I had a dream in the form of a novel. It began with a title page, and then a story unfolded, not as words on a page but as characters moving and talking as they would in a novel. The story had a rather simple but convincing plot, with a beginning, middle, and end. . . .
>
> I woke up exhilarated, hurriedly got dressed, and went out and sat on a bench in Sheridan Square as the dawn came. I felt refreshed and affirmed, confident I would write my novel, though I didn't know when.

LEAP FORWARD BY SPECIFYING THE TIME OF DAY

You can signal the passing of time by mentioning the sun was setting or rising, as in the Wakefield example—"as the dawn came." Or you can simply state the time or date as Rodriguez did when he leapt into the scene that began the excerpt above.

> It is nearly *three o'clock on a Wednesday at the Balboa Café on Fillmore Street.* No one seems in any hurry to get back to work. Our waitress intones the bucolic of the day: pasta with goat cheese, smoked duck, pine nuts, and sun-dried tomatoes. Father Huerta orders an omelet— "plain." [Italics mine.]

There are other leaping tricks, and if you start paying attention to those used by your favorite writers, you will pick them up. You have to be careful not to overuse any one device. And you don't want to leap between scenes so often that your work loses cohesion. You need to use some narrative bridges, too.

⌒BRIDGES

Bridges are time transitions that give your reader support and handrails to hold on to while crossing over time chasms. Bridges might begin with phrases like, "During the next several months . . ." or "It took longer than I'd imagined . . ." or "In the following days . . ." You lessen the danger of losing your reader if you write a bridge between time periods. You can, however, make the mistake of thinking of bridge transitions as merely a mechanical means to get you from here to there. Like flashbacks, bridges work best when they advance you from one emotional beat to the next, and when they are themselves thematically or emotionally charged. Take these before and after examples from Brason Lee's *Without My Helmet*. In the "before" example, he writes about his faltering affair with an older woman who is separated from her husband. At an office Christmas party, she has told Brason that she can't go to a motel with him afterward because she has to get back home to her kids. Then one of her co-workers comes up to them.

> "Claire, Brason," said the co-worker. "Would you two like to join us bar hopping?"
>
> "I'll go!" Claire said, coming back to life.
>
> Claire's response stunned me. It came before I could even turn to look at her. I thought that she was going to decline the offer, giving the need to be with her kids as the reason. She'd seemed so insistent about going home when I'd spoken to her. What had happened to the kids now? She had said no to me before, and I had accepted her answer. Why did she have to cover up the truth this time?
>
> A couple of weeks went by quickly.
>
> The New Year was two hours away. Claire and I were sitting on the sofa in her living room, while Rob and his girlfriend sat across from us on the love seat.

There is nothing wrong with the bridge, "A couple of weeks went by quickly." It gets you from the Christmas scene to the one on New Year's Eve without confusion. But see how in rewriting it, Brason uses the time bridge as an opportunity to enhance his storytelling, to make it an emotional as well as a time bridge.

. . . Why did she have to cover up the truth this time?

In the next two weeks, Claire continued to flip-flop, wanting me near one minute and then pushing me away the next.

The New Year was two hours away. . . .

The next example of turning a time bridge into an emotional bridge follows the crisis in Brason's memoir. He has up to this point successfully hidden from himself and others the reality that he has not and never will totally recover from his brain injury. Now, working at a V.A. hospital, he is confronted by some of his own patients, disabled vets in a discussion group he conducts.

"Mr. Lee," said one veteran with long hair and a grown beard. "Why do you hesitate with what you're trying to say? Are you unsure?"

"Mr. Lee," said yet another whose face was reddened from years of drinking, "why do you wait before you say anything?"

I never had a good answer for them. I didn't even have one for myself. . . .

"Mr. Lee," said one veteran with an amputated leg. "Why can't you remember my name?" . . .

"Yeah," said yet another. "I know your name!"

Soon almost everyone joined in and filled the room with questions. . . . They backed me into a corner of mirrors where the only person I could see was me.

"Why can't you remember our names? Are we not important?" said one veteran in his 60s.

Not one sound, not one motion, came from the room after that. Yet I could feel all of their eyes focused on me, waiting.

"You kn . . . know, every . . . body has dif . . . ficulties," I said, "wh . . . ether they want to ad . . . mit to it or not. Some pro . . . blems are hard . . . er to manage than others."

All the veterans began looking at each other, nodding their heads. Some began to point out examples, "Like coke." Another added, "Like my nightmares."

"I have a hard time with na . . . names es . . . pecially if I have to re . . . mem . . . ber a new group every few weeks. But I will always re . . . mem . . . ber a face, and I remem . . . ber every single one of you."

I never said a word about my head injury.

Most of the veterans stopped haunting me after that. A few started kidding around, "Do you remember me today, Mr. Lee?"

Over the next weeks, I returned to the safety of a university library where I had in the past researched information. I started to look up the many questions for which I had no answers—my problems with speech, attention, and memory. I read some articles word for word. Some I skimmed over.

In the privacy of my mind, in the silence of the room, I began to fight with myself . . .

Again, there is nothing really wrong with the time bridge, "Over the next weeks, I returned to the safety of a university library where I had in the past researched information." It is simply flat; it lets the air out, and when you are moving from your story's crisis to its climax, you want to sustain the emotional drive, not lose it. See how Brason's rewrite of the time bridge (simply the addition of a phrase of inner response) sustains the momentum of the preceding episode and leads into the next scene.

Shaken by these interactions, I returned to the safety of a university library where I had in the past found comfort in reading textbooks and journals.

The sentence isn't very different, but now it is an emotional as well as a time bridge.

FORESHADOWING

Foreshadowing hints at what is to come, creating anticipation, getting a reader to turn pages. Brason Lee began his memoir with foreshadowing.

January 20, 1981, was the second day of winter break, after my first semester as a freshman at San Diego State. The afternoon air felt fresh and crisp. The sky was scattered with high clouds. Never did I imagine that life, as I knew it, was about to end without notice.

Foreshadowing can be far more subtle than this; it can be a repeated image that acquires significance later in a story, an atmosphere predictive of the story's tone, or a dream or an event that turns out to be prescient.

Cliffhangers are essentially the same as foreshadowing, except that they tend to come at the end of chapters and can be melodramatic and obvious, for example: "I thought I had found security at last. But that was not to be." Daytime soaps and television series such as *Dynasty* and *Melrose Place* use obvious cliffhangers at the end of each episode.

The best cliffhangers are situations that are left unresolved from one chapter to the next. In one chapter, you set up the need for you to make a decision—should you accept this person's marriage proposal?—but you withhold the answer until a later chapter. In the beginning of your story you set up the possibility that you might participate in a jail break, and you omit what you actually did until the second half of the story.

When you foreshadow or cliffhang, you intrigue the reader by creating a question in the reader's mind—and withholding the answer. When you "telegraph" in writing, you give the answer ahead of time and deny the reader the pleasure of a surprise or a plot twist. Writers find themselves telegraphing unintentionally for what they think are good, even necessary reasons. Hanh Hoang found herself telegraphing her mother's escape from Saigon. Hanh had been writing chronologically about her mother having sent her to America three months before the fall of Saigon and about the California family that had sponsored Hanh. Hanh described how she had learned of events in her homeland by watching them on U.S. network news. During one of these broadcasts, she received a collect phone call from her mother asking if the people who had sponsored Hanh to the U.S. would help her get out of the refugee camp where she and Hanh's sister had been interned. Using the phone call as a transition into her mother's point of view, Hanh told the story of her mother's and sister's escape from Saigon. The phone call explained how Hanh knew her mother's story when she had not been there to observe.

The escape story had all the elements of an action adventure, a time bomb ticking as President Thieu abandoned South Vietnam, with North Vietnamese troops drawing near the city, rich Saigonese selling their bougainvillea-covered villas for a fraction of their value, Hanh's mother racing through the city on the back of Hanh's sister's motor scooter, begging friends and relatives for help, disappointments, betrayals, close calls, reversals. But the reader could not feel involved. We already knew from the phone conversation that Hanh's mother had escaped successfully. Hanh had inadvertently stolen the *goina* from her mother's story. How could she put it back?

Whenever you face this sort of problem, the first question to ask yourself is, What if I followed the actual chronology of events? If Hanh were simply to jump from her own adjustments to American life to her mother's attempts to escape Saigon, we would turn pages to find out if mother makes it out alive. We would keep reading to find out *what's goina happen.*

That's how it would be done in a movie, but of course this was not a movie; it was a memoir from Hanh's first person point of view. Fortunately, Hanh had moved into her mother's point of view in earlier sections of the book—for example, when she had described how her parents had met and married and how her mother had left the family to go to medical school. She had found entry through flashforward devices such as "recently I asked my mother how she had met my father and she told me . . ." and she'd used conditional phrases like "she must have felt." Now I was asking Hanh to jump not through *time,* but through space and into another character's POV as a novelist would. To write the equivalent of "Meanwhile, back at the ranch." I assured her that now that she had set the groundwork, she could trust that a reader would simply accept that she had learned her mother's story without needing to be told when or how. It was so important to save the *goina,* that Hanh had to push the parameters of what is conventionally accepted in memoir.

Hanh looked at me skeptically, the way that only the stunningly talented student can look at her less talented teacher. I stared her down. As long as she could get away with it, I insisted, it would be a literary virtue to push the boundaries into the novelist's terrain. *As long as she could get away with it,* which means never to go over the line and lose credibility with the reader, a line that is always moving and is different in each work. A line that only a sensitive reader could tell her she had or had not crossed, said I, asserting my position as teacher for a little longer.

SUSPENSE

Foreshadowing and cliffhangers are devices for creating the tension of suspense, and there are others: intimations of fear or hope, partial disclosure of information, and the gradual unfolding of character. Marguerite Duras created suspense in her work, simply through her spare voice, suggesting that something is being withheld, remains unspoken. Suspense need have nothing to do with physical jeopardy. The ultimate source of suspense in autobiographic writing is the suspension of resolution of your thematic conflict until the end of the work and our involvement with your need to come to your final realization.

Though it requires uncertainty, suspense does not require an unexpected outcome. Most of Shakespeare's plays were based upon well-known plots, so the audience knew the endings; what they enjoyed was the anticipation of getting there. As Coleridge said, Shakespeare doesn't give us surprise; he gives us expectation and then the satisfaction of perfect knowledge. So it is with memoir. If you are writing for relatives, they may already know the outlines of your story; if you are writing for publication, whatever surprises your story holds may be advertised on the dust jacket. Still, your work will have suspense if you build dramatic tension toward your story's crisis, climax, and final realization. And that suspense will give your reader pleasure. As Gwendolen, in Oscar Wilde's *The Importance of Being Earnest,* says, "The suspense is terrible. I hope it will last."

19

Humor

Humor/memoir/humor/memoir. Repeat the words three times fast and see how quickly they become indistinguishable and you sound funny. Though you don't need to be a comedian and make jokes, as a memoirist you need a comic vision. Humor helps you strip away façades and expose the imperfect bare-assed truth beneath. It's an antidote to bragging; a light that illuminates the ugly and subhuman, a salve for corrosive anger, a remedy for the lasting pain of embarrassment.

One of my students, a psychologist, helped me understand the importance of the comic view to the memoirist. We were walking to the parking lot after class when she mentioned that her autobiographic writing had first emerged within her diaries. I was interested because my autobiographic writings had started in my diaries, too, when the entries seemed to be taking the form of little stories.

I asked her, "What do you think changed in you that caused your journal to become autobiographic? I mean besides getting older."

"I stopped seeing my life as tragic," she said.

Turning one's life into memoir is inherently comic in the classic definition of comedy; it is redemptive. Memoir triumphs over the view that, because it ends in death, life is tragic. Memoir allows you to wrest meaning from life that outlasts the grave.

Humor as the Unveiling of Naked Truth

There is a correspondence between humor and New Autobiography in that they both pull away social masks to show human vulnerability. It was this brand of humor that finally brought success to comedian Rick Reynolds. In 1991, he presented an autobiographic one-man show at the Music Hall Theater in Beverly Hills to sold-out audiences. Within the show-case, he described how depressed he'd become in Hollywood because he couldn't get anywhere on the comedy circuit. In despair, he'd finally accepted defeat, gave up, and moved to the boonies—Petaluma, California—where he began to write with no purpose in mind the truth about his failed life. Those random writings had become his successful one-man show which moved audiences from hysterical laughter, to tears, and back to guffaws. All the years Reynolds had tried to be funny, had worked at his delivery, on the timing of his jokes, and had attended all the right parties in order to be seen, he had bombed because he had not yet learned the point of his show, ex-pressed in its title: "Only the Truth Is Funny."

As a comedian he knew the techniques of structuring a joke, but what he'd learned was that that wasn't enough. The best humor also points out the realities of human nature. Take that wonderful Oscar Wilde line, "The suspense is terrible. I hope it will last." Technically, it works because the first sentence leads you in one direction, that suspense is terrible, and the second sentence does a hairpin turn and goes in an unexpected direction. The sec-ond sentence is a surprise because you would expect that if something is ter-rible, you wouldn't want it to continue. The unexpected makes you feel like laughing, as when you suddenly say "boo" to a baby, she releases the tension of surprise by giggling. But it isn't just the structure that makes the line funny. It's funny because it is true; we do love suspense to last. The line is funny because it points out the absurdity of being human.

Every Joke Has a Victim

Reynolds's show also worked because he had discovered the best target for humor in autobiography—oneself. All humor has a victim. Take for example this joke:

What are the symptoms of an agnostic who has insomnia and dyslexia?
Someone who stays awake all night wondering if there's a dog.

Technically the joke is funny because the funny word comes at the very end and has hard sounds. But it wouldn't be funny unless it had a victim, in this case dyslexics. The joke is especially funny when told by dyslexics to dyslexics. Think about it, all great comedians make fun of their own foibles,

Jack Benny's stinginess, Lucille Ball's ambition, Cybill Shepherd's lustiness. The best autobiographic humor is when you are the butt of your own jokes.

⤳Satirical Humor

Which is not to say that you can't make others the victim of your humor, too. You just have to be careful that it's not out of proportion and you have to forsake any pretense of being a lady or gentleman. After all, the humorous truth often isn't pretty; it's body functions; it's failure and death; it's Newt Gingrich. It isn't very nice; it's a pie in the face, a kick in the pants, Newt Gingrich in Congress. The point is, though, if you can't be nice, the least you can do is be funny about it. If the real you is cantankerous, but you—unlike Newt—can make your ill humor capricious, as W. C. Fields did, we'll like you, at least some of us will like you, some of the time, better than a boring mealymouth.

Like Adelle who joined one of my private classes. Adelle was an elderly ingénue who wore coordinated outfits from Loehmann's and jewelry from Cartier. She was the nicest person you would ever want to meet. She was writing her memoir in short humorous pieces for herself because her daughter refused to read a word of it. Adelle was the thoughtful, generous one who brought cookies to class that were only slightly stale. She always had good advice to offer whether you wanted it or not. Adelle was sweet as the pink stuff, and beloved in her play-dough society, which, she demurely corrected me after I had mispronounced it for five months, was the Plato Society. But when she picked up a pen, Adelle spiked it with the esprit of Dorothy Parker. Freed on paper to write all the mean things she never let herself say in life, Adelle was a rascal, a dervish, a demon. She had no interest in the hassles of publishing and no patience for rewriting, but she loved making us laugh. Her judgmental sarcasm, which she concealed from everyone else, was the only thing we liked about Adelle.

Of course, you take more of a risk if you write sardonically about others; some people are going to take offense. I took a personal essay class from Bernard Cooper, who introduced us to the curmudgeonly essayist Phillip Lopate. I thought Lopate had the sexiest male literary voice I had ever read, but most of the women in the class thought he was a not very nice person and wanted nothing more to do with his work. (This tells you something about the way I choose men.) Well, you decide if you would want him. Here is Lopate in his essay "Never Live Above Your Landlord," from his collection *Against Joie de Vivre*.

Although I consider myself a good tenant, clean and quiet and un-obtrusive, my landlord and landlady, because of our close proximity, hear every sound I make, and cannot bring themselves to stop resenting the fact that I come in the door, that I take off my shoes, that I open the refrigerator—in short, that I live and breathe. The ideal tenant is, to them, someone who sends in the monthly rent check punctually but does not occupy the premises. I discovered this when they began fondly reminiscing about the previous tenant, a Hungarian architect who spent half the year building prefab condos in Barbados. Certainly their property must take much less wear and tear when no one is in it, alas, I can never live up to the standard set by my "invisible" pre-decessor, my Rebecca, as it were. . . .

The wife is both shriller and easier to get around. It's a tired liter-ary device to characterize someone with an animal metaphor, but what can I do when I have such a mutt of a landlady? After scratching on my door, she bolts into the living room, her dirty-blond-gray hair plas-tered at odd angles from her head. "Mr. Lopat!" she barks. She has a harsh way of saying my name that stops me in my tracks, like a flash-light pointed at a burglar.

I am resigned to her letting herself in with her keys whenever she wants. One time, however, it made for some embarrassment. I was en-tertaining a pretty woman visitor, on my lap. Mrs. Rourke took her in immediately—sniffed her out, I should say—and proceeded to ig-nore her. "Mr. Lopat! Were you watering your plants too much?"

"No."

" 'Cause it's leaking over our heads. Something's leaking. Did you just water your plants?"

"No!" I said, starting to get annoyed. "I wish I had; they needed it."

"Let me take a look." She bounded over to the window on her thick little ankle-socked legs and stuck her snout under the radiator. "The board's warped! It's leaking all over. I'll go get Jimmy."

Moments later, Mr. Rourke entered with his tools, grinning from ear to ear, enjoying, it would seem, the comedy of their interrupting a romantic scene. "Will you look at that?" he declared, kneeling by the radiator cap.

"Jimmy, it's leakin' all over! I thought it was the plants but he says he didn't water the plants."

"I know that! What are you telling me that for?" . . .

. . . He tinkered a minute more. "I'll have to come by tomorrow and look at it." They exited as suddenly as they had appeared, back to their kennel, I suppose. . . .

Whenever anything goes wrong with the plumbing (the pipes in the brownstone are very old), the Rourkes always try to make me feel defensive, as if it were my fault. An anally shaming connotation is given to clogged drains. One day this note was slipped under my door:

Please do not use the wash Basin to empty the dirt and cat litter in. Use a Pail and throw it *in your toilet*.

This Past week the Basin was Packed full of junk, and we used $9.95 *worth* of Drain Power . . . Please throw the stuff in the toilet and flush. Next thing the Pipes will get leaking.

Mrs. Rourke

My answer:

Dear Mrs. Rourke:

What makes you think I am emptying cat litter and dirt in the wash basin!! This is an absurd contention. Please make sure you know whereof you speak before you start making baseless and, frankly, fantastic accusations.

Sincerely,
Phillip Lopate

I held my breath for the next few days, thinking that perhaps I had gone too far this time. Yet when I ran into my landlady in the hallway, she was almost respectful. Not that our epistolary relationship ended there. I keep all the notes she slips under my door, among which is this quaintly worded favorite:

Please stop that
jungle drum music.

———————

or whatever it is.

———

I'm going out of my mind.
Bang   Bang   Bang

Mrs. Rourke

Although Lopate makes Mrs. Rourke the victim of his humor, he does so affectionately. If you read the entire essay, you will see that he shows all sides of her character. He explains, "All these skirmishes are part of the 'class struggle' that we are obliged to wage as tenant and landlord. The trouble is, underneath everything, we like each other, which complicates the purity of the antagonism." Yes, he calls her a mutt, but he takes the edge off it in advance by criticizing himself: "It's a tired literary device to characterize someone with an animal metaphor," anticipating the reader's negative reaction and beating 'em to the punch. It's a clever literary device to tell readers you are aware of their problem before they have it.

∼ Humor as Acceptance

Misanthropic humor, satire, and sarcasm thrive best in narrow plots (the personal essay and the autobiographic short story). A more spiritual side of comedy is found in the memoirs of those who have truly experienced tragedy. Humor brightens the work of Nancy Mairs's writing about her multiple sclerosis and enables Gilda Radner to look straight at her cancer in *It's Always Something*. For instance, in dealing with the humiliations of receiving chemotherapy, Radner consciously evoked her comic alter ego Roseanne Roseannadanna.

> . . . we went out to dinner at a friend's house and a clump of my hair fell in my plate at dinner. It looked disgusting. I was trying to get it out of the plate before the hostess noticed, but it wasn't like one hair, it was a little clump of hair in the poached salmon with the special Dijon sauce. It seemed like an event only Roseanne Roseannadanna could make up—me trying to get this hair off the plate and then trying to figure out what to do with the hair.

Radner uses her humor as a way to broach a hard to talk about subject. Similarly, Anne Lamott uses humor to find a way to express the frightening liability of loving a child in *Operating Instructions*.

> I am definitely aware of the huge wound that having a baby makes—in addition to the fact that your ya-ya gets so torn up. Before I got pregnant with Sam, I felt there wasn't anything that could happen that would utterly destroy me. Terminal cancer would certainly be a set-

back, but I actually thought I could get through it. And I always felt that if something happened to Steve or Pammy, if they died, it would be over for me for a long time but that I'd somehow bounce back. In a very real sense, I felt that life could pretty much just hit me with her best shot, and if I lived, great, and if I died, well, then I could be with Dad and Jesus and not have to endure my erratic skin or George Bush any longer. But now I am fucked unto the Lord. Now there is something that could happen that I could not survive: I could lose Sam. I look down into his staggeringly lovely little face, and I can hardly breathe sometimes. He is all I have ever wanted, and my heart is so huge with love that I feel like it is about to go off. At the same time I feel that he has completely ruined my life, because I just didn't used to care all that much.

Lamott knows how to use all the tricks comedians use: repetition of a word or phrase until it becomes funny (she repeatedly docks George Bush in her work; I copied off her with Newt), the use of comic builds in threes (terminal cancer would be a setback, Steve or Pammy dying would be hard to get over, life could hit me with erratic skin or George Bush), the use of funny sounding words (ya-ya), incongruity of tone ("but now I am fucked unto the Lord"). I love her deadpan journal entry, "September 7, 1989 So anyway, I had a baby last week" where the casualness of the language is incongruous with the import of the subject. Yet, as an autobiographic writer, she is able to do something comedians rarely can do: turn on a dime from humor to what is wrenchingly serious, and back again. She interweaves humor with tears, and self-parody with real distress. The juxtaposition of opposing extremes of comedy and tragedy makes each more powerful, as in this short piece by my student Lianne Clenard.

Please do not stop reading this even when you see the subject.

The subject is What Happened To Me When President Kennedy Got Shot. Everybody always wants to tell what they were doing when they heard about it. They think it will be interesting, which is usually never true. However, I think that my story really isn't boring even though I am the one telling it.

It happened at lunch time. I was ten years old. Mr. Greaves, the Art teacher, climbed on top of a table in the outside eating area and yelled, "People, can I have your attention? People! People!" Everyone just laughed and said boo because Mr. Greaves hated all of us. If you had Art, he yelled at the whole class just for nothing and said your manners stink and your manners are in your feet.

But Mr. Greaves didn't get down off the table and he didn't even get mad. He just looked smug like "oh boy you're going to feel really bad when you find out what I was trying to tell you." And he was right because finally it was quiet and he shouted, "Our President has been shot!" I didn't hear what he said after that.

Our president had been shot? Dusty Peak, president of our student body? I remembered seeing him just a few days earlier. We rode on the same school bus. His mother worked in the cafeteria and knew my mom. Dusty Peak had been shot!

All around me, the girls were crying with streaks of black mascara and blue eye shadow running down their cheeks. The boys were swearing. Some people were running. Some were gathering in groups with their friends. I just sat by myself and stared at my books. They had covers made of brown paper grocery bags with smeared blue ink drawings all over them.

When lunch was over, we went to 4th period and everyone was talking only about IT. Mrs. Trabasso brought in a radio and plugged it in so we could hear. The news was so serious that she had decided not to follow the lesson plan.

And then I realized that President Kennedy had been shot. I couldn't believe it. The coincidence was seriously blowing my mind! Who would ever have thought that the president of the student body and the president of the country would get shot on the *same day!*

Later I figured out what everybody else already knew. It was only President Kennedy that got shot. Dusty was fine and when he grew up he married my friend Anita Jensen.

Sometimes I tell people this story because I like to make them laugh at how funny was my way of thinking. But I do not ever tell them that when I was 7 years old, my oldest brother was shot and killed. And that is why I thought it was normal for kids to get shot and not only famous people.

Perhaps the most extreme example of humor enabling the author to address a difficult subject—here, humor in the sense of the absurd—is that most unusual of New Autobiographies, Art Spiegelman's *Maus: A Survivor's Tale.*

It is a memoir told in the format of a cartoon strip in which Spiegelman's father tells him a horrifying tale of how he had survived during the Holocaust, seeing family members killed, and hunted by the Nazis. In the cartoon, Jews are represented by mice and Germans are cats. The incongruity between the realism of the content and the form's artificiality creates a distance that allows Spiegelman to express what otherwise would be untellable. The incongruity is the essence of the book's black humor.

As in many experiential works, the autobiographic process is part of the work. In *A Survivor's Tale*, the narrator illustrates the discomfort his probing questions cause his father. The distance created by the narrator's reflecting on his own insensitivity and his father's embarrassment is a form of ironic humor.

∽ Using Humor for Writing Embarrassing Moments

There is something excruciating about embarrassment when it happens, yet it makes deliciously funny stories later. Take the night I almost killed my boss's mother. I had had little time to prepare for a dinner party since I'd landed a new producing deal with Phillip Mandelker's film company. But my boyfriend and I wanted to celebrate, so we splurged on buying Chinese dinnerware for ten people and ordered take-out from a good Chinese restaurant. It was a power group including then-NBC v.p. Deanne Barkley, several mega producers, among them the exec producer of *Dallas*, Phil Capice, and my very respected new boss, Mandelker, who had said his mother was in town and asked to bring her along.

We had a theme for the party since it was April Fool's Day, and everybody received funny masks to wear and handmade fool's pins. The dinner was a big success, the Chinese feast delicious, everybody laughed a lot, and afterward we had brandies, Jim played the piano, and we sang old show tunes. We were having such a good time that nobody noticed that Mandelker's mother had fallen off her chair. We just continued singing, until I got up to offer more brandy and nearly tripped over her body on the floor.

"Call the paramedics!" Mandelker was beginning to hyperventilate. "You did remember to tell the restaurant no MSG, didn't you?" he accused me.

"No," I gulped.

By the time the paramedics got there, Mandelker, too, had passed out, and they didn't know who to resuscitate first. I said Mandelker's mother. She came right to, muttering, "I must have had too much to drink," but when they brought back Mandelker, he was convinced it was the MSG in the dinner I'd served.

Seeing my consternation, my friends tried to take the blame.

"It was my piano playing," Jim said.

"No, it was my singing." Capice really meant it.

"She was sitting next to me," Deanne said, lighting another Kool.

Mandelker and his mother left hurriedly without thanking me.

That night my boyfriend and I could not sleep. We rolled on the bed in agonies of humiliation. We would repeat to each other a part of the evening, or accuse the other for forgetting to ask about the MSG, or wail, "Why did we have an April Fool's party?!" then burst out laughing, then writhe some more. To this day when I remember that night, I have both responses.

Of course, you don't need to have found your embarrassment humorous at the time to find the humor in it now. My gentle, cheerful student, young Brason Lee, author of "Without My Helmet," wrote of his embarrassment when he reentered college as a student with memory and language deficits from his head injury. Other students avoided him because he stammered and often forgot what had just been said to him. This scene records his anxiety over his memory difficulty.

> One day, my English professor, Dr. Sumler, an admirable and well-spoken Black man in tapered suits, asked me in class:
> "Brason, what is the . . ."
> "I . . I . . f . . f . . for . . got . . th . . the . . q . . ques . . tion," I responded.
> A wave of laughter filled the room before I could take another breath. The other students stared at me, pointing and laughing aloud.

Brason was pained by their laughter, yet in the way he writes the scene, he invites us to laugh, too.

Even if you have never tried to write with humor, the following exercise will enable you to begin.

EXERCISE 26: *An Embarrassing Moment*

See if you can take a humiliating or embarrassing incident and write it comedically. See if you can structure a comic build of expectation in one direction followed by a comic reverse. To be humorous, you don't need to tell jokes, but you do need to find a stance of ironic distance to disclose your own absurdity, imperfections, foolishness, or recklessness.

The comic view of life is not just a series of jokes; it is a philosophy, a form of wisdom. The comic spirit questions, is spontaneous, unpretentious, playful, and honest, all qualities you want in memoir—and in life.

20

Dressing Up before Going Out

If you've followed my advice, you'll finish a shitty first draft with "For my eyes only" scribbled at the top of every page. In the process you will have learned a lot about writing, maybe found your voice as a writer, or at least for this work, and knowing how to write as you do now, when you go back to read what you wrote in the beginning, you will want to find a tall tree and figure out how to tie a noose.

So here is my advice. Don't look at your first draft. Lock it up somewhere as if it were a bottle of expensive wine that will improve with age. It won't, but you will. Celebrate. Go on vacation. Let yourself enjoy for a while your fantasy of the work you have written. This fantasy is going to be very useful, because it is probably closer to the work you will write than that shitty first draft you have hidden from sight in a locked drawer.

Then when you feel strong enough to face the task ahead (well fed, well exercised, renewed), prepare yourself to read your shitty first draft. Tell yourself that no matter what you find, you won't allow yourself any extreme reactions. Tell yourself you are going to treat your first draft like the child only a parent could love, that you will love it for existing, no matter how badly it needs braces or corrective surgery, and you are prepared to give it thoughtful guidance.

Start yourself a new creative journal just for the work ahead, your editing journal. Keep it at your side, and as you read this draft, write in it any thoughts you want to consider. But don't get bogged down. On the first read through, you only want to gather large impressions by reading as quickly as you can in one sitting. Afterward, in your editing journal you can ruminate on overall questions such as:

- What are my themes? What is my major thematic conflict? How could I bring it forward in the work, strengthen it?
- What is the story I am really trying to tell here? What is the point I'm really trying to make? (In your editing journal write that story in three paragraphs.)
- Where in the work did I hear my voice? What were the qualities of that voice? Where in the work do I need to rewrite for this voice?
- Where was it tedious? What might I be able to do about that? Cut? Go deeper into the truth?
- Where am I still hiding the truth? Where is the whole truth more complex than what I have yet been able to express? Are there places where I use words to present an image of myself that is false or incomplete?
- Is there a final pivotal event, i.e., a climax where something dies so something can be born? Could my explosion of realization be more powerful?
- Have I built to my climax with a crisis, i.e., a narrowing of options and a final battle with myself or with an antagonist?
- Where is the chronology confusing? Are there places where I could increase suspense by changing the order in which events are presented?
- Where does my story really begin? Can I get there sooner? Do I have warm-up paragraphs that I wrote to get to the beginning of my story that now I could cut?
- Do I have more than one ending? How can I shorten the ending and make it concrete if it is abstract?

Ruminate on these questions, and any others that come to you, in your editing journal. Begin the meditative process about the work all over again. Ask yourself questions to which you don't yet have answers and let them sit there. Write a dialog with the work. Ask it where it wants to go in the next draft.

Many writers feel they are not writing unless they are putting words on the page, but the most important work goes on when they are daydreaming about the work. State your problems in your journal, leave it be, and in time you'll get creative solutions.

⁓ Feedback from Others

At this stage, many writers wish to get feedback from readers, but be very careful whom you select. Just as I warned in *The New Diary*—that most people do not know how to read diaries—here I have to warn that most people don't know how to read first drafts of autobiographic works. If the reader appears in the work, he will be looking for himself and his feedback may consist of "That isn't how it was at all" or "Why didn't you write more about me?" or "So that's the reason you treat me like you do!" or "I'd appreciate it if you would not ever call me again." This is not what you want.

You can get valuable feedback from members of a memoir club if you are in one, but understand that while other writers may be able to feel where the writing is alive and where it goes flat or doesn't ring true, they generally cannot tell you how to fix it, and you are likely to get contradictory suggestions. The best way to sift through their feedback is to see where it clings to your own instincts.

⁓ The Second Read

Now read the whole work again, this time pencil in hand, ready to mark the pages and scribble more notes in your editing journal. This time, read the work listening to it as music. Anytime you come to a passage that makes you uncomfortable, where the rhythm seems off or the melody goes awry, mark it with a question mark. You don't yet need to know what is wrong with it; that will come later.

Be mindful when your attention strays. This is how I identify writing problems when I am reading someone's manuscript: I'll be reading along and suddenly I realize that I'm wondering if there is anything in the fridge for a sandwich or should I have a salad and I forgot to call back the roofer and I have no idea what happened in this manuscript on pages 124 and 125. Do I blame my own inattentiveness? No. I blame the writing for not holding me, and I go back to find out what went wrong.

As you are rereading, make lots of notes with relevant page numbers in your editing journal. Consider these points as you read:

• Where are the areas that need development? Mark the passages that ring false: passages of blaming, self-pity, self-aggrandizement, rationalization, or avoidance of responsibility.

• Look for every opportunity to cut: deadwood, unnecessary words, adverbs and adjectives, repetitions, dialog that rambles, characters you can do without, tangents that don't move you forward, information you don't need. Can you find whole scenes to cut? Whole chapters?

• Every time you see a cliché, mark it; every time you find a word choice that is iffy, mark it. Ask yourself, Where is the writing too on the nose? Where have I killed the mystery by making it seem too resolved?

• Notice when the contours of a scene are mushy. When you come back to that scene, ask yourself, How can I give it a cleaner shape? Do I have beats that repeat themselves? Where does the scene really begin?

• Where have I narrated something when showing it with a scene would be better? Where can I replace a generalization with specific details?

• Where have I missed an opportunity to develop thematic conflict through dialog?

• Where do my transitions feel inadequate? Overdone?

• Where have I dropped the emotional story? Where do I need to add more of my own feelings and reflections?

• Where does it feel as if I am missing a beat? (You don't need to know yet what is missing; just mark it and go on, letting your unconscious work on it.)

• What types of images recur, for instance, lots of references to canines or gemstones? Without making it obvious, can you arrange these images so that they complement your thematic conflict? A system of select imagery can be very useful to the autobiographic writer. Sometimes life events provide inadequate climaxes and resolutions, but your imagination can compensate through developing and shaping of a pattern of images and metaphors that run through a work. Once you know what your image systems are, you can manipulate them to strengthen or even create a missing climax and resolution (as Pam Houston and Mary Karr do in their concluding scenes quoted in Chapter 22).

• Is there potential humor that I can make funnier by building more in one direction before the drop?

•Where is the meaning of a sentence or a paragraph unclear or garbled? Mark it. When you come back to rewrite, ask yourself, What am I really trying to say here? Say it out loud. Then write what you just said.

• Try to make a graph of character arcs, your own and those of your other major characters. On a large sheet of paper, or several taped together, identify each time you move to a new position in your story internally and externally. Your internal position is how you feel and think; your external position is your journey along your desire line, in relationship to social institutions and other people. Your movement in position, from point A to point C and all the interim pivotal points between, is your story. You want to be sure that you create consistent movement in an overall direction until you reach your first pivotal event. Then the movement may go in another direction, but it, too, should be gradual and cumulative. Do you need to rearrange or fill in parts of your story for the sake of your character arc, i.e., how you changed? Can you make character arcs for the major characters besides yourself?

When I say listen for the music in rereading, I mean listen for the emotional melody under the words, feel where the gaps are and where it goes flat from dishonesty. Feel where it should swell, where it could get quieter, where it really begins, where it really ends. After the initial stage of reading the manuscript, autobiographic rewriting cannot be a purely intellectual process. It is reengagement with your notes for an emotional symphony.

One hopes. Here is the really horrifying news. Some writers—remember Russell Baker?—some really fine writers simply have to put their first drafts away after reading them and never look again. Writing the first draft was the way they got to know what it is they were trying to say. I have to tell you to be prepared to do that. You probably won't have to dispose of the original work, completely, but be prepared to let go of anything and everything. If you want to take a moment to weep right now, please do.

Now take a deep breath. Look at the old work as a snake skin you have already shed. This is your initiation as a writer. You no longer want that creepy old skin, you want to grow a new one, and you know it won't be possible without leaving that old one behind. Rewriting is starting the writing process all over again. Doing many of the exercises in this book, all over again. Don't be parsimonious in giving it your all, all over again. Writing is rewriting and rewriting is writing, not just removing a sentence here and there, not just retouching a mixed metaphor.

Now, maybe you won't need such extreme measures. Maybe you only have to sledgehammer parts of your structure. Maybe most of it is salvageable. I'm giving the worst case here, without ever having seen your work, like a doctor giving the worst possible prognosis, because I'm afraid if I don't, you won't undergo the necessary painful treatment. I'm telling you this because I see my students so exhilarated at having completed an autobiographic work that they want to send it off to a publisher or an agent immediately. It is really hard for me, their cheerleader through the first draft, to say, Not yet; it's not ready; you have so much more to do. They feel betrayed.

On the other hand, maybe all this doesn't apply to you. Maybe you have written for your children, and a first draft is all you have energy for, and they don't want to wait any longer to get it, so fine, that's it. You're done. Don't look back. Just continue celebrating. You have given them more than most parents ever will. There's more to enjoying what remains of your life than rewriting.

Or maybe, like the pristine work of some of my students, your first draft isn't really a first draft at all. I'm talking about those smug writers who don't have to start over from scratch because secretly they've been rewriting all along, week after week, draft after draft, so that when they get to the end of what they are calling their first draft, it is really a sixth draft. Don't worry, they paid the piper, too, just earlier. No good writer gets off without having to dismantle the work at some point; and with autobiographic rewriting, it isn't just to improve the structure or the prose. It has to be done to get to the next layer of truth. First drafts are only the first layer. Your memory doesn't stop remembering once it gets going, and your imagination doesn't stop helping once you've finished a first draft. The process of self-discovery continues, if you stick with it.

But when does it end? How do you know when you are done with a work? Not when it is perfect. Even if you are on your eleventh draft, there will still be a piece of crap in it. You could keep rewriting your life for all the time that remains of it, and you'd never get it perfect.

Fortunately, writers seem to know when to stop. It's usually when the appetite for the next work has taken over, and the appetite for the present one has long been satiated. This is an amazing thing about autobiographic writing; it is self-propagating. In the beginning, you think you have one story to tell and that will be it. But this is not what I see. I see Lianne, having finished a memoir on her childhood, wanting to write one about her experience of becoming a whistle blower while working for UCLA medical school. I see Brason, having learned to write from telling his story of recovery, wanting to take a section of his memoir and turn it into an autobiographical novel. I see Lois, having delivered her autobiography to her children, wanting to write personal travel literature. I see James Ingebretsen at eighty-nine, having spent fifteen years writing his autobiography, planning a little book on death and dying. I see Marlena, having finished her collection of autobiographic short stories, turning some of the material into a performance showcase.

They're hooked. They've become writers, whether or not they ever publish. I have to admonish some of them not to quit their day jobs.

21

Emotional, Legal, and Ethical Concerns

L et me tell you about Lois. She was the first autobiographic writer with whom I worked, twenty years ago. She was writing a full autobiography for her four grown children. Lois was a homemaker who had moved to California from Indiana with her husband, Clyde, when Ralston Purina transferred him west. (In Chapter 16, you read a passage of hers about Clyde's having won them a trip to Camp Minniwanca for a Purina sales meeting.)

Lois was fifty-five when she began her autobiography. Her plan was to make a gift of her life story as a wife and mother, just as she intended to pass on to her offspring the heirloom Quaker furniture that graces the living room of her tract house. It took Lois two years of dedicated work to write a full autobiography which reveals that there is vast emotion, beauty, and human drama in the most ordinary human life if it is perceived with depth. An avid reader of *The New Yorker,* Lois wrote gorgeous, clear prose; her characters came alive on the page, embraced by her humor and love; her night dreams and her understanding of Jungian psychology added a mythic level to chapters on closing up the Indiana homestead after her mother's death, on the duties of being a corporate wife, on rediscovering the companionship of marriage after her children's departure for college. I was a little envious of Lois's children, that they had a mother who could articulate and share her life with them so eloquently.

Lois had four volumes of her autobiography bound, and she presented a copy to each of her grown children for Christmas. Her son to this day has never read it. One daughter has never said anything to Lois about it, if she did read it. The other two children offered their mother only a few cursory sentences of appreciation. It took two years of waiting before Lois realized there would not be more. Her children were either intimidated because they did not experience their lives with the depth Lois brought to hers or because it is so difficult for children to accept their parents as autonomous individuals.

Lois does not for a moment regret the two years she spent writing her autobiography. It was, most importantly, she realizes, a gift to herself. Her experience taught me to anticipate something I never would have expected—that one's children are sometimes the worst audience for an autobiography. It can be such a struggle for children to separate their identities from a parent's, that the gift of an autobiography from that parent can be overwhelming. The mother who so clearly has defined herself by recreating her world on paper may be threatening to the child still trying to individuate.

Since the time of Lois's Christmas surprise, I have heard similar tales from other mothers and fathers who have written autobiographies for their adult children. What I have come to realize is that there is nothing wrong with the inclination to pass on the benefit of one's life experience to one's descendants; it is as natural as wanting your children to be well. However, to reach a receptive audience for a family autobiography, you may need to skip a generation. If you have grandchildren, they are more likely to be the true audience for your work.

Of course, that leaves some out in the cold, doesn't it? Those without children, let alone grandchildren. On the contrary. If every one of my friends wrote a memoir, I would happily take a vacation from the bookstores. All the better if it were a limited edition only to be read by a privileged few. God, what fun to read my friends' life stories as perceived by them, and what a kick to see how they would portray me! We'd be just like celebrities who rush out to buy each other's books and, before the driver leaves the parking lot, turn to the index to see how many pages are devoted to *moi*.

But, of course, maybe I wouldn't like what my friend wrote about me, my *ex*-friend. Maybe she would tell something that I didn't want anyone to know, or that would hurt me terribly, or that was untrue and I would *sue* her and take her every dime, that bitch! These are our fears, aren't they?

"I want to write about my relationship with my father, but it would kill him." "If my mother read this and found out how I was living in the 1970s, it would break her heart." "I'd like to tell my story, but it would embarrass my children and they would never forgive me." "I can't tell my story without telling my husband's story, and he doesn't want it told."

Every conference, every workshop, every class, the hands shoot up. People have paid their money; they want an answer. How can I teach autobiographic writing, how can I advocate it, without having the answer? How can the writer be faithful to self and not hurt others?

Well I don't have *the* answer; each of these questions is the premise for a drama, a thematic conflict, and each will play itself out to a different crisis, climax, and resolution. (Notice how once you start seeing the dramatic structure in life, it becomes an ongoing construct?) Something is going to have to die for something to be born. Something or someone is going to have to give. I can't know who or what that will be in your case: your ambition or your mother's sense of propriety, your artistic integrity or your relationship with your beloved.

What I do have to offer is a number of scenarios that I have seen work successfully; perhaps one of them will fit your situation.

Getting Permission

Anaïs Nin said that she tried to get written permission from all the people she portrayed in her published *Diaries* to enable her publisher and editor to feel secure against lawsuits. She would let the subject read what she had written about them before publication and take out or alter whatever offended them—as long as it did not destroy the integrity of the portrait. If Anaïs did not want to change her portrait to appease the subject's objections, she would give them the option of not appearing in the published *Diary* at all. This gave her considerable leverage, since most people did not want to be cut out. Her first husband, Hugh Guiler, initially wished not to appear in the published *Diary*. He told me near the end of his life that he regretted that decision. (Now that he is dead, he appears in the more recently published unexpurgated portions.)

Almost every person Anaïs Nin asked gave permission to publish what she had written about them, but I know that she didn't really bother to ask everyone for permission, because she didn't ask me. If she had, I would have corrected a very important mistake: *She made me older than I am. I am not as old as Henry Jaglom!* To say that I am that old could be considered *damaging* and I could have *sued* her!

Now the point here is that I would not sue her, even if she had made me another ten years older than I really am. You don't sue your friends; and given how unpleasant I find the idea of having to talk to a lawyer on a regular basis, I wouldn't even sue an enemy. Besides, I think that suing someone for libel or defamation is a very aggressive thing to do, and I agree with Supreme Justice Hugo Black, who stated that he considered the entire law of libel contrary to the basic principles of free speech. (Of course, I could not have won a libel suit against Anaïs Nin, even if I'd wanted to, because I would never be able to prove malice—ill intent. I know very well that she had none toward me, and now that I am getting past the age she mistakenly said I was, I can see how all younger people begin to look the same.)

Anaïs Nin knew that asking permission to use sensitive material is a gracious and smart thing to do. Besides offering the writer legal protection, it makes the person portrayed feel that you care enough about them to want to know what they would like changed; it gives them an opportunity to consider whether they would prefer to have their identity disguised; and it shields the subject from the blow of seeing something in print that could take them by surprise.

You're better off letting people read your work in manuscript because it looks less alarming than it will in print, as Russell Baker warns in this story about his getting permission from his wife, Mimi, to keep in *Growing Up* details about their relationship, including that she was pregnant before he married her.

...When I told her that I thought the book needed this, she was very supportive. I said, "Do you mind if I write about it?" and she said, "No, go ahead." And I interviewed her just the way I did everybody else. She was a terrible interview. She lied like a politician. But I interviewed her and I went up and wrote those concluding chapters. They went very quickly. And I brought it to her finally and said, "Read through it, and if there's anything you want cut, I'll cut it." Well, after reading it she said she thought I had left out certain events that would make it more interesting. I was sort of shocked at some of the things she suggested ought to be added, and I said, "Look, I'm a writer who's used to dealing with sensitive material—let me make the decision." And my decision was not to add a thing.

Well, after several months we got the first copies of the book in the mail, and Mimi immediately grabbed one, took it to the bedroom, closed the door and read all afternoon. When she came out she looked appalled. "Well, what do you think?" I said to her, and she said, "It looks different in print."

"That's what they always say," I told her.

Of course, if you ask permission of someone in advance of finishing (or even beginning) your work, you take the risk that they will forbid you to portray them. Even so, you may have more powers of persuasion than you realize. One of my students informed her reclusive billionaire boyfriend that she was writing her autobiography and he was part of it. He told her in no uncertain terms to disguise his identity and she assured him that she could do that, but perhaps, she suggested, he might change his mind. He insisted that was out of the question. So she proceeded with her writing, every now and then suggesting that he might be sorry that he wasn't in her book; he might actually find it titillating. Gradually he began to agree, because he realized she was the only person who had good things to say about him!

Most of the time, a memoir writer's concern is not that a loved one will sue (even for divorce). The writer's real fear is of hurting or embarrassing someone she cares about or of violating the implicit loyalty one feels toward family. Susan Golant, despite encouragement from an interested editor for whom she had written another book, was reluctant to begin her memoir on being the daughter of Holocaust survivors. She knew it would cause her parents pain if she wrote how the horrors they had known had affected her. Nevertheless, she found she could not *not* write her memoir, so gently she informed her parents that she was going to be writing about her childhood memories. They loved her, so they would not tell her not to, but it did cause them pain. Susan did not offer them any of her writing to read as she wrote, but she did speak with them about its progress week by week. Gradually her parents evolved from feeling negative and frightened to feeling excited about her book. They began to offer her memories of their own. Instead of alienating Susan from her parents, the memoir became a vehicle through which they were able to share intimate knowledge and feelings.

As so often happens, the process of writing autobiographically entered the work. One of Susan's chapters, "Entitlement," dramatizes how sharing the progress of her writing began to change her relationship with her parents.

As I have been doing with some regularity lately, I went to my parents' house for dinner one night recently while my husband was out of town. As usual, the subject of the war came up. After we had cleared the dishes and were drinking our tea, I decided to share with my folks my progress on this book.

"Soap?" my father said, incredulously. "You're writing about soap?"

But a knowing, almost sly smile slid across my mother's face.

"Don't you remember how much soap we used to keep in the basement?" I asked him, glancing at her.

He seemed nonplussed.

"Oy, I suffered so from the dirt," my mother chimed in, wringing her hands. "Some people didn't, but I really did."

"I know. That's what I wrote about."

"Can you imagine what it's like not being able to wash for six months at a time?"

"Yes. And I also talk about the symbolism of being clean or dirty. The shame of it."

She nodded decisively and smiled again, this time proudly. I had understood. But I could also detect pain in her eyes. I had understood.

In the meantime, my father seemed to become agitated. Clearly, he was working on something. He pushed his chair away from the table impatiently. "She used to keep soap, you say, but she still does." With that, he ran to the linen closet in the hallway and brought back two boxes of gift soap, one from Neiman-Marcus, the other, a still-wrapped carton of French hand-milled vetiver soap. Soon, the kitchen, still redolent with the warm scent of frying potato pancakes, filled with the fragrance of sandalwood and spices.

"Oh that," my mother said, caressing the smooth oval bars from the department store. "That's not soap. Those were presents. You know, someone came to dinner and brought me a gift."

"So why don't you use them?" I asked. But my father didn't await her reply. He ran back to the closet, and now produced a treacly-sweet box of purple, orange, and pink soaps shaped into little fruits and shells.

"See," he said in triumph, holding it aloft, "she still collects it."

"Nah," she replied. "Those are garbage."

"But why do you keep them?" I asked. "And why didn't you use the nice soap? What are you saving it for?"

"I don't know," she said with a shrug. *"Sis meir a shued.* It's a shame to use them. I thought I would maybe give them as a gift. Look," she pointed at the box of French soap. It still had the price tag on it. "Fifteen dollars reduced to $11.95. Would I use a soap that costs five dollars a bar?"

"Why not? Millions of other women do. Besides, whoever gave it to you probably bought it at the Price Club for $7.00. Anyway, why shouldn't you use it? Don't you deserve it?"

At this, my mother flushed. "You know, you're right," she said after a moment. And like a little child opening a box of chocolates, she pulled off the cellophane. Inside we found three round bars, each neatly wrapped in pleated beige tissue secured with shiny labels. My mother slowly brought the box up to her nose and inhaled its perfume.

"Go ahead," I said. "Enjoy yourself. What have you got to lose?" What, indeed, if not a lifetime of self-denial and deprivation.

Susan goes on to realize that she, too, for many years had felt disentitled, not only to enjoy material things, but also disentitled to personal fulfillment. I wonder how many of us prevent ourselves from writing our stories in the name of not wanting to hurt someone else, when really it is because we don't feel entitled to express our own truth?

⁓Libel and Invasion of Privacy

"No," you protest, "I feel entitled, but if I write about my ex-boyfriend he'll sue me!" "My marriage to the famous rock star is the best part of my story (and the main reason it would be published) but he has lawyers with nothing to do but file suits!" Actually, I did have a student who had been married to a famous rock star. Even though he was a public figure and thereby, according to the law, had already forgone much of his right to privacy, she was obsessively worried how he might retaliate if she published. Given what this man did on stage and said to the press, it's hard to imagine that she could have written anything that would damage his reputation, but reason had little to do with it; she was intimidated into silence. In the end, she would have had no problem at all because he died of an overdose, and the law says the dead cannot be libeled, famous or otherwise. But after he died, she found another reason not to finish the memoir and moved to Czechoslovakia to study parapsychology.

In fact, I have only had two students who had to be concerned about a lawsuit, although many of them worried about it. I've found that when a writer's fear of legal consequences is tying them in knots, most of the time what's really at issue is an emotional fear.

Still, the laws forbidding libel and invasion of privacy can be a nuisance and a constraint for all kinds of writers, including novelists. I don't mean to get on a soapbox about it—well, yes I do. Some of these laws remind me of what a friend tells me about the inner circles of EST in the bad old days. Gossip was frowned upon and highly discouraged. Now, on the surface, prohibiting gossip may seem like a good idea. Gossip can be cruel and hurtful. But forbidding gossip (as Mao did in China) is a totalitarian strategy, because when members of a group cannot talk about what is really going on around them, especially about the misdeeds of their leaders, they will remain ignorantly in thrall. Similarly, libel laws prevent false gossip, but they can also intimidate us from writing and sharing our true life experiences. If we aren't free to write the truth about our own lives, where is our freedom of speech?

Anaïs Nin wrote in *The Novel of the Future,* "The necessity for fiction was probably born of the problem of taboo on certain revelations. It was not only a need of the imagination but an answer to the limitations placed on portrayal of others." Many novels we read are simply New Autobiographies that have been labeled fiction in order to circumvent emotional or legal concerns about portraying others. Ironically, it was the attempt to fictionalize a real person in order to avoid legal problems that led to the most disturbing libel case in America. Published writers tell initiates about psychologist Paul Bindrim's lawsuit against novelist Gwen Davis in hushed tones like kids telling horror stories around the campfire.

It seems that Davis had participated in a nude encounter group led by Bindrim, who had the foresight to make her sign an agreement that she would not write about it. (This perhaps should have been a clue to her that Bindrim would get upset if she did write about him.) But Davis thought that since she was writing a *novel* about a "crude, aggressive and unprofessional" therapist who conducts nude encounter groups and because she'd made him fat with long white hair and sideburns when, in fact, the real Bindrim was clean-shaven with short hair, there wouldn't be a problem. Nevertheless, Bindrim won a judgment of $75,000 in damages against Doubleday, Davis's publisher, who in turn sued her and made her pay it. An appeals court had decided that just because Davis's book was a novel, that did not insulate her from libel laws. If even a single reader saw Bindrim and his fictional counterpart as the same person, the work could be considered libelous—because Davis had distorted the events of his group! This is, you see, a catch-22. If you fictionalize, you can be said knowingly to be telling an untruth about a person; and if you don't fictionalize enough, someone may be able to recognize who that person is! Because of this case, publishers now take out libel insurance for themselves and can purchase insurance on the writer's behalf.

Since that horrific decision, things in the courts have been going better for writers. Novelist Terry McMillan's former boyfriend, Leonard Welch, took her to court for allegedly basing a character on him in her novel *Dis-*

appearing Acts. He said she'd defamed him because the character drank and did drugs and beat his girlfriend, and she'd given the character Leonard's line of work and education. The judge dismissed the case, writing, "a reasonable reader couldn't possibly attribute the defamatory aspects of the character to Mr. Welch, even though the character seems to be modeled on Mr. Welch . . . the man in the novel is a lazy, emotionally disturbed alcoholic who uses drugs and sometimes beats his girlfriend, while Leonard Welch is none of these things." This time the catch-22 went in the writer's favor.

More recently, journalist Janet Malcolm was sued for libel by psychiatrist Jeffrey Masson, whom she quoted in a *New Yorker* piece as calling himself an "intellectual gigolo" who wanted to turn the Sigmund Freud archives into "a place of sex, women, fun." Masson denied that he had ever said such things, and unfortunately Malcolm, who had tape recordings of the other self-incriminating things he had said, could not produce evidence of these two quotes. "A fabricated quotation may injure reputation," the Supreme Court held. In a retrial, though, the court reversed the finding of libel, saying that Jeffrey Masson had failed to prove that Malcolm deliberately or recklessly falsified his statements.

Some of the writers I work with were alarmed by the Malcolm case. As memoirists, we fabricate quotes all the time, and we don't have tape recordings of any of them. How can we write in scenes without making up dialog, which we can't possibly remember word for word? I had to remind them, we are not journalists. We are not asserting that this is what the person said. We are saying that this is what we honestly remember them saying, this is just our *opinion*. The law says that if a statement is one of opinion, not fact, it's protected under the First Amendment, and it can't be libelous. So it's a good idea to remind a reader that your writing is just your opinion. You can do that in a disclaimer at the beginning of a work, something like: "This is not a work of journalism; the only claim I make regarding interchanges with the people portrayed here is the recreation of my own emotions and memory." If you are really worried that a particular passage could be actionable as defamation, you could as gracefully as possible work a disclaimer right into the text, perhaps as a reflection, "Did he really say that? Hurt has resided so long in my heart; can I be sure what I remember is how it was? All I can know is these are the words that so many years later resound in my memory." Well, something a little more graceful than that, I hope.

Yes, it's a nuisance, but we have to protect our margin of free speech as autobiographic writers. So what else can we writers learn from these cases?

• *Do not write about shady shrinks.*

• *Follow the Ninth Commandment, "Thou shalt not bear false witness against thy neighbor." In other words, write the truth of events, actions, and conversations; don't exaggerate, don't lie, except to disguise someone's identity.*

• *If you do disguise someone's identity, do a damn good job of it—make sure that no one can guess who the person is.*

•*You probably should not write about a former lover for the sake of revenge, if he or she has the money to sue you, is litigious, and doesn't hold you in the highest regard either. (Though Nora Ephron in her* roman à clef, Heartburn, *seems to have gotten her digs in without legal repercussions from her former husband Carl Bernstein.)*

• *Don't accuse someone of a criminal act unless he or she has already confessed or been convicted. You can recreate the scene of misdeeds and describe the person's actual behavior and words in your presence, but stick to what you can verify, and remind the reader that this is your recollection, not a statement of fact.*

• *Don't attribute a mental or physical disease to someone without having evidence that you can prove your statement. Again, instead dramatize the person's actual behavior from your point of view and offer your opinion.*

• *Don't accuse someone of being incompetent or dishonest in his job; instead, show his behavior in particular situations. Don't accuse a woman of being in a cult or of being a prostitute; show her behavior as you observed it and describe your feelings, making sure the reader knows you are giving opinion only.*

The comforting truth is that most people will never sue for libel, if only because it is so expensive. Not to mention that if something you wrote embarrassed someone, a lawsuit would bring even more attention to it. Besides, libel suits are not easy to win. In most states, the plaintiff must be able to show that not only is what you wrote not true, but that a reader could recognize whom the character is based on, that the subject of your writing had been damaged by it in some demonstrable way, and that you wrote the lie with malicious intent.

Of course, anyone can sue for anything whether or not they are justified in doing so, and if this worries you, you can believe that it worries a publisher even more. So in addition to their insurance underwriters, the large publishing houses will have their own attorneys "vet" your manuscript line by line for risk of copyright infringement, libel, invasion of privacy, obscenity, or other possible legal claims. Then they will ask you to omit or change whatever they consider too risky to print.

If you are so concerned about your legal liability that you can't even begin your memoir without being reassured, you can pay for the opinion of a literary attorney before you sit down to write your story. I can nearly promise you, without even knowing your situation, however, that you won't get reassurance. You will get an informed *opinion* from a lawyer, because without the final manuscript before her, this is all she can give you, and because this area of law is changing so rapidly no attorney knows how the courts will rule next. Most likely, the lawyer you consult will say, "It all depends . . ." It is her job to tell you all the possible consequences of what could happen if someone takes offense at your portrayal. It is not her intent to discourage you, but after you speak with her, I can pretty much assure you, you will not be able to write more than a shopping list.

My job is to tell you *not* to let your fear of being sued stop you from writing your first draft for your eyes only. Writers use worrying about the legal questions as a way of justifying writer's block and not writing the embarrassing, discomfiting, or strong stuff that makes for the best writing. I say, when in doubt, put it all in your first draft and then figure out what to do with it. You can always leave it to a publisher's attorney to tell you what to cut or change, if you are lucky enough to get published.

Ethical Concerns

An attorney can give you an opinion on legal concerns, but when it comes to ethical concerns you are on your own. I can give you an opinion, so can just about anyone else, but there's no getting away from the responsibility of making your own moral decisions. And the ethical problems presented by autobiographic writing are often much more serious than the legal ones, though frequently writers confuse one for the other. If someone has told you something in confidence, or even if they haven't *said* it was in confidence, but you know that putting it in print will cause them pain, which do you put first, your own need to tell the story or the unspoken trust of friends or family?

The problem is that drama deals with moments of crisis and with secrets. In order to write a short story, a memoir, a novel, any narrative work, you need to deal with exactly the kinds of things people don't want known about them. You can make the decision for yourself to admit to being human in print, but can you make that decision for someone else? There simply is no answer to this question; it must be agonized afresh by every person and with each new work. Nancy Mairs writes in the preface to *Remembering the Bone House:*

It is one thing to expose one's own life, taking responsibility for the shock and ridicule such an act may excite, and quite another to submit the people one loves to the same dangers. I can't resolve this dilemma to anyone's full satisfaction. But I have tried to keep my focus tight, speaking only for myself. The others all have stories of their own, some of which differ radically from mine, I'm sure.

Mairs deals with the dilemma by trying to keep her focus narrowly on herself.

David Huddle, in *The Writing Habit,* addresses the problem differently.

I believe the writer must do whatever he can to avoid . . . trouble, to keep from hurting feelings, but I believe finally he cannot allow the opinions and feelings of others to stop or to interfere with his writing. Maybe this is the ultimate selfishness, to say that one's own work is more important than the feeling of family and friends. Autobiographical writing will bring you to the point of having to make not just one but a number of hard choices between the life and the work.

Some writers will decide that there are many stories they can tell; the one that would break a mother's heart can wait. Others will put ambition first, as did William Faulkner, who said a writer is "completely amoral in that he will rob, borrow, beg or steal from anybody and everybody to get the work done." But I think Faulkner was posing when he said that; an amoral man did not write *The Sound and the Fury.*

We live in a callous era; people scream each other's secrets on tabloid talk shows. Journalists who work for the *National Enquirer* do not draw a moral line at all. Publishers will print whatever they can legally get away with. If you write sensitively and responsibly, trying to capture the complexity of human relationships, you will be in a very different moral world than that of the popular culture. If you write the whole truth with love, a celebration of real life, you may find that the person whose reaction you feared will thank you.

You can never know how someone will actually be affected by your work. Some writers tell of the friend omitted from a work who sees himself in it anyway, and others laugh about the one who refuses to recognize herself in the work even when told. People will take offense who have no right to, and others will forgive almost any trespass. You cannot control how others will react; all you can command is your intent. Do you intend to lie? Do you intend to hurt? Or do you wish to heal? Is your commitment to humor at any cost? Is it to truth transmuted through love? These are ethical questions you need to ask yourself.

Do not forget that family and friends have some ethical responsibility to your need to write your truth, as you have a responsibility to respect their feelings. Writing your version of how you experienced your life—owning your own truth—will often be threatening to others. But remember they may write their version, too. They have that right. So do you.

Even if you ultimately decide to cut out portions of your writing to protect another or fictionalize for the sake of disguise, you should not censor yourself in your first draft. Once you start blocking, even for good and rational reasons, the unconscious doesn't know how to discriminate what is O.K. and what isn't O.K. to express. If you censor yourself too soon, you'll never get to much of your best material that would have presented no ethical or legal problems. Once you have a draft "for your eyes only," you can choose from the alternatives that follow for dealing with ethical or legal concerns.

⌒ Disguising Identities in Memoir

Because you are writing creative *nonfiction*, my recommendation is to use actual names and identifiers unless you have a strong reason not to do so. Readers like to feel they are reading the true story, and altered names, especially of well-known people, can diminish your credibility. There was no way for Molly Haskell to disguise the identity of her husband, well-known film critic Andrew Sarris, in *Love and Other Infectious Diseases: A Memoir,* and fortunately she had no reason to.

Nevertheless, you are writing New Autobiography, not journalism, so if the only way you can write your truth is through disguising a character, by all means do it; you will still be writing creative nonfiction. Some writers change the names of their lovers, friends, and family members—not from concern about lawsuits, but out of desire to retain a margin of privacy for themselves and others. Although Phillip Lopate turns the sleeve of his life inside out, he does alter people's names in his personal essays. Many of his readers may know when he refers to his brother by another name that it is really Leonard Lopate on WNYC radio, and certainly some people know the real names of his parents and siblings and who his girlfriend Kay really was. It is Lopate's policy to fictionalize only the names of these people, not their other identifying characteristics.

It is worth considering how much privacy you want to protect, your own and that of others. Despite the clichéd aspersions that autobiographic writers are narcissists or exhibitionists, usually both, I haven't found that to be the case. Narcissists are not keen observers, and exhibitionists are more interested in forcing a reaction from an audience than in exploring their own responses. Sometimes narcissists and exhibitionists are attracted to the idea of autobiographic writing, but they don't stick with it and rarely distinguish themselves in the field.

For most successful autobiographic writers, the desire to protect one's privacy and the impulse to bare personal truths elbow each other and have to find a mutual accommodation. Nancy Mairs writes of the polarity between a desire to publish and a desire to remain anonymous in *Voice Lessons*.

> If the very thought of taking off all your clothes in the middle of the Washington Mall during a school holiday makes you blush, you haven't even begun to dream what it feels like to publish a book. . . .
>
> The fact that I am by nature reclusive strikes people as incongruous with the personal candor I display in my books. But frankness itself functions as a kind of screen more effective in some ways than the legendary obsession with privacy of J. D. Salinger or Thomas Pynchon, say, because it deflects rather than kindles curiosity. *If she tells me all this*, a reader is likely to reason, *what can be left to say?* Behind this public Nancy, the introvert curls up with her books and computer, two cats and a corgi her only company, for hours every day.

Many autobiographic writers, especially those just beginning, feel they must go much farther in disguising identities than Lopate or Mairs. Perhaps they do not yet live in a world that accepts their avocation, and perhaps they do not have the luxury enjoyed by personal essayists to pick and choose which personal fragments of their lives to expose. In ongoing narrative, you can't just skip over a very sensitive pivotal event if it is necessary for your story to make emotional sense.

So here is the trick you need to know in disguising characters for strong emotional, legal, or ethical reasons. First of all, it is not enough to change a person's name and appearance. You have to make more radical changes. You have to take some characteristic of this person that is readily recognizable and delete it, and you have to replace it with some personal habit or other trait that makes it impossible to believe your character and its source are one and the same. Let's say that the real Mavis has a yappy little dachshund, which she dotes on and takes everywhere with her. Your character, Leona (who is really Mavis), will function in your story as Mavis did, but Leona hates animals, is allergic to dog and cat hair, and will not enter a house where there are pets. You can have a lot of fun with this, as you can see from Anne Lamott's suggestions on how to write about a man you lived with who is easily recognizable to his associates by his personal habits.

> If he dyed his hair black, have him use foundation instead and maybe the merest hint of blusher. However, if he revealed himself through his actions toward you to be a sociopathic narcissist, you can attempt to capture his character and use actual conversations, just as long as this specific man is not identifiable by your descriptions. Change everything that would point to him specifically. Leave out his kleptomaniac leanings. Leave out the kind of car he really drove and the fact that he hated smokers so much that he planted a tiny tree in the ashtray. Make yourself the first wife or the girlfriend, instead of the third wife, and do not include his offensive children, especially the red-haired twins. If you disguise this person carefully so that he cannot be recognized by the physical or professional facts of his life, you can use him in your work. And the best advice I can give you is to give him a teenie little penis so he will be less likely to come forth.

Helpful as these tricks are, they still may be insufficient for some autobiographic writers. One of my students, Moreen, a college administrator who describes herself as a Jewish princess, wanted to publish a memoir about her affair with an African-American man who was thirty years younger than she, mostly unemployed, and living with another woman who was the mother of his child. Not only that, Moreen had been the one to initiate the affair. She worried what her professional colleagues would think, but most of all she worried what her mother would say. She needed to disguise not only her lover's identity, but also her own, so she had to publish under a pseudonym and call her story a novel.

When the Novel Is Your Best Solution

There are novels and short stories that only the author knows are autobiographic; there are novels that everyone knows are autobiographic; and there are novels that are not autobiographic at all, but truly works of the imagination. If you are turning your memoir into a novel for ethical, emotional, or legal reasons, yours will be the first variety and you will not want to identify it as autobiographic. You can still write in the first person and the narrator can have uncanny resemblances to you, but when anyone says, "This is really your story, isn't it? That character Ray is really Joe, isn't it?" you must look shocked, and say, "It's fiction, you ignoramus," or in some more polite way make them feel boorish for asking such a question. If you are at a cocktail party and someone says, "Better not get too intimate with Bridget, you'll end up a character in her next novel," you bat your eyelashes, and say, "I only write fiction, and all fiction writers draw something from real life," and turn your back on the bonehead. Students writing autobiographic fiction in my classes practice their shocked look on other students who make the mistake of confusing the novelist with her protagonist.

You may call this deceptive, but, my dear, illusion is what the novel is all about, and, as is often the case, deception is a clever defensive strategy employed by the powerless. I am reminded of the virtual bondage of a Japanese-American woman who took one of my classes. She had been raised in the States but had met in college and married a very wealthy Japanese man from one of the most powerful families in Tokyo. I thought her story publishable because it allowed us into a hidden world and because of its powerful theme of conflicting cultural expectations within a marriage. But this writer feared, and I believe her fears were well-founded, that if she were to expose her husband's family and how they had treated her, that she would not only be thrown out of the community in which she had lived most of her adult life, but her children would be taken from her as well. This was a consequence too great to risk. Yet she felt her very survival as the person she knew herself to be depended upon her writing her memoir. For years she had been writing it secretly in stolen moments, and her intention was to continue to do so. When her book was complete, she would rewrite it as a novel, try to publish it under a pen name, and never let on to her family that she had done so. What other choice did she have? Fiction and deception were her only doors to freedom.

If you wish to publish your true story as a novel, however, you must keep in mind that your writing must be more skillful and your story more intriguing than it need be for a memoir. When we know we are reading the truth in Russell Baker's *Growing Up*, we are interested. If it were a novel, we would find it lacking. In general, writers with newsworthy or high-concept stories will find it easier to find a publisher if they can identify their work as nonfiction. If you hope to publish your story as a novel, you will need to take it to a higher level of artifice and craft. All that you have learned about story and technique in this book will serve you well.

When the Memoir Wants to Become a Novel

Sometimes, once you have found the story in your life you want to tell, it takes on a life of its own and begins to transform itself into fiction. Cristina Garcia, author of *Dreaming in Cuban,* says that she began writing the novel as a memoir; that her first draft was completely autobiographic, but that she allowed her imagination to take over in subsequent drafts.

Since the advice to young novelists is usually "write what you know," it's not surprising that the undisguised autobiographic novel is a breakthrough genre for young writers. Ralph Ellison's *Invisible Man,* Erica Jong's *Fear of Flying,* Jay McInerney's *Bright Lights, Big City,* and Bret Easton Ellis's *Less Than Zero* were best-selling autobiographic first novels.

J. D. Salinger offers advice on the form of the autobiographic novel, indirectly through the main character, Holden Caulfield, at the opening of *Catcher in the Rye.*

> If you really want to hear about it, the first thing you'll probably want to know is where I was born, and what my lousy childhood was like, and how my parents were occupied and all before they had me, and all that David Copperfield kind of crap, but I don't feel like going into it, if you want to know the truth.

If you want to publish an autobiographic novel, you must realize nobody wants all that crap. Yes, your grandchildren do if you are writing an autobiography for them. But if you have any hope of publishing a novel, your allegiance must be to keeping the reader hooked on the story first and to literal fact last. The magic phrases for the writer transforming her life into fiction are "What if?" "How can I up the stakes?" "What if I made up . . . ?" and "Why not . . . ?"

The memoirist and the novelist can travel into each other's lands because they speak a similar language of story, character, theme, setting, scene, and dialog. In this book, you have learned most of the tools a novelist needs. If you decide ultimately that you want the greater invention and tightening of fiction, your work will resonate with truth if you begin with the autobiographic process.

22

Finishing the Unfinished Story

All autobiographic writing tells an unfinished story, one that continues as life continues. You create an ending by finding a resolution to your thematic conflict. It may be only a momentary resolution; sometimes it can only be achieved artistically through manipulation of descriptive imagery and internal responses. For instance, in her autobiographic short story "Selway," Pam Houston uses nature imagery to resolve her conflict between wanting to marry some steady guy and being afraid she'd be bored out of her wits. Her need to pursue a man sufficiently exciting to keep her interested has in this story caused her nearly to lose her life river-rafting. Caught in a washing machine torrent of rapids, the river, which had been associated in her image system with freedom, takes a reverse association of captivity. At the end of the story, Houston's nature imagery rises from river to mountains as her conflict between needing love and loving freedom rises to a crises. In her image system, the high wind's motion merges with stillness, finally synthesizing the narrator's desires for both romance and peace.

> ...I could see the light behind the mountains in the place where the moon would soon rise, and I thought about all the years I'd spent saying love and freedom were mutually exclusive and living my life as though they were exactly the same thing.
>
> The wind carried the smell of the mountains, high and sweet. It was so still I could imagine a peace without boredom.

In all likelihood the narrator woke up the next day and her conflict, though perhaps transformed in some way, was still with her. The story ends by focusing on a moment in which resolution, or at least a vision of it, is possible.

Sometimes the ending of a work can only be found in the writing of it. The death and rebirth of a climactic conflagration, and the final realization that emerges from it like the phoenix, never happened during the slice of time you chose to write about. It may happen, though, to that self who now, engaged in the autobiographic process, understands events in a way that was not possible at the time. This is how Mary Karr creates a climax to end *The Liar's Club.* The climactic scene is preceded by a scene in which Karr's mother unexpectedly reveals the secret of her lifelong unhappiness to her daughter. When she was a young woman, before Karr was born, her mother tells her, she'd been forced to give up two children she couldn't afford to care for. After this cathartic scene set in a restaurant, mother and daughter drive home to where Karr's father, attended by a nurse, lies wasting away, paralyzed. Karr transforms that commute into the climax of her memoir.

> Dark was closing in. We hit a long stretch of roadside bluebonnets that broadened to a meadow. Here and there in the flowers you could make out small gatherings of fireflies. How odd, I thought, that those bugs lived through the refinery poisons. Beyond Mother's tired profile, the fireflies blinked in batches under spreading mist like little birthday cakes lighting up and getting blown out.
>
> I didn't think this particularly beautiful or noteworthy at the time, but only do so now. The sunset we drove into that day was luminous, glowing; we weren't.
>
> Though we should have glowed, for what Mother told absolved us both, in a way. All the black crimes we believed ourselves guilty of were myths, stories we'd cobbled together out of fear. We expected no good news interspersed with the bad. Only the dark aspect of any story sank in. I never knew despair could lie. So at the time, I only felt the car hurtling like some cold steel capsule I'd launched into onrushing dark.
>
> It's only looking back that I believe the clear light of truth should have filled us, like the legendary grace that carries a broken body past all manner of monsters. I'm thinking of the cool tunnel of white light the spirit might fly into at death, or so some have reported after coming back from various car wrecks and heart failures and drownings,

courtesy of defib paddles and electricity, or after some kneeling samaritan's breath was blown into stalled lungs so they could gasp again. Maybe such reports are just death's neurological fireworks, the brain's last light show. If so, that's a lie I can live with.

Through language and imagery, Karr creates a climax, a transformative death and rebirth, which didn't happen at the time, though, she says, it should have.

In such a way, the story on paper may be finished, even as our memory of its events continues to transmute. This is why Marguerite Duras could keep writing the same set of memories repeatedly, each time finding within them a different story, a different meaning. Why Doris Lessing reflects in *Under My Skin*, "I am trying to write this book honestly. But were I to write it aged eighty-five, how different would it be?" If only in our imaginations, throughout our lives we continue to rewrite our important stories.

In yet another sense, our stories do not end—if they reach another person. Just as those I have loved and my important teachers live in me, so the books that have touched me, especially those in which the writing is most intimate, live now within me. I am different after reading Nancy Mairs, Diane Ackerman, and Bernard Cooper, enlarged by their vision of the world and capable now of perceiving more keenly my own world.

If you publish your writing, if you self-publish or distribute your writing to a few people, or simply share its progress in a writing group, yours may be the words that relieve another's isolation, that open a door to understanding, that influence the course of another's path. If you write an autobiography for a great-great-grandniece not yet born, perhaps she will find it in her mother's drawer, and she will be altered, perhaps even saved, through the wisdom you have sent her.

Your work continues within you, too, for not only do you write it, it rewrites you. The unconscious story that has driven your life is now made conscious and you choose another. You discover your true self behind your masks, and henceforth are fierce with reality. You change your history that once was tragic into a human comedy or a passionate drama, and your past now fuels rather than diminishes your future. You see yourself as the protagonist of your life, and you know it is your choices that determine your character, your values, and your story. Or you now perceive as a writer does, and you dedicate yourself to precision of thought and feeling and language, finding the world around you filled with meaningful detail and underlying drama.

Some, having learned here the writer's craft, will go on to write more stories, more memoirs, perhaps fiction. Others, closer to the end of life, will lie down in peace, having at last put it all in order, having made of it something worthwhile and meaningful, an offering. Despite the best intentions, someone will die without finishing a work. Be consoled; as a part of the dream contains the whole, so the fragment of a life recorded contains the essence and voice of the self. What wouldn't I give for just a paragraph from my great-great-grandmother?—she who had time only to feed the livestock and the children, clean up against the rats, and collapse in a straw bed with the husband she loved.

We the human race are connected on this fragile spinning planet, not only geographically across national and race boundaries, but also through time by our scratchings with rock on stone, blood on papyrus, quill on parchment, and laser printer on paper. Unlike our forebears, we no longer need autobiographic writing to record history and public deeds. Newspapers and TV are more than happy to do that. What will not exist unless we record it is the personal life, how ordinary people thought and felt, what exquisite dreams we had in the dark, how passionately we loved, how pained we were by the human devolution in our times. If future generations remember us only by the images preserved by our media, they will not know the goodness of our hearts, the way we continued to cherish culture in books and music, how we struggled to find and tell the truth, how we found God in nature and one another, how we divined meaning within our individual stories, how we revered the mysteries of death and rebirth within our own lives. If we do not leave behind the gift of our inner selves, how will future generations know us? By our tax returns, our hit movies and sitcoms, a NASA time capsule, a factual genealogical chart?

It is not the job of future generations to make sense of our lives from the remnants of the marketplace, scrap snapshots, refurbished heirlooms, electronic bits of bits. Only we can make of it all a song of self, a story with the power of myth, to leave somewhere the best of what we were and what we learned.

Appendix 1

❧

Forming or Finding a Memoir Group

Many groups come together spontaneously from friends discovering they have similar interests. You can also form or find a memoir club by putting a notice for other interested parties in your local newspaper, at your neighborhood library, church, or community center. Or ask a bookstore to sponsor a memoir club, publicize it, and give you a space in which to meet.

At your first meeting, discuss ground rules: how often you will meet (once every two weeks is good), how you will take turns reading (bring photocopies), how large you want the group to become (more than ten is cumbersome, but remember, not everyone shows up every time). Decide on how strict you want to be about confidentiality. My rule is that no one reveals the content of another member's writing outside the group without permission from the individual.

If you all agree, you could start by reading this book chapter by chapter, discussing it, doing the exercises, and bringing the results into the group to share. The eventual purpose, though, is for you to give each other encouragement and feedback on your autobiographic works in progress.

❧ Guidelines for Giving Feedback

Here are my guidelines:

• I like writers to read aloud what they have written in the two weeks between meetings as listeners follow along from photocopies. You hear things in the work by reading it for others that you can notice no other way—where the humor is, and isn't, where you have overwritten, where you have repeated yourself, where your voice is.

• All feedback should begin with what you liked about another's writing. If you then point out a weakness, offer a suggestion for how to fix it.

• Do point out where the writing seems insincere or stretches credulity, where you feel the writer hasn't dared risk enough, and where you don't have enough information to understand what the writer is trying to say.

• Allow the writer to ask questions to solicit specific feedback from the group members, such as, "Was it clear that there was only one door out of the house?"

• Maintain a spirit of nurturing, encouragement, and mutual commitment.

This quote from Nancy Mairs's collection of personal essays, *Voice Lessons: On Becoming a Woman Writer,* captures the generosity of spirit required in an autobiographic writing group. She is speaking of the nature of feedback given in her women's writing group, but it's also apt for men.

I want to give her the courage to say the next hard thing, without fear of ridicule or expulsion if she strays across the borders of good taste, good sense, or good judgment. . . . I want her to do the same for me.

This is what we can all do to nourish and strengthen one another; listen to one another very hard, ask hard questions, too, send one another away to work again, and laugh in all the right places.

For help in finding, creating, or registering a memoir club in your area, arranging for memoir classes, lectures, workshops or to learn about our center's efforts in facilitating the creation, study, and conservation of diaries and autobiographic works, please write:

CENTER FOR AUTOBIOGRAPHIC STUDIES
260 S. LAKE AVENUE, SUITE 220
PASADENA, CALIFORNIA 91101

You may also visit the Center for Autobiographic Studies website at: storyhelp.com

Appendix 2

Selling Your Story
for Fame and Fortune
and Other Good Alternatives

This is the section some writers turn to first, like the kid who can't think about anything but dessert when he sits down to dinner. So just to make sure that you know where it belongs, I've put it as near the end as possible. However, since some of you can't get that big banana split out of your head, let's go for it now.

The Big Book Deal

Some autobiographic works are more attractive to a publisher than others, and needless to say, those by celebrities in or out of jail are the most attractive. But there are also memoirs by no-names that have the potential to go from book to TV movie or theatrical film and make a nice pocket of change for the author. In order for an autobiographic work to be published by one of the large conglomerates, it needs a hook with which they can promote it. Here's a little quiz to see if your work might have what it takes for a big publisher to be interested.

- Do you provide a glimpse into a unique world?
- Do you write of events so unusual or dramatic that others will be fascinated?
- Does your story embody the social issues of a larger group, whether distinguished by race, gender, era, class, political persuasion, occupation, life style, religion, or national, regional, or ethnic identity?

• Do you write with such humor or depth and skill about a certain aspect of life that it will distinguish your work?

• Do you represent a new voice that needs to be heard from, for example, inner city youth, domestic workers, displaced career military, and those who are living "blended" racial identities?

Certain experiences such as having been raped or a victim of child abuse, while important for the author to write about for her own healing, are not publishable now unless you have something very new to say on the subject. For instance, one of my students wrote a book on a topic that is now so familiar that even the talk shows are bored with it—why it took her so long to leave a husband who beat her. She did have a new angle on it: contrary to the assumptions of pop psychology, she had not been an abuse victim as a child, nor had her mother. In fact, she had had a fairly normal '50s childhood. Her angle was that the assumptions of that era predisposed her to stay in a tyrannical marriage. Because of her feminist angle, her work will be published by a small feminist press. It's not the sort of memoir that would be published by a large house that can only choose books that will fiercely compete in the marketplace, but it found a home.

Here's the good news. If your true story is newsworthy or timely, it doesn't have to be all that well written to get published and optioned. Here's the other good news. If you have crafted your autobiographic work as literature, and developed a distinctive writer's voice, you may find an agent or an editor who wants it for that reason.

Here's the bad news. If your goal is publication by a big house and you are not already famous or an established writer, you must complete a full manuscript, and rewrite several times, and polish it as though you were a scullery maid the night before a visit from the queen. Then you must send a query letter to an appropriate agent or publisher, following the guidelines given in books like these:

• *The Writer's Market,* published and updated every year by Writer's Digest Books, Cincinnati, OH.

• *The Insider's Guide to Book Editors, Publishers, and Literary Agents,* edited and updated yearly by Jeff Herman, Prima Publishing, Rocklin, CA.

After querying an agent or publisher, you must then act like Cinderella, who waited patiently for her life to be transformed. Generally everything takes much longer than you expect. It can take many months for an agent to read the work and decide if he/she wants to represent it. It can take another Sahara of time for editors to respond to your agent. Neither editors nor agents like to be nudged by a no-name. Which is what you are until your book has sold 100,000 copies, and then you qualify for lunch with your agent at a pizzeria.

The Big Movie Deal

If you get a big book deal, or even a little one, you may get interest for a film. Suddenly you have a hot property. You will get calls and visits from dozens of producers all at once, who will take you to posh restaurants on their expense accounts, which will make you think that you are a very important person. Your personality will change, you will get greedy, and you will sign a deal promising you a lot of money *if* the movie gets made, but you will only get a tiny bit of the money as an option, which reserves the producer's right to own your story, and then all the excitement will be over as soon as you sign, except, *if* the property goes into development, you will occasionally get a call from an empathetic screenwriter (you will not be able to write the script, so forget that), and then you will hear nothing at all until you find out your option was not picked up. (The odds are it won't be because approximately only one out of five television movie scripts developed are filmed and fewer than one out of twenty-five features developed are filmed.) If you were counting on collecting the full hundred thousand for the TV movie rights to support you as the writer you've become, or you've already spent it using credit cards, or you planned to divide it amongst your children as a bribe to get them to finish reading the book you originally wrote just for them, you'll be in for a letdown. Funny, isn't it, what you thought would be the answer to all your dreams never turns out that way? Life just keeps making story.

So if you want to go through this, here's some idea of what your work has to have: high concept. Now, high concept is difficult to define because to a large extent it has to do with changing fashions and fads. It means a dramatic story with a good hook that hasn't been told yet, or at least within recent memory, or if it has been told it was hugely successful and yours is a little different; in other words, it has to be fresh, *and* it has to be promotable in the mass media; you have to be able to say it in one sentence that is so gripping that we just have to know more. One sentence. Or less.

Boutique Publishers

If you realistically set your sights on a specialty publisher, one who only publishes books on aviation, or from people in the navy, or religious works, or World War II history, or one of hundreds of ethnic or regional specialties—the variety of such publishers will amaze you—and your memoir fits into the publisher's area of interest, then your chances of publication are good. The specialty publisher can do a smaller first printing than a larger house, yet the physical book—its paper, print, binding, and dust jacket—often look indistinguishable from those of a big publisher. The limitations have traditionally been in distribution and promotion, but you may have a unique way to help promote your work to its audience. Moreover, today's megabookstores such as Barnes and Noble are more than happy to buy from small publishers. Some stores that feature alternative books, such as Tower, prefer to promote writers who publish through a small press or who self-publish.

You can look in the geographic index in *The Literary MarketPlace* and in the Nonfiction Book Publisher's Index in *The Writer's Market* for names, addresses, and information on how to submit to specialty publishers. Another resource is:

• *The International Directory of Little Magazines and Small Presses,* edited by Len Fulton, Dustbooks, P.O. Box 100, Paradise, CA 95967.

Magazine Submissions

The *International Directory of Little Magazines and Small Presses* is also a wonderful resource if you want to publish a short autobiographic piece in a periodical. It lists 5,500 markets for writers, and when you look through, it seems as if there is a publisher for every writer in America. There are periodicals and magazines whose franchise is to publish only autobiographic pieces such as:

• *Reminisce Magazine,* editor/publisher Roy J. Reiman, 5400 S. 60th St., Greendale, WI 53129.
• *Life Story: A Magazine of Writing Personal and Family History,* editor Charles Kempthorne, Letter Rock Publications, Manhattan, KS.

Well-written autobiographic short stories can pass as fiction in order to get published in magazines that pay well, such as *Ladies' Home Journal, Es-*

quire, Seventeen, Mademoiselle, or *Vogue.* Anecdotal pieces have the easiest time of it in magazines such as *Reader's Digest* and specialized or regional periodicals, but you have to make your style and approach match that of the magazine. In the "His" and "Hers" sections of *The New York Times Magazine,* brevity is required, but personal essays in just about any tone and voice appear. Morning Edition on National Public Radio broadcasts personal essays and stories read by the author, submitted on audio tape, and likes regional voices. Literary personal essays and stories have to compete for high honors with some of the best contemporary writers in the most unapproachable forums such as *The New Yorker* and *Harper's.*

Self-Publishing

Fortunately for New Autobiography, it appears at a time when we are going through a technological communications revolution, a turning point comparable to the advent of the printing press or television. Desktop publishing has made it possible to typeset your own work, or simply hand your floppy disk to someone who does computer layout and typesetting, and Kinko's can help you produce a book of sorts in whatever number of copies you wish. If you want a really professional-looking book, you can go directly to a printing house that will print and bind a hundred copies of your typeset book either in soft or hardcover for as little as a thousand to three thousand dollars. (It will cost more if you are including photos.)

Vanity presses are becoming passé. They still exist and you can recognize them by their come-on in the backs of magazines where you may mail-order an instant face-lift for $69, or a kitty cover to teach your cat how to crouch on the toilet.

Along with alternatives to the old vanity presses have come new attitudes toward self-publishing. Today it can be fun, hip, and entrepreneurial to self-publish. Buyers at boutique bookstores will often sell self-published books on consignment, especially if the author is a local. And big publishers now scout successful books that are self-published or printed by small presses. They consider them a good risk because they are already market-tested. The new legend in publishing today is mega best-seller *The Celestine Prophecy,* which originally was self-published. For detailed information on self-publishing refer to:

• *The Complete Guide to Self-Publishing,* Tom and Marilyn Ross, Writer's Digest Books, Cincinnati, OH.

Internet Publishing

The New Autobiography could bring to the Internet what it is presently missing: quality and intimacy. Say you were rearing a Down's syndrome child; think if on the Internet you could find readable memoirs of four other parents who had been through this experience? Think what a gift to give and to receive. It's true that people already set up web sites offering documents about their personal experiences, but the works are so poorly crafted that no one actually reads them. If you make your memoir a story that reads like a novel, you will find readers, not just browsers. Through the many web sites of the Internet, you can inform the specific audiences who would be interested in your autobiographic work. You can publish it from your own web site or use an Internet publisher.

In the future, we will see a new form of memoir that takes advantage of the multimedia possibilities of computer technology. When you are reading Uncle Bill's CD about his high-school years at the beginning of the 1970s you will be able to listen to Santana's *Abraxas* while looking at pages from his yearbook, which he has scanned in. If Uncle Bill wrote his memoir with hypertext, you will be able to double-click on his first date with Tina, a subject only briefly mentioned in his main story. On your screen you'll see a picture of Tina with long hair parted in the middle and a short story about Bill's crazy date with her. If you want to know about the date from Tina's point of view, you will double-click on her picture and see the story she wrote at Bill's request.

Book Art

I think that the high tech of the Internet is one direction in which New Autobiography will expand in the future. Simultaneously, it will develop in the opposite direction of low tech—custom books. If you want only a small number of copies of your autobiographic work as gifts for a few very fortunate people, think about the pleasures of bookmaking, and I don't mean the ponies. Think about smoothing your fingers over handmade paper speckled like a robin's egg. Think about taking a class in book art at your local college or adult school. Think about including copies of photos and drawings with borders made of dried leaves, tiny pebbles, or bubble gum wrappers; think about what you could do with a book's shape; think about bindings made of corn husks, or leather, or silk, or muslin; think of covers made of hammered gold, or fur, or collaged playbills, or a yellowed wedding dress.

Even if your initial goal was to be published by Simon and Schuster and to become rich and famous, and you bit the bullet and finished a complete book, and rewrote and polished and submitted and you didn't get a big publisher, you may turn out to feel as some of my students do. They say, as though they were being interviewed by *People* magazine, that along with having their children, writing their memoir was the most satisfying thing they ever did. Except they really mean it.

Bibliography of
Autobiographic Works and Critical Works
on Memoir Cited in the Text

Ackerman, Diane. *A Natural History of the Senses.* New York: Random House, Inc., 1990.

Adams, Henry. *The Education of Henry Adams.* Boston: Houghton Mifflin, 1982.

Allende, Isabel. *Paula.* New York: HarperCollins Publishers, 1994.

Allison, Dorothy. *Bastard out of Carolina.* New York: Plume, 1992.

Angelou, Maya. *I Know Why the Caged Bird Sings.* New York: Random House, Inc., 1969.

Aristotle. *The Poetics of Aristotle.* Chapel Hill: The University of North Carolina Press, 1942.

Atwan, Robert, ed. *The Best American Essays of 1994.* Boston: Houghton Mifflin. (New collections for each year, 1995, 1996, etc.)

Augustine, Saint, Bishop of Hippo. *Confessions,* Books I–IV. New York: Cambridge University Press, 1995.

Bachelard, Gaston. *The Poetics of Space.* Boston: Beacon Press, 1958.

Baker, Russell. *Growing Up.* New York: Congdon & Weed, Inc., 1982.

Baldwin, James. *Nobody Knows My Name, More Notes of a Native Son.* New York, Dial Press, 1961.

Barber, Phyllis. *How I Got Cultured: A Nevada Memoir.* Athens: University of Georgia Press, 1961.

Bateson, Mary C. *Composing a Life: Life as a Work in Progress—The Improvisations of Five Extraordinary Women.* New York: Plume, 1989.

———. *With a Daughter's Eye: A Memoir of Margaret Mead and Gregory Bateson.* New York: William Morrow and Company, Inc., 1984.

Berendt, John. *Midnight in the Garden of Good and Evil.* New York: Random House, Inc., 1994.

Bombeck, Erma. *If Life Is a Bowl of Cherries, What am I Doing in the Pits?* New York: Fawcett Books, 1990.

———. *The Grass Is Always Greener Over the Septic Tank.* New York: McGraw-Hill, 1976.

Bradbury, Ray. *Dandelion Wine.* Random House, Inc., 1975.

Braxton, Joanne M. *Black Women Writing Autobiography: A Tradition Within a Tradition.* Philadelphia: Temple University Press, 1989.

Brown, Cecil. *Coming Up Down Home.* Hopewell, New Jersey: Ecco Press, 1993.

Brown, Claude. *Manchild in the Promised Land.* New York: Macmillan, 1965.

Buchwald, Art. *Leaving Home: A Memoir.* New York: G. P. Putnam's Sons, 1993.

Bunyon, John. *The Pilgrim's Progress.* Pennsylvania: Franklin Library, 1976.

Campbell, Joseph. *The Power of Myth.* New York: Doubleday, 1988.

Casteneda, Carlos. *The Teachings of Don Juan: A Yaqui Way of Knowledge.* Berkeley: University of California Press, 1968.

Cellini, Benvenuto. *Autobiography of Benvenuto Cellini.* Translated by John Addington Symonds. New York: Garden City Publications, 1979.

Cisneros, Sandra. *The House on Mango Street.* New York: Random House, Inc., 1989.

———. *Woman Hollering Creek and Other Stories.* New York: Random House, Inc., 1991.

Cleaver, Eldridge. *Soul on Ice.* New York: Dell Publishing Company, 1968.

Clenard, Lianne. *Why I'm Glad I'm Not a Boy.* Unpublished memoir, 1995.

Colette. *Sido.* Paris: J. Ferenczi & Fils, 1930.

Conroy, Frank. *Stop-Time.* New York: Penguin, 1993.

Conroy, Pat. *The Great Santini.* Boston: Houghton Mifflin, 1976.

———. *The Prince of Tides.* Boston: Houghton Mifflin, 1986.

Cooper, Bernard. *Maps to Anywhere.* New York: Penguin Books, 1990.

———. *Truth Serum: Memoirs.* Boston: Houghton Mifflin, 1996.

Cousins, Norman. *Anatomy of an Illness as Perceived by the Patient.* New York: W. W. Norton & Co., 1979.

Crone, Joan. *Letters of My Life.* Edition of 25. 4 1/2″/7 1/2″, tea-stained paper, photocopied and water colored, inside 10 oragami folded envelopes. San Diego, 1995.

Davis, Angela. *An Autobiography.* New York: Random House, Inc., 1974.

Davis, Patti. *The Way I See It: An Autobiography.* New York: G.P. Putnam's Sons, 1992.

de Beauvoir, Simone, *Cérémonie des adieux.* English title: *Adieux: A Farewell to Sartre.* Translated by Patrick O'Brian. New York: Pantheon Books, 1984.

Delany, Sarah, and Elizabeth Delany, with Amy Hill. *Having Our Say. The Delany Sisters' First 100 Years.* New York: Kodansha Int., 1993.

de Mille, Agnes. *Dance to the Piper.* Boston: Little, Brown & Co., 1952.

De Quincey, Thomas. *Confessions of an English Opium-Eater.* London: Taylor and Hessey, 1822.

Didion, Joan. *Slouching Towards Bethlehem.* New York: Farrar, Straus, & Giroux, 1968.

Dillard, Annie. "To Fashion a Text," in *Inventing the Truth: The Art and Craft of Memoir.* Edited by William Zinsser. Boston: Houghton Mifflin, 1987.

————. *Pilgrim at Tinker Creek.* New York: Harper's Magazine Press, 1974.

Dinesen, Isak. *Out of Africa.* New York: Crown, 1987.

Douglass, Frederick. *Life and Times of Frederick Douglass, Written by Himself: His Early Life as a Slave, His Escape from Bondage, and His Complete History to the Present Time.* With an introduction by George L. Ruffin. Hartford, Conn: Park Pub. Co., 1881.

DuBois, W. E. B. *The Autobiography of W. E. B. DuBois: A Soliloquy on Viewing My Life from the Last Decade of Its First Century.* New York: International Publishers, 1968.

Duras, Marguerite. *The Lover.* Translated by Barbara Bray. New York: Pantheon Books, 1985.

————. *The North China Lover.* New York: The New Press, 1992.

Durrell, Lawrence. *Justine.* New York: E. P. Dutton, 1957.

Eakin, John Paul. *Fictions in Autobiography: Studies in the Art of Self-Invention.* Princeton, New Jersey: Princeton University Press, 1985.

Eliot, T.S. *The Four Quarters.* New York: Harcourt Brace & World, 1971.

Emmons, Nuel. *Manson in His Own Words.* New York: Grove Weidenfeld, 1986.

Esquivel, Laura. *Como agua para chocolate.* English title: *Like Water for Chocolate.* México, D.F.: Planeta, 1989.

Fontenay, Marlena. *Torch Songs.* Unpublished memoir, 1995.

Frame, Janet. *To the Is-Land: An Autobiography.* New York: George Braziller, 1982.

Franklin, Benjamin. *The Autobiography.* Boston: Houghton, Mifflin & Co., 1886.

Gandhi, Mahatma. *An Autobiography: The Story of My Experiments with Truth.* Translated by Mahadev Desai. London: Phoenix Press, 1949.

Gilmore, Mikal. *Shot in the Heart.* New York: Doubleday, 1994.

Golant, Susan Kleinhandler. *The Mansion of Our Soul: Essays on Pain and Healing from the Daughter of Holocaust Survivors.* Unpublished memoir, 1996.

Goldberg, Natalie. *Writing Down to the Bones: Freeing the Writer Within.* Boston: Shambhala. Distributed by Random House, 1986.

Gordon, Barbara. *I'm Dancing as Fast as I Can.* New York: Harper & Row, 1979.

Gordon, Mary. *The Shadow Man.* New York: Random House, Inc., 1996.

Gornick, Vivian. *Fierce Attachments: A Memoir.* New York: Farrar, Straus, & Giroux, 1987.

Greene, Melissa Fay. *Praying for Sheetrock.* Massachusetts: Addison-Wesley, 1991.

Griffin, John Howard. *Black Like Me.* Boston, Houghton Mifflin, 1961.

Haley, Alex. *The Autobiography of Malcolm X.* New York: Ballantine Books, 1965.

Hamill, Pete. *A Drinking Life: A Memoir.* Boston: Little, Brown, 1994.

Hayden, Tory L. *One Child.* New York: Avon Books, 1980.

Heilbrun, Carolyn G. *Writing a Woman's Life.* New York: Ballantine Books, 1988.

Hellman, Lillian. *An Unfinished Woman.* Boston: Little, Brown, 1969.

————. *Scoundrel Time.* Boston: Little, Brown, 1976.

Hemingway, Ernest. *A Moveable Feast.* London: J. Cape, 1964.

Henley, Lois. *The Choice or the Privilege.* Unpublished autobiography, 1983.

Hoang, Hanh. Untitled, unpublished memoir, 1996.

Hotchner, A. E. *King of the Hill.* New York: Harper & Row, 1972.

Houseman, John. *Final Dress.* New York: Simon and Schuster, 1983.

———. *Front & Center.* New York: Simon and Schuster, 1979.

———. *Run-Through: A Memoir.* New York: Simon and Schuster, 1972.

Houston, Pam. *Cowboys Are My Weakness.* New York: W. W. Norton, 1992.

Hurston, Zora Neale. *Dust Tracks on a Road: An Autobiography.* Philadelphia: Lippincott, 1942.

Hyman, Barbara Davis. *My Mother's Keeper.* New York: Morrow, 1985.

Iacocca, Lee, with William Novak. *Iacocca: An Autobiography.* New York: Bantam Books, 1984.

Ingebretson, James. *Apprentice to the Dawn.* Unpublished memoir, 1995.

Isherwood, Christopher. *Berlin Stories.* Norfolk, Connecticut: New Directions, 1963.

Jackson, Rebecca. *Gifts of Power: The Writings of Rebecca Jackson, Black Visionary, Shaker Eldress.* Edited, with an introduction, by Jean McMahon Humez. Amherst: University of Massachusetts Press, 1981.

Jacobs, Harriet Brent. *Incidents in One Life of a Slave Girl, Written by Herself.* Edited by L. Maria Child. Boston, Pub. for the author, 1861.

Jelinek, Estelle C. *The Tradition of Women's Autobiography from Antiquity to the Present.* Boston: Twayne Publishers, 1986.

Jones, James. *From Here to Eternity.* New York: C. Scribner, 1952.

Jong, Erica. *Fear of Flying.* New York: Signet/NAL, 1973.

Joyce, James. *Portrait of the Artist as a Young Man.* New York: B. W. Huebsch, 1916.

Jung, C. G. *Memories, Dreams, Reflections.* Random House, Inc., 1963.

Karr, Mary. Essay in *New York Times Magazine,* May 1996.

———. *The Liar's Club: A Memoir.* New York: Viking, 1995.

Kaysen, Susanna. *Girl, Interrupted.* New York: Random House, Inc., 1993.

Kazan, Elia. *Elia Kazan: A Life.* New York: Knopf, 1988.

Kazin, Alfred. *New York Jew.* New York: Knopf, 1978.

———. *A Walker in the City.* London: Victor Gollancz, 1952.

Keckley, Elizabeth. *Behind the Scenes: Or, Thirty Years a Slave and Four Years in the White House.* New York: Oxford University Press, 1987.

Kempe, Margery. *The Book of Margery Kempe.* Translated by B. A. Windeatt. New York: Viking Penguin, 1985.

Kerouac, Jack. *On the Road.* New York: Viking Press, 1957.

Kingsolver, Barbara. *High Tide in Tucson.* New York: HarperCollins Publishers, Inc., 1995.

Kingston, Maxine H. *The Woman Warrior: Memoirs of a Girlhood Among Ghosts.* New York: Alfred A. Knopf, Inc., 1989.

Kirkland, Gelsey, with Greg Lawrence. *Dancing on My Grave: An Autobiography*. Garden City, New York: Doubleday, 1986.

Kite, Joan. *Witness Dismissed*. Unpublished memoir, 1995.

Knapp, Caroline. *Drinking: A Love Story*. New York: Dial Press, 1996.

Konner, Melvin. *Becoming a Doctor: A Journey of Initiation in Medical School*. New York: Viking, 1987.

Lamott, Anne. *Bird by Bird: Some Instructions on Writing and Life*. New York: Pantheon Books, 1994.

———. *Operating Instructions: A Journal of My Son's First Year*. New York: Pantheon Books, 1993.

Lee, Jarena. *Religious Experience and Journal of Mrs. Jarena Lee, Giving an Account of Her Call to Preach the Gospel, Revised and Corrected from the Original Manuscript Written by Herself*. Philadelphia: Pub. for the author, 1849.

Lessing, Doris. *Under My Skin: Volume One of My Autobiography*. New York: Harper-Collins Publishers, 1994.

Long, Philomene. *Memoirs of a Nun on Fire*. Unpublished memoir, 1996.

Lopate, Philip. *Bachelorhood: Tales of the Metropolis*. New York: Poseidon Press, 1981.

Lopate, Phillip, ed. *Against Joie de Vivre: Personal Essays*. New York: Poseidon Press, 1989.

———. *The Art of the Personal Essay: An Anthology from the Classical to the Present*. New York: Anchor Books, 1994.

Mairs, Nancy. *Ordinary Time: Cycles in Marriage, Faith, and Renewal*. Boston: Beacon Press, 1993.

———. *Remembering the Bone House: An Erotics of Place and Space*. New York: Harper & Row, 1989.

———. *Voice Lessons: On Becoming a (Woman) Writer*. Boston: Beacon Press, 1994.

Martin, Martha. *O Rugged Land of Gold*. New York: Macmillan Publishing Company, 1981.

Matousek, Mark. *Sex Death Enlightenment: A True Story*. New York: Riverhead Books, 1996.

Mayle, Peter. *A Year in Provence*. New York: Knopf, 1990.

McCall, Nathan. *Makes Me Wanna Holler: A Young Black Man in America*. New York: Random House, Inc., 1994.

McCarthy, Mary. *Memories of a Catholic Girlhood*. San Diego: Harcourt Brace & Company, 1974.

McInerney, Jay. *Bright Lights, Big City*. New York: Vintage Contemporaries, 1984.

Meredith, James. *Three Years in Mississippi*. Bloomington: Indiana University Press, 1966.

Metzger, Deena. *Writing for Your Life: A Guide and Companion to the Inner Worlds*. San Francisco: Harper San Francisco, 1992.

Mill, John Stuart. *Autobiography of John Stuart Mill*. New York: The New American Library of World Literature, Inc., 1964.

Miller, Henry. *Tropic of Cancer*. New York: Grove Press, 1961.

———. *Tropic of Capricorn*. New York: Grove Press, Inc., 1961.

Millett, Kate. *Flying*. New York: Simon & Schuster, 1990.

Moffat, Mary Jane. *City of Roses: Stories from Girlhood*. Santa Barbara, CA: J. Daniel, 1986.

Morris, Willie. *New York Days*. Boston: Little, Brown and Co., 1993.

Nery, Adrianna. *Split at the Root*. Unpublished memoir, 1995.

Nin, Anaïs. *The Diary of Anaïs Nin*. Vols. 1–7. New York: Harcourt, Brace & World, Inc., 1967.

———. *The Novel of the Future*. New York: Macmillan Company, 1968.

O'Higgins, Patrick. *Madame: The Very Intimate Biography of the Despot of Beauty, Helena Rubinstein*. New York: The Viking Press, 1971.

Orwell, George. *Down and Out in Paris and London*. Complete ed., London: Secker & Warburg, 1986.

Parks, Gordon. *A Choice of Weapons*. New York: Harper & Row, 1966.

Perelman, Sidney Joseph, *The Swiss Family Perelman*. Drawings by Hirschfeld. New York: Simon and Schuster, 1950.

Phillips, Julia. *You'll Never Eat Lunch in This Town Again*. New York: Random House, 1991.

Pirsig, Robert M. *Zen and the Art of Motorcycle Maintenance: An Inquiry into Values*. New York: Morrow, 1974.

Plath, Sylvia. *The Bell Jar*. London: Faber and Faber, 1966.

Proust, Marcel. *A la recherche du temps perdu*. English title: *Remembrance of Things Past*. Translated by C. K. Scott Moncrieff and Terence Kilmartin. New York: Random House, 1981.

Rainer, Tristine *The New Diary: How to Use a Journal for Self-Guidance and Expanded Creativity*. Los Angeles: J. P. Tarcher, 1978.

Rodriguez, Richard. *Days of Obligation: An Argument with My Mexican Father*. New York: Penguin Books USA, Inc., 1992.

———. *Hunger of Memory: The Education of Richard Rodriguez An Autobiography*. New York: David R. Godine Publisher, Inc., 1982.

Roth, Phillip. *Operation Shylock: A Confession*. New York: Simon & Schuster, 1993.

———. *Portnoy's Complaint*. New York: Random House, 1969.

Rousseau, Jean-Jacques. *Confessions*. English title: *The Confessions* (and correspondence, including the letters to Malesherbes), edited by Christopher Kelly, Roger D. Masters, and Peter G. Stillman; translated by Christopher Kelly. Hanover: Published by University Press of New England [for] Dartmouth College, 1995.

Sacks, Oliver. *A Leg to Stand On*. New York: Summit Books, 1984.

———. *The Man Who Mistook His Wife for a Hat*. London: Duckworth, 1985.

Salinger, J. D. *The Catcher in the Rye*. New York: Buccaneer Books, 1991.

Sarris, Greg. *Mabel McKay, Weaving the Dream.* Berkeley: University of California Press, 1994.

Sartre, Jean-Paul. *Nausée.* English title: *Nausea.* Translated by Lloyd Alexander. Norfolk, Conn.: New Directions, 1959.

Schank, Roger. *Tell Me a Story: A New Look at Real and Artificial Memory.* New York: Scribner, 1990.

See, Carolyn. *Dreaming: Hard Luck and Good Times in America.* New York: Random House, Inc., 1995.

Smith, Sidonie. *Subjectivity, Identity, and the Body: Women's Autobiographical Practices in the Twentieth Century.* Bloomington: Indiana University Press. 1993.

Spiegelman, Art. *Maus: A Survivor's Tale.* New York: Pantheon Books, 1986.

Stanton, Elizabeth Cady. *Eighty Years and More (1815–1897). Reminiscences of Elizabeth Cady Stanton.* New York: European Publishing Company, 1898.

Steedman, Carolyn. *Landscape for a Good Woman: A Story of Two Lives.* London: Virago, 1986.

Stein, Gertrude. *Everybody's Autobiography.* New York: Random House, Inc., 1937.

———. *The Autobiography of Alice B. Toklas.* New York: Random House, Inc., 1960.

Stepto, Robert. *From Behind the Veil: A Study of Afro-American Narrative.* Urbana: University of Illinois Press, 1979.

Sterling, Joy. *A Cultured Life: A Year in a California Vineyard.* New York: Villard Books, 1993.

Stuhlmann, Gunther, ed. *A Literate Passion: Letters of Anaïs Nin & Henry Miller: 1932–1953.* San Diego: Harcourt, Brace Jovanovich, Publishers, Inc., 1987.

Styron, William. *Darkness Visible: A Memoir of Madness.* New York: Random House, Inc., 1990.

Talese, Gay. *Thy Neighbor's Wife.* Garden City, New York: Doubleday, 1980.

Thatcher, Margaret. *The Downing Street Years.* London: HarperCollins, 1993.

Theroux, Paul. *The Great Railway Bazaar: By Train Through Asia.* Boston: Houghton Mifflin, 1975.

———. *Old Patagonian Express: By Train Through the Americas.* Boston: Houghton Mifflin, 1979.

———. *Riding the Iron Rooster: By Train Through China.* New York: G. P. Putnam's Sons, 1988.

Thomas, Elizabeth M. *The Hidden Life of Dogs.* Boston: Houghton Mifflin Company, 1993.

Thoreau, Henry David. *Walden.* Edited by J. Lyndon Shanley. Introduction by Joyce Carol Oates. Princeton, New Jersey: Princeton University Press, 1989.

Tisdale, Sallie. *Lot's Wife: Salt and the Human Condition.* New York: H. Holt & Co., 1988.

Trump, Donald, with Tony Schwartz. *Trump: The Art of the Deal.* New York: Random House, Inc., 1987.

Wakefield, Dan. *New York in the 50's.* New York: Houghton Mifflin Company, 1992.

———. *Returning: A Spiritual Journey.* New York: Penguin Books, 1988.

Walker, Alice. *You Can't Keep a Good Woman Down.* New York: Washington Square Press, 1983.

Weber, Nancy. *The Life Swap.* New York: Dial Press, 1974.

Wells, Ida B. *Crusade for Justice: The Autobiography of Ida B. Wells.* Edited by Alfreda M. Duster. Chicago: University of Chicago Press, 1970.

Williams, Donna. *Nobody Nowhere: The Extraordinary Autobiography of an Autistic.* New York: Times Books, 1992.

Williams, Terry Tempest. *Refuge: An Unnatural History of Family and Place.* New York: Random House, Inc., 1991.

Wingo, Josette D. *Mother Was a Gunner's Mate: World War II in the Waves.* Annapolis: Naval Institute Press, 1994.

Wolfe, Tom. *The New Journalism.* New York: Harper & Row, Publishers, Inc., 1973.

Wolff, Geoffrey. *The Duke of Deception: Memories of My Father.* New York: Random House, Inc., 1979.

Wolff, Tobias. *This Boy's Life: A Memoir.* New York: Atlantic Monthly Press, 1989.

Wood, Beatrice. *I Shock Myself.* San Francisco: Chronicle Books, 1988.

Woolf, Virginia. "A Sketch of the Past," in *Moments of Being: Unpublished Autobiographical Writings.* Edited with an introduction and notes by Jeanne Schulkind. London: Chatto and Windus for Sussex University Press, 1976. First American ed. New York: Harcourt Brace Jovanovich, 1976.

Wright, Richard. *Black Boy: A Record of Childhood and Youth.* New York: Harper & Row, 1969.

Yogananda, Paramhansa. *Autobiography of a Yogi.* New York: The Philosophical Library, 1946.

Zinsser, William, ed. *Inventing the Truth: The Art and Craft of Memoir.* Boston: Houghton Mifflin Company, 1987.

Ackerman, Diane, 249, 325; *A Natural History of the Senses*, 91, 117, 204
Actions: description of, 244; and time leaps, 280
Adams, Henry, *The Education of Henry Adams*, 88
Adieux: A Farewell to Sartre, Beauvoir, 87
Adventure stories, 25–26, 53, 88
Adversaries, 80, 157; struggle with, 66, 69–70
Adversity, memoirs of, 89
African-American tradition, 26–27, 95–96, 137–38
African-American women, 120
Against Joie de Vivre, Lopate, 91, 291–94
Ahuri (ancient Egyptian), 22
Allende, Isabel, *Paula*, 63, 227–28
Allison, Dorothy, *Bastard Out of Carolina*, 86, 158
America, autobiography in, 24–27, 95–98
An American Childhood, Dillard, 212–16, 218
Anatomy of an Illness, Cousins, 89
Ancestors, imagining of, 120–21
Angelou, Maya; 137; *I Know Why the Caged Bird Sings*, 32, 85, 86, 96, 136–37, 165, 261–62
Anglo-Saxon men, memoirs by, 67
Antagonists, 152–53, 157, 265; fairness to, 158–62
Apprentice to the Dawn, Ingebretsen, 148
The Arabian Nights, 275–76
Aristotle, 71, 103; *Poetics*, 65
The Armies of the Night, Mailer, 32
The Art of the Personal Essay, Lopate, 90, 91
Asian-American tradition, 97, 138
Atlas, James, 10
Atwan, Robert, ed., *The Best American Essays*, 91
Audience, 12; and poetic license, 176
Augustine, Saint, 15, 90; *Confessions*, 22–23
Autobiographic writing, 2–3, 7, 8, 15–16, 34, 37–38, 189–90, 198, 243, 305, 325–26; basic components, 66–82; chronology in, 278; climax in, 74; composite voice,

129–35; ending of, 323–26; feminists and, 7–8; language of, 127–29; theme in, 212–30; and traumatic memories, 192–93; truth in, 173–83; types of, 84–99; voice in, 123
Autobiography, 10, 20–36; traditional, 49–53, 85–86, 231; falsified, 25. *See also* New Autobiography
The Autobiography of Alice B. Toklas, Stein, 28–29
The Autobiography of Malcolm X, Haley, 35
Awareness, levels of, 268

Bachelard, Gaston, *The Poetics of Space*, 117–18
Bachelorhood, Lopate, 91
Bacon, Sir Francis, 65
Baker, Russell, 38–39, 147, 212; *Growing Up*, 67–68, 70, 71–72, 75, 77, 86, 159–61, 165, 220, 309
Baldwin, James, *Nobody Knows My Name*, 96, 244–45
Barber, Phyllis, *How I Got Cultured: A Nevada Memoir*, 86
Baryshnikov, Mikhail, 88
Bastard Out of Carolina, Allison, 86, 158
Bateson, Mary Catherine, 60; *Composing a Life*, 5, 6
Beats, 79, 250–53, 265, 270; in dialog, 255, 258; emotional, 81, 150, 265, 268, 278–79; in relationships, 153–55
Beauvoir, Simone de, *Adieux: A Farewell to Sartre*, 87
Becoming a Doctor: A Journey of Initiation in Medical School, Konner, 87
Beginnings of works, 274
Behavior, character definition by, 166
Behind the Scenes, or, Thirty Years a Slave and Four Years in the White House, Keckley, 96
Beige voice, 125

Being Brett, Hobbie, 133
The Bell Jar, Plath, 92
Berendt, John, *Midnight in the Garden of Good and Evil*, 141
Berlin Stories, Isherwood, 60, 92
Bernstein, Carl, 315
The Best American Essays, Atwan, ed., 91
Big book deals, 329–31
Bindrim, Paul, 312
"Biography of a Prose Style," Harris, 126–27
Bird by Bird, Some Instructions on Writing and Life, Lamott, 186
Black, Hugo, 309
Black Boy, Wright, 96
Black Like Me, Griffin, 93
Blumenthal, Michael, "The New Story of Your Life," 14–15
Body, physical, writing of, 202–11
Body movements, memory of, 119
Bombeck, Erma, personal essays, 94
Book art, 61–63, 334–35
Bookends, 274–75
Book-length memoirs, 226
Boring parts of narrative, 278
Boutique publishers, 332
Boylan, Clyde, 173–74
Boylan, Helen (Martha Martin), 173–76
Brackets, 275–77
Bradbury, Ray, *Dandelion Wine*, 92
Bragging, fear of, 147–48
Braxton, Joanne, 96
Bridges, in narrative, 282–84
Bright Lights, Big City, McInerney, 322
Brown, Cecil, *Coming Up Down Home*, 96
Brown, Claude, *Manchild in the Promised Land*, 96
Buchwald, Art, *Leaving Home*, 94
Bunyan, John, *The Pilgrim's Progress*, 90

Campbell, Joseph, 2, 41–42, 66, 175
Capote, Truman, *In Cold Blood*, 31
Castaneda, Carlos, *The Teachings of Don Juan*, 90
The Catcher in the Rye, Salinger, 322
The Celestine Prophecy, 333
Cellini, Benvenuto, 23
Censoring of self, 150
Central character, self as, 140–51
Change, autobiographic writing and, 147
Character arc, 38, 39, 47, 60, 61, 303–4
Characters, 152–72; composite, 180–81; dialog and, 255–57
Childhood memoirs, 53
Children, 307; as antagonists, 153
Chinese-American autobiography, 97
A Choice of Weapons, Parks, 96
The Choice or the Privilege, Henley, 232–33
Chopra, Deepak, 267
Chronology, 267, 278; changes in, 180
Ciardi, John, 248
Cinderella, 41, 67–74
The Cinderella Complex, Dowling, 40–41

Cisneros, Sandra, 204–5; *The House on Mango Street*, 97, 124
City of Roses, Moffat, 107
Cixous, Helene, 208
Cleaver, Eldridge, 137–38; *Soul on Ice*, 96
Clenard, Lianne, 295–96, 305; *Why I'm Glad I'm Not a Boy*, 133–34
Cliches, 135, 203, 248–49, 250
Cliffhangers, 285–86
Climax, 66, 67, 73–76, 81; of scene, 266
Coleridge, Samuel Taylor, 287
Colette (Sidonie-Gabrielle), *Sido*, 87
Collective wisdom, feminine, 120
The Color Purple, Walker, 96
Coming-of-age memoirs, 86
Coming Up Down Home, Brown, 96
Complaint, autobiographic, 93
Composing a Life, Bateson, 5, 6
Composite characters, 180–81
Composite voice, 129–35
Conceptual autobiography, 32, 35, 93–94
Conclusion, 72–78; of scene, 265–66. *See also* Endings
Conditional statements, 161–62
Confessional writing, 22–23, 85, 90
Confessions, Saint Augustine, 15, 22–23
Conflict, 56–59, 66, 79, 217–30, 286–87, 323; characters and, 155–56; dialog and, 255; in scene, 266, 273–74
Conroy, Frank, *Stop-Time*, 86, 101
Conroy, Pat, 29, 35, 92; *The Prince of Tides*, 63–64, 111, 271
Contemporary readers, 35
Conversation, 253, 257, 259
Cooper, Bernard, 291, 325; *Maps to Anywhere*, 91; "Truth Serum," 206–7
Courage in writing, 151, 189–91
Cousins, Norman, *Anatomy of an Illness*, 89
Cowboys Are My Weakness, Houston, 60, 92, 240–42, 259–61, 264–66
Crawford, Christina, *Mommie Dearest*, 93
Creative journal, 9, 49, 54, 78–79, 105, 118, 213; behaviors, 165–66; character lists, 155–56; for editing, 300–305; thematic conflict, 219–20
Creative nonfiction, 183, 318
Credibility, 179–80, 183, 286; disguised identities and, 318
Crisis, 66, 67, 72–73, 81, 266
Crone, Joan, 61–63
Crowe, Cameron, *Fast Times at Ridgemont High*, 32, 93
Crusade for Justice, Wells, 88
A Cultivated Life, Sterling, 88
Culture, and voice, 137–39
Custom books, 334–35

Dance to the Piper, de Mille, 18, 135
Dancing on My Grave, Kirkland, 88
Dandelion Wine, Bradbury, 92
Darkness Visible, Styron, 13, 89

Dark periods, light spots in, 194–95
Davis, Angela, *An Autobiography*, 96
Davis, Gwen, 312
Davis, Patti, *The Way I See It*, 93
Davis, Philip, *Memory and Writing*, 267
Days of Obligation, Rodriguez, 97, 177, 280, 281
Delany, Elizabeth and Sarah, *Having Our Say*, 95
de Mille, Agnes, *Dance to the Piper*, 18, 135
Description, 244–50, 265, 280
Desire, as story element, 51–53, 76, 80; scenes and, 238–39
Desire line, 5, 42, 66, 68–69, 218; bends in, 52, 69–70, 80–81; of women, 7
Desktop publishing, 333
Details, 136–39, 162–63, 234, 248; invention of, 105–10
Dialog, 244, 253–64, 279–80; imagined, 314; in scenes, 234, 242, 265
Diaries, 2, 6, 104, 125–27, 169
Didion, Joan, *Slouching Towards Bethlehem*, 86, 138
Dillard, Annie, 223; *An American Childhood*, 212–16, 218; *Pilgrim at Tinker Creek*, 86; "To Fashion a Text," 102
Dinesen, Isak, *Out of Africa*, 86
Direct dialog, 258–59
Disappearing Acts, McMillan, 313–14
Disclaimers, 176–79, 181–82, 314
Disguised identities, 318–20
Distortions of memory, 101–2
Divisions, periodic, of life, 49–53
Donneé (disclaimer), 176–79
Doty, Mark, *Heaven's Coast*, 13
Douglass, Frederick, 96
Dowling, Colette, *The Cinderella Complex*, 40–41
Down and Out in Paris and London, Orwell, 32, 93
The Downing Street Years, Thatcher, 88
Drama, 95; life and, 74–76
Dramatic conflict, scene of, 273–74
Dramatic structure, 65–82, 195, 263–66
Dreaming: Hard Luck and Good Times in America, See, 13, 32, 55, 129–30, 138–39
"Dream police" technique, 112–13
Drinking: A Love Story, Knapp, 89
A Drinking Life, Hamill, 90, 116
Druks, Renate, 34, 144–45
Du Bois, W. E. B., *Autobiography*, 88
The Duke of Deception, Wolff, 93, 272–73
Duras, Marguerite, 286, 325; *The Lover*, 110–11, 115, 130–32
Dysfunctional families, 172

Eakin, Paul John, *Fictions in Autobiography*, 29
Earth, wounds of, 196–97
Ecological memoirs, 85–87, 210
Editing: of autobiographical writing, 300–305; of dialog, 263–64
The Education of Henry Adams, Adams, 88
Egypt, ancient, autobiographies, 21–22
Eliot, T. S., 76; *Four Quartets*, 79
Ellis, Bret Easton, *Less Than Zero*, 322

Ellison, Ralph, *Invisible Man*, 322
Embarrassment, humor and, 297–99
Embroidery Thread technique, 55–59
Emotional authenticity, 140
Emotional beats. *See* Beats, emotional
Emotional flooding, 200–201, 239
Emotional honesty, 183, 184
Emotional memory, and description, 245
Emotional time, 234
Emotions, 78, 250, 252–53; fear of libel suits and, 312
Endings, 79, 195–96, 323–26
Ephron, Nora, *Heartburn*, 315
Esquivel, Laura, *Like Water for Chocolate*, 95
Estés, Clarissa Pinkola, 2, 175
Estroff, Sue, *Making It Crazy*, 94
Ethical concerns, 316–18
Everybody's Autobiography, Stein, 100
Exercises: character sorting, 155–56; description writing, 247, 249; disclaimers, 176–79; fairy tale, 42–45; finding of themes, 226–27; free intuitive writing, 111–12; humor in embarrassment, 298–99; indicative behaviors, 165–66; life sorting, 213–14; light spots in dark periods, 194–95; memory of house, 118; original wound, 196–97; periods of life, 49–54; relationship beats, 153–55; reveries 105–6; story splits, 224–25; telling details, 163; thematic conflict, 219–20; writing of feelings, 203
Exhibitionists, 319
Experience, 211
Experiential writing, 123
Expositional writing, 251
Extremes, avoidance of, 198

Fact, 179; truth and, 175, 180
Fairy tale, 39–40, 66, 231; writing of, 42–45, 196
Family histories, 94, 115–16, 121–22
Family relationships, 152, 172, 181
Fantasy, and memory, 120
Fast Times at Ridgemont High, Crowe, 32, 93
Faulkner, William, 317
Fear of Flying, Jong, 322
Fear of truth, 190–91
Feedback, 145, 302, 327–28
"Feeding Time in L.A.," Fontenay, 187–90
Feelings, 202–11, 246–47; thoughts and, 251
Fels, Luisa, 146–47
Feminism, 7–8, 25
Fern, Fanny, 190
Fiction, 27, 29, 35, 312, 322
Fictions in Autobiography: Studies in the Art of Self Invention, Eakin, 29
Fierce Attachments, Gornick, 97
Film scripts, 95, 236–40
First, You Cry, Rollin, 89
First drafts, 155, 185–87, 252, 305, 316, 318; editing of, 300–305
First person, use of, 132–35
Flashbacks, 268–71

Flashforwards, 271–73
Fleishenberg, Liesal, 237–38
Floor plans, memories of, 117–18
Fontenay, Marlena, 83–84, 276–77, 305;
    "Feeding Time in L.A.," 187–90
Foreshadowing, 284
Formal essays, 215, 216
Formula for writing, 78–82
Four Quartets, Eliot, 79
Frame, Janet, To the Is-Land, 178
Franklin, Benjamin, Autobiography, 86
Free association, 111–12
French Symbolists, 249
Freud, Sigmund, 15, 110, 119, 192
Full autobiography, 85–86

Gaia concept, 210
Gandhi, Mohandas K., Autobiography: The Story of
    My Experiments With Truth, 87
Garcia, Cristina, 322
Genres, of self, 83–99
Gestures, 164–67; and dialog, 259, 262
Gilmore, Gary, 135
Gilmore, Mikal, Shot in the Heart, 13, 32,
    134–35, 193, 256–59
Girl, Interrupted, Kaysen, 32, 53, 60, 95, 142, 253–55
Gists of memory, 102–3
Goina of story, 237–38
Golant, Susan, 114–17, 194–95, 310–12
Goldberg, Natalie, Writing Down the Bones, 136
Golden, Marita, Migrations of the Heart, 96
Goodman, Ellen, 95
Gordon, Barbara, I'm Dancing as Fast as I Can, 89
Gordon, Mary, The Shadow Man, 97
Gornick, Vivian, Fierce Attachments, 97
Gossip, 313
Grabbers, 273–74
Graham, Martha, 18
Grandchildren, 43–45, 307
Gray, Dorothy Randall, 120
The Great Railway Bazaar, Theroux, 91
The Great Santini, Conroy, 92
Green, Hannah, I Never Promised You a Rose
    Garden, 89
Greene, Melissa Fay, Praying for Sheetrock, 88–89
Griffin, John Howard, Black Like Me, 93
Growing Up, Baker, 38–39, 67–68, 70–72, 75, 77,
    86, 159–61, 165, 220, 309
Guidelines in New Autobiography, 179–83
Guiler, Hugh, 308

Haley, Alex: Roots, 94; The Autobiography of
    Malcolm X, 35, 87
Hamill, Pete, A Drinking Life, 90, 116
Hammerstein, Oscar, 179
Happy endings, 76, 195
Harris, Daniel, "Biography of a Prose Style,"
    126–27
Haskell, Molly, Love and Other Infectious Diseases,
    53, 318
Having Our Say, Delany sisters, 95

Hawthorne, Nathaniel, 190
Hayden, Torey, One Child, 279
Healing process, autobiography as, 14–15
Heaven's Coast, Doty, 13
Hegel, Georg Wilhelm Friedrich, The Science of
    Logic, 217
Heisenberg's uncertainty principle, 101
Hellman, Lillian: Scoundrel Time, 86; An
    Unfinished Woman, 104, 113–14, 180
Hemingway, Ernest, A Moveable Feast, 87
Henley, Lois, 219, 305, 306–7; The Choice or the
    Privilege, 232–33
Hero, self as, 140–51
Hidden dialog, subtext as, 259–62
The Hidden Life of Dogs, Thomas, 55
High Tide in Tucson, Kingsolver, 91, 280
"High-water," Houston, 163, 259–61
Hillman, James, 5, 196
Historical memoirs, 88
Hoang, Hanh, 142–43, 150, 162, 163–64, 218,
    246–47, 285–86
Hobbie, Douglas, Being Brett, 133
Hoffman, Jack, Run, Run, Run, 273
Honesty, 101–2; emotional, 183, 184
Horizontal time devices, 267, 278–87
Hotchner, A. E., King of the Hill, 86
The House on Mango Street, Cisneros, 97, 124, 204
Houston, Pam, Cowboys Are My Weakness, 60, 92,
    264–66; "High-water," 163, 259–61;
    "Jackson Is Only One of My Dogs,"
    240–42; "Selway," 323–24
How I Got Cultured: A Nevada Memoir, Barber, 86
Huddle, David, The Writing Habit, 317
Humor, 94, 289–99; in character portrayals,
    167–69
Hunger of Memory: The Education of Richard
    Rodriguez, Rodriguez, 97
Hybrid literary forms, 95, 99
Hyman, Barbara Davis, My Mother's Keeper, 93

Ideas: opposing, 218; writing about, 215–16, 219
Identities, disguised, 181, 318–20
Ideology, 101
I Know Why the Caged Bird Sings, Angelou, 32,
    85, 86, 96, 136–37, 165, 261–62
Illness, memoirs of, 89
I'm Dancing as Fast as I Can, Gordon, 89
Imagery, 203, 303
Imagination, 76, 104–10, 119–21
The Importance of Being Earnest, Wilde, 287, 290
Incidents in the Life of a Slave Girl: Written by
    Herself, Jacobs, 96
In Cold Blood, Capote, 31
Indian captivity narratives, 25
Indirect dialog, 258
I Never Promised You a Rose Garden, Green, 89
Information, in scenes, 241–42, 265
Ingebretsen, James, 228–29, 274–75, 305;
    Apprentice to the Dawn, 148
Initiating incident, 3, 66, 67–68, 79–80; in scene,
    265

Inner responses, 250–53, 256, 281

Insights, 234, 250

Inspirational memoirs, 26–27, 89

Interesting parts of narrative, 278–79

Intergenerational sagas, 55

Internal responses, 244

Internal voices, negative, 184–85

Internet publishing, 17, 334

Intimacy, 140, 208

Introduction of characters, 163–64

Inventing the Truth, Zinsser, 38

Invisible Man, Ellison, 322

Isherwood, Christopher, 29; *Berlin Stories*, 60, 92

I Shock Myself, Wood, 86

It's Always Something, Radner, 294

Jackson, Rebecca Cox, 96

"Jackson Is Only One of My Dogs," Houston, 240–42

Jacobs, Harriet "Linda Brent," *Incidents in the Life of a Slave Girl*, 96

Japanese autobiographic writing, 35, 175

Jelinek, Estelle, 21

Jewish-American autobiography, 97

Johnson, Robert A., 175

Johnson, Samuel, 249

Johnstone, Jill, 10–11

Jong, Erica, *Fear of Flying*, 322

Journalism, 36, 141

Journal writing, 61, 263

Joyce, James, *A Portrait of the Artist as a Young Man*, 86

Judgment, avoidance of, 157–58, 162–63

Jung, Carl, 14; *Memories, Dreams, Reflections*, 90

Karr, Mary, 172; *The Liar's Club*, 101, 227, 324–25

Kaysen, Susanna, *Girl, Interrupted*, 32, 53, 60, 95, 142, 253–55

Kazan, Elia, *A Life*, 86, 123, 229–30

Kazin, Alfred: *New York Jew*, 97; *A Walker in the City*, 86

Keckley, Elizabeth, *Behind the Scenes*, 96

Kempe, Margery, 91

The Kingdom and the Power, Talese, 31

Kingsolver, Barbara: *High Tide in Tucson*, 91, 280; *Pigs in Heaven*, 164–65

Kingston, Maxine Hong, 32, 138; *The Woman Warrior*, 30–31, 121

Kirkland, Gelsey, *Dancing on My Grave*, 88

Kite, Joan, 157

Knapp, Caroline, *Drinking*, 89

Konner, Melvin, *Becoming a Doctor*, 87

Lamott, Anne, 320; *Bird by Bird*, 186; *Operating Instructions*, 123, 294–95

Landscape for a Good Woman, Steedman, 11

Language, attention to, 198–200

Latino-American tradition, 97

Lawsuits, 308–9

Leaving Home, Buchwald, 94

Lee, Brason, *Without My Helmet*, 182–83, 218, 222–23, 268–70, 282–84, 298, 305

Lee, Jarena, 96

A Leg to Stand On, Sacks, 69, 246, 250–52

Lessing, Doris, *Under My Skin*, 119, 271–72, 325

Less Than Zero, Ellis, 322

Letters of My Life, Crone, 61–63, *162*

The Liar's Club, Karr, 101, 227, 324–25

Libel laws, 309, 312–16

Life, 1; dramatic structure of, 65–82; stories in, 5–7, 37–46, 47–49

The Life and Religious Experience of Jarena Lee, 96

The Life Swap, Weber, 93

Light spots, in dark periods, 194–95

Like Water for Chocolate, Esquivel, 95

Listener, hiring of, 125

Literary memoir. *See* New Autobiography

A Literate Passion, Miller and Nin, 205

Literature of adversity, 89

Long, Philomene, *Memoirs of a Nun on Fire*, 191

Lopate, Phillip, 206, 215, 291–94, 318; *Against Joie de Vivre*, 91; *The Art of the Personal Essay*, 90, 91; *Bachelorhood*, 91; "My Drawer," 181–82

Lot's Wife, Tisdale, 91, 117

Love, of self, 145–46, 148, 150

Love and Other Infectious Diseases, Haskell, 53, 318

The Lover, Duras, 110–11, 115, 130–32

Lovers, as antagonists, 153

Love story, adversary in, 69

Lying, 176

Mabel McKay: Weaving the Dream, Sarris, 98

McCall, Nathan, *Makes Me Wanna Holler*, 14, 127–28, 150–51, 252–53

McCarthy, Mary, *Memories of a Catholic Girlhood*, 30, 86, 158, 166–69, 177

McGinniss, Joe, *The Selling of the President*, 31

McInerney, Jay, *Bright Lights, Big City*, 322

McKay, Mabel, 98

McMillan, Terry, 312–13

Madame: An Intimate Biography of Helena Rubenstein, O'Higgins, 93

Magazines, publication in, 95, 332–33

Mailer, Norman, *The Armies of the Night*, 32

Mairs, Nancy, 89, 206, 294, 325; *Ordinary Times*, 198–200, 234; *Remembering the Bone House*, 178, 208–10, 316–17; *Voice Lessons*, 132, 202, 319, 328

Major events, invention of, 180

Makes Me Wanna Holler, McCall, 14, 127–28, 150–51, 252–53

Making It Crazy, Estroff, 94

Malcolm, Janet, 213, 314

Malcolm X, 87

Mallon, Thomas, personal essay, 117

Manchild in the Promised Land, Brown, 96

Mandelker, Phillip, 297–98

Manson, Charles, 141

The Man Who Mistook His Wife for a Hat, Sacks, 87

Maps to Anywhere, Cooper, 91
Martin, Martha, *O Rugged Land of Gold*, 173–75
Masson, Jeffrey, 314
Matousek, Mark, *Sex Death Enlightenment: A True Story*, 89
Maus: A Survivor's Tale, Spiegelman, 95, 296–97
Mayle, Peter, *A Year in Provence*, 91, 221
Meaning: in story, 77–78; from traumatic memory, 192
Media for New Autobiography, 13
Medical memoirs, 87
Meditations, 90, 223
Memoir groups, 144, 302, 327–28
Memoirs, 53, 71, 86–89, 175–76, 180, 289; by Anglo-Saxon men, 67; phony, 25
Memoirs of a Nun on Fire, Long, 191
Memories: emotional, and descriptions, 245; and reminiscence, 100–104; repressed, 110–12; retrieval tricks, 114–22; writing of, 112–14
Memories, Dreams, Reflections, Jung, 90
Memories of a Catholic Girlhood, McCarthy, 30–31, 86, 158, 166–69, 177
Memory and Writing, Davis, 267
Metafictions, 30
Metzger, Deena, *Writing for Your Life*, 112–13, 119
Midnight in the Garden of Good and Evil, Berendt, 141
Migrations of the Heart, Golden, 96
Miller, Henry, 29, 205
Minority groups, and autobiography, 11
Misanthropic humor, 294
Modern life, pivotal events, 75
Modesty, 148
Modifiers, overuse of, 248, 250
Moffat, Mary Jane, 107
Mommie Dearest, Crawford, 93
The Money Game, Smith, 31
Montaigne, Michel de, 90
Morris, Willie, *New York Days*, 86
Morrison, Toni, 109
Mother Was a Gunner's Mate, Wingo, 128–29
A Moveable Feast, Hemingway, 87
Movie, life as, 236–40
Music, and memories, 116
"My Drawer," Lopate, 181–82
My Favorite Year, Palumbo, 95
My Mother's Keeper, Hyman, 93
Myth, 37, 41–42, 65–66, 196; personal, invention of, 121; truths in, 175

Names, alteration of, 181
Narcissists, 319
Narrative, 2–3, 8, 38, 192, 251–53
Narrative of the Life of Frederick Douglass, An American Slave, 96
Narrative summary, 232–35, 240, 241–43
Narrator, in autobiography, 129
Nash, Michael, 120
Native American autobiography, 97–98
A Natural History of the Senses, Ackerman, 91, 117, 204

Nausea, Sartre, 88
Near death encounters, 88
Negative memories, repressed, 110
Nery, Adrianna, 218
"Never Live Above Your Landlord," Lopate, 291–94
New Autobiography, 1–3, 7, 9–19, 28–36, 55, 89, 120, 130, 198, 231, 253; disclaimers, 176–77; evolution of, 20–36; historical memoirs as, 88–89; humor and, 289–90; self as hero, 140–51; and truth, 178–83
The New Diary, Rainer, 3, 82, 184
New Journalism, 13, 31–32, 36, 141
The New Journalism, Wolfe, 27–28
"The New Story of Your Life," Blumenthal, 14–15
New York in the Fifties, Wakefield, 281
New York Jew, Kazin, 97
The New York Times Magazine, 10
Nichols, John, 29
Nin, Anaïs, 147–48, 308–9; *Diaries*, 1, 61, 205; *Novel of the Future*, 158, 312
Nobody, Nowhere, Williams, 13, 89
Nobody Knows My Name, Baldwin, 96, 244–45
Nonfiction, creative, 31, 318
Novels, 23, 27–28, 55, 130, 322; autobiographic, 92, 312, 320–22

Objective correlative, 76
Objects, and memories, 116–17
Observation, and writing, 136–39
Occupational memoirs, 87–88
O'Higgins, Patrick, *Madame: An Intimate Biography of Helena Rubenstein*, 93
O'Keeffe, Georgia, 87
The Old Patagonian Express, Theroux, 91
One Child, Hayden, 279
O'Neill, Eugene, 95
Operating Instructions, Lamott, 123, 294–95
Operation Shylock, Roth, 29–30
Ordinary Times, Mairs, 198–200, 234
Orgasmic structure, 66, 67, 255
Original wound, 196–97
O Rugged Land of Gold, Martin, 173–75
Orwell, George, *Down and Out in Paris and London*, 32, 93
Others, portrayal of, 152–72
Out of Africa, Dinesen, 86
Oxenberg, Jan, *Thank-You and Good-Night*, 195

Painful experiences, writing about, 193
Palumbo, Dennis, *My Favorite Year*, 95
Panthermania, Sheehy, 31
Parents, as antagonists, 152–53
Parks, Gordon, *A Choice of Weapons*, 96
Passages, Sheehy, 52
Past, missing, imagination of, 119–21
Pathetic fallacy, 246
Paula, Allende, 63, 227–28
Perception, credibility and, 179
Perelman, S. J., 94

Perfectionism, 186
Permission for portrayal, 308–12
Personal essays, 90–91, 117, 215–16, 223;
    magazine publication, 333
Personal nonfiction narrative. *See* New
    Autobiography
Phillips, Julia, *You'll Never Eat Lunch in This Town
    Again*, 24, 90, 123, 177
Philosophic memoirs, 88
Photos, memories and, 114–16
Physical feelings, writing of, 202–11
The Piano (film), 74
Pieces of White Shell, Williams, 41–42
Pigs in Heaven, Kingsolver, 164–65
The Pilgrim's Progress, Bunyan, 90
Pirsig, Robert, *Zen and the Art of Motorcycle
    Maintenance*, 88
Pivotal events, 51–53, 54, 66, 70–71, 75, 79,
    80–81, 265
Place, memoirs of, 86
Plath, Sylvia, *The Bell Jar*, 92
Plebeian autobiography, 10–11
Poe, James, 237
Poetic license, 176
The Poetics of Space, Bachelard, 117–18
Poetry, reminiscence and, 103
Pornography, 209
Portraits, 93, 152, 166, 169–72
Power, in relationships, 258–59
Power of Myth, Campbell, 41
Praying for Sheetrock, Greene, 88–89
Precipitating event, 66, 71–72, 81, 265
Precision in description, 248, 250
Preliminary structure, 79
The Prince of Tides, Conroy, 63–64, 92, 111, 271
Problem, as story element, 66, 68, 80
Progoff, Ira, 226
Protagonist, self as, 67, 132–33, 141–52
Proust, Marcel, 271
Prozac Nation: Young and Depressed in America,
    Wurtzel, 89
Pseudo memoirs, 25
Psychological illness, memoirs of, 89
Psychotherapy, 14–15, 147
Publication, 16–17, 86, 91–94, 176, 321, 325,
    329–35
Puritans, 20, 24
Purpose of autobiography, 9, 195

Quakers, autobiographical writings, 24
Quests, 59–60, 90
Quilts, life structure as, 60–63
Quindlen, Anna, 95
Quotes, fabrication of, 314

Radical Chic & Mau-Mauing the Flak Catchers,
    Wolfe, 31
Radner, Gilda, 294
Rainer, Tristine, 3–8
Reading aloud, 125
Reagan, Ronald, 147

Realistic novels, 27–28
Reality, truth and, 175–76
Realizations, 48, 53, 67, 76–78, 82, 266
Reason for writing, 12–13, 146, 195
Reflections, 90, 223
Refuge: An Unnatural History of Family and Place,
    Williams, 87, 210–11
Relationships, 56–59, 87, 152
Relativity of memory, 101
Religious autobiography, 88
Remembering the Bone House, Mairs, 178, 208–10,
    316–17
Reminiscences, 90, 100–104
Repressed memories, 110–12
Resolution, 66, 82, 323
Retrieval of memories, 112–22
Returning, Wakefield, 84–85
Revenge, writing for, 93, 158, 315
Reveries, 90, 105, 231, 245
Rewriting, 304–5
Reynolds, Rick, 290; "Only the Truth Is Funny,"
    94
Riding the Iron Rooster, Theroux, 91
Rodriguez, Richard: *Days of Obligation*, 97, 177,
    280, 281; *Hunger of Memory*, 97
Rollin, Betty, *First, You Cry*, 89
Roots, Haley, 94
Roth, Philip, 29–30
Rousseau, Jean-Jacques, *Confessions*, 24
Rules, breaking of, 266
Run, Run, Run: The Lives of Abbie Hoffman,
    Hoffman and Simon, 273

Sacks, Oliver: *A Leg to Stand On*, 69, 246,
    250–52; *The Man Who Mistook His Wife for a
    Hat*, 87
Sale of writing, 329–35
Salinger, J. D., *The Catcher in the Rye*, 322
Sarris, Andrew, 53, 318
Sarris, Greg, *Mabel McKay*, 98
Sartre, Jean-Paul, *Nausea*, 88
Satirical humor, 291–94
Scenes, 180, 229–66; imagined, 181–82
Schank, Roger, 102
Schindler's List (film), 74
The Science of Logic, Hegel, 217
Screenplays, 235
See, Carolyn, *Dreaming*, 13, 32, 55, 129–30,
    138–39
Selectivity in description, 247, 250
Self, 140–51, 193–94, 210–11; genres of, 83–99;
    as protagonist, 132–33, 152; as target of
    humor, 290–91
Self-discovery, 79, 88
Self-publishing, 17, 333
The Selling of the President, McGinniss, 31
"Selway," Houston, 323–24
Sensate details, 103–10
Senses, writing of, 204–5, 249
Sex Death Enlightenment, Matousek, 89
Sex, writing about, 205–10

The Shadow Man, Gordon, 97
Shakespeare, William, plays of, 287
Shapiro, Judy, 47–48
Sheehy, Gail: *Panthermania*, 31; *Passages*, 52
Short stories, 71, 92, 320
Shot in the Heart, Gilmore, 13, 32, 134–35, 193,
    256–59
Siblings, as antagonists, 153
Simenon, Georges, 158
Similes, 136
Simon, Daniel, *Run, Run, Run*, 273
"A Sketch of the Past," Woolf, 15–16
Slave narratives, 26, 96
Slouching Towards Bethlehem, Didion, 86, 138
Smith, Adam, *The Money Game*, 31
Snortland, Ellen, 95
Society, conflicts with, 89–90, 97
Soul on Ice, Cleaver, 96
Speakers, identification of, 262–63
Spiegelman, Art, *Maus*, 95, 296–97
Spiritual autobiography, 90, 88
Spouses, as antagonists, 153
Stanton, Elizabeth Cody, 26
Stayton, Richard, "Waiting for Dennis," 274
Steedman, Carolyn Kay, *Landscape for a Good
    Woman*, 11
Stein, Gertrude: *Everybody's Autobiography*, 100;
    The Autobiography of Alice B. Toklas, 28–29
Stepto, Robert, 96
Sterling, Joy, *A Cultivated Life*, 88
Stop-Time, Conroy, 86, 101
Story, 1, 32–34, 37–49, 153–55, 195–98, 212,
    222, 270–71; structure of, 8, 65–82
Stream of consciousness, 111–12
Struggle with adversary, 66, 69–70
Stutz, Phil, 186
Styron, William, *Darkness Visible*, 13, 89
Subtext, as hidden dialog, 259–62
Suffragists, 26–27
Summaries, 231–34, 257–58
Supporting characters, 155–57
Suspense, 286–87
Swiss Family Perelman, Perelman, 96
Synthesis of conflict, 219–20, 222

Talese, Gay: *The Kingdom and the Power*, 31; *Thy
    Neighbor's Wife*, 32
Taping of voice, 125
Tarcher, Jeremy, 144
Taylor, Deborah, 43–44
The Teachings of Don Juan, Castaneda, 90
Telling details, 162–63
Tell Me a Story, Schank, 102
Teresa of Avila, Saint, 87
Thank-You and Good-Night, Oxenberg, 195
Thatcher, Margaret, 88
Thematic conflict, 79, 155–56, 255, 323
Thematic memoirs, 55–59, 87–88, 97
Theme, autobiographic, 13–14, 212–30
Therapeutic writing, 109, 111
Theroux, Paul, travel memoirs, 91

Third person, use of, 132–33
This Boy's Life, Wolff, 86, 158
Thomas, Elizabeth Marshall, *The Hidden Life of
    Dogs*, 55
Thoreau, Henry David, *Walden*, 87
Thoughts, feelings and, 251
A Thousand and One Nights, 275–76
Thrilling memoirs, 25–26, 88, 174
Thy Neighbor's Wife, Talese, 32
Time: alternations of, 267–87; emotional, 234;
    for writing, 239–40
Tisdale, Sallie, *Lot's Wife*, 91, 117
"To Fashion a Text," Dillard, 102
Torch Songs, Fontenay, 276–77
To the Is-Land, Frame, 178
Traditional autobiography, 95–98
Transparency technique, 63–64
Trauma, memories of, 109, 111, 192–93
Travel memoirs, 91
"Treatments," 235
Tribute portraits, 169–72
Truth, 35–36, 109, 146, 159, 173–83, 315;
    humor and, 289–90; reminiscence and, 104
"Truth Serum," Cooper, 206–7
Turning points. *See* Pivotal events

Under My Skin, Lessing, 119, 271–72, 325
Understatement, 149–50, 167–69
An Unfinished Woman, Hellman, 104, 113–14,
    180
Useful phrases, 130

Values, conflicts of, 56–57, 218
Vanity presses, 333
Vernacular, writing in, 127–29
Vertical time devices, 267–77
Vidal, Gore, 125
Viewpoints, multiple, 146, 268
Villains, 157–58
Vocational memoirs, 87–88
Voice, personal, finding of, 123–39
Voice Lessons, Mairs, 132, 202, 319, 328

"Waiting for Dennis," Stayton, 274
Wakefield, Dan: *New York in the Fifties*, 281;
    Returning, 84–85
Walden, Thoreau, 87
Walker, Alice, *The Color Purple*, 96
War stories, 88
The Way I See It, Davis, 93
Weber, Nancy, *The Life Swap*, 93
Welch, Leonard, 312–13
Wells, Ida B., *Crusade for Justice*, 88
Why I'm Glad I'm Not a Boy, Clenard, 133–34
Wilde, Oscar, *The Importance of Being Earnest*,
    287, 290
Wilder, Thornton, 212
Williams, Donna, *Nobody, Nowhere*, 13, 89
Williams, Tennessee, 95
Williams, Terry Tempest: *Pieces of White Shell*,
    41–42; *Refuge*, 87, 210–11

Wingo, Josette Dermody, *Mother Was a Gunner's Mate*, 128–29
Without My Helmet, Lee, 222–23, 282–84
Wolfe, Tom, 13; *The New Journalism*, 27–28; *Radical Chic*, 31
Wolff, Geoffrey, *The Duke of Deception*, 93, 272–73
Wolff, Tobias, *This Boy's Life*, 86, 158
Woman Hollering Creek, Cisneros, 204
The Woman Warrior, Kingston, 30–31, 121
Women, 7, 21–26, 60, 120, 141, 271; African-American, 96; and sex, 208; white, 96–97
Woolf, Virginia, 75; "A Sketch of the Past," 15–16
Wordsworth, William, 103

Wright, Richard, *Black Boy*, 96
Writer's block, 184
Writing Down the Bones, Goldberg, 136
Writing for Your Life, Metzger, 112–13, 119
Writing groups, 125, 144
The Writing Habit, Huddle, 317
Wurtzel, Elizabeth, *Prozac Nation*, 13, 89
Wyler, Marie, 235–36, 239–40

A Year in Provence, Mayle, 91, 221
Yogananda, Paramhansa, 88
You'll Never Eat Lunch in This Town Again, Phillips, 24, 90, 123, 177

Zen and the Art of Motorcycle Maintenance, Pirsig, 8

Copyrights and Permissions